American Negro Slavery

American Negro Slavery

• A MODERN READER

EDITED BY

ALLEN WEINSTEIN AND FRANK OTTO GATELL

NEW YORK

OXFORD UNIVERSITY PRESS

LONDON TORONTO

PRINTED IN THE UNITED STATES OF AMERICA

ᴛᴏ David Potter

Table of Contents

AMERICAN NEGRO SLAVERY

Introduction

Historians writing on American Negro slavery have usually begun with some general moral judgment of the institution. Over the past century, slavery in the United States has found its share of apologists and detractors among scholars. Just as James Ford Rhodes and other late nineteenth-century writers indicted the system as evil and intrinsically corrupt, a number of Progressive era historians, most notably Ulrich B. Phillips, viewed the institution instead through the eyes of white Southerners and created the image of a benign and patriarchal system of bondage. Phillip's sympathetic portrait of slavery in the ante-bellum South dominated historical response to the subject up to World War II, partly because it embodied prevailing American beliefs in Negro inferiority and in the black man's subordinate place within the society.[1] The work of anthropologists like Franz Boas earlier in the century had undermined the intellectual respectability of racist ideas among social scientists but had failed to affect significantly the ordinary white American's stereotypes of the Negro—those alternately cheerful and buffonish Mammies and Sambos. Public rejection of overt racism in the United States, as Eugene D. Genovese noted, "probably had more to do with [Adolph Hitler] than Franz Boas." Some Americans, in other words, finally recognized the discomfiting analogy between their own assumptions about the Negro and the Nazi's attitudes toward the Jews.

Confronted with the genocidal handiwork of German racists, American scholars began reassessing their own perspectives on slavery. Even before the end of World War II, some historians, Herbert Aptheker for one, had challenged sharply the mythology of the ante-bellum South, but a critical appraisal of Phillip's work in 1944 by Richard Hofstadter served as a starting point in the re-examination of slavery among liberal scholars.[2] "Let the study of the Old South be undertaken by other scholars," Hofstadter wrote, "who have absorbed the viewpoint of modern cultural anthropology, who have a feeling for social psychology. . .who will concentrate upon the neglected rural (i.e. non-slaveholding) elements that formed the great majority of the

Southern population, who will not rule out the testimony of more critical observers, and who will realize that any history of slavery must be written in large measure from the standpoint of the slave. . . ." [3] Subsequent research on American slavery has reflected these concerns.

The process of reassessment remains in its earliest stage, and historians still disagree about the nature of the system itself. Passionate neo-abolitionist scholars like Kenneth B. Stampp and Herbert Aptheker have attempted to refute, point by point, the milder picture of plantation bondage, drawn earlier by Phillips, of submissive, carefree slaves who endured their servitude with little protest. Phillips's use of evidence as well as his racism have undergone critical scrutiny by Hofstadter, Stampp, and other post-World War II commentators. Stanley Elkins has pointed out, however, that Stampp's own synthesis of Southern slavery, *The Peculiar Institution,* remained bound by the older moral argument with historians like Phillips over the question of whether slavery was good or evil, whether it had been harsh or gentle for those black men who lived under it. "The coercions of a century-old debate remain irresistible," Elkins noted. Stampp "has joined the debate; he may even have won it, but it is still very much the same debate. In spite of its outcome, the strategy of *The Peculiar Institution* was still dictated by Ulrich Phillips." [4] A similar observation can be made of Eugene D. Genovese's recent efforts to restore both Ulrich B. Phillips's declining reputation among historians and Phillips's concept of a patriarchal slave society. No more fervent and thoughtful historical defense of ante-bellum Southern society has appeared in the past two decades than Genovese's. This Northern Marxist views slavery as "a social system within which whites and blacks lived in harmony as well as antagonism with little evidence of massive organized Negro opposition to the regime. . . ." [5] Where Stampp, along with other liberal and radical historians, found most bondsmen hating both their masters and slavery itself, Genovese—like Phillips—has discerned instead a smoothly functioning, semifeudal social order, distinct in many essentials from the rest of American society during the ante-bellum period. On this disputed problem of slavery as a social system, most historians have taken their stand somewhere between the Aptheker-Stampp and Phillips-Genovese models of "the peculiar institution."

Profound disagreements among historians also remain on the question of how the slaves behaved in bondage. Only a few scholars, however, have attempted to analyze carefully the impact of American slavery upon Negro personality, the most controversial work in this area being Stanley M. Elkins's *Slavery, A Problem in American Institutional and Intellectual Life*, probably the most influential study of slavery in the United States to be published since World War II.[6] Elkins's book remains, a decade after its publication, the baseline for present historical work in the field, and students should be familiar with the entire volume. The excerpts contained in this collection discuss some but not all of Elkins's most subtle and challenging concepts: his belief in the slave's acceptance of his own inferiority or "Sambo-ness" through the deliberate efforts of slaveholders to encourage Negro infantilism; the absence in the United States of an adequate institutional framework in the areas of law, religion, and political authority to protect the slave's status as a human being, especially when compared with the institutional buffers of Latin America's slave cultures; the vulnerability of Negro slaves in the English mainland colonies to total manipulation by the master caste because of the absence of institutional controls on the system of "unopposed capitalist" agriculture; finally, the author's controversial analogy suggesting that the master's absolute power over his bondsmen in the United States had destructive effects on slave personality comparable to the impact of Nazi concentration camps on their inmates. Many of these ideas are examined, criticized, or defended by other authors in this collection. Elkins's over-all impact on the modern study of American slavery remains singular. Applying concepts of social psychology and Frank Tannenbaum's comparative analysis of English and Latin American slave societies, he opened up lines of investigation into the study of master and slave personalities that few other recent historians have shown sufficient daring to exploit.

The comparative study of slave societies, unlike the question of slave personality, has become a popular and productive field of inquiry among recent scholars. In the first volume of his projected history of antislavery movements, *The Problem of Slavery in Western Culture*, David Brion Davis traced the evolution of beliefs and social patterns on the subject from antiquity to colonial North and South America in a careful comparative discussion of ideologies and institutions.[7] Another important recent work, Herbert Klein's *Slavery in the Americas, a Comparative Study of Cuba and Virginia*, found considerable evidence to support the Tannenbaum-Elkins hypothesis that English and Spanish American colonies developed distinctly different slave cultures, thereby shaping remarkably dissimilar behavior patterns among Negro slaves in each culture.[8] David Brion Davis and other writers have challenged the Tannenbaum-Elkins hypothesis on the basis of research into existing Spanish and Portugese scholarship, but Klein's examination of the Cuban and Virginian experiences remains one of the few available studies of the actual operation of slave institutions in two distinct societies. Hopefully, other such studies will follow, which will allow for more confident assessment of the argument.

Certain older questions regarding slavery in the United States continue to receive fresh treatment from scholars. Controversy over slavery's profitability in the ante-bellum South has been "a historical perennial" among American writers. In this collection, Harold Woodman reviews the relevant literature on slavery as an economic institution; works such as Eugene D. Genovese's *The Political Economy of Slavery* and Alfred H. Conrad and J. H. Meyer's *The Economics of Slavery* are important recent contributions to more precise understanding of Southern economic development under slavery.[9] Race relations under the slave system have also attracted recent attention from writers such as Kenneth Stampp and Richard Wade. A selection from Wade's *Slavery in the Cities: The South, 1820–1860* traces the patterns of racial accommodation in the urban South; Robert Starobin's article examines Negro-white relations among non-agricultural workers in the South.[10] Despite previous studies, the extent to which racial segregation existed in the ante-bellum South and the forms which it took remain important questions for future investigators. In time, a work similar to Leon Litwack's *North of Slavery: The Negro in the Free States, 1790–1860* may detail the complexities of social adjustment between the races in the slaveholding South.[11] Recent historians have also disputed the origins of American slavery, debating whether race prejudice, economic necessity, or some combination of these and other factors led to the enslavement of Negroes in the English mainland colonies. In this collection, Winthrop D. Jordan reviews recent literature on the controversy, and David Brion Davis compares the factors which conditioned slavery's emergence in various parts of the Western Hemisphere during the era of colonization.

The discussion above suggests only some of the major questions dealing with American Negro slavery which have preoccupied scholars. Most of the readings in this book concern slavery in the South, even though the institution existed in every English mainland colony until after the American Revolution. The editors chose not to focus on the problem of slavery in the North, but not because it lacks either importance or a growing body of literature. On the contrary, recent works such as Arthur Zilversmit's *The First Emancipation: The Abolition of Negro Slavery in the North* and Edgar J. McManus's *A History of*

Negro Slavery in New York reveal the continuing interest of scholars in the evolution of slavery north of the Mason-Dixon line.[12] Yet within a few decades after the Revolution, the North had abandoned the institution, leaving to the South alone the dilemma which slavery posed. For the next century and a half, the problem of white over black in America would be centered in the states of the Old South.

The question of race, which Ulrich B. Phillips called the "central theme of Southern history," has re-emerged in the 1960's from its regional base to become again the central theme of our national experience. No collection of readings on American slavery can do more than suggest some of the historical background of present racial conflict, but the road from Samboism to Black Power began within the confines of ante-bellum Southern slavery. If many slaveholders viewed their Negro chattels as child-like, shiftless, and content, others were tormented by images of less accommodating bondsmen. South Carolinians during the Nullification Crisis of the 1830's knew, for example, as William W. Freehling has shown, that for every Sambo there might also exist a Spartacus. Freehling's recent study of South Carolinian society, *Prelude to Civil War: The Nullification Crisis in South Carolina, 1816–1836*, showed that fear of Negro revolts played a major role in causing the Southern shift from apologetic embarrassment for slavery to aggressive defense of it against antislavery advocates.[13] Although in the United States the incidence of slave uprisings remained remarkably low compared with Latin American and West Indian slave societies, Southerners believed in their possibility and prepared systematically to prevent their occurrence. As many Northerners, who for generations have had little concern for the black ghettoes in their midst, have now come to realize, those to whom evil is done, in W. H. Auden's phrase, do evil in return (or at least might be expected to).

Modern historical reassessment of American Negro slavery remains far from complete. Much more has been promised than has been fulfilled, even by writers included in this collection. In some important instances, their major works on the subject remain in progress, and the selections printed here often suggest new directions that scholars are taking rather than offer an individual historian's final or conclusive ideas on a topic. For example, students of American slavery eagerly await Eugene D. Genovese's forthcoming elaboration and synthesis of his theories on Southern ante-bellum society and David Brion Davis's future volumes on antislavery movements. Comparative studies of Latin American, West Indian, and North American slave cultures currently in progress should help to clarify the patterns which slavery *in practice* took in each culture—the degree of similarity and the precise quality of the differences. Scholars are also re-examining the influence of the Negro's varied African tribal origins on his behavior under American slavery, continuing the work of Melville Herskovits and other anthropologists who pioneered in this area. No doubt other historians will extend and reshape Elkins's theories on slave personality after careful and imaginative use of available primary source materials in Southern archives, materials which Elkins himself did not exploit in his book.

Hopefully, scholars will also begin to abandon the self-imposed insularity of many previous writers on American slavery and begin studying the institution within the context of broader developments in American life. This would involve supplementing single-minded concern for how the system functioned with more curiosity about the impact of events on the course of Southern slave society. William W. Freehling's superb *Prelude to Civil War: The Nullification Crisis in South Carolina, 1816–1836* contributed notably to such a re-assessment. This approach would view slavery not as an unchanging or relatively fixed set of institutional patterns, but as an unstable regional culture, subject to shock waves both from outside and within, whether in the form of abolitionist propaganda, Andrew Jackson's tariff messages, or Nat Turner's calls for slave rebellion. More monographs like Freehling's, combining hard political and economic research with skillful social psychological analysis, are needed in order to appraise the shifting moods and habits of slave society. Historians might examine more carefully the impact on the South of such important cultural developments and events as Northern industrial growth, the Compromise of 1850, the rise of political antislavery groups, and John Brown's raid. Parallel studies concerning the changing patterns of slave life wrought by Southern or national developments are also needed. Earlier syntheses of American Negro slavery such as Phillips's and Stampp's have presented different versions of the institution's operation by studying its *intact* structure. Any future synthesizer faces the even more complex task of piecing together the changing patterns of Southern slave society *in process*.

The reader should be sufficiently aware by this time that, on most questions concerning American slavery, a century of historical research has left more to be undertaken and explored than to be catalogued and filed away. Until the paperback revolution, recent literature on slavery in the United States often remained hidden in scholarly journals, largely inaccessible to most students of American history. Even today, only a few leading historians of the subject, notably Phillips, Stampp, and Elkins, have become familiar to students. The present collection offers a sampling of their work and of many other recent contributors to the re-assessment of American slavery. It also contains a bibliographic guide to further reading. Although slavery no longer exists in this country, Americans continue to confront the problems it left unresolved, not the smallest of which was its long duration. Slavery lasted for 240 years in the South and for almost 180 years in the North. In the South, the institution did not die out or collapse ultimately from inner weakness: it was crushed by superior force. The residual effects of slavery on both black and white people in America today remain profound. The ordeal of black men in the United States spans our entire colonial and national past, two-thirds of which time they spent as slaves. In the readings which follow, historians treat the major dimensions of this experience—its origins, the slave, the master, and the system itself.

NOTES

1. See, for example, Ulrich Bonnell Phillips, *American Negro Slavery* (New York, 1918, reprinted 1967 by Louisiana State University Press).

2. Herbert Aptheker, *American Negro Slave Revolts* (New York, 1943); see also Joseph C. Carroll, *Slave Insurrections in the United States, 1800–1865* (Boston, 1938).

3. Richard Hofstadter, "U.B. Phillips and the Plantation Legend," *Journal of Negro History*, XXIX (April 1944).

4. Stanley M. Elkins, *Slavery, A Problem in American Institutional and Intellectual Life* (Chicago, 1959); Kenneth M. Stampp, *The Peculiar Institution: Slavery in the Ante-bellum South* (New York, 1956).

5. Eugene D. Genovese, "The Legacy of Slavery and the Roots of Black Nationalism," *Studies on the Left*, Vol. 6, No. 6 (November-December 1966), p. 3. See also Eugene D. Genovese, *The Political Economy of Slavery: Studies in the Economy and Society of the Slave South* (New York, 1965).

6. Elkins, *Slavery, passim.*

7. David Brion Davis, *The Problem of Slavery in Western Culture* (Ithaca, 1966).

8. Herbert S. Klein, *Slavery in the Americas: A Comparative Study of Cuba and Virginia* (Chicago, 1967).

9. Alfred H. Conrad and J. R. Meyers, *The Economics of Slavery and Other Studies in Economic History* (Chicago, 1964).

10. Richard C. Wade, *Slavery in the Cities, The South, 1820–1860* (New York, 1964; Robert Starobin, "Race Relations in Old South Industries" (unpublished manuscript, 1967).

11. Leon Litwack, *North of Slavery: The Negro in the Free States, 1790–1860* (Chicago, 1961).

12. Arthur Zilversmit, *The First Emancipation: The Abolition of Negro Slavery in the North* (Chicago, 1967); Edgar J. McManus, *A History of Negro Slavery in New York* (Syracuse, 1966).

13. William W. Freehling, *Prelude to Civil War: The Nullification Crisis in South Carolina, 1816–1836* (New York, 1966).

I: THE ORIGINS

• *The settlers of the mainland colonies had not held slaves in England. How then did the institution of slavery emerge in the New World setting? What factors led to the difference in treatment accorded European indentured servants and that accorded Africans, with the automatic relegation of Negroes to slave status by the end of the seventeenth century? Winthrop Jordan discusses this problem and offers his own views on the development of Negro slavery in the American colonies.*

Modern Tensions and the Origins of American Slavery

WINTHROP D. JORDAN

Thanks to John Smith we know that Negroes first came to the British continental colonies in 1619.[1] What we do not know is exactly when Negroes were first enslaved there. This question has been debated by historians for the past seventy years, the critical point being whether Negroes were enslaved almost from their first importation or whether they were at first simply servants and only later reduced to the status of slaves. The long duration and vigor of the controversy suggest that more than a simple question of dating has been involved. In fact certain current tensions in American society have complicated the historical problem and greatly heightened its significance. Dating the origins of slavery has taken on a striking modern relevance.

During the nineteenth century historians assumed almost universally that the first Negroes came to Virginia as slaves. So close was

From Winthrop D. Jordan, "Modern Tensions and the Origins of American Slavery," *Journal of Southern History,* XXVIII (February 1962), 18-30, with omissions. Copyright © 1962 by the Southern Historical Association. Reprinted by permission of the Managing Editor. A somewhat modified and much more complete description of the origin of American slavery is in Winthrop D. Jordan, *White Over Black: The Development of American Attitudes Toward the Negro, 1550–1812* (Chapel Hill, 1968).

their acquaintance with the problem of racial slavery that it did not occur to them that Negroes could ever have been anything but slaves. Philip A. Bruce, the first man to probe with some thoroughness into the early years of American slavery, adopted this view in 1896, although he emphasized that the original difference in treatment between white servants and Negroes was merely that Negroes served for life. Just six years later, however, came a challenge from a younger, professionally trained historian, James C. Ballagh. His A *History of Slavery in Virginia* appeared in the *Johns Hopkins University Studies in Historical and Political Science*, an aptly named series which was to usher in the new era of scholarly detachment in the writing of institutional history. Ballagh offered a new and different interpretation; he took the position that the first Negroes served merely as servants and that enslavement did not begin until around 1660, when statutes bearing on slavery were passed for the first time.[2]

There has since been agreement on dating the statutory establishment of slavery, and differences of opinion have centered on when enslavement began in actual practice. Fortunately there has also been general agreement on slavery's distinguishing characteristics: service for life and inheritance of like obligation by any offspring. Writing on the free Negro in Virginia for the Johns Hopkins series, John H. Russell in 1913 tackled the central question and showed that some Negroes were indeed servants but concluded that "between 1640 and 1660 slavery was fast becoming an established fact. In this twenty years the colored population was divided, part being servants and part being slaves, and some who were servants defended themselves with increasing difficulty from the encroachments of slavery."[3] . . .

. . . Yet despite disagreement on dating enslavement, the earlier writers—Bruce, Ballagh, and Russell—shared a common assumption which, though at the time seemingly irrelevant to the main question, has since proved of considerable importance. They assumed that prejudice against the Negro was natural and almost innate in the white man. It would be surprising if they had felt otherwise in this period of segregation statutes, overseas imperialism, immigration restriction, and full-throated Anglo-Saxonism. By the 1920's, however, with the easing of these tensions, the assumption of natural prejudice was dropped unnoticed. Yet only one historian explicitly contradicted that assumption: Ulrich Phillips of Georgia, impressed with the geniality of both slavery and twentieth-century race relations, found no natural prejudice in the white man and expressed his "conviction that Southern racial asperities are mainly superficial, and that the two great elements are fundamentally in accord." [4]

Only when tensions over race relations intensified once more did the older assumption of natural prejudice crop up again. After World War II American Negroes found themselves beneficiaries of New Deal politics and reforms, wartime need for manpower, world-wide repulsion at racist excesses in Nazi Germany, and growingly successful colored anticolonialism. With new militancy Negroes mounted an attack on the citadel of separate but equal, and soon it became clear that America was in for a period of self-conscious reappraisal of its racial arrangements. Writing in this period of heightened tension (1949) a practiced and careful scholar, Wesley F. Craven, raised the old question of the Negro's original status, suggesting that Negroes had been enslaved at an early date. Craven also cautiously resuscitated the idea that white men may have had natural distaste for the Negro, an idea which fitted neatly with the suggestion of early enslavement. Original antipathy would mean rapid debasement.[5]

In the next year (1950) came a sophisticated counterstatement, which contradicted both Craven's dating and implicitly any suggestion of early prejudice. Oscar and Mary F. Handlin in "Origins of the Southern Labor System" offered a case for late enslavement, with servitude as the status of Negroes before about 1660. Originally the status of both Negroes and white servants was far short of freedom, the Handlins maintained, but Negroes failed to benefit from increased freedom for servants in mid-century and became less free rather than more.[6] Embedded in this description of diverging status were broader implications: Late and gradual enslavement undercut the possibility of natural, deep-seated antipathy toward Negroes. On the contrary, if whites and Negroes could share the same status of half freedom for forty years in the seventeenth century, why could they not share full freedom in the twentieth?

The same implications were rendered more explicit by Kenneth M. Stampp in a major reassessment of Southern slavery published two years after the Supreme Court's 1954 school decision. Reading physiology with the eye of faith, Stampp frankly stated his assumption "that innately Negroes *are*, after all, only white men with black skins, nothing more, nothing less." [7] Closely following the Handlins' article on the origins of slavery itself, he almost directly denied any pattern of early and inherent racial antipathy: ". . . Negro and white servants of the seventeenth century seemed to be remarkably unconcerned about their visible physical differences." As for "the trend toward special treatment" of the Negro, "physical and cultural differences provided handy excuses to justify it." [8] Distaste for the Negro, then, was in the beginning scarcely more than an appurtenance of slavery.

These views squared nicely with the hopes of those even more directly concerned with the problem of contemporary race relations, sociologists and social psychologists. Liberal on the race question almost to a man, they tended to see slavery as the initial cause of the Negro's current degradation. The modern Negro was the unhappy victim of long association with base status. Sociologists, though uninterested in tired questions of historical evidence, could not easily assume a natural prejudice in the white man as the cause of slavery. Natural or innate prejudice would not only violate their basic assumptions concerning the dominance of culture but would undermine the power of their new Baconian science. For if prejudice was natural there would be little one could do to wipe it out. Prejudice must have followed enslavement, not vice versa, else any liberal program of action would be badly compromised. One prominent social scientist suggested in a UNESCO pamphlet that racial prejudice in the United States commenced with the cotton gin! [9]

Just how closely the question of dating had become tied to the practical matter of action against racial prejudice was made apparent by the suggestions of still another historian. Carl N. Degler grappled with the dating problem in an article frankly entitled "Slavery and the Genesis of American Race Prejudice." [10] The article appeared in 1959, a time when Southern resistance to school desegregation seemed more adamant than ever and the North's hands none too clean, a period of discouragement for those hoping to end racial discrimination. Prejudice against the Negro now appeared firm and deep-seated, less easily eradicated than had been supposed in, say, 1954. It was Degler's view that enslavement began early, as a result of white settlers' prejudice or antipathy toward the first Negroes. Thus not only were the sociologists contradicted but the dating problem was now overtly and consciously tied to the broader question of whether slavery caused prejudice or prejudice caused slavery. A new self-consciousness over the American racial dilemma had snatched an arid historical controversy from the hands of an unsuspecting earlier generation and had tossed it into the arena of current debate.

Ironically there might have been no historical controversy at all if every historian dealing with the subject had exercised greater care with facts and greater restraint in interpretation. Too often the debate entered the realm of inference and assumption. For the crucial early years after 1619 there is simply not enough evidence to indicate with any certainty whether Negroes were treated like white servants or not. No historian has found anything resembling proof one way or the other. The first Negroes were sold to the English settlers, yet so were other Englishmen. It can be said, however, that Negroes were set apart from white men by the word *Negroes*, and a distinct name is not attached to a group unless it is seen as different. The earliest Virginia census reports plainly distinguished Negroes from white men, sometimes giving Negroes no personal name; and in 1629 every commander of the several plantations was ordered to "take a generall muster of all the inhabitants men woemen and Children as well *Englishe* as Negroes."[11] Difference, however, might or might not involve inferiority.

The first evidence as to the actual status of Negroes does not appear until about 1640. Then it becomes clear that *some* Negroes were serving for life and some children inheriting the same obligation. Here it is necessary to suggest with some candor that the Handlins' statement to the contrary rests on unsatisfactory documentation.[12] That some Negroes were held as slaves after about 1640 is no indication, however, that American slavery popped into the world fully developed at that time. Many historians, most cogently the Handlins, have shown slavery to have been a gradual development, a process not completed until the eighteenth century. The complete deprivation of civil and personal rights, the legal conversion of the Negro into a chattel, in short slavery as Americans came to know it, was not accomplished overnight. Yet these developments practically and logically depended on the practice of hereditary lifetime service, and it is certainly possible to find in the 1640's and 1650's traces of slavery's most essential feature.[18]

The first definite trace appears in 1640 when the Virginia General Court pronounced sentence on three servants who had been retaken after running away to Maryland. Two of them, a Dutchman and a Scot, were ordered to serve their masters for one additional year and then the colony for three more, but "the third being a negro named John Punch shall serve his said master or his assigns for the time of his natural life here or else where." No white servant in America, so far as is known, ever received a like sentence.[14] Later the same month a Negro was again singled out from a group of recaptured runaways; six of the seven were assigned additional time while the Negro was given none, presumably because he was already serving for life.[15] After 1640, too, county court records began to mention Negroes, in part because there were more of them than previously—about two per cent of the Virginia population in 1649.[16] Sales for life, often including any future progeny, were recorded in unmistakable language. In 1646 Francis Pott sold a Negro woman and boy to Stephen Charlton "to the use of him . . . forever." Similarly, six years later William Whittington sold to John Pott "one Negro girle named Jowan; aged about Ten yeares and with her Issue and produce duringe her (or either of them) for their Life tyme. And their Successors forever"; and a Maryland man in 1649 deeded two Negro men and a woman "and all their issue both male and Female." The executors of a York County estate in 1647 disposed of eight Negroes—four men, two women, and two children—to Captain John Chisman "to have hold occupy posesse and inioy and every one of the afforementioned Negroes forever[.]"[17] The will of Rowland Burnham of "Rapahanocke," made in 1657, dispensed his considerable number of Negroes and white servants in language which clearly differentiated between the two by specifying that the whites were to serve for their "full terme of tyme" and the Negroes "for ever." [18] Nor did anything in the will indicate that this distinction was exceptional or novel.

In addition to these clear indications that some Negroes were owned for life, there were cases of Negroes held for terms far longer than the normal five or seven years.[19] On the other hand, some Negroes served only the term usual for white servants, and others were completely free.[20] One Negro freeman, Anthony Johnson, himself owned a Negro.[21] Obviously the enslavement of some Negroes did not mean the immediate enslavement of all.

Further evidence of Negroes serving for life lies in the prices paid for them. In many instances the valuations placed on Negroes (in estate inventories and bills of sale) were far higher than for white servants, even those servants with full terms yet to serve. Since there was ordinarily no preference for Negroes as such, higher prices must have meant that Negroes were more highly valued because of their greater length of service. Negro women may have been especially prized, moreover, because their progeny could also be held perpetually. . . .

Wherever Negro women were involved, however, higher valuations may have reflected the fact that they could be used for field work while white women generally were not. This discrimination between Negro and white women, of course, fell short of actual enslavement. It meant merely that Negroes were set apart in a way clearly not to their advantage. Yet this is not the only evidence that Negroes were subjected to degrading distinctions not directly related to slavery. In several ways Negroes were singled out for special treatment which suggested a generalized debasing of Negroes as a group. Significantly, the first indications of debasement appeared at about the same time as the first indications of actual enslavement. . . .

Virginia law set Negroes apart in a second way by denying them the important right and obligation to bear arms. Few restraints could indicate more clearly the denial to Negroes of membership in the white community. This action, in a sense the first foreshadowing of the slave codes, came in 1640, at just the time when other indications first appear that Negroes were subject to special treatment.[22]

Finally, an even more compelling sense of the separateness of Negroes was revealed in early distress concerning sexual union between the races. In 1630 a Virginia court pronounced a now famous sentence: "Hugh Davis to be soundly whipped, before an assembly of Negroes and others for abusing himself to the dishonor of God and shame of Christians, by defiling his body in lying with a negro."[23] While there were other instances of punishment for interracial union in the ensuing years, fornication rather than miscegenation may well have been the primary offense, though in 1651 a Maryland man sued someone who he claimed had said "that he had a black bastard in Virginia."[24] There may have been nothing racial about the 1640 case by which Robert Sweet was compelled "to do penance in church according to laws of England, for getting a negroe woman with child and the woman whipt."[25] About 1650 a white man and a Negro woman were required to stand clad in white sheets before a congregation in Lower Norfolk County for having had relations, but this punishment was sometimes used in ordinary cases of fornication between two whites.[26]

It is certain, however, that in the early 1660's when slavery was gaining statutory recognition, the colonial assemblies legislated with feeling against miscegenation. Nor was this merely a matter of avoiding confusion of status, as was suggested by the Handlins. In 1662 Virginia declared that "if any christian shall committ ffornication with a negro man or woman, hee or shee soe offending" should pay double the usual fine. Two years later Maryland prohibited interracial marriages:

> forasmuch as divers freeborne English women forgettfull of their free Condicōn and to the disgrace of our Nation doe intermarry with Negro Slaves by which alsoe divers suites may arise touch-

ing the Issue of such woemen and a great damage doth befall the Masters of such Negros for prevention whereof for deterring such freeborne women from such shamefull Matches . . . , strong language indeed if the problem had only been confusion of status. A Maryland act of 1681 described marriages of white women with Negroes as, among other things, "always to the Satisfaccōn of theire Lascivious & Lustfull desires, & to the disgrace not only of the English butt allso of many other Christian Nations." When Virginia finally prohibited all interracial liaisons in 1691, the assembly vigorously denounced miscegenation and its fruits as "that abominable mixture and spurious issue." [27]

One is confronted, then, with the fact that the first evidences of enslavement and of other forms of debasement appeared at about the same time. Such coincidence comports poorly with both views on the causation of prejudice and slavery. If slavery caused prejudice, then invidious distinctions concerning working in the fields, bearing arms, and sexual union should have appeared only after slavery's firm establishment. If prejudice caused slavery, then one would expect to find such lesser discriminations preceding the greater discrimination of outright enslavement.

Perhaps a third explanation of the relationship between slavery and prejudice may be offered, one that might fit the pattern of events as revealed by existing evidence. Both current views share a common starting point: They predicate two factors, prejudice and slavery, and demand a distinct order of causality. No matter how qualified by recognition that the effect may in turn react upon the cause, each approach inevitably tends to deny the validity of its opposite. But what if one were to regard both slavery and prejudice as species of a general debasement of the Negro? Both may have been equally cause and effect, constantly reacting upon each other, dynamically joining hands to hustle the Negro down the road to complete degradation. Mutual causation is, of course, a highly useful concept for describing social situations in the modern world.[28] Indeed it has been widely applied in only slightly altered fashion to the current racial situation: Racial prejudice and the Negro's lowly position are widely accepted as constantly reinforcing each other.

This way of looking at the facts might well fit better with what we know of slavery itself. Slavery was an organized pattern of human relationships. No matter what the law might say, it was of different character than cattle ownership. No matter how degrading, slavery involved human beings. No one seriously pretended otherwise. Slavery was not an isolated economic or institutional phenomenon; it was the practical facet of a general debasement without which slavery could have no rationality. (Prejudice, too, was a form of debasement, a kind of slavery in the mind.) Certainly the urgent need for labor in a virgin country guided the direction which debasement took, molded it, in fact, into an institutional framework. That economic practicalities shaped the external form of debasement should not tempt one to forget, however, that slavery was at bottom a social arrangement, a way of society's ordering its members in its own mind.

NOTES

1. "About the last of August came in a dutch man of warre that sold us twenty Negars." Smith was quoting John Rolfe's account. Edward Arber and A. G. Bradley (eds.), *Travels and Works of Captain John Smith* . . . (2 vols., Edinburgh, 1910), II, 541.

2. Philip A. Bruce, *Economic History of Virginia in the Seventeenth Century* (2 vols., New York, 1896), II, 57-130; James C. Ballagh, A *History of Slavery in Virginia* (Baltimore, 1902), 28-35.

3. John H. Russell, *The Free Negro in Virginia, 1619-1865* (Baltimore, 1913), 29.

4. Phillips, *American Negro Slavery*, viii.

5. Wesley F. Craven, *The Southern Colonies in the Seventeenth Century, 1607-1689* (Baton Rouge, 1949), 217-19, 402-403.

6. *William and Mary Quarterly*, s. 3, VII (April 1950), 199-222.

7. Kenneth M. Stampp, *The Peculiar Institution: Slavery in the Ante-Bellum South* (New York, 1956), vii-viii, 3-33.

8. *Ibid.*, 21-22.

9. Arnold Rose, "The Roots of Prejudice" in UNESCO, *The Race Question in Modern Science* (New York, 1956), 224. For examples of the more general view see Frederick G. Detweiler, "The Rise of Modern Race Antagonisms," *American Journal of Sociology*, XXXVII (March 1932), 743; M. F. Ashley Montagu, *Man's Most Dangerous Myth: The Fallacy of Race* (New York, 1945), 10-11, 19-20; Gunnar Myrdal, *An American Dilemma: The Negro Problem and Modern Democracy* (New York, 1944), 83-89, 97; Paul Kecskemeti, "The Psychological Theory of Prejudice: Does it Underrate the Role of Social History?" *Commentary*, XVIII (October 1954), 364-66.

10. *Comparative Studies in Society and History*, II (October 1959), 49-66. See also Degler, *Out of Our Past: The Forces that Shaped Modern America* (New York, 1959), 26-39.

11. H. R. McIlwaine (ed.), *Minutes of the Council and General Court of Colonial Virginia, 1622-1632, 1670-1676* (Richmond, 1924), 196. See the lists and musters of 1624 and 1625 in John C. Hotten (ed.), *The Original Lists of Persons of Quality* . . ., (New York, 1880), 169-265.

12. "The status of Negroes was that of servants; and so they were identified and treated down to the 1660's." ("Origins," 203.) The footnote to this statement reads, "For disciplinary and revenue laws in Virginia that did not dis-

O., 1917–1919), I, 42, which turns out to be one quotation from John Milton. However, "spurious" was used in colonial laws with reference only to unions between white and black, and never in bastardy laws involving whites only. Mulattoes were often labeled "spurious" offspring.

28. For example, George C. Homans, *The Human Group* (New York, 1950).

• Negro slavery quickly became established not only in North America but in the British West Indies and in the Spanish, Portugese, and French colonies of the Western Hemisphere. David Brion Davis compares the evolution of slavery and the special characteristics of the institution in British America with slavery in Latin America.

The Evolution of Slavery in British America and Latin America: A Comparison

DAVID BRION DAVIS

The slave trade itself was a powerful agent of acculturation—one might say, of Americanization—which tended to blur distinctions in custom and give a more uniform character to Negro slavery than would have been found among earlier forms of European serfdom and villenage. With the acquisition of important Caribbean islands by Holland, Britain, and France, and with the development of sugar planting in the 1640's, the mounting demand for slaves made it impossible for mercantilist governments to prevent the growth of a vast system of smuggling and illicit trade. The same slave ships brought cargoes to mainland and island colonies, and competed with one another in supplying the Spanish. Planters of various nationalities bought slaves at reduced prices at the great Dutch entrepôts at Saint Eustatius and Curaçao. From their forts on the African coast to their colonies in America, the Dutch, French, English, Danes, and Portuguese were thrown together in a common enterprise that doubtless produced some blending of customs and attitudes toward the Negro slave.[1] Barbadians not only studied and imitated Brazilian methods of sugar cultivation, but possessed slaves by the 1650's who knew the language and customs of Brazil. In Guadeloupe and Martinque, Dutch émigrés from Brazil introduced the Portuguese practice of allowing

From David Brion Davis, *The Problem of Slavery in Western Culture* (Ithaca: Cornell University Press, 1966), pp. 244-53. Copyright © 1966 by Cornell University. Used by permission of Cornell University Press.

slaves to grow their own provisions. During the seventeenth century there were close ties between Barbados and the mainland colonies of North America; and many of the Negroes in the continental colonies had lived for a time in the West Indies. Some of them spoke French, Dutch, or Spanish.²

Much is yet to be learned about this process of cultural exchange and its possible influence on the evolution of systems of slavery in the various colonies. Few questions in American history have been so controversial or so charged with moral significance as the origin of chattel slavery and its relation to racial prejudice. The most convincing recent studies suggest that the mainland colonists adopted from Barbados the view that Negroes were especially suited for perpetual slavery; and that while the early status of some Negroes was close to that of white servants, an increasingly degraded position was both a source and result of racial prejudice.³ But however unfamiliar perpetual servitude may have been to most Elizabethan Englishmen, as early as 1617 a noted Puritan writer could assume that "slavish" servants were "perpetually put under the power of the master, as blackamores with us." ⁴ The problem is considerably complicated by the ambiguity of seventeenth-century terms. Some historians have assumed that a "servant" was not a slave, and yet Samuel Purchas and Thomas Hobbes, to mention only two writers of that century, used the word "servant" to refer to the most absolute slaves.⁵ In the French and Spanish colonies, as well as in the English, the word for "Negro" was frequently used as a synonym for "slave." But Richard Ligon considered the condition of white servants in Barbados worse than that of the Negroes. Although white men were not subject to perpetual and inheritable servitude, it would be a mistake to think they were free from all burdens of slavery. In many colonies white servants could be sold, inherited, wagered, or recovered for a debt; Gabriel Towerson, an eminent English divine, complained that too many servants confused service with a profession and thought they needed to obey only when assigned a specific task.⁶

There were two historical circumstances, however, which differentiated the white from the Negro servant. As Oscar and Mary Handlin have observed, the emigration of white laborers was in large part voluntary, and the demand for their services was great enough to induce colonial legislators to offer them various protections and rewards: this was not only true on the mainland, but also in the West Indies, where there was the additional incentive of increasing public safety and avoiding a rebellious union of Negroes and lowly whites. We should also remember that white servitude was based on the customs and laws of particular countries. The English servant was not ordinarily an article of international commerce, nor was he subject to the ancient laws of slavery, as incorporated in the *jus gentium*.[7] Yet it was a general belief that Christianity permitted the enslavement of men "of infidel origin," and that Negroes purchased on the African coast had either been convicted of crime or captured, hopefully in a just war, and were therefore slaves by virtue of the law of nations. Hence Sir Edward Coke could affirm, in *Calvin's Case*, that infidels could either be put to death or enslaved; and Cotton Mather, doubtless drawing on Aristotle, could tell Massachusetts Negroes that they were "the *Animate, Separate, Active Instruments* of other men." [8]

Even if colonists were inclined to apply ancient concepts of slavery to the Negro, there was nothing, of course, to prevent individual masters from evolving their own rules and practices. First in Barbados and the Leeward Islands, then in Virginia and Maryland, and finally in Pennsylvania, New York, New England, and French Canada, societies accepted the perpetual slavery of Indians and Negroes without specific legislative sanction. In some areas the actual status of Negroes differed little from that of white servants; in New England, where the Confederation of 1643 recognized the slavery of captives, bondsmen were considered for a time to be under the protective regulations of the Old Testament. But the fact that stands out from all the variations in temporary custom is the cumulative debasement of the Negro in every British and French colony. Whether he served the Puritans of Old Providence Island or the French of Martinique, the Jamaica overseer or the Virginia farmer, the Pennsylvania Quaker or the Canadian convent, his person was the property of his owner, and he and his progeny, if they were born of a slave woman, were condemned to eternal bondage.[9]

From 1680 to 1710 virtually every English and French colony from the Saint Lawrence to South America acquired laws that attempted to define the slave's peculiar position as conveyable property, subject to rules respecting debt, descent, and taxation; and as a man who might be protected, punished, or prevented from exercising human capacities. Given the wide range of differences in colonial societies, the surprising fact about these laws is their underlying similarity. Everywhere they embodied ambiguities and compromises that arose from the impossibility of acting consistently on the premise that men were things. The basic contradiction was elucidated much later by a Virginia court, which echoed the doctrine of Seneca: "Slaves are not only property,

but they are rational beings, and entitled to the humanity of the
Court, when it can be exercised without invading the rights of property; and as regards the owner, their value is much enhanced by the
mutual attachment of master and slave; a value which cannot enter
into the calculation of damages by a jury." [10]

Both French and English colonial law assumed that the slave had
essentially the attributes of personal property, and like a horse or cow
could be moved, sold, or rented out at the will of his owner. In several
colonies, however, there was doubt whether for purposes of taxation
slaves should be rated as persons, personal property, or real estate.
And while no colony presumed to infringe upon the slaveholder's right
to move or sell his property, it was widely recognized that, in the interests of both the slave and society, there should be special rules
regarding debt and inheritance.[11]

As early as the 1660's planters in the Leeward Islands were disturbed by the fact that merchant creditors could force the sale of Negroes and other chattels at auction, and thus deprive an estate of its
productive capacity. In addition, the death of a planter sometimes resulted in the ruin of his estate when executors or minor heirs
needlessly disposed of slaves. To prevent these evils, colonial legislators
tried to invest bondsmen with some of the attributes of real estate,
and thus provided lawyers with a subject for endless debate and confused litigation. In 1669 an Antigua law ruled that if a debtor's
chattels, including white servants, were insufficient to satisfy a claim,
the creditor must accept slaves as "estates of inheritance," attached to
the freehold, and assume management of the plantation. In the previous year Barbados had defined slaves as freehold property, although
in 1672 they were deemed chattels for the payment of an owner's
debts. For more than a century, legislators in Jamaica and the Leeward
Islands sought to make the descent of slaves conform to the law for
freehold property, and to prevent Negroes from being seized for debt
when claims could be satisfied by other means. But in all other respects, as a Nevis statute of 1705 made clear, there was no question
that slaves were chattels.[12]

The French islands, Virginia, and South Carolina all experienced
the same difficulties in trying to reconcile the notion of a slave as personal property with the desire to protect the integrity of estates. Under
the *Code Noir* the slave was unmistakably a chattel; but a royal decree
of 1721 prohibited heirs under the age of twenty-five from selling
slaves from their estates.[13] After 1705 bondsmen in Virginia were
accounted real estate for purposes of descent, but chattels, by an act of

1727, with respect to gifts and devises. Three years later a court decided that, regardless of previous statutes, executors were to consider slave property as no different from horses or cattle, a view which the assembly endorsed in 1748, when it was decided that confusion could be lessened by reducing bondsmen to their "natural condition" as personal goods. This new law was nullified, however, by the crown. There is evidence that Negroes in Virginia were sometimes annexed to the land and entailed, and were considered by courts as in some sense bound to the soil in inheritance. But in 1794 it was held, in Walden v. Payne, that though the law had protected bondsmen from unnecessary sale for the payment of debts and levies, they were chattels by nature. We might note that the confusion was carried across the mountains into Kentucky, which adopted the Virginia law of 1705 defining slaves as real estate for certain purposes. In colonial South Carolina bondsmen were regarded as chattels personal, notwithstanding an attempt in 1690 to class them as real estate; and yet as late as 1837 a court upheld an action of trespass against the captain of a patrol who had whipped a slave belonging to the plaintiff, but hired out to another man, on the ground that a slave was more analogous to land than to personal property. In addition to appealing to the analogy of an easement, the court maintained that a master possessed all the legal means of protecting his slave that the slave himself would have, had he been a freeman.[14]

It is not quite accurate, then, to think of chattel slavery as a well-defined status which put the Negro on precisely the same footing as other personal property. In no American colony was he attached to the soil in the sense of the *colonus*, or in a way that limited the freedom of his owner. But for both economic and humanitarian reasons, judges and lawmakers recognized that the slave was something more than a private and expendable possession.

The ambiguity was more pronounced when it came to regulating the bondsman's daily life and defining his relations with other people. If we think of freedom as a power to act or cause others to act, then it is clear that even the most authoritarian master, supported by the most oppressive laws, was to some extent limited by the will of his slaves, who had the power to appeal, flatter, humiliate, disobey, sabotage, or rebel. Richard Ligon reported that Barbadian Negroes not only persuaded planters to improve their diet, but complained so long about a shortage of women that their owners felt obliged to purchase more, the coveted females being apportioned by the slaves themselves in accordance with their own social hierarchies.[15] Courts and legislatures were farther removed from the direct influence of slaves, and had, besides, the mission of maintaining the standards and morale of slaveholders; yet in few instances could the law ignore the human capacities of slaves.

We have already seen that there were formidable obstacles to the religious conversion of slaves. By and large, Catholics showed far more concern for the souls of Negroes than did Protestants; and yet a number of British colonies, including New York, Jamaica, and South Carolina, gave official encouragement to such missionary work. If this amounted to little more than pious lip-service, the same could be said of the religious provisions in the *Code Noir*. The Spanish and Portuguese were more successful in winning converts, but it is doubtful whether the mass of slaves in any colony enjoyed a meaningful religious life.[16]

Whether a Negro worked on Sunday or had an opportunity to marry were largely matters of local custom and circumstance. An article in the *Code Noir* forbidding Sunday work was apparently no better enforced than similar laws in colonial Georgia and South Carolina. But in many British colonies it was customary to reserve Sundays for leisure and marketing, and to grant days of respite at Christmas, Easter, and Whitsuntide.[17] Since even Pennsylvania prohibited the marriage of white servants without their masters' consent, it is not surprising that this was a minimal restriction for slaves under both English and French law. A Massachusetts statute said that so long as servants were of the same "nation," their marriage should not be unreasonably denied. But in French Canada, where slave marriages were legally valid when permitted by a master, infants were disposed of at the will of the mother's owner, and when they died, were listed only as the property of a master, with no indication of their parentage. In the British West Indies and Southern mainland colonies, slave marriages were no more legal than under Roman law. But as in Roman law, nineteenth-century Louisiana courts acknowledged that such a *contubernium* had legal consequences, and could become valid as a contract after manumission. In 1871 a judge of the supreme court of Tennessee delivered the opinion that slave marriages had always been valid in that state, though not followed by all the legal consequences of a marriage between freemen. This somewhat questionable view simply underlines the essential point: it was impossible to ignore the fact that slaves could and did marry; but even where given legal sanction, such marriages were radically altered by the effects of bondage.[18]

NOTES

1. Evidence of the mixing of nationalities in the slave trade, and of the frequent contact between Dutch, English, French, Spanish, Portuguese, Danes, and Swedes, can be found throughout Elizabeth Donnan's *Documents Illustrative of the History of the Slave Trade to America* (Washington, 1930–35). Fernando Romero stresses that the entire slave trade was a single process divided into various branches. (Romero, "The Slave Trade and the Negro in South America," *Hispanic American Historical Review*, XXIV [Aug., 1944], 371. See also, Scelle, *Traite négrière*, I, 707; Basil Davidson, *Black Mother: The Years of the African Slave Trade* [Boston, 1961], *passim*; Daniel P. Mannix and Malcolm Cowley, *Black Cargoes: A History of the Atlantic Slave Trade*, 1518–1865 [New York, 1962], *passim*.

2. Richard Ligon, *A True & Exact History of the Island of Barbados* (London, 1757), pp. 52, 85; Vincent T. Harlow, *A History of Barbados, 1625–1685* (Oxford, 1926), pp. 268-91; Jean-Baptiste Du Tertre, *Histoire générale des Antilles habitées par les François* (Paris, 1667–71), II, 515; Frank Wesley Pitman, *The Development of the British West Indies, 1700–1763* (New Haven, 1917), pp. 6-15; Frank Wesley Craven, *The Southern Colonies in the Seventeenth Century, 1607–1689* (Baton Rouge, 1949), pp. 18, 25; "Eighteenth-Century Slaves as Advertised by Their Masters," *Journal of Negro History*, I (Apr., 1916), 163-216; Pierre-François-Xavier de Charlevoix, *Histoire de l'Isle Espagnole ou de Saint-Domingue . . .* (Amsterdam, 1733), III, 162-63; Winthrop D. Jordan, "The Influence of the West Indies on the Origins of New England Slavery," *William and Mary Quarterly*, 3rd ser., XVIII (Apr., 1961), 248-49.

3. See especially the following articles: Winthrop Jordan, "Influence of West Indies," pp. 243-50; Jordan, "American Chiaroscuro: The Status and Definition of Mulattoes in the British Colonies," *William and Mary Quarterly*, 2nd ser., XIX (Apr., 1962), 183-200; Jordan, "Modern Tensions and the Origins of American Slavery," *Journal of Southern History*, XXVIII (Feb., 1962), 18-30; M. Eugene Sirmans, "The Legal Status of the Slave in South Carolina, 1670–1740," *Journal of Southern History*, XXVIII (Nov., 1962), 462-73; Carl N. Degler, "Slavery and the Genesis of American Race Prejudice," *Comparative Studies in Society and History*, II (Oct., 1959), 49-67. The seminal study which raised issues that have not yet been resolved is Oscar and Mary Handlin, "Origins of the Southern Labor System," *William and Mary Quarterly*, 3rd ser., VII (Apr., 1950), 199-222.

4. Paul Baynes, *An Entire Commentary upon the Whole Epistle of the Apostle Paul to the Ephesians*, reprinted in *Nichol's Series of Commentaries*, XI (Edinburgh, 1865), pp. 365-69. Although this work was not published until 1643, Baynes died in 1617. I am indebted to Lawrence W. Towner for supplying me with a copy of this document.

5. Thomas Hobbes, *De Cive, or the Citizen* (ed. and with introd. by Sterling P. Lamprecht, New York, 1949), ii, viii; Samuel Purchas, *Purchas His Pilgrimes in Five Bookes* (London, 1625), III, 419 (Purchas refers to the "cholopey" of Novograde both as "bondslaves" and "servants").

6. Ligon, *True & Exact History*, pp. 43-44; Abbot Emerson Smith, *Colonists*

in Bondage: White Servitude and Convict Labor in America, 1607–1776
(Chapel Hill, 1947), pp. 224, 233; Richard B. Schlatter, *The Social Ideas of Religious Leaders, 1660–1688* (Oxford, 1940), p. 66.

7. Oscar and Mary Handlin, "Origins of the Southern Labor System," pp. 210-21; *Acts of Assembly . . . Charibbee Leeward Islands*, pp. 159-63; Harlow, *History of Barbados*, pp. 303-5; *Journals of the Assembly of Jamaica*, I (Jamaica, 1811), 120-21, 125; Smith, *Colonists in Bondage*, pp. 227-38. The servitude of English and Irish convicts and prisoners was not, of course, contractual in character; it was mitigated only by the traditional belief that "Christians," meaning men who were not of "infidel" origin, should not be held in perpetual slavery. My interpretation differs from that of the Handlins with respect to the origins of chattel slavery and the degree of similarity between West Indian and mainland colonies.

8. W. S. Holdsworth, *A History of English Law*, VII (London, n.d.), 484; Lawrence W. Towner, " 'A Fondness for Freedom': Servant Protest in Puritan Society," *William and Mary Quarterly*, 2nd ser., XIX (Apr., 1962), 210.

9. J. H. Lefroy, *Memorials of the Discovery and Early Settlement of the Bermudas or Somers Islands, 1515–1685, Compiled from the Colonial Records and Other Original Sources* (n.p., 1932 reprint ed.), I, 526-27; II, 70, 166; Degler, "Slavery and the Genesis of American Race Prejudice," pp. 49-67; Ligon, *True & Exact History*, pp. 22-37; Lucien Peytraud, *L'Esclavage aux Antilles françaises avant 1789* (Paris, 1897), pp. 144-45; Ulrich Bonnell Phillips, *American Negro Slavery: A Survey of the Supply, Employment and Control of Negro Labor as Determined by the Plantation Regime* (reprint ed., Gloucester, Mass., 1959), pp. 46, 52, 98-99; Trudel, *L'Esclavage au Canada français*, pp. 99-100; Almon W. Lauber, *Indian Slavery in Colonial Times Within the Present Limits of the United States* (New York, 1913), pp. 214-16; Susie M. Ames, *Studies of the Virginia Eastern Shore in the Seventeenth Century* (Richmond, 1940), pp. 101-6; Towner, "Fondness for Freedom," pp. 201-19; Lorenzo J. Greene, *The Negro in Colonial New England, 1620–1776* (New York, 1942), pp. 124-26, 167-90; Edward R. Turner, *The Negro in Pennsylvania: Slavery, Servitude, Freedom, 1639–1861* (Washington, 1911), pp. 18-26; Jordan, "Influence of West Indies," pp. 243-50; Jordan, "Modern Tensions," pp. 23-30. For interpretations which place more emphasis on local conditions and differences, see Handlin, "Origins of Southern Labor System," pp. 199-22; John M. Mecklin. "The Evolution of the Slave Status in American Democracy," *Journal of Negro History*, II (Apr., 1917), 105-25; (July, 1917), 229-51; James C. Ballagh, *History of Slavery in Virginia* (Baltimore, 1902), *passim*. Stanley Elkins provides an excellent summary and discussion of the entire question in *Slavery*, pp. 37-52.

10. Helen T. Catterall (ed.), *Judicial Cases Concerning American Slavery and the Negro* (Washington, 1926-1937), I, 142, 144.

11. Peytraud, *L'Esclavage aux Antilles français*, pp. 144-45; 213-41, 253-65; Trudel, *L'Esclavage au Canada français*, pp. 99-102; Lauber, *Indian Slavery*, pp. 216-17, 226-29; Greene, *Negro in Colonial New England*, p. 126; George H. Moore, *Notes on the History of Slavery in Massachusetts* (New York, 1866), pp. 62-65.

12. *Acts of Assembly . . . Charibbee Leeward Islands*, pp. 18-19, 82; *The Laws of the Island of Saint Vincent, and Its Dependencies, from the First Establishment of a Legislature to the End of the Year, 1809* (Bridgnorth, Eng-

land, 1811), pp. 24-49; C. S. S. Higham, *The Development of the Leeward Islands Under the Restoration, 1660–1688: A Study of the Foundations of the Old Colonial System* (Cambridge, England, 1921), pp. 157-59; *Journals of the Assembly of Jamaica*, II (London, 1824), 16-17, 30-31; *The Statutes and Laws of the Island of Jamaica* (rev. ed., Jamaica, 1889), pp. 115-16; Lawrence Henry Gipson, *The Triumphant Empire: New Responsibilities Within the Enlarged Empire, 1763–1766* (New York, 1956), p. 259. There was considerable conflict between British and colonial governments on the precise legal character of slave property. This was especially true after 1732, when Parliament enacted a law to facilitate the recovery of colonial debts. Although British law defined slaves as real estate, and the government disallowed a Virginia statute classing them as personal goods, the dispute involved the interests of debtors and creditors and had nothing to do with the general status of slaves as conveyable property. For this reason I think that M. Eugene Sirmans exaggerates the moral significance of slaves being defined as freehold property for purposes of descent in Barbados and South Carolina ("The Legal Status of the Slave in South Carolina, 1670–1740," *Journal of Negro History*, XXVIII [Nov., 1962], 462-73). Even in Louisiana, where slaves were long classed as real estate, they retained most of the characteristics of chattels personal (Kenneth M. Stampp, *The Peculiar Institution: Slavery in the Ante-Bellum South* [New York, 1956], p. 197). I have seen no evidence to show that a definition of slaves as freehold property implied that an owner had a right only to the services of his slave and not to the slave himself. Regardless of rules on descent and seizure for debt, slaves in both British and French colonies could be sold or otherwise conveyed apart from the land on which they worked.

13. *Le Code Noir, ou recueil des reglemens rendus jusqu'à présent. Concernant le gouvernement, l'administration de la justice, la police, la discipline & le commerce des negres dans les colonies françoises* (Paris, 1742), pp. 308-9; Peytraud, *L'Esclavage aux Antilles français*, pp. 247-65. Article 44 of the *Code Noir* classed slaves as *meubles*, but the law prohibited seizure and separate sale of husbands and wives, or of children under the age of puberty.

14. John Codman Hurd, *The Law of Freedom and Bondage in the United States* (Boston, 1858–62), I, 239, 242-43, 297, 303; II, 15-16; Sirmans, "Legal Status of the Slave in South Carolina," pp. 462-73; Catterall (ed.), *Judicial Cases*, I, 83-86, 93, 99-103, 269, 312, 318; II, 365, 393-96.

15. Ligon, *True & Exact History*, pp. 43, 47-48. A thoughtful dicussion of the meanings and complexities of liberty is Oscar and Mary Handlin, *The Dimensions of Liberty* (Cambridge, Mass., 1961), pp. 18-20.

16. Hurd, *Law of Freedom*, I, 232, 281, 297, 300; *Journals of the Assembly of Jamaica*, I, 120-25; Peytraud, *L'Esclavage aux Antilles français*, pp. 243-45; Martin, "Slavery and Abolition in Brazil," p. 168; Stein, *Vassouras*, pp. 196-99. In some English colonies, such as Pennsylvania, the proportion of converted Negroes may have been as high as that in any of the Spanish and Portuguese colonies (Turner, *Negro in Pennsylvania*, pp. 43-45).

17. Peytraud, *L'Esclavage aux Antilles français*, pp. 213-41; Hurd, *Law of Freedom*, I, 306-7; Ruth Scarborough, *The Opposition to Slavery in Georgia Prior to 1860* (Nashville, Tenn., 1933), p. 84; *Laws of Island of Saint Vincent*, p. 46; [Long], *History of Jamaica*, II, 491. Unlike the *Code Noir*, the laws of many of the British colonies, both on the mainland and in the West Indies, attempted to limit the number of hours a slave could work each day.

18. Smith, *Colonists in Bondage*, p. 271; Peytraud, *L'Esclavage aux Antilles français*, pp. 244-45; Turner, *Negro in Pennsylvania*, pp. 45-46; Hurd, *Law of Freedom*, I, 263; Trudel, *L'Esclavage au Canada français*, pp. 267-73; Cobb, *Law of Negro Slavery*, p. 243; Catterall (ed.), *Judicial Cases*, II, 479, 592. Although the Catholic Church had long accepted the right of slaves to marry even without their masters' permission, this measure was still being demanded by Brazilian reformers of the nineteenth century (José Bonifácio, *Memoir Addressed to the General, Constituent and Legislative Assembly*, pp. 45-46). There is considerable evidence to suggest that slaves benefited very little from having their marriages recognized by law. In Brazil, Saint Domingue, Québec, and Massachusetts such legal sanction did not prevent the separation of families or the independent sale of small children (Williams, "Treatment of Negro Slaves in Brazilian Empire," p. 325; Greene, *Negro in Colonial New England*, p. 211). William Huskisson, as Secretary of State for the British Colonial Office, pointed out that a Jamaican law of 1826 permitting slave marriages was largely meaningless because it required baptism and permission from masters, and because, in any event, the integrity of slave families was unprotected. And yet in certain regions of the South, Christian marriages of slaves were widely sanctioned by public opinion even if not by law (*Slave Law of Jamaica*, pp. 62, 145-58; Edward W. Phifer, "Slavery in Microcosm: Burke County, North Carolina," *Journal of Southern History*, XXVIII [May, 1962], p. 148).

II: THE SLAVE

• Ulrich B. Phillips produced the classic historical defense of American Negro slavery. His research uncovered a wealth of important material concerning the institution and, although more recent scholars have challenged his racist beliefs and his sympathetic attitude toward slavery, Phillips's writings remain extremely important for any student of slavery. The following selection offers a good summary of his perspectives on slavery as a social system and on the character of the Negro slave.

Southern Negro Slavery: A Benign View

ULRICH BONNELL PHILLIPS

The simplicity of the social structure on the plantations facilitated Negro adjustment, the master taking the place of the accustomed chief.[1] And yet these black voyagers experienced a greater change by far than befell white immigrants. In their home lands they had lived naked, observed fetish, been bound by tribal law, and practiced primitive crafts. In America none of these things were of service or sanction. The Africans were thralls, wanted only for their brawn, required to take things as they found them and to do as they were told, coerced into self-obliterating humility, and encouraged to respond only to the teachings and preachings of their masters, and adapt themselves to the white men's ways.

In some cases transported talent embraced the new opportunity in extraordinary degree. . . . But in general, as always, the common middle course was passive acquiescence.

To make adaptation the more certain, it was argued that "no Negro should be bought old; such are always sullen and unteachable, and frequently put an end to their lives." [2] And indeed planters who could afford an unproductive period were advised to select young children

From Ulrich Bonnell Phillips, *Life and Labor in the Old South* (Boston: Little, Brown and Company, 1927), pp. 194-217. Copyright © 1927, by Little, Brown and Company. Reprinted by permission of Little, Brown and Company.

from the ships, "for their juvenile minds entertain no regrets for the loss of their connections. They acquire the English language with great ease, and improve daily in size, understanding and capacity for labour." [3] The proportion of children in the cargoes was great enough to permit such a policy by those who might adopt it.[4] But the fact that prices for imported Negroes, even after seasoning, ranged lower than for those to the American manner born is an evidence that the new habituation as a rule never completely superseded the old. Thanks, however, to plantation discipline and to the necessity of learning the master's language if merely to converse with fellow slaves of different linguistic stocks, African mental furnishings faded even among adult arrivals.

To the second and later generations folklore was transmitted, but for the sake of comprehension by the children an American Brer Rabbit replaced his jungle prototype. If lullabies were crooned in African phrase their memory soon lapsed, along with nearly all other African terms except a few personal names, Quash, Cuffee, Cudjoe and the like.[5] And even these may have owed such perpetuation as they had to the persistence of the maritime slave trade which long continued to bring new Quashes and Cuffees from the mother country. In short, Foulahs and Fantyns, Eboes and Angolas begat American plantation Negroes to whom a spear would be strange but a "languid hoe" familiar, the tomtom forgotten but the banjo inviting to the fingers and the thumb. Eventually it could be said that the Negroes had no memories of Africa as a home.[6] Eventually, indeed, a Virginia freedman wrote after thirteen years of residence in Liberia, "I, being a Virginian," rejoice that "the good people of my old state are about to settle a colony on the coast of Africa"; and went on to say of himself and his compatriots, "there is some of us that would not be satisfied in no other colony while ever there was one called New Virginia." [7] His very name, William Draper, is an index of his Anglo-Americanization; and a pride which he expresses that Virginia Negroes have been the founders and the chief rulers "of almost all the settlements" in Liberia proves him a true son of the Old Dominion, "the mother of states and of statesmen." But William Draper was an exceptional specimen. In the main the American Negroes ruled not even themselves. They were more or less contentedly slaves, with grievances from time to time but not ambition. With "hazy pasts and reckless futures," they lived in each moment as it flew, and left "Old Massa" to take such thought as the morrow might need.

*   *   *

The plantation force was a conscript army, living in barracks and on constant "fatigue." Husbands and wives were comrades in service under an authority as complete as the commanding personnel could wish. The master was captain and quartermaster combined, issuing orders and distributing rations. The overseer and the foreman, where there were such, were lieutenant and sergeant to see that orders were executed. The field hands were privates with no choice but to obey unless, like other seasoned soldiers, they could dodge the duties assigned.

But the plantation was also a homestead, isolated, permanent and peopled by a social group with a common interest in achieving and maintaining social order. Its régime was shaped by the customary human forces, interchange of ideas and coadaptation of conduct. The intermingling of white and black children in their pastimes was no more continuous or influential than the adult interplay of command and response, of protest and concession. In so far as harmony was attained—and in this the plantation mistress was a great if quiet factor —a common tradition was evolved embodying reciprocal patterns of conventional conduct.

The plantation was of course a factory, in which robust laborers were essential to profits. Its mere maintenance as a going concern required the proprietor to sustain the strength and safeguard the health of his operatives and of their children, who were also his, destined in time to take their parents' places. The basic food allowance came to be somewhat standardized at a quart of corn meal and half a pound of salt pork per day for each adult and proportionably for children, commuted or supplemented with sweet potatoes, field peas, sirup, rice, fruit and "garden sass" as locality and season might suggest. The clothing was coarse, and shoes were furnished only for winter. The housing was in huts of one or two rooms per family, commonly crude but weather-tight. Fuel was abundant. The sanitation of the clustered cabins was usually a matter of systematic attention; and medical service was at least commensurate with the groping science of the time and the sparse population of the country. Many of the larger plantations had central kitchens, day nurseries, infirmaries and physicians on contract for periodic visits.[8] The aged and infirm must be cared for along with the young and able-bodied, to maintain the good will of their kinsmen among the workers, if for no other reason. Morale was no less needed than muscle if performance were to be kept above a barely tolerable minimum.

*   *   *

The plantation was a school. An intelligent master would consult his own interest by affording every talented slave special instruction and by inculcating into the commoner sort as much routine efficieny, regularity and responsibility as they would accept. Not only were many youths given training in the crafts, and many taught to read and write, even though the laws forbade it, but a goodly number of planters devised and applied plans to give their whole corps spontaneous incentive to relieve the need of detailed supervision. . . .

The civilizing of the Negroes was not merely a consequence of definite schooling but a fruit of plantation life itself. The white household taught perhaps less by precept than by example. It had much the effect of a "social settlement" in a modern city slum, furnishing models of speech and conduct, along with advice on occasion, which the vicinage is invited to accept. . . . The bulk of the black personnel was notoriously primitive, uncouth, improvident and inconstant, merely because they were Negroes of the time; and by their slave status they were relieved from the pressure of want and debarred from any full-force incentive of gain.

Many planters, however, sought to promote contentment, loyalty and zeal by gifts and rewards, and by sanctioning the keeping of poultry and pigs and the cultivation of little fields in off times with the privilege of selling any produce. In the cotton belt the growing of nankeen cotton was particularly encouraged, for its brownish color would betray any surreptitious addition from the master's own fields. Some indeed had definite bonus systems. A. H. Bernard of Virginia determined at the close of 1836 to replace his overseer with a slave foreman, and announced to his Negroes that in case of good service by the corps he would thereafter distribute premiums to the amount of what had been the overseer's wages. . . .

But any copious resort to profit-sharing schemes was avoided at large as being likely to cost more than it would yield in increment to the planter's own crop. The generality of planters, it would seem, considered it hopeless to make their field hands into thorough workmen or full-fledged men, and contented themselves with very moderate achievement. Tiring of endless correction and unfruitful exhortation, they relied somewhat supinely upon authority with a tone of kindly patronage and a baffled acquiescence in slack service. . . .

It has been said by a critic of the twentieth century South: "In some ways the negro is shamefully mistreated—mistreated through leniency," which permits him as a tenant or employee to lean upon the whites in a continuous mental siesta and sponge upon them habitually, instead of requiring him to stand upon his own moral and economic legs.[9] The same censure would apply as truly in any preceding generation. The slave plantation, like other schools, was conditioned by the nature and habituations of its teachers and pupils. Its instruction was inevitably slow; and the effect of its discipline was restricted by the fact that even its aptest pupils had no diploma in prospect which would send them forth to fend for themselves.

* * *

The plantation was a parish, or perhaps a chapel of ease. Some planters assumed the functions of lay readers when ordained ministers were not available, or joined the congregation even when Negro preachers preached.[10] Bishop Leonidas Polk was chief chaplain on his own estate, and is said to have suffered none of his slaves to be other than Episcopalian; [11] but the generality of masters gave full freedom as to church connection.

The legislature of Barbados, when urged by the governor in 1681 to promote the Christianization of slaves on that island, replied, "their savage brutishness renders them wholly incapable. Many have endeavored it without success." [12] But on the continent such sentiments had small echo; and as decades passed masters and churches concerned themselves increasingly in the premises. A black preacher might meet rebuke and even run a risk of being lynched if he harped too loudly upon the liberation of the Hebrews from Egyptian bondage; [13] but a moderate supervision would prevent such indiscretions. The Sermon on the Mount would be harmless despite its suggestion of an earthly inheritance for the meek; the Decalogue was utterly sound; and "servants obey your masters," "render unto Caesar the things that are Caesar's," and "well done, thou good and faithful servant" were invaluable texts for homilies. The Methodists and Baptists were inclined to invite ecstasy from free and slave alike. Episcopalians and Presbyterians, and the Catholics likewise, deprecating exuberance, dealt rather in quiet precept than in fervid exhortation—with far smaller statistical results.[14]

The plantation was a pageant and a variety show in alternation. The procession of plowmen at evening, slouched crosswise on their mules; the dance in the new sugarhouse, preceded by prayer; the bonfire in the quarter with contests in clogs, cakewalks and Charlestons whose fascinations were as yet undiscovered by the great world; the work songs in solo and refrain, with not too fast a rhythm; the baptizing in the creek, with lively demonstrations from the "sisters" as they came dripping out; the torchlight pursuit of 'possum and 'coon, with full-voiced halloo to baying houn' dawg and yelping cur; the rabbit hunt, the log-rolling, the house-raising, the husking bee, the quilting party, the wedding, the cock fight, the crap game, the children's play, all punctuated plantation life—and most of them were highly vocal.[15] A funeral now and then of some prominent slave would bring festive sorrowing, or the death of a beloved master an outburst of emotion.[16]

*   *   *

The plantation was a matrimonial bureau, something of a harem perhaps, a copious nursery, and a divorce court. John Brickell wrote of colonial North Carolina: "It frequently happens, when these women have no Children by the first Husband, after being a year or two co-habiting together, the Planters oblige them to take a second, third, fourth, fifth, or more Husbands or Bedfellows; a fruitful Woman amongst them being very much valued by the Planters, and a numerous Issue esteemed the greatest Riches in this Country." [17] By running on to five or more husbands for a constantly barren woman Brickell discredits his own statement. Yet it may have had a kernel of truth, and it is quite possible that something of such a policy persisted throughout the generations. These things do not readily get into the records. I have myself heard a stalwart Negro express a humorous regret that he was free, for said he in substance: "If I had lived in slavery times my master would have given me half a dozen wives and taken care of all the children." This may perhaps voice a tradition among slave descendants, and the tradition may in turn derive from an actual sanction of polygamy by some of the masters. A planter doubtless described a practice not unique when he said "that he interfered as little as possible with their domestic habits except in matters of police. 'We don't care what they do when their tasks are over—we lose sight of them till next day. Their morals and manners are in their own keeping. The men may have, for instance, as many wives as they please, so long as they do not quarrel about such matters.' " [18] But another was surely no less representative when he instructed his overseer: "Marriages shall be performed in every instance of a nuptial contract, and the parties settled off to themselves without encumbering other houses to give discontent. No slave shall be allowed to cohabit with two or more wives or husbands at the same time; doing so shall subject them to a strict trial and severe punishment." [19]

Life was without doubt monogamous in general; and some of the matings were by order,[20] though the generality were pretty surely spontaneous. . . .

In the number of their children the Negro women rivaled the remarkable fecundity of their mistresses. One phenomenal slave mother bore forty-one children, mostly of course as twins; [21] and the records of many others ran well above a dozen each. As a rule, perhaps, babies were even more welcome to slave women than to free; for childbearing brought lightened work during pregnancy and suckling, and a lack of ambition conspired with a freedom from economic anxiety to clear the path of maternal impulse.

Concubinage of Negro women to planters and their sons and overseers is evidenced by the census enumeration of mulattoes and by other data.[22] It was flagrantly prevalent in the Creole section of Louisiana, and was at least sporadic from New England to Texas. The régime of slavery facilitated concubinage not merely by making black women subject to white men's wills but by promoting intimacy and weakening racial antipathy. The children, of whatever shade or paternity, were alike the property of the mother's owner and were nourished on the plantation. Not a few mulattoes, however, were manumitted by their fathers and vested with property.

Slave marriages, not being legal contracts, might be dissolved without recourse to public tribunals. Only the master's consent was required, and this was doubtless not hard to get. On one plantation systematic provision was made in the standing regulations: "When sufficient cause can be shewn on either side, a marriage may be annulled; but the offending party must be severely punished. Where both are in the wrong, both must be punished, and if they insist on separating must have a hundred lashes apiece. After such a separation, neither can marry again for three years." [23] If such a system were in general effect in our time it would lessen the volume of divorce in American society. But it may be presumed that most plantation rules were not so stringent.

The home of a planter or of a well-to-do townsman was likely to be a "magnificent negro boarding-house," at which and from which an indefinite number of servants and their dependents and friends were fed.[24] In town the tribe might increase to the point of embarrassment. . . .

Each plantation had a hierarchy. Not only were the master and his family exalted to a degree beyond the reach of slave aspiration, but among the Negroes themselves there were pronounced gradations of rank, privilege and esteem. An absent master wrote: "I wish to be remembered to all the servants, distinguishing Andrew as the head man and Katy as the mother of the tribe. Not forgetting Charlotte as the head of the culinary department nor Marcus as the Tubal Cain of the community, hoping that they will continue to set a good example and that the young ones will walk in their footsteps." [25] The foreman, the miller and the smith were men of position and pride. The butler, the maid and the children's nurse were in continuous contact with the white household, enjoying the best opportunity to acquire its manners along with its discarded clothing. The field hands were at the foot of the scale, with a minimum of white contact and privileged only to plod, so to say, as brethren to the ox.

At all times in the South as a whole perhaps half of the slaves were owned or hired in units of twenty or less, which were too small for the full plantation order, and perhaps half of this half were on mere farms or in town employment, rather as "help" than as a distinct laboring force. Many small planters' sons and virtually all the farmers in person worked alongside any field hands they might possess; and indoor tasks were parceled among the women and girls white and black. . . .

However the case may have been as to relative severity on farms and plantations, there can be no doubt that the farmers' slaves of all sorts were likely to share somewhat intimately such lives as their masters led [26] and to appropriate a considerable part of such culture as they possessed—to be more or less genteel with their gentility or crude with their crudity, to think similar thoughts and speak much the same language. On the other hand, the one instance of wide divergence in dialect between the whites and the Negroes prevailed in the single district in which the scheme of life was that of large plantations from the time when Africans were copiously imported. On the seaboard of South Carolina and Georgia most of the blacks (and they were very black) still speak Gullah, a dialect so distinct that unfamiliar visitors may barely understand it. And dialect, there as elsewhere, is an index to culture in general.

*   *   *

The life of slaves, whether in large groups or small, was not without grievous episodes. A planter's son wrote to his father upon a discovery of mislaid equipment: "The bridle and martingal which you whipped Amy so much for stealing was by some inattention of Robert's left in Mr. Clark's stable." Again, an overseer, exasperated by the sluggishness of his cook, set her to field work as discipline, only to have her demonstrate by dying that her protestations of illness had been true.

Grievances reinforced ennui to promote slacking, absence without leave, desertion and mutiny. The advertising columns of the newspapers bristled with notices of runaways; and no detailed plantation record which has come to my hand is without mention of them. . . .

Certain slaves were persistent absconders, and the chronic discontent of others created special problems for their masters. . . .

By one means or another good will and affection were often evoked. When his crop was beset with grass and the work strenuous, a Mississippian wrote of his corps as being "true as steel." [27] A Georgian after escaping shipwreck on his way to Congress in 1794 wrote: "I have ever since been thinking of an expression of Old Qua's in Savannah a few days before I sailed. The rascal had the impudence to tell me to stay at home & not fret myself about Publick—'What Publick care for you, Massa? God! ye get drowned bye & bye, Qua tell you so, and what going come of he Family den?'" [28] An Alabama preacher while defending slavery as divinely ordained said of the Negro: "He is of all races the most gentle and kind. The *man*, the most submissive; the *woman*, the most affectionate. What other slaves would love their masters better than themselves?" [29] And a British traveler wrote from his observation of slaves and masters: "There is an hereditary regard and often attachment on both sides, more like that formerly existing between lords and their retainers in the old feudal times of Europe, than anything now to be found in America." [30]

On some estates the whip was as regularly in evidence as the spur on a horseman's heel.[31] That cruelties occurred is never to be denied. Mrs. Stowe exploited them in *Uncle Tom's Cabin* and validated her implications to her own satisfaction in its *Key*. Theodore D. Weld had already assembled a thousand more or less authentic instances of whippings and fetters, of croppings and brandings, of bloodhound pursuits and the break-up of families.[32] Manuscript discoveries continue to swell the record. . . .

Most of the travelers who sought evidence of asperity in the plantation realm found it as a rule not before their eyes but beyond the horizon. Charles Eliot Norton while at Charleston in 1855 wrote home to Boston: "The slaves do not go about looking unhappy, and are with difficulty, I fancy, persuaded to feel so. Whips and chains, oaths and brutality, are as common, for all that one sees, in the free as the slave states. We have come thus far, and might have gone ten times as far, I dare say, without seeing the first sign of Negro misery or white tyranny." [33] Andrew P. Peabody wrote of the slaves of his host at Savannah: "They were well lodged and fed, and could have been worked no harder than was necessary for exercise and digestion." [34] Louis F. Tasistro remarked of the slaves on a plantation at the old battle field below New Orleans: "To say that they are underworked and overfed, and far happier than the labourers of Great Britain would hardly convey a sufficiently clear notion of their actual condition. They put me much more in mind of a community of grown-up children, spoiled by too much kindness, than a body of dependants, much less a company of slaves." [35] Frederika Bremer had virtually nothing but praise for the slave quarters which she visited or their savory food which she tasted.[36] Welby, Faux, Lyell, Basil Hall, Marshall Hall, Robert Russell, William Russell, Olmsted [37] and sundry others concur in their surprise at finding slavery unsevere, though some of them kept seeking evidence to the contrary without avail.

The surprise was justified, for tradition in the outer world ran squarely opposite. And the tradition was reasonable. Slavery had been erected as a crass exploitation, and the laws were as stringent as ever. No prophet in early times could have told that kindliness would grow as a flower from a soil so foul, that slaves would come to be cherished not only as property of high value but as loving if lowly friends.[38] But this unexpected change occurred in so many cases as to make benignity somewhat a matter of course. To those habituated it became no longer surprising for a planter to say that no man deserved a Coromantee who would not treat him rather as a friend than as a slave; [39] for another to give his "people" a holiday out of season because "the drouth seems to have afflicted them, and a play day may raise their spirits"; [40] or for a third to give one of his hands an occasional week-end with a dollar or two each time to visit his wife in another county,[41] and send two others away for some weeks at hot springs for the relief of their rheumatism.[42]

The esteem in epitaphs, whether inscribed in diaries or on stone, was without doubt earned by their subjects and genuinely felt by their composers. . . .

On the other hand slaves in large numbers were detached from their masters, whether by sale, by lease to employers or by hire to themselves. The personal equation was often a factor in such transactions. Some slaves were sold as punishment, for effect upon the morale of their fellows. On the other hand some whose sales were impelled by financial stress were commissioned by their masters to find buyers of their own choice; some purchases were prompted by a belief that the new management would prove more congenial and fruitful than the old; [43] and still more transfers were made to unite in ownership couples who desired union in marriage.

In the hiring of slaves likewise the personal equation often bulked large, for the owner's desire for a maximum wage was modified by his concern for assured maintenance of physique and morale, and the lessee on his part wanted assurance from the slave of willing service or of acquiescence at least.[44] The hiring of slaves to the slaves themselves was a grant of industrial freedom at a wage. It was an admission that the slave concerned could produce more in self-direction than when under routine control, a virtual admission that for him slavery had no industrial justification. In many cases it was a probationary period, ended by self-purchase with earnings accumulated above the wages he had currently paid his owner.

Slave hiring and self-hire were more characteristic of town than of country. Indeed urban conditions merely tolerated slavery, never promoted it. And urban slaveholders were not complete masters, for slavery in full form required a segregation to make the master in effect a magistrate. A townsman's human chattels could not be his subjects, for he had no domain for them to inhabit. When a slave ran an errand upon the street he came under the eye of public rather than private authority; and if he were embroiled by chance in altercation with another slave the two masters were likely to find themselves champions of opposing causes in court, or partisans even against the constables, with no power in themselves either to make or apply the law.[45]

Town slaves in a sense rubbed elbows with every one, high and low, competed with free labor, white and black, and took tone more or less from all and sundry. The social hierarchy was more elaborate than on the plantations, the scheme of life more complex, and the variety wider in attainment and attitude. The obsequious grandiloquence of a barber contrasted with the caustic fluency of a fishwife. But even the city chain gang was likely to be melodious, for its members were Negroes at one or two removes from the plantation. All in all, the slave régime was a curious blend of force and concession, of arbitrary disposal by the master and self-direction by the slave, of tyranny and benevolence, of antipathy and affection.

NOTES

1. *Cf.* N. S. Shaler, "The Nature of the Negro", in the *Arena*, III, 28.

2. *Gentleman's Magazine*, XXXIV, 487 (London, 1764).

3. *Practical Rules*, reprinted in *Plantation and Frontier Documents*, II, 133.

4. For example there were 102 below ten years of age among the 704 slaves brought by five ships to South Carolina between July and October, 1724.—British transcripts in the South Carolina archives, XI, 243.

5. A table of the names most common among imported Negroes, which were derived from the days of the week, is printed in Long's *Jamaica*, II, 427.

6. Charleston *Courier*, July 8, 1855.

7. Letter of William Draper, Bassa Cove, Liberia, August 17, 1837, to

William Maxwell, Norfolk, Va. T. C. Thornton, *An Inquiry into the History of Slavery* (Washington, 1841), 272.

8. For example, James Hamilton, Jr., while Congressman from South Carolina, engaged Dr. Furth of Savannah to make visits on schedule to his plantation a few miles away. In 1828 he wrote from Washington to his factor at Savannah: "I have just received a letter from Mr Prioleau, informing me that the eyes of my old and faithful Servant Peter were in a perilous condition. I will [thank] you to request Dr Furth to attend to them promptly and effectually. . . . I will thank you to supply for my Hospital on his requisition all that may be necessary *in his opinion* to make my negroes comfortable when they are sick. I will thank you to request him to drop me a line occasionally of the health of my people and the success of the reform I propose thro him to institute in attention to the sick. . . . Be so good as to give to Peter the value of a couple of Dollars monthly for comforts to his family." Manuscript in private possession.

On rations, quarters, work schedules and the like see [Ebenezer Starnes] *The Slave-holder Abroad* (Philadephia, 1860), appendix; *DeBow's Review*, VIII, 381, X, 621, XI, 369; *Southern Literary Messenger*, VII, 775; and travelers' accounts at large.

9. Howard Snyder in the *Atlantic Monthly*, CXXVII, 171.

10. E.g., Rev. I. E. Lowery, *Life on the Old Plantation in Ante-bellum Days* (Columbia, S. C., 1911), 71, 72. The author was an ex-slave.

11. Olmsted, *Back Country*, 107 note.

12. *Calendar of State Papers, Colonial*, 1681-1685, p. 25.

13. E.g., letter of James Habersham, May 11, 1775, to Robert Kean in London, in the *Georgia Historical Society Collections*, VI, 243, 244.

14. Surveys of religious endeavor among the slaves: Rev. Charles C. Jones, *The Religious Instruction of the Negroes in the United States* (Savannah, 1842): C. F. Deems, ed., *Annals of Southern Methodism for 1856* (Nashville [1857]); W. P. Harrison, ed., *The Gospel among the Slaves* (Nashville, 1893).

15. Doubtless many a plantation was blessed, or cursed as the case might be, with a practical joker such as Jack Baker, who kept himself and his whole neighborhood in Richmond entertained by his talent in mimicry. "Jack's performances furnished rare fun in the dog-days, when business was dull, and his pocket was furnished by the same process." One of his private amusements was to call some other slave in the tone of his master, and vanish before the summons was answered. "His most frequent dupe was a next door neighbor, whose master, a Scotchman, took frequent trips to the country on horseback. During his absence Jack would, before retiring to bed, rap on the gate and call 'Jasper! come and take my horse.' Jasper, aroused from his nap, came, but found neither master nor horse, and well knew who quizzed him. One night the veritable master made the call, some time after Jack had given a false alarm. Jasper was out of patience, and replied in a loud voice, 'D——n you, old fellow, if you call me again I'll come out and thrash you!' After that, poor Jasper was at Jack's mercy, unless he resorted to 'thrashing.' "—*DeBow's Review*, XXVIII, 197.

16. *Cf.* Catherine Bremer, *Homes of the New World*, I, 374.

17. John Brickell, *The Natural History of North Carolina* (Dublin, 1737), 275.

18. Basil Hall, *Travels*, III, 191.

19. *Southern Agriculturist*, III, 329. These instructions continued: "All my slaves are to be supplied with sufficient land, on which I encourage and even compel them to plant and cultivate a crop, all of which I will, as I have hitherto done, purchase at a fair price from them."

20. An instance of coercive breeding is reported by Frederick Douglass, in *Narrative* (Boston, 1849), 62. For this item I am indebted to Mr. Theodore Whitfield of Johns Hopkins University.

21. Phillips, *American Negro Slavery*, 298, 299.

22. It is hinted, for example, by the exclamation point in this Virginian letter of 1831: "P. P. Burton has quit his wife, sent her to her father's and gone off with Sandy Burton to Texas and taken a female slave along!" Manuscript in private possession.

23. Plantation manual of James H. Hammond. Manuscript in the Library of Congress.

24. A. P. Peabody, in the *Andover Review*, XVI, 156.

25. P. Carson, *Life of James Louis Petigru* (Washington, 1920), 431. In another letter Petigru conjured his sister: "Do not allow the little nigs to forget that their hands were given them principally for the purpose of pulling weeds." —*Ibid.*, 23.

26. *Cf.* Basil Hall, *Travels*, III, 279.

27. *Mississippi Historical Society Publications*, X, 354.

28. T. U. P. Charlton, *Life of James Jackson* (Augusta, 1809, reprint Atlanta, n. d.), 154 of the reprint.

29. Fred A. Ross, *Slavery Ordained of God* (Philadephia, 1859), 26.

30. Sir Charles Lyell, *Second Visit*, 2d ed., I, 352.

31. *E.g.*, J. W. Monette in [J. H. Ingraham] *The South-West*, II, 286-288.

32. *American Slavery as it is: Testimony of a Thousand Witnesses* (New York, 1839).

33. *Letters of Charles Eliot Norton* (Boston, 1913), I, 121.

34. *Andover Review*, XVI, 157.

35. *Random Shots and Southern Breezes* (New York, 1842), II, 13.

36. *Homes of the New World*, I, 293 *et passim*.

37. Some of these are quoted in Phillips, *American Negro Slavery*, 306-308.

38. A Virginia woman, talking in 1842 with a visiting preacher from the North, said that her superannuated cook was "as pious a woman, and a lady of as delicate sensibilities as I ever saw; she is one of the very best friends I have in the world." The visitor wrote on his own score: "I am more and more convinced of the injustice we do the slaveholders. Of their feelings toward their negroes I can form a better notion than formerly, by examining my own toward the slaves who wait on my wife and mind my children. It is a feeling most like that we have to near relations." And again as to the slaves: "They are unspeakably superior to our Northern free blacks, retaining a thousand African traits of kindliness and hilarity, from being together in masses. I may say with Abram [Venable, a planter whom he visited], 'I love a nigger, they are better than we.' So they are: grateful, devoted, self-sacrificing for their masters." —John Hall ed., *Forty Years' Familiar Letters of James W. Alexander, D. D.* (New York, 1860), I, 351-353.

39. Christopher Codrington, in *Calendar of State Papers, Colonial*, 1701, p. 721.

40. Diary of Landon Carter, in the *William and Mary College Quarterly,*

XIII, 162.

41. "The Westover Journal of John A. Seldon," in *Smith College Studies,* VI, 289 *et passim.*

42. *Ibid.,* 308.

43. For a striking example see *Plantation and Frontier,* I, 337, 338.

44. For a vivid account of a tripartite negotiation see Robert Russell, *North America* (Edinburgh, 1857), 151.

45. *E.g.,* Carson, *Petigru,* 348; Phillips, *American Negro Slavery,* 414, 415.

• *The most important recent synthesis of American slavery is Kenneth M. Stampp's* The Peculiar Institution. *Stampp has criticized severely both Phillips's handling of evidence connected with Southern slave society and his tolerant moral outlook regarding its practices. The historical issues which divide Stampp and Phillips reflect, to a great extent, American assumptions concerning the Negro at the time of their writing. Phillips, a benign Southern racist, believed that, despite excesses on the part of some slaveholders, the institution had served a useful civilizing purpose for the Negro. Stampp, on the other hand, viewed the institution as a thoroughly cruel and brutal system of social control. The following selection from the chapter entitled "To Make Them Stand in Fear" discusses some aspects of slavery which helped produce Stampp's moral outrage over Phillips's gentle apology for slaveholding.*

Southern Negro Slavery:

"To Make Them Stand in Fear"

KENNETH M. STAMPP

A realistic Arkansas slaveholder once addressed himself to the great problem of his class, "the management of Negroes," and bluntly concluded: "Now, I speak what I know, when I say it is like 'casting pearls before swine' to try to *persuade* a negro to work. He must be *made* to work, and should always be given to understand that if he fails to perform his duty he will be punished for it." Having tested the "*persuasion* doctrine" when he began planting, he warned all beginners that if they tried it they would surely fail.[1]

From *The Peculiar Institution: Slavery in the Ante-Bellum South*, by Kenneth M. Stampp, pp. 171-91. Copyright © 1956 by Kenneth M. Stampp. Reprinted by permission of Alfred A. Knopf, Inc.

Most masters preferred the "persuasion doctrine" nevertheless. They would have been gratified if their slaves had willingly shown proper subordination and wholeheartedly responded to the incentives offered for efficient labor. They found, however, that some did not respond at all, and that others responded only intermittently. As a result, slaveholders were obliged to supplement the lure of rewards for good behavior with the threat of punishment for bad. One Virginian always assumed that slaves would "not labor at all except to avoid punishment," and would "never do more than just enough to save themselves from being punished." Fortunately, said a Georgian, punishment did not make the Negro revengeful as it did members of other races. Rather, it tended "to win his attachment and promote his happiness and well being." [2]

Without the power to punish, which the state conferred upon the master, bondage could not have existed. By comparison, all other techniques of control were of secondary importance. Jefferson Davis and a few others gave their bondsmen a hand in the chastisement of culprits. On Davis's Mississippi estate trusted slaves tried, convicted, and punished the violators of plantation law. [3] But this was an eccentric arrangement. Normally the master alone judged the seriousness of an offense and fixed the kind and amount of punishment to be administered.

Slaveholders devised a great variety of penalties. They demoted unfaithful domestics, foremen, and drivers to field labor. They denied passes to incorrigibles, or excluded them from participating in Saturday night dances. An Arkansas planter gave his bondsmen a dinner every Sunday and required those on the "punishment list" to wait on the others without getting any of the food themselves. Masters forced malingerers to work on Sundays and holidays and at night after the others had finished. They penalized them by confiscating the crops in their "truck patches," or by reducing the sums due them. They put them on short rations for a period of time, usually depriving them of their meat allowances. And they sold them away from their families and friends.

Some of the penalties were ingenious. A Maryland tobacco grower forced a hand to eat the worms he failed to pick off the tobacco leaves. A Mississippian gave a runaway a wretched time by requiring him to sit at the table and eat his evening meal with the white family. A Louisiana planter humiliated disobedient male field-hands by giving them "women's work" such as washing clothes, by dressing them in women's clothing, and by exhibiting them on a scaffold wearing a red flannel cap.[4]

A few slaveholders built private jails on their premises. They knew that close confinement during a working day was a punishment of dubious value, but they believed that it was effective during leisure hours. "Negroes are gregarious," explained a small planter, "they dread solitariness, and to be deprived from the little weekly dances and chitchat. They will work to death rather than be shut up." Accordingly, a Louisianian locked runaways in his jail from Saturday night until Monday morning. When he caught a cotton picker with a ten pound rock in his basket, he jailed him every night and holiday for five months.[5]

Others made use of public jails, paying the jailer a fee for the service. One South Carolinian put a runaway in solitary confinement in the Charleston workhouse; another had a slave "shut in a darkcell" in the same institution. A Georgia Planter advised his overseer to take a disobedient slave "down to the Savannah jail, and give him prison discipline and by all means solitary confinement for 3 weeks, when he will be glad to get home again." [6]

The stocks were still a familiar piece of equipment on the plantations of the ante-bellum South. . . .

"Chains and irons," James H. Hammond correctly explained, were used chiefly to control and discipline runaways. "You will admit," he argued logically enough, "that if we pretend to own slaves, they must not be permitted to abscond whenever they see fit; and that if nothing else will prevent it these means must be resorted to." [7] Three entries in Hammond's diary, in 1844, indicated that he practiced what he preached. July 17: "Alonzo runaway with his irons on." July 30: "Alonzo came in with his irons off." July 31: ". . . re-ironed Alonzo."

Hammond was but one of many masters who gave critics of the peculiar institution a poignant symbol—the fettered slave. A Mississippian had his runaway Maria "Ironed with a shackle on each leg connected with a chain." When he caught Albert he "had an iron collar put on his neck"; on Woodson, a habitual runaway, he "put the ball and chain." A Kentuckian recalled seeing slaves in his state wearing iron collars, some of them with bells attached. The fetters, however, did not always accomplish their purpose, for numerous advertisements stated that fugitives wore these encumbrances when they escaped. For example, Peter, a Louisiana runaway, "Had on each foot when leaving, an iron ring, with a small chain attached to it." [8]

But the whip was the most common instrument of punishment—

indeed, it was the emblem of the master's authority. Nearly every slaveholder used it, and few grown slaves escaped it entirely. Defenders of the institution conceded that corporal punishment was essential in certain situations; some were convinced that it was better than any other remedy. If slavery were right, argued an Arkansas planter, means had to be found to keep slaves in subjugation, "and my opinion is, the lash—not used murderously, as would-be philanthropists assert, is the most effectual." A Virginian agreed: "A great deal of whipping is not necessary; *some* is." [9]

The majority seemed to think that the certainty, and not the severity, of physical "correction" was what made it effective. While no offense could go unpunished, the number of lashes should be in proportion to the nature of the offense and the character of the offender. The master should control his temper. "Never inflict punishment when in a passion," advised a Louisiana slaveholder, "but wait until perfectly cool, and until it can be done rather in sorrow than in anger." Many urged, therefore, that time be permitted to elapse between the misdeed and the flogging. A Georgian required his driver to do the whipping so that his bondsmen would not think that it was "for the pleasure of punishing, rather than for the purpose of enforcing obedience." [10]

Planters who employed overseers often fixed the number of stripes they could inflict for each specific offense, or a maximum number whatever the offense. On Pierce Butler's Georgia plantation each driver could administer twelve lashes, the head driver thirty-six, and the overseer fifty. A South Carolinian instructed his overseer to ask permission before going beyond fifteen. "The highest punishment must not exceed 100 lashes in one day and to that extent only in extreme cases," wrote James H. Hammond. "In general 15 to 20 lashes will be a sufficient flogging." [11]

The significance of these numbers depended in part upon the kind of whip that was used. The "rawhide," or "cowskin," was a savage instrument requiring only a few strokes to provide a chastisement that a slave would not soon forget. A former bondsman remembered that it was made of about three feet of untanned ox hide, an inch thick at the butt end, and tapering to a point which made it "quite elastic and springy." [12]

Many slaveholders would not use the rawhide because it lacerated the skin. One recommended, instead, a leather strap, eighteen inches long and two and a half inches wide, fastened to a wooden handle. In Mississippi, according to a visitor, the whip in general use consisted of a "stout flexible stalk" covered with a tapering leather plait, about three and a half feet in length, which formed the lash. "To the end of the lash is attached a soft, dry, buckskin cracker, about three eights of an inch wide and ten or twelve inches long, which is the only part allowed to strike, in whipping on the bare skin. . . . When it is used by an experienced hand it makes a very loud report, and stings, or 'burns' the skin smartly, but does not bruise it." [13]

How frequently a master resorted to the whip depended upon his temperament and his methods of management. On some establishments long periods of time elapsed with relatively few whippings—until, as a rice planter explained, it seemed "as if the devil had got into" the hands, and for a time there was "a good deal of it." Or, occasionally, a normally amiable slave got out of hand and had to be flogged. "Had to whip my Man Willis for insolence to the overseer," wrote a Tennesseean. "This I done with much regret as he was never whipped before." [14]

On other establishments the whip was in constant use. The size of the estate may have had some relationship to the amount of whipping, but the disposition of the proprietor was decidedly more crucial. Small farmers, as well as large planters, often relied upon corporal punishment as their chief method of enforcing discipline. Southern women were sometimes equally prone to use the lash upon errant domestics.

Some overseers, upon assuming control, thought it wise to whip every hand on the plantation to let them know who was in command. Some masters used the lash as a form of incentive by flogging the last slave out of his cabin in the morning.[15] Many used it to "break in" a young slave and to "break the spirit" of an insubordinate older one. "If the negro is humble and appears duly sensible of the impropriety of his conduct, a very moderate chastisement will answer better than a severe one," advised a planter. "If however, he is stubborn . . . a slight punishment will only make bad worse." Slaves had to be flogged, explained an Alabamian, until they manifested "submission and penitence." [16]

In short, the infliction of stripes curbed many a bondsman who could not be influenced by any other technique. Whipping had a dispiriting effect upon most of them. "Had to administer a little rod to Bob this morning," reported a Virginian. "Have seen for more than 3 months I should have to humble him some, hope it may benefit him." [17]

"To manage *negroes* without the exercise of too much passion, is next to an impossibility. . . . I would therefore put you on your guard, lest their provocations should on some occasions transport you beyond the limits of decency and christian morality." The Reverend Charles Pettigrew, of North Carolina, gave this advice to his sons when he willed them his estate. John H. Cocke, of Virginia, cautioned the overseer on his Bremo Plantation: "Most persons are liable to be thrown into a passion by the improper conduct of those they have to govern." After traveling through the South, Olmsted wondered "whether humanity and the accumulation of wealth, the prosperity of the master and the happiness and improvement of the subject, are not in some degree incompatible." [18] Physical cruelty, as these observations suggest, was always a possible consequence of the master's power to punish. Place an intemperate master over an ill-disposed slave, and the possibility became a reality.

Not that a substantial number of slaveholders deliberately adopted a policy of brutality. The great majority, in fact, preferred to use as little violence as possible. Many small slaveholders, urban and rural, who had close personal contacts with their bondsmen and knew them as human beings, found it highly disagreeable to treat them unkindly. Large planters, in their instructions to overseers, frequently prohibited barbarous punishments. Thomas Affleck's plantation record book advised overseers that the "indiscriminate, constant and excessive use of the whip" was "altogether unnecessary and inexcusable." A Louisiana proprietor was very explicit on this point. In whipping a slave the overseer was never to be "cruel or severe," though he could repeat the whipping at intervals "until the most entire submission" was achieved. "I object to having the skin cut, or my negroes marked in any way by the lash. . . . I will most certainly discharge any overseer for striking any of my negroes with a club or the butt of his whip." [19]

A master who gave some thought to his standing in the community certainly wished to avoid a reputation for inordinate cruelty. To be counted a true Southern Gentleman one had to be humane to his bondsmen, to exercise self-control in dealing with them, to know how to give commands without raising his voice. Plenty of masters possessed these qualities. A European visitor marveled at the patience, the "mild forbearance," some of them exhibited. It seemed that every slaveholder's temper was subjected to a discipline which either ruined or perfected it. And more than a few met the test with remarkable success. [20]

Many openly censured those who were guilty of inhumanity. A Georgian told a Northerner that the government of slaves was necessarily despotic, but that Southerners despised ruthless masters. A South

Carolinian wrote in a published letter, "The overseer whose constant and only resort is to the lash . . . is a brute, and deserves the penitentiary." And a North Carolinian denounced a neighbor as a *"moral miasma"* because of the way he treated his slaves.[21]

Those who were destitute of humane instincts might still be restrained by the slave's economic worth. To injure by harsh punishment a prime field-hand valued at a thousand dollars or more was a costly indulgence. It may be, therefore, that rising slave prices encouraged a decline in the incidence of brutality.

But these restraints were not always enough. Some masters, made irascible by the endless irritations which were an inevitable part of owning slaves, were unmerciful in exercising their almost unlimited powers. Some were indifferent about their reputations among neighbors, or hoped to conceal the conditions that existed on their isolated estates. Some were as prodigal in the use of human chattels as they were in the use of other property. Neither law, nor social pressure, nor economic self-interest made Southern Gentlemen out of all slaveholders. As long as the peculiar institution survived, the master class contained a group of unfeeling men.

Few who knew southern slavery intimately denied that there existed within it an element of savagery. No apologist disputed the evidence published by Theodore Dwight Weld, the abolitionist, for he gathered it from southern newspapers and public records.[22] It is unnecessary, however, to turn to the abolitionists—or to former slaves—for proof. Daniel R. Hundley, a Southerner who admired and defended his section's institutions, agreed that the South was "no second paradise." He knew that slaves were "badly treated" on some estates, and that masters were sometimes unconcerned about it. Moreover, "he must be a very bold man who will deny that the overseers on many southern plantations, are cruel and unmercifully severe." [23]. . .

Southerners themselves having established the fact of cruelty, it only remains to estimate its extent and to examine its nature. Proslavery writers asserted that cases of cruelty were the rare exceptions to the general rule of humanity by which slaves were governed. Travelers in the South gave conflicting testimony. Abolitionists and ex-slaves insisted that cruelty was far more common than defenders of the institution would admit.

The exact truth will never be known, because surviving records are fragmentary and sometimes hint only vaguely at conditions. There is no way to discover what went on in the "voiceless solitudes" where no records were kept, or on hundreds of plantations where visitors were unwelcome and the proprietors were in residence only part of the year. (In 1860, several large planters in Rapides Parish, Louisiana, would not even permit the census takers to trespass upon their estates.) Even so, the public and private records that do survive suggest that, although the average slaveholder was not the inhuman brute described by the abolitionists, acts of cruelty were not as exceptional as pro-slavery writers claimed.

As a South Carolina judge sadly confessed, there were "men and women on earth who deserved no other name than *fiends*," for they seemed to delight in brutality.[24] No southern state required masters to be tested for their competence to rule slaves. Instead, they permitted slaves to fall willy-nilly into the hands of whoever inherited them or had the cash or credit to buy them. As a result, bondsmen were owned by persons of unsound minds, such as the South Carolin-ian who had his chattels "throw dirt upon [his] roof . . . to drive off witches." They were owned by a woman "unable to read or write, . . . scarcely able to count ten," legally incompetent to contract marriage.[25] They were owned by drunkards, such as Lilburne Lewis, of Livingston County, Kentucky, who once chopped a slave to bits with an ax; and by sadists, such as Madame Lalourie, of New Orleans, who tortured her slaves for her own amusement. It would be pointless to catalogue the atrocities committed by psychopaths.

Cruelty, unfortunately, was not limited to the mentally unbalanced. Men and women, otherwise "normal," were sometimes corrupted by the extraordinary power that slavery conferred upon them. Some made bondsmen the victims of their petulance. (The repentant wife of a Louisiana planter once wrote in her diary: "I feel badly got very angry and whipped Lavinia. O! for government over my temper." [26]) Others who were reasonably humane to most of their slaves made the ones who annoyed them beyond endurance the targets of their animosity. Still others who were merely irresponsible, rather than inherently brutal, made slaves the objects of their whims. In other words, masters were seldom consistent; they were apt to be indulgent or harsh depend-ing upon their changing moods, or their feelings toward individual slaves. In truth, said one Southerner, "men of the right stamp to man-age negroes are like Angels visits few and far between." [27]

Kindness was not a universal trait among small slaveholders, especi-ally among those who were ambitious to climb the economic ladder. Both a shoemaker and a carpenter, each of whom owned a single slave, were guilty of atrocities.[28] Southern farmers with modest holdings were also, on occasion, capable of extreme cruelty toward slaves.

But brutality was more common on the large plantations. Overseers, almost all of whom were native-born Southerners, seldom felt any personal affection for the bondsmen they governed. Their inclination in most cases was to punish severely; if their employers prohibited severity, they ignored such instructions as often as not. Planters complained that it was difficult to find an overseer who would "condescend to take orders from his employer, and manage according to the system of another man." The typical overseer seemed to have little confidence in the use of incentives as a method of governing slaves; he had a decided preference for physical force.[29]

Illustrations of this problem sometimes found their way into the records of southern courts. Overseers sued masters for their wages when discharged for cruelty; masters sued overseers for injuring slave property; occasionally the state intervened to prosecute an overseer for killing or maiming a bondsman.[30] Most of these cases never reached the courts, as the planter dealt with the problem himself. An Alabamian discovered that he had found no solution even when he employed a relative to oversee. "I want you to distinctly understand me," he scolded, "withhold your rushing whipping and lashing—for I will not stand it any longer." A Louisiana planter, returning to his estate after a year's absence, related in his journal the "most terrible account of the severity [and] cruelty" of his overseer. At least twelve slaves had died from "negligence and ill treatment." Discharging this overseer and employing another, he was dismayed to find that the new one also "punished severely without discretion." [31]

A planter was often in a quandary when his overseer was both brutal and efficient. "I do not know whether I will keep Harris another year or not," a Mississippian told his wife. "He is a first rate manager except he is too cruel. I have had my feelings greatly shocked at some of his conduct." But he re-employed Harris after exacting from him a promise to be less harsh. Harris, he explained, made big crops, and he did not wish "to break it all up by getting a new manager."

A few years later this same planter, having transferred his operations to Arkansas, viewed the problem of slave management in a different light. While Harris was away on a month's leave of absence, the proprietor ran the estate himself. He found governing slaves to be a "pretty rough business" and waited impatiently for his overseer to return.[32]

Ordinarily the owner of a large plantation was realistic enough to know that controlling a gang of field-hands was at best a wretched business, and that a certain amount of savagery was inevitable. There seemed to be no other way to keep certain bondsmen under control. "Experience and observation have taught me that some negroes require a vast deal more punishment than others to be brought to a performance of their duties," wrote an Arkansas planter. And a Louisiana sugar planter assured his distressed wife that he would not sanction the admitted cruelty of his overseer unless there was "a *great* necessity for it." Indeed, he found the management of slaves "exceedingly disagreeable . . . under any and all circumstances." [33]

Although cruelty was endemic in all slaveholding communities, it was always most common in newly settled regions. Along the rough southern frontier thousands of ambitious men were trying swiftly to make their fortunes. They operated in a frantically competitive society which provided few rewards for the virtues of gentility and almost put a premium upon ruthlessness. In the eastern tobacco and rice districts brutality was unquestionably less prevalent in the nineteenth century than it had been during the colonial period. But in the Southwest only limited areas had developed a mellowed gentry as late as 1860. In the Alabama-Mississippi Black Belt, in the cotton and sugar parishes of Louisiana, along the Arkansas River, and in eastern Texas the master class included the "parvenus," the "cotton snobs," and the "Southern Yankees." If these planters failed to observe the code of the patrician, they apparently thought none the less of each other for it.

The hired slave stood the greatest chance of subjection to cruel punishments as well as to overwork. His employer, a Kentucky judge confessed, had no incentive to treat him kindly "except the mere feelings of humanity, which we have too much reason to believe in many instances . . . are too weak to stimulate the active virtue." [34] This was no exaggeration.

Southerners who were concerned about the welfare of slaves found it difficult to draw a sharp line between acts of cruelty and such measures of physical force as were an inextricable part of slavery. Since the line was necessarily arbitrary, slaveholders themselves disagreed about where it should be drawn. Was it barbarous to "correct" a slave by putting him in the stocks, or by forcing him to wear chains or an iron collar? How severely might a slave be flogged before the punishment became brutal? These were matters of personal taste.

But no master denied the propriety of giving a moderate whipping to a disobedient bondsman. During the seventeenth and eighteenth centuries the lash was used to punish free men as well as slaves. By mid-nineteenth century, however, it was seldom used upon any but slaves, because public opinion now considered it to be cruel. Why it was less cruel to whip a bondsman was a problem that troubled many sensitive masters. That they often had no choice as long as they owned slaves made their problem no easier to resolve. . . .

Beyond this were cases of pure brutality—cases of flogging that resulted in the crippling, maiming, or killing of slaves. An early nineteenth-century Charleston grand jury presented "as a serious evil the many instances of Negro Homicide" and condemned those who indulged their passions "in the barbarous treatment of slaves.[35] "Salting"—washing the cuts received from the whip with brine—was a harsh punishment inflicted upon the most obstinate bondsmen. Though all but a few deplored such brutality, slaveholders found themselves in a dilemma when nothing else could subdue a rebel.

If a master was too squeamish to undertake the rugged task of humbling a refractory bondsman, he might send him to a more calloused neighbor or to a professional "slave breaker." John Nevitt, a Mississippi planter not averse to the application of heroic remedies, received from another master a young chattel "for the purpose of punishing him for bad conduct." Frederick Douglass remembered a ruthless man in Maryland who had a reputation for being "a first rate hand at breaking young negroes"; some slaveholders found it beneficial to send their beginning hands to him for training.[36]

The branding of slaves was a widespread custom in colonial days; it was less common in the nineteenth century. But as late as 1838, a North Carolinian advertised that Betty, a fugitive, was recently "burnt . . . with a hot iron on the left side of her face; I tried to make the letter M." In 1848, a Kentuckian identified his runaway Jane by a brand mark "on the breast something like L blotched." [37] Mutilation as a form of punishment also declined without disappearing entirely. A Louisiana jailer, in 1831, gave notice that he had a runaway in his custody: "He has been lately gelded, and is not yet well." Another Louisianian recorded his disgust for a neighbor who had "castrated 3 men of his." [38]

Some masters who were otherwise as humane as the peculiar institution would permit tolerated almost anything that might "cure" habitual runaways. Andrew Jackson once offered fifty dollars reward for the capture of a fugitive, "and ten dollars extra for every hundred lashes any person will give him to the amount of three hundred.". . . The tracking of runaways with dogs was no figment of abolitionist imaginations; it was a common practice in all slave states, defended and justified in the courts. Groups of slaveholders sometimes rode through the swamps with their dogs and made the search for fugitives a sport comparable to fox hunting. Others preferred to hire professional slave catchers who provided their own "Negro dogs.". . .

The dogs could give a fugitive a severe mauling if the owner was willing to permit it. After a Mississippi master caught an escaped slave he allowed his dogs to "bite him very severely." A Louisiana planter "treed" a runaway and then "made the dogs pull him out of the tree, Bit him very badly, think he will stay home awhile." On another occasion his dogs tore a slave naked; he then "took him Home Before the other negro[es] . . . and made the dogs give him another over hauling." [39]

The angry mobs who dealt extra-legal justice to slaves accused of serious crimes committed barbarities seldom matched by the most brutal masters. . . .

Mobs all too frequently dealt with slaves accused of murder or rape. They conducted their own trials or broke into jails or court rooms to seize prisoners for summary execution. Their more fortunate victims were hanged; the others were burned to death, sometimes in the presence of hundreds of bondsmen who were forced to attend the ceremony. . . .

The abolition of slavery, of course, did not bring to a close the record of brutality in the South any more than it did elsewhere. But it did make less tenable the argument that brutality was sometimes in the public interest. And it did rescue many a master from the dilemma he faced when his desire to be humane was compromised by the demands of proper discipline.

NOTES

1. *Southern Cultivator*, XVIII (1860), pp. 130-31, 239-40.
2. Olmsted, *Seaboard*, pp. 104-105; *Southern Cultivator*, XII (1854), p. 206.
3. Walter L. Fleming, "Jefferson Davis, the Negroes and the Negro Problem," *Sewanee Review*, XVI (1908), pp. 410-11.
4. John Thompson, *The Life of John Thompson, A Fugitive Slave* (Worcester, Mass., 1856), p. 18; Sydnor, *Slavery in Mississippi*, p. 89; Davis (ed.), *Diary of Bennet H. Barrow*, pp. 112, 154, 175.
5. *De Bow's Review*, XI (1851), p. 371; Davis (ed.), *Diary of Bennet H. Barrows*, pp. 165, 269.
6. Gaillard Plantation Journal, entry for May 22, 1849; Gavin Diary, entry for March 26, 1856; Phillips (ed.), *Plantation and Frontier*, II, pp. 31-32.
7. *De Bow's Review*, VII (1849), p. 500.
8. Nevitt Plantation Journal, entries for November 9, 1827; March 28, 1831; July 18, 1832; Coleman, *Slavery Times in Kentucky*, pp. 248-49; New Orleans *Picayune*, December 26, 1847.
9. *Southern Cultivator*, XVIII (1860), p. 239-40; *Southern Planter*, XII (1852), p. 107.
10. *De Bow's Review*, XXII (1857), pp. 376-79; *Southern Agriculturist*, IV (1831), p. 350.

11. Kemble, *Journal*, pp. 42-43; Phillips (ed.), *Plantation and Frontier*, I, pp. 116-22; Plantation Manual in Hammond Papers.

12. Douglass, *My Bondage*, p. 103.

13. *Southern Cultivator*, VII (1849), p. 135; [Ingraham], *South-West*, II, pp. 287-88.

14. Olmsted, *Seaboard*, pp. 438-39; Bills Diary, entry for March 30, 1860.

15. *Southern Cultivator*, II (1844), pp. 169-70; Davis, *Cotton Kingdom in Alabama*, pp. 54-55.

16. *Southern Cultivator*, VIII (1850), p. 164; William P. Gould Ms. Plantation Rules.

17. Adams Diary, entry for July 2, 1860.

18. Johnson, *Ante-Bellum North Carolina*, p. 496; John H. Cocke Ms. Plantation Rules, in N. F. Cabell Collection of Agricultural Papers; Olmsted, *Seaboard*, pp. 367-68.

19. *De Bow's Review*, XXII (1857), pp. 376-79.

20. Martineau, *Society in America*, II, pp. 109-10.

21. Lester B. Shippee (ed.), *Bishop Whipple's Southern Diary 1843–1844* (Minneapolis, 1937), pp. 31-32; *Southern Cultivator*, II (1844), p. 107; William S. Pettigrew to James C. Johnston, September 24, 1846, Pettigrew Family Papers.

22. Theodore Dwight Weld, *American Slavery As It Is: Testimony of a Thousand Witnesses* (New York, 1839).

23. Hundley, *Social Relations*, pp. 63-64, 187-88, 203-205.

24. Charleston *Courier*, May 14, 1847.

25. Catterall (ed.), *Judicial Cases*, II, pp. 336, 427.

26. Quoted in Taylor, "Negro Slavery in Louisiana," p. 254.

27. Moore Rawls to Lewis Thompson (n.d.), Lewis Thompson Papers.

28. New Orleans *Picayune*, March 16, 1858; Northup, *Twelve Years a Slave*, pp. 105-16.

29. *Southern Cultivator*, II (1844), p. 107; Bassett, *Plantation Overseer*, pp. 3-5.

30. Catterall (ed.), *Judicial Cases, passim*.

31. James P. Tarry to Samuel O. Wood, November 27, 1853; July 1, 1854, Samuel O. Wood Papers; Haller Nutt Ms. Journal of Araby Plantation, entries for November 1, 1843, *et seq.*

32. Gustavus A. Henry to his wife, December 12, 17, 1848; December 7, 1857, Henry Papers.

33. *Southern Cultivator*, XVIII (1860), p. 287; Sitterson, *Sugar Country*, p. 105.

34. Catterall (ed.), *Judicial Cases*, I, p. 284.

35. Henry, *Police Control*, pp. 67-68.

36. Nevitt Plantation Journal, entry for June 5, 1828; Douglas, *My Bondage*, p. 203; Sydnor, *Slavery in Mississippi*, pp. 69-70.

37. Johnson, *Ante-Bellum North Carolina*, pp. 493-94; Coleman, *Slavery Times in Kentucky*, pp. 248-49.

38. Taylor, "Slavery in Louisiana," p. 236; Davis (ed.), *Diary of Bennet H. Barrow*, pp. 173-74.

39. William Read to Samuel S. Downey, August 8, 1848, Downey Papers; Davis (ed.), *Diary of Bennet H. Barrow*, pp. 369-70, 376.

• The first slave code in the United States was enacted in Massachusetts, not in a Southern colony, and slavery existed in every Northern province during the colonial period. Edgar J. McManus describes some of the distinctive features of slavery in New York and suggests some of the reasons for its abolition in the North without social upheaval following the American Revolution.

The Negro Slave in New York

EDGAR J. MC MANUS

"Another instance in which I conceive I and my fellow servants are more hardly dealt with than the Negroes, is that they universally almost have one day in seven whether to rest or to go to church or see their country folks—but we are commonly compelled to work as hard every Sunday."
—*Richard Cain to William Kempe, October 23, 1754.*

Slave relations after the English occupation were not as good as under the Dutch, for the rapid progress of the colony and the growth of the slave population created regulatory problems which were unknown in New Netherland. Nevertheless, relations were generally good by the standards of the times, and the government took measures to protect the slaves as well as regulate them. A law enacted in 1686 made the willful killing of a slave a capital offense.[1] And in 1709 Governor Hunter was instructed by England to see to it that private slave discipline was not unduly severe and that the physical needs of slaves were not neglected by masters.[2] Owners were forbidden to allow their slaves to beg under penalty of a fine of £10 for each offense.[3] Moreover, slaves were encouraged to report abusive treatment to the provincial council.[4] All in all, the English authorities strove to keep the slave system as humane as possible.

The rationale of slavery of course was race, but the test of race really applied only to the first slaves. With the passage of time and the

From Edgar J. McManus, *A History of Negro Slavery in New York* (New York: Syracuse University Press, 1966), pp. 59-73. Copyright © 1966 by Syracuse University Press.

growth of a racially mixed population, the simple racial test became obsolete from a legal standpoint. By the end of the seventeenth century slave status no longer depended upon Negro blood but upon slave blood on the maternal side. The offspring of a male slave and a free woman was free, and the offspring of a free man and a slave woman was a slave.[5] Thus slavery was not confined exclusively to Negroes but included anyone with slave blood on the maternal side. The slightest admixture of slave blood was legally sufficient to subject a person to slavery regardless of complexion or physical appearance.[6] Persons of predominantly Negro ancestry were often free, whereas persons visibly white were slaves. By the eighteenth century the latter had become quite numerous. Advertisements for fugitive slaves make it clear that some runaways gained freedom simply by passing over into the white population.[7]

In cases where the status of racially mixed persons was in doubt, the courts had to decide who were to be treated as Negroes and who were to be treated as whites. The resolution of this question could be vitally important, for Negroes as a class were presumed to be slaves. A Negro claimed as a slave had the burden of rebutting the claim, whereas a white had no burden of proof because the law presumed him to be free. The test was physical appearance, and persons visibly white or Negro were treated as such for the purpose of allocating the burden of proof.[8] When Thomas Thatcher, a resident of New York City, claimed a predominantly white mulatto as a slave in 1677, the court gave him eight days to prove his claim; in the meantime the mulatto was presumed to be free.[9] Although the visibility test could and did result in injustice, it was the only practical test available for a slave system based upon race. Moreover, it was not conclusive as to the ultimate question of status, for in every case the putative slave had the right of rebuttal.

Although the formal structure of slavery was not unusual, its everyday operation was in some ways unique. For one thing, the efficiency of the system required a high degree of collaboration between masters and slaves. Since a large proportion of the bondsmen were highly skilled workers who could not be managed efficiently through coercion alone, concessions had to be made in order to obtain their cooperation. Masters who owned such slaves were usually willing to close their eyes to minor breaches of discipline and even to pay bribes in the form of clothing, liquor, and small sums of money in order to obtain loyal service. There were few concessions within reason that could not be extorted from the masters. The most highly skilled slaves bargained for manumission and were even able to prevent unwanted sales by indicating their reluctance to work for a prospective buyer.[10] The value of skilled slaves of course depended largely on their willingness to work. Threats which might be sufficient to compel physical exertion could not on the other hand guarantee the quality of the performance. Such was their bargaining power that skilled slaves were known to break up auctions merely by announcing their unwillingness to work for any of the bidders.[11]

The concessions won by the skilled slaves set precedents which affected the entire slave system. Not every slave of course was able to bargain effectively for freedom; only skilled slaves could do so, for without occupational skill a slave had nothing with which to bargain. The privileges enjoyed by the skilled bondsmen nevertheless brought a spirit of give and take to slave relations in general that made the system more humane in everyday operation. Slaves usually received adequate food, clothing, medical care, and time off for rest and relaxation.[12] With one day off in every seven, they often had more leisure time than white indentured servants, who were usually required to work a full seven-day week.[13] Nor is there any evidence that the mortality rate was higher among Negroes than among whites. Indeed, against the most dreaded epidemic disease of colonial times, smallpox, Negroes often fared better than whites.[14]

Perhaps the most unusual privilege enjoyed by the slaves was the privilege of owning private property. Slaves were allowed to accumulate property for their own purposes without fear that it might be taken from them by the masters. Although the privilege had no legal standing, in practice it was universally respected and protected. Evidence of this can be found in the numerous legacies given to slaves in the eighteenth century.[15] These legacies, made by persons with first-hand knowledge of slavery, could easily have been conditioned on the slave's right of enjoyment if there had been the slightest chance that the proceeds might be taken by the masters. The fact that testators did not make use of this obvious protective device is convincing evidence that they did not regard it as necessary. The property privilege was in fact so well established that the slaves themselves often drew up wills leaving their possessions to friends and relatives.[16]

What use they made of property that came their way depended on the character and outlook of the individual slave. Some bondsmen sedulously saved every penny in order to buy their freedom.[17] Others, however, sought immediate satisfactions and wasted whatever came into their possession on frivolous luxuries. A mania for fine clothing, for example, caused many slaves to squander the wages earned during their free time on the latest fashions. Tailors and bootmakers in New York City did a profitable business outfitting slaves with fancy shoes and fine clothing.[18] The desire to own such apparel was responsible for much petty crime, for slaves unable or unwilling to hire their free time often resorted to theft and burglary.[19] The sartorial mania inspired so much petty theft that some masters tried to protect themselves against pilferage by rewarding loyal slaves with special clothing.[20]

The exaggerated importance given to fine clothing was a natural reaction of the slaves to the general deprivations inherent in bondage. Slaves obtained in expensive attire an illusion of importance that their real condition denied them. Classed as property, it was difficult if not impossible for them to grasp normal social values. Marital and family ties, for example, meant little or nothing to most of the slaves. The average slave lived for satisfactions as ephemeral as the fine clothing which he yearned to own. Perhaps the greatest tragedy of slavery was the way it distorted the outlook of the Negro bondsman and imposed on him a mean and frivolous view of himself. In place of the stabilizing ties of family life, slavery conditioned the Negro to values which were petty and inferior by the standards of the whites.[21]

Not that every master was indifferent to the family ties of his slaves, for many of them were obviously troubled by the destructive effect of slavery on the slave family. Some tried to improve conditions by solemnizing slave marriages with civil or religious ceremonies calculated to upgrade the significance of the marital relationship.[22] Curfew regulations were frequently relaxed to permit married slaves to visit their spouses in the evening.[23] Men were often released from their regular duties to spend extra time with their wives and children.[24] It was not unusual, either, for a master to refuse to sell married slaves unless the buyer promised to keep the spouses together.[25]

But for most of the slaves family attachments were casual and impermanent. The slave system was simply not structured to support slave families and no amount of good will could surmount this fact or mitigate its effects. Slave families that were somehow kept together inevitably burdened slaveholders with costly and unmanageable numbers of slave children.[26] Another difficulty was that the typical slave family was divided among several owners. Although one of the owners might be willing, even eager, to protect family ties, he was powerless to do so without cooperation from the others. Since it was economically unfeasible for slaveholders as a class to subordinate their buying and selling to the stability of the slave family, it was inevitable that families should disintegrate.

Even when slave families were not physically disrupted, the absence of normal economic conditions weakened their stability. The men could not support their families, for they spent most of their time at tasks which benefited the masters. Most of them in fact had no desire or motivation to support their wives and children, for they understood this to be the responsibility of the masters. Whatever economic significance the slave family had involved the sort of responsibilities which fell entirely to the women. Men neither were the head of the family, nor did they have anything to do with the raising of children. It was the mother who provided the children with the essentials of life and with a symbol of authority and protection.[27] Indeed, newspaper advertisements of slaves for sale make it clear that women with dependent children were looked upon as complete family units without the father.[28]

Such conditions created a bad climate of sexual morality. Most slaves regarded monogamy as an aberration when they regarded it at all, for spouses who might be separated at any time by sale were not likely to develop deep emotional loyalties to one another.[29] And the example of the whites was certainly not a source of moral edification. Slavery bound whites and Negroes in a relationship debasing to the standards of both races. For one thing, the defenseless condition of the slave woman was a constant invitation to sexual exploitation. How much of this took place cannot be estimated with much precision, for disreputable practices of this sort were carefully kept out of sight. But evidence that such contacts were common can be found in the emergence of a mixed race with various degrees of white and Negro blood. By the middle of the eighteenth century large numbers of mulattoes could be found in all parts of the province.[30]. . .

But the most important point of contact between the races after the English occupation was not blood but religion. Racial intermixture was always tainted with an element of sexual exploitation which disturbed the conscience of the community. This explains in part the reluctance of masters to legitimize offspring for whom they obviously felt deep affection. Religion, on the other hand, carried no illicit taint; rather, it was respectable and, superficially at least, provided a point of contact between the races not blighted by exploitation. It is not surprising therefore that attempts to indoctrinate the slaves in the religious beliefs of the whites not only had wide support but reassured the whites of their own moral superiority. And the colonial authorities were strongly in favor of proselytization, for they equated Christianity with civil stability.[31] As early as 1686 Governor Dongan was instructed by England "to find out the best means to facilitate and encourage the conversion of Negroes." [32] Many slaveholders proselytized their bondsmen, at least to the extent of bringing them to religious services and encouraging them to conform outwardly to Christianity.[33]

The masters, however, were generally unwilling to have their slaves indoctrinated by anyone but themselves. They did not want them to receive catechetical instruction from either clergy or lay preachers, for they were morbidly suspicious of activities affecting their slaves over which they did not have direct personal control.[34] Thus it is not surprising that the main impetus to organized proselytization came not from the slaveholders but from a missionary group in England known as the Society for the Propagation of the Gospel in Foreign Parts. This organization had the support of the highest civil and ecclesiastical officials in England and was probably the most powerful branch of organized philanthropy in the eighteenth century.[35] Founded to save souls, both white and black, the S.P.G. provided much of the drive and most of the money behind the missionary effort in New York.[36]. . .

The S.P.G. nevertheless encountered stubborn resistance to its activities in all parts of the province. Most slaveholders were bitterly opposed to the indoctrination of their slaves by professional proselytizers. Many of them warned their slaves that they would be sold outside New York if they had anything to do with the missionaries.[37] They preferred instead to indoctrinate the slaves themselves in a safe version of Christianity with dangerous ideas carefully deleted. Slaveholders were well aware that some of the evangelical sects, particularly the Baptists and Quakers, preached an equalitarian gospel inimical to slaveholding. The hostility of these sects toward slavery compromised even the conservative denominations in the eyes of the slaveholding class. Clergymen and lay catechists who attempted to proselytize slaves invariably aroused suspicion regardless of religious affiliation or standing in the community.[38]

Another reason for resistance to the missionary effort was the fear that formal conversion to Christianity might give the slaves a legal claim to freedom.[39] This fear sprang mainly from the fact that in colonial times civil status was tied closely to religion. The right to vote, to hold public office, and to own real property were all subject to religious tests. Moreover, the legal basis of slavery was somewhat unclear, for even after legalization it rested exclusively on local municipal law. Since the English common law did not recognize chattel bondage, the legal premises of the slave system were in fact extremely shaky.[40] Indeed, on some points the system conflicted directly with the common law. For one thing, the rule that the status of a child followed the status of its mother was borrowed from the civil law, not from the common law, which fixed status by paternal descent.[41] The uncertainty surrounding the legal status of slavery made masters morbidly suspicious of attempts to change the status of the bondsmen in any respect.

Slaveholders were also worried by the judicial decisions in England which equated civil status with religion. In several cases the courts held that no Christian could be kept in slavery regardless of race or prior condition of servitude.[42] Although these decisions were not strictly binding outside of England, they were a source of great anxiety to the master class. This anxiety was especially acute in New York, where the bungling of local officials created the impression that the colonial government favored the English rule. Carelessly drafted statutes and slipshod census taking seemingly equated Christianity with freedom. A statute of 1686, for example, outlawed the enslavement of Christians "except such who shall be judged thereto by authority, or such as willingly have sold or sell themselves." [43] This was meant to apply only to indentured servants, but imprecise draftsmanship gave it a more sweeping meaning. Likewise the census of 1712 identified the free population as the "Christian" population.[44] Obviously not every non-Christian was a slave nor was every Christian free, but the careless overlapping of categories implied a relation between religion and freedom.

With so much to feed their suspicions—the English decisions, ambiguous statutes, and equivocal census returns—it is easy to understand why so many slaveholders were hostile to any attempt to proselytize the slaves. Nothing could dissuade them from believing that the missionary effort was basically inimical to their interests. Even assurances from the Solicitor and Attorney General of England that their legal rights would not be impaired in any way failed to move them, for their anxiety was not confined to legal consequences alone.[45] Many of them were convinced that any change brought about by the proselytizers—and this included the moral improvement of the slaves—would only work to undermine the slave system. One master in New York City pointed out that such improvement might fill the slaves with "dangerous conceits." [46] They might, for instance, be led to question the premises of a system which subjected them to morally inferior masters. Slaveholders did not forget for a moment that Christian slaves had played a leading role in the bloody insurrection of 1730 in Virginia. Many believed that proselytization had been responsible for the Virginia uprising, and even those who did not share this belief did not want to put the theory to a test in New York. . . .[47]

NOTES

1. N.Y. *Col. Docs.*, III, 374.
2. *Ibid.*, V, 138.
3. Flick, ed., *History of the State of New York*, II, 300.
4. O'Callaghan, ed., *Cal. Hist. MSS.*, II, 371.
5. Cobb, *Inquiry into the Law of Slavery*, p. 67.
6. A statute of 1706 provided that "all and every Negro, Mulatto, and mestee bastard child and children, who is, are, and shall be born of any Negro, Indian, or mestee, shall follow the state and condition of the mother." *Col. Laws N.Y.*, I, 597-98.
7. *New York Weekly Post-Boy*, August 27, 1759; June 18, 1761; March 18, 1771; *New York Mercury*, July 17, 1758; June 15, 1761; May 10, August 30, 1762; October 10, 1763; November 19, 1764; July 20, 1772; October 12, 1776.
8. Cobb, *Inquiry into the Law of Slavery*, p. 67.
9. O'Callaghan, ed., *Cal. Hist. MSS.*, II, 56.
10. Register of Manumissions, pp. 65-66, 73, MS. coll. Museum of the City of New York; *John Watts Letter Book*, p. 151; *Huntington Town Records*, III, 142; *New York Weekly Post-Boy*, March 23, 1746/47; March 30, 1747; August 30, 1756; January 8, 1758; September 1, 1763; *New York Mercury*, September 5, 1763; May 27, 1765; February 26, June 1, 1772; January 18, April 26, 1773; March 4, November 10, 1777.
11. Schermerhorn to Clinton, January 13, 1788, in Beekman Papers, Box 32, MS. coll. N.Y. Hist. Soc.
12. Philip Evertse Wendell's Day Book, p. 30; *Lloyd Papers*, I, 341, 309-10, II, 719.
13. Richard Cain to William Kempe, October 23, 1754, in John Tabor Kempe Papers, Box 4, Folio A-C, MS. coll. N.Y. Hist. Soc. See Richard B. Morris, *Government and Labor in Early America*, pp. 478-79.
14. During the New York City epidemic of 1730, only 71 of the 509 persons who died were Negroes. Although Negroes constituted at least 20 per cent of the population, their mortality rate was only 12 per cent. John Duffy, *Epidemics in Colonial America* (Baton Rouge: Louisiana State University, 1953), pp. 78-80.
15. *Abstracts of Wills*, VII, 129, 380-81, 407; IX, 72; XII, 155-57; XIV, 1-3; XV, 112-13, 127-28.
16. Register of Manumissions. p. 87.
17. *Jamaica Town Records* (New York: Long Island Historical Society, 1914), III, 346-47, 349-55; *Abstracts of Wills*, XV, 114-16.
18. Charles Nicoll's Account Book (1753-1758), January 27, October 24,

1756; October 2, 1760; March 21, 1761; Ledger (1759-1765), pp. 4, 9, 11, 13-16, 33.

19. Joel Munsell, ed., *Collections on the History of Albany* (Albany: J. Munsell, 1865), II, 382-83; *New York Weekly Post-Boy*, April 15, 1762.

20. Hendrick Denker's Account Book (1747-1758), *passim*, MS. col. N.Y. Hist. Soc.; Charles Nicoll's Ledger (1759-1765), p. 11; *Lloyd Papers*, II, 725.

21. This frivolous attitude toward life in general and toward themselves in particular tends to support Stanley M. Elkins' thesis that slavery "infantilized" the values of many bondsmen. Elkins, *Slavery* (New York: Grosset & Dunlap, 1963), pp. 103-15.

22. Grant, *Memoirs*, I, 265-67.

23. William S. Pelletreau, ed., *Records of the Town of Smithtown* (Huntington; Long Islander Print, 1898), p. 170.

24. David Humphreys, *An Account of the Endeavours Used by the Society for the Propagation of the Gospel in Foreign Parts to Instruct the Negro Slaves in New York* (London, 1730), p. 7.

25. *New York Weekly Post-Boy*, March 23, 1746/47; March 21, November 28, 1765; *New York Mercury*, March 5, November 19, 1770; February 8, 1779; *Abstracts of Wills*, V, 99-100; VI, 97-98; XII, 374-75.

26. *New York Weekly Post-Boy*, April 9, 1750; *Abstracts of Wills*, VI, 459-62; Shonnard and Spooner, *History of Westchester County*, p. 153.

27. This was typical of Negro family life everywhere under the American slave system. See Kenneth Stampp, *The Peculiar Institution* (New York: Alfred A. Knopf, 1956), pp. 343-44.

28. *New York Weekly Post-Boy* (1743-73); *New York Mercury* (1752-83).

29. *Revolutionary and Miscellaneous Papers*, in New-York Historical Society, *Collections*, XI-XIII (1878-80), III, 355. Hereinafter cited as *Rev. and Misc. Papers*.

30. Grant, *Memoirs*, I, 85-87.

31. *N.Y. Eccles. Recs.*, II, 916, 954, 1034; *Cal. State Papers, Col.*, XVII (1699), 176.

32. *N.Y. Col. Docs.*, III, 374.

33. *N.Y. Eccles. Recs.*, I, 489.

34. Humphreys, *Account of the Endeavours by the S.P.G.*, pp. 9-10. See also Morgan Dix, *A History of the Parish of Trinity Church* (New York: vols. I-IV, The Knickerbocker Press; vol. V, Columbia University Press, 1898-1950), I, 349-50.

35. Humphreys, *Account of the Endeavours by the S.P.G.*, p. 3.

36. *Rev. and Misc. Papers*, III, 357. See Humphreys, *Account of the Endeavours by the S.P.G.*, p. 18.

37. Hawkins, *Historical Notices of the Church of England*, p. 271.

38. *Ibid.*, pp. 50, 73.

39. *Cal. State Papers, Col.*, XVII (1699), 176.

40. William Goodell, *The American Slave Code* (New York: The American and Foreign Anti-Slavery Society, 1853), pp. 260-61; Hurd, *Law of Freedom and Bondage*, I, 278.

41. *Col. Laws N.Y.*, I, 597-98. See George M. Stroud, *A Sketch of the Laws in Relation to Slavery in the United States of America* (Philadelphia: Kimber & Sharpless, 1827), pp. 2-3, 10-11.

42. The English rule was that Negroes could be held as slaves "until they

become Christians and thereby they are enfranchised." See *Butts v. Penny*, 3 Kemble's Reports 785, I Lord Raymond's Reports 147.

43. *Col. Laws N.Y.*, I, 18.

44. *N.Y. Col. Docs.*, V, 339-40.

45. Cobb, *Inquiry into the Law of Slavery*, pp. 153, 162. See *New York Packet*, April 25, 1788.

46. Hawks' Records, I, 639. See Dix, *History of Trinity Church*, I, 185-86.

47. Hawks' Records, II, 33-34.

• Both Ulrich B. Phillips and Kenneth M. Stampp, along with most other historians of American slavery, have relied heavily on available records of large plantations. Slaves worked also in other economic settings in the ante-bellum South: on small family farms, in factories, and in a number of mercantile establishments. Generalizations made concerning the nature of plantation bondage may not apply without modification to other patterns of slavery. Edward W. Phifer examines the institution as it affected life in a single North Carolina county.

Slavery in Microcosm:
Burke County, North Carolina

EDWARD W. PHIFER

The local historian, casting about for an approach to a local historical situation which will enable him to make a contribution to general history—be it ever so trivial—finds himself in a particularly favorable position when he turns his attention to American Negro slavery. One would naturally suppose that the local and regional historian would exert his greatest efforts here where his potential is particularly great. Such has not been the case. For example, most historians of counties and regions in western North Carolina who mention the institution of slavery at all are content to refer to it in an occasional oblique reference, as if such a condition hardly existed. Neither imagination nor intuition is brought into play in an attempt to fathom the attitudes and thoughts of slaves or slaveholders, nor does the historian use to best advantage the bits of local information he has accumulated, the relevant experiences he has undergone, the wicked old tales he has been told, or his knowledge of a thousand and one happenings that go

From Edward W. Phifer, "Slavery in Microcosm: Burke County, North Carolina," *Journal of Southern History*, XXVIII (May 1962), 137-60. Reprinted by permission.

to make up the personality of a community. The fact remains, however, that if the local historian is, in a manner of speaking, indigenous
to the area which he is studying, if he springs from a curious admixture
of all socioeconomic groups, if he is cognizant of this admixture and
has an awareness of the bad and good qualities of all and of the endless
intermingling of families and family groups, then he is better able to
attack the problem, objectively but without being wholly impersonal,
than is the general historian.

Furthermore, the local historian of slavery is in a better position to
develop the technique of dealing with minutiae than is the general
historian, who likely lacks both the taste and the time for the study of
a locality. Generalization is often the pitfall that traps the scholar trying to analyze the many facets of slavery, an area in which minute
details can be particularly revealing. "We think in generalities," says
Whitehead, "but we live in detail. To make the past live, we must
perceive it in detail in addition to thinking of it in generalities." This
then is the province of the local historian of slavery: To focus down
upon a high-power field and examine the cellular structure of this so-
ciopathological process, hoping that an understanding of slavery may
be reached in this painstaking fashion after grosser methods have
failed. The historian of locality, even if without formal training, may
find himself uniquely qualified to detect nuances when information
comes reticently and only through innuendo, to utilize familiarity for
breaking down the barriers of the mind, and to exploit knowledge of
family traits and idiosyncrasies in order to release his intuitive understanding. If this were not so, Wilbur J. Cash could not have written
The Mind of the South and Faulkner could not have created Yokna-
patawpha County. "You can't understand it," Quentin Compson says
to his friend Shreve who is puzzled by the South, "you would have to
be born there."

The local historian who turns his attention to slavery can not fail to
note, after he has floundered about in the great mass of material
scholars have marshaled on the institution that, by and large, general
historians have utilized source materials from restricted geographical
areas much as if to say that these areas were representative of the entire slaveholding South. They have found it much easier to study the
records of the great plantations than to search the crumbling annals
of the small slaveholding farmer of the backcountry. Anyone thumb-
ing through the much-used eyewitness accounts of travelers in the
slave states will find the itineraries, more often than not, following
the better traveled routes through Maryland, Virginia, and the Caro-

lina tidewater, or up the Mississippi from New Orleans into the heart of the Black Belt of the New South—in other words they tended to visit the areas that were more accessible, where they could see the most slavery with the least travel. Furthermore, those newspapers that continued to operate with any degree of permanency—and remain most available to scholars—were located in the larger coastal towns, not in the sparsely settled interior. In short, the critical analyses of the institution of slavery have not been derived, to any extent, from the study of regions occupied by the self-sufficing small slaveholding farmer but rather almost entirely from the study of the areas dominated by the rice, tobacco, and cotton planters, who, having large slaveholdings, farmed commercially—and this notwithstanding the fact that roughly half the slavery territory of the United States was the domain of small farmers, most of whom owned no slaves, many of whom owned only a few slaves, and none of whom for reasons largely geographical farmed commercially or grew a staple crop.[1] Here, obviously, is an area for study peculiarly suited to the talents of the local historian of slavery.

Admittedly slavery throughout the South had a certain uniformity, but it was far from complete. Certainly, slavery in the nonstaple-producing area—to which the county under study belongs—was not exactly the same as slavery in the staple-producing areas. Each of the two regions had certain general characteristics which served to set it apart from the other, as all the great historians of slavery have understood and duly emphasized. The nonstaple regions were usually inland with poor farm-to-market transportation facilities. As the regions were broken by streams and mountains, with a markedly restricted amount of alluvial soil in the valleys, farms were, of necessity, small. Climate and soil conditions were unsuited to the cultivation of cotton or rice and usually poorly adapted to the cultivation of tobacco. The slave population was ordinarily less than thirty per cent of the total population, and there were few large slaveholders. Treatment of the slaves was reputedly much less stringent than on the large cotton plantations of the Black Belt; the farmer lived in closer relationship to his "black family," often worked in the fields with them, and knew them intimately. The crops produced were not sold but were used to feed livestock, feed and clothe the slaves, and "keep body and soul together." Little money came in or went out. The small farmers lived on the farm and off the farm produce.

In summary, the history of slavery has been neglected by county historians; trivialities contribute to the story of slavery, and it falls to the local historian to present them; and, lastly, historians of slavery have not adequately studied the large areas where staples were not produced but where slavery nevertheless existed. Also the subject needs to be studied from an early nineteenth-century posture, rather than— as has been repeatedly done—from a twentieth-century moral position or from a position of "complete detachment."

Created from the western part of Rowan County, North Carolina, in the early days of the Revolution, Burke County initially encompassed a huge pie-shaped region lying entirely north of the Lord Granville line and including all of the present counties of Burke, Catawba, Mitchell, Madison, and Yancey; most of the present counties of Caldwell, Avery, and McDowell; large portions of the present counties of Buncombe, Haywood, and Alexander; and in addition small parts of the present counties of Lincoln, Cleveland, Rutherford, and Swain. First fragmented in 1791 to form Buncombe in the west, Burke by 1842 approximated its present size and shape, with an area of slightly more than 500 square miles.[2] . . . Shaped like the upward-tilted head of a lonely wolf with her open mouth baying toward the northwest and the tip of her ear pointing in the direction of Old Salem, her nose and high, broad collar line are deeply corrugated by mountains. Her major stream, the Catawba River, flowing east, divides the county into two roughly equal parts, and the numerous tributaries create a herringbone pattern as they course down the slopes from the mountains. Significantly, the streams that feed into the Catawba from the north are more numerous and much larger than those that feed from the south. The northern mountains are higher and create a greater watershed than do the South Mountains; and furthermore the eastern end of these South Mountains drain into streams which flow south into Lincoln County to join the North Fork River, rather than north into the Catawba.

The map of the county makes it apparent why there was a very definite relationship, on the one hand, between the stream pattern and size of these watercourses and, on the other hand, the number of slaves owned by each slaveholder engaged in farming, as, of course, most were. The largest, flattest, richest land areas lay in the crotches between two or even three larger streams or up the broad river valleys which ordinarily existed for only a few miles above the mouths. The largest slaveholders had their plantations located on these rich alluvial deltas at the juncture between two major streams such as the junctures of Linville River, Johns River, Upper Creek, Lower Creek, Canoe Creek, Silver Creek, or Muddy Creek with the Catawba, or the juncture of Upper Creek with Irish Creek. Slaveowners with moderate holdings were also distributed along these major streams but not at the mouths, although most were situated at a point where a branch entered a major stream. Small slaveholders occupied the land along smaller streams, not at junctures, and the nonslaveholders had to be content with narrow bottoms high up on the creeks or with upland which was unsuited for serious farming. One might almost say, then, that the number of slaves stationed at a given point was directly proportional to the volume of water flowing by that point in a given period of time.

In 1860, 921 families in the country were engaged in farming, but only 548 persons were landowners, and only nine of these were listed as owning as many as 300 improved acres. Slaveholders, who held the best situated and most fertile land, comprised only thirty-eight per cent of the 548 landowners of the county, and sixteen per cent of these slaveholders owned but one slave. One farmer on the Linville River, Barnet H. Moore, owned seventeen slaves in 1860 but no land. He farmed the land of relatives and friends and was thus, if you like, a tenant-planter or slaveholding sharecropper. Apparently there was never a Negro slaveholder in Burke.[3] In 1860, sixty family heads owned ten or more slaves, but a large segment of the population was almost untouched by slavery. Particularly was this true in the southern and southeastern parts of the county, settled largely by Germans.

A number of questions immediately come to mind. What was the origin of the slave system in Burke County? How did it develop? Or, even, why did it develop at all if slavery was as unprofitable in the nonstaple crop regions as many historians imply that it was? Very few of the early immigrants brought slaves with them when they moved into the county, and those that did brought only a few. . . . These early slaveholders were almost all Scotch-Irish or English, not Germans, and they came to the county from regions where the slave system was well-established, usually from Virginia or eastern North Carolina and not directly from Pennsylvania or other Northern states. Once the germ of slavery had found its way into Burke County, the practice of slaveholding gradually spread through the purchase of slaves from other states and from North Carolina counties to the east.[4] "Drovers" or slave traders, at intervals, brought slaves through the county for sale, and inhabitants could attend slave sales customarily held in certain localities such as nearby Huntsville in southeastern Yadkin County.[5]

There is no evidence that the people of Burke resisted the development of slavery. Manumissions were few and far between. The only case of manumission recorded by the county court between 1796 and

1830 was on May 26, 1797, when one Ben was freed by Dr. Thomas Bouchelle, a native of Delaware, who at the time had probably been a resident of Burke County for less than a year.[6] The small number of free Negroes in the county is further evidence of the reluctance of Burke slaveholders to free their slaves. Slavery gradually but steadily became more and more prevalent up to 1860. . . . Although the statistics . . . are somewhat distorted by the population loss resulting from the formation of new counties (generally speaking, the territory ceded was to the west where the proportionate number of slaves was smaller than in the territory which remained a permanent part of the county), a slave population of twenty-six per cent in 1860 offers little support to the argument that the institution would have in the foreseeable future been abolished by local initiative, nor does it lend credence to the popular concept that this region exported large numbers of slaves to the Deep South in the decades before the Civil War.

Considerable insight into the attitude of the white inhabitants of Burke County toward the institution of slavery can be gained by the historian from the behavior and the tone of the personal correspondence of these people. One thing is certainly crystal clear: It never occurred to them to attempt to justify slavery on moral grounds. The valley of the Catawba was settled by two Protestant groups—the Scotch-Irish and the Germans. They had been molded for generations by almost identical historical experiences which had made them into hardened realists, the Scotch-Irish in particular. Having known only hard labor and grinding poverty and now engaged in the struggle to make their way on the frontier, they gave first priority to the acquisition of wealth. Property was paramount; they had a fanatical respect for it. Slavery appeared to them as a bonanza, and a pseudo-salutary freedom from sentimentality permitted them to accept it as such. There was little time for contemplation in their lives, nor did abstractions tempt the unlettered mind. Besides, these comparatively recent arrivals had found slavery a well-established institution in America. As newcomers, who were they to express moral indignation?

The Scotch-Irish and German upcountrymen turned to legalism, already a component of their thought process, to justify the institution of slavery. The law and the law courts were at the center of their cultural and intellectual life. They looked forward to court week as the prime source of amusement. The lawyers were the actors of the day, and the courtroom their stage. Backwoodsman or yeoman farmer, the citizen of Burke was remarkably aware of his legal rights and was ready to go to court on the slightest provocation. The prosperous had no qualms about using the courts to drive a poverty-stricken debtor to the wall, and the leading men of the locality learned as justices of the county court the pompous ways and sententious language of the courtroom. In truth, all the white men of the county were exceedingly "courthouse conscious." For their purposes, legality was synonomous with morality. If the idea ever occurred to them that laws were human instruments and therefore imperfect, they rejected it. Slavery did not make of them a guilt-ridden people.

Accepting slavery as the *fait accompli* that it most certainly was, and seeing it as providing relief from backbreaking labor and a means for gaining property and wealth or advancement in social status, they were not inclined to question the instrument of "progress." All of which is not to say that there were not among the Scotch-Irish and Germans of the county those who disapproved of slavery; [7] but the point is that the basis of disapproval was essentially *economic*, not moral.

A good indication of how little opprobium was attached to slavery by the local citizenry is to be found in the identity of the slaveholders themselves. Professional people and church officers, as well as farmers and merchants, owned slaves. A Methodist minister on Paddy's Creek, William Fullwood, owned as many as nineteen slaves at one time, and the Presbyterian minister at Morganton and Quaker Meadows, John McKamie Wilson, Jr., had ten slaves in 1850. In fact, the slave census shows conclusively that among slaveholders were the most highly respected people in the community, the people who provided its moral and ethical leadership. . . .

It appears, from a local coign of vantage, that one thing which has tended to lead scholars astray in their analyses of the economics of slavery has been their failure to probe the mind of the slaveholder.[8] What must be understood is that the slaveholder was not at heart an investor; he was a speculator. His primary interest was not in yearly income on an investment; his primary interest was in appreciàtion. "The self-sufficing farmer was not seeking profits, but a living." [9] True, but through capital accumulation he hoped to endow his progeny for generations to come. The answer to the question of whether the man with capital and credit who was seeking to establish his family's fortunes believed that slaves were a good speculative risk is, of course, "Yes, he most certainly did." [10] Was he correct in this assumption? Were slaves a good speculative risk? The answer again is an unavoidable "Yes." Barring any radical changes in the economic system, slaves were an excellent speculative risk, as the record shows. After 1800 the price of slaves generally rose steadily except during the depression period of 1837–1845. In 1799, John James of Brunswick County sold Thomas McEntire of Burke a twenty-year-old male for $400. Thirty-six years later W. A. Lenoir wrote his grandfather in Happy Valley, "I will just say to you and Father that $1,100.00 is about the lowest price for Negroe fellows in Morganton and 8 or 900 for women. Some have sold for a good deal more." [11] By 1860 "Negroe fellows" were selling for not a great deal less than double this amount.[12] The slave had great mobility and therefore wide marketability, while natural increase provided a built-in growth component. Furthermore, the investment field was sharply limited for these provincial investors. Securities of canal and railroad companies did not perform well, and banking stocks— although stockholders, on the whole, fared better—were not popular in the western counties. Land, of course, was the commonest form of investment, but arable land was scarce in Burke County; and, as an investment, landholding was complementary to slaveholding, for slaves provided the labor to make productive the richer land of the county. During most of this period, the slaveholder in North Carolina also enjoyed a highly favored tax position. The slave tax as administered under the poll principle was smaller than if the ad valorem principle had been applied, as it was to real property.[13] The tax on slaves, furthermore, was confined to a highly productive age group, with exemptions allowable if the slave were, for physical or mental reasons, a burden on the owner.[14]

Few of the large slaveholders of Burke confined their activities to farming. Of the twenty leading slaveowners in the county in 1850, at least thirteen had occupations unassociated with agriculture. They were lawyers, physicians, merchants, ministers, innkeepers, building contractors, bankers, surveyors, postmasters, and county office holders. Artisans, innkeepers, and manufacturers owned slaves and employed them in their shops; planters employed their slaves not only on their farms but also in household manufacturing, gold mining, public works such as road maintenance and river clearance, and, toward the end of the period, in railroad construction.[15] Slaveholders farmed as part of their way of life and in order to "make a living," but the fiscally sophisticated rarely depended on it for more than this. Cash and liquid assets were derived from other sources.

> I am without an overseer [wrote a large slaveholder who was also a bank cashier], and trying to farm, with a rather smaller force than usual, having some hands mining. Am afraid I shall not

succeed very well, not having it in my power to devote as much of my personal attention to it as I could wish. [1]

Emphasis must be placed upon the unvarnished fact that slave breeding was what made slavery an attractive long-term investment. The subject, approached with diffidence by some and with self-righteous horror by others, has engendered much profitless and naive debate. Again, it would seem that the key lies in the mind and conscience of the slaveowner. Fully realizing that active breeding was an indispensable requisite to successful slaveownership, the investor made certain, insofar as he was financially able, that the female of childbearing age was an integral part of his slave family and that the male slave in turn was a part of her environment. No additional planning or plotting was necessary; the natural processes of reproduction went on without urging or prompting. Occasionally an owner would, in an unguarded moment, betray his true feelings on this matter, as in the optimistic phrase, "three Breeding Wenches and another wench nearly Grown," found in a private letter.[17]

It must be remembered that the class structure of Burke County was by no means entirely determined by slave ownership, nor was slave ownership a hallmark of nobility. *Noblesse oblige* did not hold then any more than it holds with the wealthy industrial and commercial classes today. The delineations of certain of the larger slaveholders in the county that filter down to us are disenchanting to say the least. A number, although clever enough to become financially successful, were uneducated and even illiterate.[18] Some have been portrayed as small, mean men—shrewd, tricky bargainers, greedy in the extreme, unscrupulous sharpers with a penchant for penury; a few as vulgar ruffians intermittently involved in drunkenness, lechery, or violence. On the whole, though, one gets the impression from the court records, that the conduct of the slaveholders was superior to that of their nonslaveholding neighbors.

Strictly speaking there was never a real slaveholding or planter class in Burke County. Slavery flourished in it for little more than sixty years—about three generations. This is hardly sufficient time for the development of a stable aristocracy, even if other factors did not militate against it. A scrutiny of genealogical patterns goes a long way toward making clear why a slave aristocracy did not develop in Burke County. Without provisions for primogeniture and entail, the man seeking to found a slave dynasty had to assure that he lived a long time and that he left behind few children, preferably only one. It is as simple as that. For instance, five Greenlee brothers owned a total of 184 slaves in 1820; by 1850 there were no large slaveholders among the Greenlee heirs residing in Burke County. . . . Of course, there was always the heir who, completely outstripping his brothers and sisters, built his own slave empire by ingenuity and energy, or by marriage, while the rest of his family ineluctably slipped into a lower stratum. More abruptly devastating to the incipient slave dynasty than frequent division of property was the failure of business ventures. For more than one Burke County slaveholder, among the most disastrous of these ventures was investment in gold mines. John E. Butler, a victim of business reverses, owned fifty slaves in 1830 and was the seventh largest holder in the county; in 1860 his widow did not own a single slave. . . . All of this is to say that Burke County had a fluid society, and that what class stratification did develop was not necessarily based on slave wealth.

Slavery, as practiced in Burke County and elsewhere in the South, was grounded on a matriarchal system, a system rooted in the legal concept that the children of slaves were the property of the mother's owner, not the father's. In actual practice, the slave family unit was always designated by the name of the mother; for example, one would refer to "Viney's house" or "Viney's children." The point that has not been stressed, however, is that slavery, although matriarchal in this sense, was also a major component of a patriarchal system.[19] The peculiar twist here is that the slave husband was not the patriarch. The white master was. It is a gross understatement to say that this both denigrated the slave husband and tended to undermine the integrity of the slave family. Nevertheless, even though slave marriages had no legal status whatsoever, Christian marriage between slaves was widely practiced in Burke, and it was countenanced by the master and encouraged by the church. Nor was it uncommon for the slave husband and wife to have different masters who belonged to different churches.[20]

At this point in such a discussion, the horrid specter, miscegenation, inevitably raises its head. In Burke County, as elsewhere, race mixing between male members of an owner's family and his female slaves did occur. In Burke, the condition appears to have been just about as commonplace as one would expect considering the intimate relationship that existed in the county between the slave and the slaveholding family.[21] The slavehouses were in the yard of the slaveholder's dwelling, and younger male members of the owner's family in nearly every case played and worked in the fields year after year with slaves of their own age.[22] The attitude of the community toward race mixing was complex, but in Burke County a general pattern is discernible. If a bachelor slaveholder entered into an intimate relationship with a female slave and raised a family by her, but never became promiscuous, the situation did not become a topic of polite conversation it is true, yet there is very little evidence that he was censured for his conduct or that he lost status in the community. Again, if a young boy of a slaveholding family had a child by a female slave, later married, and engaged in no further indiscretions, the incident was usually considered lightly and quickly forgotten. But the married slave owner who promiscuously or openly consorted with his slaves became a social outcast, and he was never forgiven nor his actions forgotten so long as his name was remembered.

The close relationship that often existed between slave and slaveholding family was not always sordid in its implication. Both master and mistress ordinarily were conscientious about caring for the sick—even for the aged who no longer had commercial value.[23] Religion strengthened the bond between slave and free. Local churches, both rural and town, received slaves into membership, baptized their infants, and buried their dead in the plots reserved for their master's family. Although the slave customarily affiliated with the church of his master, on the whole he had considerable freedom of choice in his religious life. Furthermore, he was fairly treated by the church courts of conduct which seem to have taken their work seriously during this period. At church gatherings, slaves were expected to sit together, separate from the white members. Slave graves were poorly marked or not marked at all, but so frequently were white graves.[24] Twentieth-century segregation is not a by-product of slavery but rather a reactionary aftermath to Reconstruction.

And yet in spite of all that has been said—that the slaveholder did not feel a sense of guilt, did not consider himself morally reprehensible; that close association between master and slave often promoted a feeling of reciprocal admiration and affection just as it might, by the same token, promote a feeling of hatred or disdain; that treatment of slaves was less harsh and the institution itself more informal than in the areas of commercial farming—in spite of all this, incidents did occur now and then which broke the seeming pastoral calm and created an atmosphere of tension. From the correspondence of Burke County people one senses that there ordinarily existed an atmosphere not of emotional tension but of slight restraint marked by a failure to express emotions that would otherwise have found free expression, a reticence born of circumspection. Perhaps the emotional tone of the community was set as much by the character and disposition of the inhabitants as by the presence of slavery, but a contemporary suggests otherwise when he speaks of "the unhappy excitement and the great sensitiveness of the community to everything connected with slavery." [25]

The underlying tension comes through to us in the reactions of the community to incidents of violence in the slave population and in the precautions it took to keep the slaves under strict surveillance. In the summer of 1813, a slave named Jerry, with the complicity of a female slave named Betsey, allegedly murdered his master, John W. Taggart, a small slaveholder from the eastern part of the county, south of Lovelady Ford. Tried together in the county court of pleas and quarter sessions before three justices of the peace and a jury of twelve men, most of whom were slaveholders, the two were found guilty and sentenced to be hanged. At the same term of court, a slave belonging to William McGimsey was found guilty of trespassing and was sentenced to stand one hour in the public pillory "thence to be taken down, confined to the public whipping post and there receive thirty-nine lashes on his bear [*sic*] back well laid on." Several years later, Bolin Brantley, a free Negro, was required by the court to give bond in the amount of $300 with "two good Securities" or else be placed in custody by the sheriff because of his reputation as "a black man of bad fame." [26]

Perhaps prompted by the San Domingo revolt of 1791, patrolling was established in Burke County at least as early as mid-year 1792, and, contrary to reports of other localities, it was apparently performed faithfully and with vigor. The county court supported the patrols by administering very strictly the law that allowed a slave to carry a gun on his master's plantation only if his master posted bond and security.[27] When a slave belonging to a resident of neighboring Wilkes County failed to identify himself satisfactorily to the Burke patrol and was severely cowhided, the owner of the slave entered a complaint against the patrol, but the court ruled in 1821 that if a patroller punished with discretion he was not liable to the slave's master unless malice against the master was evident.[28] The Nat Turner revolt of late August 1831 occurred in Southampton County, Virginia, only a short distance from those North Carolina border counties supplying slave labor for the gold mines of Burke and Rutherford counties. Repercussions in Burke County from this are described in this way:

In consequence of letters, received last week from Rutherfordton stating that a Negro Preacher, and three or four other slaves had been examined and committed to Prison charged with meditating an insurrection in the neighborhood of the mines, the Community to some extent, but the Citizens of Morganton particularly, have been in a state of uncommon excitement for a few days past—the great number of Slaves employed about the mines, would render vigilance among Managers and Patrollers, proper at all times; but from the best information I can get, there is no Just ground for the Panic that has existed—the Negroes of the County are as orderly and submissive, as I ever knew them. . . .[29]

Several months later, one John Hay was arrested and lodged in the Burke County jail "under charge of exciting the negroes to insurrection." The community had hardly settled down from this episode when two slaves, Giles and Billy, were arrested on charges of conspiracy but were acquitted by jury trial. After this, there apparently was no further panic in the county, but we do have occasional indications of continued slave unrest and white hypersensitivity. In early 1844 Isaac, a runaway slave belonging to James Upton, was said to be "lurking hid committing various and sundry depredations upon stock and other property." The county court issued a proclamation calling on him to surrender at once, with warning that should he fail to do he would be declared an outlaw, and "it shall be lawful for any person or persons to kill or destroy said slave Isaac by such ways and means as he or they shall think fit with out accusation or impeachment of any crime of the same." A second order states that Isaac "is suspected of being harboured by evil disposed persons" and therefore "that Daniel J. Forney and the patrollers in his neighborhood acting with him are permitted to search the house or houses of any persons whom they may have reason to suspect for harbouring said slave." [30]

Other cases on record indicate that the court could be as lenient as it was sometimes harsh in dealing with a slave. In an action against Sam, a slave owned by David Greenlee, the indictment for petit larceny was quashed, and a vindictive white prosecutor was taxed with court costs. In 1827, a slave Abram was hailed into court on an unspecified charge to which he submitted and prayed for benefit of clergy; it was "extended to him," the judgment of the court being that "the Defendant be taken to the public whiping [sic] post and there receive one stroke." [31] Early in the spring of 1830 two slaves belonging to the clerk of the superior court, William W. Erwin, were tried for murder. One was found not guilty, and the other, Solomon, being found guilty of manslaughter, prayed for and was given benefit of clergy, whereupon the court ordered that "Solomon be Branded with the letter M on the brawn of the left thumb . . . and that the owner of said slave pay the costs of the prosecution and the Prisoner be discharged." [32]

All of this makes one conclusion inescapable: When the crime of the slave threatened the institution of slavery or otherwise encroached on the economic welfare of the slaveholder, the punishment meted out was as harsh as the law allowed; but, if, in contrast, the crime was of no economic consequence, or, if severe punishment would have been contrary to the economic interest of the slaveholder, mitigation was the rule. This is not to say that some particularly heinous crime, such as assault on a white female, would not have invoked the maximum penalty however it affected the interests of the slaveholder, but certainly property rights strongly influenced the courts of the county when dealing with slave crime. None of this contradicts the contention that "the master was more important than the law in determining the extent to which the activities of the slaves were curtailed." [33] The jeremiad of Mrs. E. C. Alexander of southwestern Burke County is in point: "The servants will not obey me. John ran away six weeks since. . . . Last week he returned and says he intends to leave again whenever he pleases." [34] While this may have been an uncommon situation, there is other evidence that slaves enjoyed considerable freedom of movement—occasionally to their own detriment, like Charles McDowell's Jerry who "came by his death by a stab or stabbing with a knife from the hand of some other person than himself in an affray in Mr. Fleming's Island on Friday night last in which said Jerry and others were engaged." [35]

More productive for study at the county level than the legal aspects of slavery is the problem of slave transfer, even though this has also received a great deal of attention from scholars. Slave transfer may, for our purposes, be divided into the three categories of sale, transfer through inheritance, and hiring. Slave sale or slave trading, "slave mongering," has generally been considered the most odious of the three. Yet, it is certainly altogether possible that often hiring or transfer by inheritance created the greater hardship and grief for the slave. Slave sales in Burke County were infrequent in comparison with land sales. The county court records of deeds and bills of sale reveal approximately twenty land transactions to every slave transaction, and in one year when over a hundred land deeds were recorded only two slave transactions were recorded.[37] Careful analysis of slave transactions, when the analysis is illuminated by some knowledge of the general characteristics of the persons involved in the sales, enables one to gain a very clear understanding of the prevailing ethics of slave trading. It becomes immediately apparent that there was no stigma attached to strictly local trades in which buyer and seller were both residents and intended to remain so. The local Presbyterian minister, John Stilliman, for instance, did not hesitate to sell in 1831 a Negro boy to Samuel P. Carson, a resident of the area.[38] Also, it was considered all right for a local buyer to purchase a slave from a seller who lived in another state, but a local seller who sold slaves to a buyer from another state was often censored. The buyer, unless he was a professional trader, was generally less subject to criticism than the seller. One wonders whether the odium heaped upon the seller stemmed more from the fact that the sale was a heartless act or from the fact that it was evidence of his failure as a businessman, while the buyer was admired as a symbol of aggressiveness and affluence. The most objectionable act was to sell to an itinerant trader or agent who obviously intended to transfer the Negroes to a distant market; [39] but even the most conservative of local slaveholders sometimes hankered to speculate in the slave market as indicated by a few lines that a Burke County businessman-farmer scrawled covertly at the end of a letter to his brother-in-law, Thomas Lenoir:

> I will apprize you while I think of it of another circumstance. Negro property has taken a very considerable rise in Norfolk and every other place where purchases result in consequence of the number of purchasers for the Louisiana Market—this I learned at Raleigh and I mention it because you talked of selling property of that description[.] Women are quoted at $500.[40]

Some years later, however, Colonel Lenoir cautioned his son in Alabama against selling "property of that description" unless the slave family was kept together and was willing to be sold. He also strongly advised the young trader to sell to a friend rather than to a stranger if at all possible.[41] It is easy to overlook the fact that sometimes the slave was not only willing to be sold but wished to be sold, hoping, as it is one's nature to hope, that he might improve his lot or knowing that at the very least he would experience a change in scenery. Such apparently was the case when a male slave belonging to Mrs. Thomas Espy, the widow of a Presbyterian minister, accosted one Charles Stanlee, a nonresident who happened to be in Morganton, and told the white man that he was anxious to be traded and requested that Stanlee buy him.[42]

Even from the standpoint of the slaveholder, slave trading did not present a pretty picture. Many individuals who prided themselves on being "smart" or "close" traders seemed to have derived satisfaction from "getting the best of the other fellow," from "driving a hard bargain." An example of a victim of such trickery and greed is William Alberto Erwin, who bought a Negro at a public sale after having accepted the statement of an interested party that the boy was intelligent, only to find that he was an idiot.[43] Fragmentation of slave families, common as the result of slave trades can be easily illustrated from the slave records. For example, James Murphy, highly respected in the county, bought two small children from Richard Owens of Wilkes County, without acquiring either parent.[44] Fragmentation of slave families was in fact inevitable, particularly in the transfer of slaves by inheritance. Wills were principally concerned with equitable distribution of property to rightful heirs, and administrators of estates were compelled by law to manage the affairs of the deceased in a manner which would produce the greatest revenue. Auction sales at the courthouse door—a necessary part of the institution—were unaffected by sentimental considerations.[45] Individual slaves went to the highest bidder. The law went so far as to provide even that "Negroes willed to be free" were to be sold "with the Stock and other property on hand" if necessary in order to pay the debts and settle the estate of the testator.[46]

A distasteful and tragic story of transfer by inheritance is that of the little slave girl Ony. Waightstill Avery, a large property owner of Burke County, provided in his will, in addition to large bequests to his children, that his niece, Margaret Avery, should receive "a likely negro slave of nine or ten years old or four hundred dollars in money" and made a bequest to his son-in-law, William B. Lenoir, contingent upon his payment of this legacy. When Colonel Avery died, Margaret Avery was the wife of John Murphy of Burke County; and Lenoir was living in Roane County, Tennessee. To comply with the terms of the will, Lenoir had a relative conduct a young female slave, Ony, from Tennessee to North Carolina. When the little girl reached Murphy's plantation in Burke County, she was found to have acquired a limp. Because of this defect that apparently developed during her journey, Murphy refused to accept the girl as full payment of his wife's legacy. At his insistence, the question was submitted to a select committee of arbitration, which ruled that if the lameness had not disappeared within three months Murphy would be entitled to an adjustment.[47] Once it is understood that Avery's bequest to his niece was obviously intended as an affectionate gesture, that Lenoir had a reputation for scrupulous honesty, and that Murphy was a man of wealth and the sole heir of one of the largest slaveholders in the county, it becomes clear that this is a prime example of a reverence for the law which tended to blunt moral perception. Legalism did not provide for a sense of gratitude or of sympathy for a little ten-year-old girl who had been abruptly taken from her accustomed surroundings and transferred almost 200 miles over rough mountain trails only to find she was unwanted when she arrived at her destination.

Transfer by inheritance, although of necessity usually impersonal, was sometimes relieved of its harshness by the provisions of testator, most of whom tried to see that a mother and her smaller children were kept together. One expressed the "desire that my Servants, John and his wife Sally Should not be Sold if it can be avoided, especially to persons out of this County, and that they Should not be alloted to any Legatee who will take them out of the State unless they wish to go." [48] Another stipulated that his "servant Rufus and Alcy" be allowed to choose their owner from among his children or relatives at a value set by the executors should his wife die or marry again.[49] Still another required that to pay his debts his town lots be sold before any Negroes and that his wife should designate the order in which the slaves would be sold should this become necessary.[50] Jesse Moore arranged that a man and his wife were not to be sold but were to have the privilege of living with whichever of his children they chose.[51] Individual slaves were occasionally willed their freedom, but these bequests were always subject to the laws relating to manumission, strictly construed by the courts. Daniel Jones willed that his "negro girl Lizzie be set free on account of her good and faithful service to me and I give her my tract of land and my desire is that Dr. Jones should build her a house and see that she should be taken care of." [52] At her death, Mary Probit, widow of John Probit, freed her slaves in accordance with her deceased husband's wishes, leaving one slave to a friend, Alexander Glass, to "have and enjoy . . . for 11 years," with the proviso that "at the end of said term" he was "to set her free." To four other slaves, she bequeathed her plantation on Cain Creek, with furniture sufficient "that they may live comfortably." [53] In a very general way, it may be said that the small slaveholder more commonly made special provisions in his will for his slaves than did the

large slaveholder with multiple heirs, whose will was usually more impersonal in order to make it more easily administered.[54]

Slave hiring, the third form of slave transfer, was by definition, a
temporary arrangement. A common practice in Burke, the hiring out
of slaves was conducted on a large-scale contractual basis during the
gold rush of the early 'thirties and during the railroad construction
boom beginning in the late 'fifties. Slaves were employed in railroad
construction either by slaveholders entering into contracts themselves
and using their own slave labor or by slaveholders hiring out their
slaves to other contractors. In either case, the slaves were put under
the immediate direction of an overseer who "followed the road" and
was frequently a hard taskmaster.[55] Except in the cases of these big
projects, Frederic Bancroft's generalization that it was "usually necessary" to hire out slaves "when slave property was in probate, or possessed by a life-tenant unable to employ it, or belonged to orphan
children or other wards in chancery" holds true for Burke County.[56]
For instance, when Samuel Greenlee died intestate in 1848, leaving
five minor children, a wife (who died three years later), and more than
twenty slaves, a local lawyer who was appointed administrator managed to hire out the slaves belonging to the minor children to various
individuals for periods of one year.[57]

The system of hiring to individuals seemed to work out more satisfactorily for all concerned than mass hiring for industrial purposes.
One slaveholder noted, "Hands came Home from Mines several days
ago—said they were mistreated." And on the following day he wrote
that he had "declined sending the boys back to the mines." [58] Other
holders were reluctant to hire out their slaves even to individuals,
particularly to town residents. As one wrote ironically, "the largest
boy is still in Morganton where his morals I suspect are not improving
much." [59] Slaves themselves ordinarily did not object to being hired
out to other citizens. One reason for this, perhaps, is that the practice
sometime gave a slave considerable independence and responsibility, as
indicated by the diarist's remark, "Jerry came over from Burnsville and
brought me $18.75 for his hire from M. Penland." [60] It must be
stated in conclusion, however, that nothing in the records of slave hiring in Burke County supports Professor Clement Eaton's thesis that
this was a major step toward freedom for the slave. Apparently the
slaveholders of Burke looked upon the practice simply as an important
and profitable part of the system of slavery itself.[61]

"The more you press in toward the heart of a narrowly bounded historical problem," Arthur O. Lovejoy says, "the more likely you are to encounter in the problem itself a pressure which drives you outward beyond those bounds." Certainly this has been true in this study of slavery at the local level. What has been the residual impact of slavery upon the mind and character of the people of the county used in this study? What has been the effect of the legacy of slavery upon the freedman, the Negro? Upon the descendants of the nonslaveholding white yeoman? Upon the progeny of the slaveholder?

That the long enslavement of the Negro led to the retardation of the development of the Negro throughout the South is a notorious historical fact. But there can be no contradicting that the slave of Burke County had a distinct advantage over his brothers in the various black belts. If nothing else, his closer association with his master and his master's family permitted him to learn more about the white man's society in which he and his descendants were to live. But there remained the spiritual ignominy of slavery, the effect of which does not disappear in a day, and the local Negro's advancement has been slowed by his continued affiliation with the people of the old slaveholding class, most of whom were themselves held back by their inability to come to terms with the facts of postwar life. In fact, the effect of slavery upon the slaveholder and his progeny, if not so dramatic, was almost as disastrous as upon the Negro. Slavery created households of specialization in which the two diverse elements, whites and Negroes, became reciprocally dependent. As slaves developed in skill, mastered various crafts and manual arts, the slaveholder became more and more dependent upon the slave for goods and services. The classical disciplines were of no help to him in the new world where he found himself after Appomattox, and he failed to take the lead in the new age's industrialism. His descendants were left to nurture their pride and find justification in a pretense to nobility and high morality, while others did the work of the world.

It was the yeoman farmer who suffered least from the incubus of slavery, who might be said, in the end, positively to have profited from it. Not dependent upon slaves, he maintained the vigor, the independence, the mechanical resourcefulness, and the shrewd adaptability of the traditional frontiersman.[62] When the crutch of slavery was taken from his betters, the nonslaveholding yeoman was able to wrest economic, social, and cultural leadership from the soft and indolent victims of slavery.

A Burke County man, once a slaveholder, attempted to evaluate, in retrospect the peculiar institution in this way:

I had over thirty slaves—all good and faithful. I would often leave things in their charge and they took good care. Some could read and write a tolerable legible hand, and keep ordinary accounts. Some were members of the church, and I would gather them together [sic] on the Sabbath read to them and instruct them about the future and there [sic] responsibility to there [sic] Maker. Some were impressed, outhers [sic] seemed unmoved. In this part of the country slaves were well treated, fed, and clothed. There was probably some rigid treatment where there were large numbers on a plantation, and where it required rigid treatment to keep all straight and in there [sic] places. I do not think emancipation has been such a boon for the colored race in this land . . . . I never was a great advocate of slavery, but I believe that the question of slavery, if justice an[d] righteousness had ruled, could have been more satisfactorily adjusted, without the loss of the thousands of precious lives and the millions of money.[63]

NOTES

1. See particularly Ulrich B. Phillips, *American Negro Slavery* (New York, 1918), and Kenneth M. Stampp, *The Peculiar Institution: Slavery in the Ante-Bellum South* (New York, 1956). See also Guion G. Johnson, *Ante-Bellum North Carolina; a Social History* (Chapel Hill, 1937), 468-612; Francis B. Simkins, *A History of the South* (New York, 1953), 116-52; and John S. Bassett, *Slavery in the State of North Carolina* (Baltimore, 1899).

2. David L. Corbitt, *The Formation of the North Carolina Counties, 1663–1943* (Raleigh, N. C., 1950), 42-48.

3. See John Hope Franklin, *The Free Negro in North Carolina, 1790–1860* (Chapel Hill, 1943), 234-37.

4. See the following bills of sale: William Price to Henry Reid, September 12, 1793, in Austin-Reid Papers (Manuscript Department, Library, Duke University, Durham, N.C.); John McLean to Benjamin Burgin, February 27, 1798, and John James to Thomas McEntire, September 8, 1799, in Burke County Miscellaneous Papers (North Carolina State Department of Archives and History, Raleigh), Bills of Sale 1781–1815–1833 (C. R. 14.009); Hance Hamilton and others to Waightstill Avery, December 26, 1793, in Burke County Court Minutes (North Carolina State Department of Archives and History), July 1791–1834, January Session 1794; and Thomas Patton to Ben Smith, July, 1804, *ibid.*, July Session 1804.

5. See U. S. Census, 1850, North Carolina, Schedule 1 (National Archives), Surrey County (South Division); U. S. Census, 1860, North Carolina Schedule 1 (National Archives), Yadkin County; and Yadkin County, Tax Lists, 1851–1862 (office of Clerk, Superior Court, Yadkinville, N. C.). One resident of Burke County established himself as a slave trader in Charleston, South Carolina, about 1804 and apparently carried on a commerce in slaves in Burke County until 1808. Memoirs of Col. Thomas G. Walton (typescript, Southern

Historical Collection, University of North Carolina, Chapel Hill), 10; County Court Minutes, October Session 1804.

6. *Ibid.*, July Session 1798.

7. See Franklin, *Free Negro in North Carolina*, 8.

8. In his excellent summation of the historiography of the subject, Stanley M. Elkins directs attention to a new approach to the question of the profitability of slavery made by Alfred H. Conrad and John R. Meyer, who persuasively argue that conventional accounting methods applied to plantation records should be abandoned and replaced by "general economic theory." Elkins, *Slavery; a Problem in American Institutional and Intellectual Life* (Chicago, 1959), 231-37; Conrad and Meyer, "The Economics of Slavery in the Ante Bellum South," *Journal of Political Economy*, LXVI (April 1958), 95-130. For examples of the application of conventional accounting methods, see Thomas P. Govan, "Was Plantation Slavery Profitable?" *Journal of Southern History*, VIII (November 1942), 513-35, and Rosser H. Taylor, *Slaveholding in North Carolina; an Economic View* (Chapel Hill, 1926), 98.

9. Lewis C. Gray, *History of Agriculture in the Southern United States to 1860* (2 vols., Washington, 1933), I, 451.

10. See Isaac T. Avery to Isaac T. Lenoir, September 30, 1833, in Lenoir Family Papers (Southern Historical Collection, University of North Carolina).

11. See W. A. Lenoir to William Lenoir, September 1, 1836, *ibid.*

12. Phillips, *American Negro Slavery*, 370-71, insert.

13. The ad valorem principle was not applied to slaves until 1858. See George R. Woolfolk, "Taxes and Slavery in the Ante Bellum South," *Journal of Southern History*, XXVI (May 1960), 180-200. In Burke County, all land was taxed according to acreage until 1808 when town property was taxed ad valorem. In 1819, the ad valorem principle was applied to all real property; the tax rate on land was set at 18¢ per $100 valuation and the poll tax at 44¢. The rate gradually rose to 27½¢ per $100 valuation on real property and 80¢ a poll in 1848. County Court Minutes, 1798–1834, 1844–1848.

14. For examples, see exemption granted to John Erwin by the July 1795 session of the county court and to George Corpening by the January 1848 session. County Court Minutes. The slaveholder was not so favored in the capitation tax which was levied only on free white males over twenty-one and under forty-five but on all slaves, male and female, over twelve and under fifty.

15. For example, Robert H. Erwin, a blacksmith, Joseph Hilton (Helton?), a saddler, William M. D. Howard, a tanner, and William S. Moore, a carriagemaker, each owned slaves to help in his shop. U. S. Census, 1850, North Carolina, Schedule 2 (National Archives), Burke County.

16. Isaac T. Avery to Selina L. Lenoir, March 16, 1833, in Lenoir Papers.

17. Waightstill Avery to James Avery, January 23, 1816, in Waightstill Avery Papers (Southern Historical Collection, University of North Carolina).

18. Many small slaveholders were illiterate, but the largest Burke County slaveholder who could not read and write was Sara Van Horn, widow of John and owner of sixteen slaves in 1850. Burke County Records, Wills 1793-1905 (North Carolina State Department of Archives and History), II, 58.

19. See Keith F. McKean, "Southern Patriarch: A Portrait," *Virginia Quarterly Review*, XXXVI (Summer 1960), 376-89.

20. Register of Grace Episcopal Church, Morganton, N. C. (church office, Morganton), II, 113-14.

21. Illicit relations between the races were largely between white males and slave females. The writer knows of only two instances in which white women bore children by slaves, and in both the woman was unrelated to the master's family.

22. For example, see Diary of James Hervey Greenlee (in possession of J. Harvey Greenlee, Morganton; copy, Library, University of North Carolina), I, 51.

23. See for example I. T. Avery to Thomas Lenoir, November 28, 1820, and Avery to Selina Lenoir, February 18, 1835, in Lenoir Papers.

24. Register of Grace Episcopal Church, II, 21, 83, 123; Minutes of Globe Church, Burke County (Southern Historical Collection, University of North Carolina), 1808, 1816, 1824, 1825, 1829–1831, 1833, 1834, 1840; Morganton Presbyterian Church Sessional Book of Minutes, 1835–1852 (church office, Morganton), 11-12, 66, 70.

25. Records of Morganton Presbytery, 1836–1840 (Historical Foundation, Montreat, N. C.), 35 (3 Sess., March 16-17, 1837).

26. County Court Minutes, July Session 1813, and October Session 1817.

27. *Ibid.*, July Session 1792; July Session 1818; January and April Sessions 1817.

28. *Tate v. O'Neal* in Helen T. Catterall (ed.), *Judicial Cases Concerning American Slavery and the Negro* (5 vols., Washington, 1926–1937), II, 40, citing 8 N. C. 220 (1821).

29. Isaac T. Avery to Selina Lenoir, September 26, 1831, in Lenoir Papers. See also Johnson, *Ante-Bellum North Carolina*, 520.

30. County Court Minutes, January Session 1832; Burke County Superior Court Minutes, 1830–1854 (North Carolina State Department of Archives and History), March 29, 1832; County Court Minutes, January Session 1844.

31. *Ibid.*, July Session 1819, and January Session 1827. Benefit of clergy had been extended to slaves as well as freemen in eighteenth-century Virginia, and North Carolina recognized the plea for some years after independence. See G. MacLaren Brydon, "Random Gleanings from the Virginia Gazette," *Historical Magazine of the Protestant Episcopal Church*, XVIII (December 1949), 428, and *Cyclopedia of Law and Procedure* (40 vols., New York, 1901–1912), XII, 778n.

32. Superior Court Minutes, March 26, 1830. Whether the victim was white, free nonwhite, or slave can not be determined.

33. Katherine Ann McGeachy, The North Carolina Slave Code (unpublished M.A. thesis, University of North Carolina, 1948).

34. Mrs. E. C. Alexander to W. L. Alexander, April 2, 1850, in Hoke Papers (Southern Historical Collection, University of North Carolina), cited in Johnson, *Ante-Bellum North Carolina*, 496.

35. Burke County Miscellaneous Papers (North Carolina State Department of Archives and History), Coroners's Inquest, 1806–1847 (C. R. 14.099), November 29, 1829.

36. For detailed treatments of the legal aspects of slavery in North Carolina, see Bassett, *Slavery in the State of North Carolina*, 10-28, *passim*; Johnson, *Ante-Bellum North Carolina*, 493-521; Rosser H. Taylor, "Humanizing the Slave Code of North Carolina," *North Carolina Historical Review*, II (July 1925), 323-31; Julius Yanuck, "Thomas Ruffin and North Carolina Slave Law," *Journal of Southern History*, XXI (November 1955), 456-75; Mc-

Geachy, North Carolina Slave Code; and Ernest J. Clark, Jr., Slave Cases Before the North Carolina Supreme Court (unpublished M.A. thesis, University of North Carolina, 1959).

37. County Court Minutes, April Session 1821. Possibly not all slave transactions were recorded, particularly where the chattel was removed from the county, but neither were all land titles recorded.

38. *Ibid.*, October Session 1831. The purchaser, Samuel Price Carson (1789–1838), son of John, was first secretary of state of the Republic of Texas. Louis Wiltz Kemp, *The Signers of the Texas Declaration of Independence* (Houston, 1944), 45-56.

39. The only professional trader who made Morganton his headquarters was Z. D. Lancaster who operated in this area after 1850 and was undoubtedly an agent for a larger trader from one of the commercial centers. U. S. Census, 1860, North Carolina, Schedule 1, Burke County.

40. Isaac T. Avery to Thomas Lenoir, December 17, 1821, in Lenoir Papers.

41. Thomas and Selina Lenoir to William Lenoir, March 28, 1837, *ibid.*

42. Charles Stanlee to J. E. Erwin, undated, in Burke County Miscellaneous Papers, Correspondence of the Clerk of the Court, 1812–1868.

43. *Erwin v. Greenlee* in Catterall, *Judicial Cases*, II, 69, citing 18 N. C. 39 (1834).

44. County Court Minutes, July Session 1803.

45. For example, see Rutherfordton, N. C., *Spectator*, August 6, 1830; Rutherfordton *North Carolina Spectator and Western Advertiser*, February 11, 1832; County Court Minutes, January Session 1832, 1833, and 1848.

46. See references to the will of William Probert (*i.e.* Probit), *ibid.*, October Session 1811, and January Session 1812.

47. Will of Waightstill Avery, February 20, 1819, a certified unfiled copy (office, Register of Deeds, Morganton), and in Burke County Records, Wills, 1793–1805, I (folio 15), 1-4; report of arbitrators, June 1, 1822, and Isaac T. Avery to William B. Lenoir, June 3, 1822, both in Lenoir Papers.

48. Item 6, will of Mary E. Patton, Burke County Records, Wills, 1793–1905, II (folio 4), 28.

49. Will of William W. Avery, *ibid.*, I (folio 3), 6.

50. Will of William L. McRee in Burke County Miscellaneous Papers, Wills, 1787–1900 (C. R. 14.103).

51. Will of Jesse Moore, *ibid.*

52. Will of Daniel Jones, *ibid.*

53. Will of Mary Probat (*i.e.* Probit), *ibid.*

54. For example, see wills of William W. Erwin, Burke County Records, Wills, 1793–1905, I (folio 2), 44, and of Thomas Walton in William Carson Erwin Papers (Southern Historical Collection, University of North Carolina); partition report, estate of Margaret C. Tate, in County Court Minutes, October Session 1825.

55. For names of local slaveholders who employed slaves in railroad construction, see *Reports and Proceedings of Western North Carolina Railroad Company for 1858* (Raleigh, 1858). For a contemporary account of the treatment of slave railroad construction workers, see typewritten statement on inner back cover of a bound collection of Western North Carolina Railroad reports, 1855–1866 (in possession of C. V. Walton, Morganton).

56. Frederic Bancroft, *Slave-Trading in the Old South* (Baltimore, 1931), 147.

57. Five of Eph Greenlee's slaves were hired out in 1849 for a total of $149, four of Elizabeth's for $141, four of Alex's for $148.50, five of George's for $185.75, and seven of Emily's for $149.45. Sixteen persons hired one or more of these slaves. Record of accountability, estate of Samuel Greenlee, in Tod R. Caldwell Papers (Library, Duke University).

58. Greenlee Diary, I, 128-29.

59. Isaac T. Avery to William B. Lenoir, December 17, 1821, in Lenoir Papers.

60. Greenlee Diary, III, 88.

61. Clement Eaton, "Slave Hiring in the Upper South: A Step Toward Freedom," *Mississippi Valley Historical Review*, XLVI (March 1960), 663-78.

62. See Frank L. Owsley, *Plain Folk of the Old South* (Baton Rouge, 1949), and Robert R. Russell, "The Effects of Slavery upon Nonslaveholders in the Ante Bellum South," *Agricultural History*, XV (April 1941), 112-26.

63. Ralph S. and Robert L. Greenlee, *Genealogy of the Greenlee Families* . . . (Chicago, 1908), 249.

• *Slavery was an urban as well as a rural phenomenon in the nineteenth-century South. Furthermore, the presence of large numbers of freed Negroes in the cities created a distinctly liberating atmosphere among the many slaves who worked in Southern industries and commerce. Richard C. Wade, one of the country's foremost urban historians, describes the institution's practices and customs in the urban South.*

Slavery in the Southern Cities

RICHARD C. WADE

By 1860 the institution of slavery was in great disarray in every Southern city. The number of Negroes had declined precipitously. Discipline over those remaining proved difficult to sustain. The network of restraint so essential to bondage no longer seemed to control the blacks nor wholly govern the whites. The distance between the races as well as separation of free colored from slave could not be maintained in the kinetic world of the city. In the most dynamic towns the whites overwhelmed the Negro population; even places with a larger proportion of slaves and less impressive growth tended to slough off at least their male blacks. In any case an institution which had been an integral part of urban life in Dixie in 1820 was languishing everywhere in 1860.

The census figures outlined the story. Though the number of slaves rose throughout the South, the proportion living in cities declined. In addition, the Negroes lost their earlier share of the urban population. In 1820, 37 per cent of all town dwellers were blacks; by 1860 that portion had dropped below 17 per cent. Urban slaves fell from 22 per cent to 10. The most dramatic shifts came, of course, in the border area, but everywhere the same pattern appeared. The New

Orleans statistics demonstrated the tendency most clearly. In 1820 one out of two residents was Negro; in 1860 only one in seven. To be sure, the black populations of smaller and newer cities, like Montgomery or the Texas towns, showed some vitality, but there is no reason to believe they would not have shared the same attrition as they expanded.

This decline did not stem from any economic reasons. There was plenty of work which whites had traditionally considered appropriate to blacks and particularly suited to slaves. Industrial employment, moreover, had proved feasible in a variety of enterprises. Hiring rates continued to rise throughout the last ante-bellum decades. And, perhaps most conclusively, the price of urban slaves on the market more than matched the general increase. In short, the usual indices suggested the continuing profitability of slavery as an economic institution. "In all departments of mechanical labor, the slaves of the South are profitably employed," the *Richmond Enquirer* asserted confidently in 1853. "As carpenters, as blacksmiths, as shoe-makers, as factory hands, they are far more valuable than field-laborers—indeed, intellectual expertness and manual dexterity are much more important elements in the price of a slave, than mere physical strength and power of endurance." [1] Or, as a visitor put it, "those whom good treatment has rendered most fit for freedom, are the most desired as slaves." [2]

Slavery's compelling problem in the city was not finding work for bondsmen, but controlling them when they were off the job. While busy, in the house or around the yard, on the docks or driving a dray, toiling in a factory or cotton press, they caused little trouble. When the task was finished or the supervision lifted, however, when the slaves became idle or contrived some free time, when dusk fell and the demand for service slackened, then the system weakened. And when the Negroes gathered by themselves, beyond the eye of masters and police, in homes, churches, or grog shops, the "peculiar institution" itself was jeopardized.

It was the total environment rather than industrial or commercial employment which eroded slavery in the cities. The problem was not what happened in the factory or shop but what happened in the back street, the church, the grocery store, the rented room, and the out-of-the-way house. It was not contact with machines or an industrial process which broke the discipline, it was contact with people of all kinds in numerous ways which generated the corrosive acids.

"The city, with its intelligence and enterprise, is a dangerous place for the slave," wrote a shrewd analyst. "He acquires knowledge of human rights, by working with others who receive wages when he receives none; who can come and go at their pleasure, when he from the cradle to the grave must obey a master's imperious will. . . . It is found expedient, almost necessary, to remove the slave from these influences, and send him back to the intellectual stagnation and gloom of the plantation." [3] Bondage "does not thrive with master or slave when transplanted to cities," a Louisiana planter observed, adding that in such surroundings "the slaves become dissipated, acquire the worst habits," and were generally "corrupted." [4] . . .

Slaves, on the other hand, found urban life to their liking. "The negroes are the most social of all human beings," De Bow asserted, "and after having hired in town, refuse to live again in the country." [5] Slavery's most famous refugee to attack the institution in all its aspects made the same point with eloquent simplicity: "Life in Baltimore, when most oppressive, was a paradise" compared to "plantation existence," Frederick Douglass wrote.[6] When masters were forced to sell, their bondsmen pleaded to be kept in the city because—in the words of some Richmond blacks—"they had acquired town habits." [7] And often those sent into the country headed back at the first opportunity to run away. In short, how could you keep them down on the plantation once they had seen Mobile?

The slave's preference was easily understood. Not only was urban life more congenial, but the alternative was especially grim. Solomon Northup found that every Negro sharing his Washington pen "dreaded the thought of being put into the cane and cotton fields." [8] Douglass, too, remembered that it was "a source of deep consternation" to him and his friends in Maryland that "we should be hurried away to the cotton fields and rice swamps, of the sunny south." [9] A sympathetic Northern traveler caught both the white and Negro perspectives when he observed that "The atmosphere of the city is too life-giving, and creates thought. It is the doom of them all to be sent back to the gloom of the plantation cabin." [10]

The cause of slavery's difficulty in the city was the nature of urban society itself. In the countryside physical isolation comprised one dimension of a successful discipline. Another was the simple division between master and slave, with virtually no other important element. The distinction between field hand and house servant, while important to the Negroes involved, constituted no significant fracture in the system. Treatment and comforts might vary, privileges could be more extensive, and everyday tasks quite different, but no area of independence was thus created. Indeed, a house servant often fell more directly under the eye of his owner than the black in the field. Nor did the overseer create a new interest among the whites. Employed by the master, usually a short-term resident, living apart from the colored quarters, and only occasionally a confidant of the owner, the overseer had at most a marginal influence on the structure.

Between black and white the social distance was immense. Slaves were confined to primitive work at worst or acquired rudimentary skills at best. Their contacts with whites were few and seldom lasting. An occasional visitor sometimes broke the isolation; nearby white families were seen just often enough to be recognized; overseers came and went. Except for the infrequent trip to town or a neighboring farm, the possibilities of outside stimuli scarcely existed. Even on small plantations or farms, the contacts with the surrounding world were circumscribed. Indeed, without other slaves about he was deprived of even the most elementary association. Rural life had always involved some social remoteness; for the plantation slave, isolation, next to his servitude, was the most compelling fact of life.

The cities, on the other hand, developed more complex structures. Both white and Negro communities included many different parts, and in the larger places a highly sophisticated system evolved with almost endless groupings and distinctions. This fragmentation, which, of course, characterized urban life nearly everywhere, had a special significance for slavery. It meant that the great gap between owner and chattel would be filled with all kinds of diverse elements, inevitably disturbing the institution's ordinary relationships. The Louisiana planter who so feared town life saw this process clearly. "The distance is so vast between slave and master" under bondage, he argued, that in the city "the interval is filled up immediately by corrupting influences." And the slaveholder was helpless. He could perceive "the evil of his slave without being able to prevent it," since it sprang from the intractable nature of urban life itself.[11]

The most obvious added ingredient in the urban scene was the free Negro. He was, to be sure, also a rural resident, but the distance and detachment of the countryside greatly diluted his influence on slavery. Often living in a remote spot, sometimes as a yeoman, more often a hired hand, he was bound to have a modest role. His opportunity there moreover was limited. Without resources he found it hard to buy land; without many others of his own kind his social life was sparse. Hence he gravitated toward the metropolis.

Freedmen constituted the most highly urbanized group in Dixie.

By 1860 they outnumbered slaves ten to one in Baltimore and 9209 to 1774 in Washington. In the deep South, too, their numbers grew with each census. New Orleans always had a considerable contingent; on the eve of the Civil War it exceeded 10,000. Yet even the places which had tried hardest to limit their free colored population could not alter the trend. Charleston had 1475 in 1820 and over 3200 in 1860, while Mobile's figures in the same span were 183 and 817. Across the South nearly a third of the free blacks were found in the larger urban centers. The report of a visitor in 1836 that "the emancipated negroes generally leave the country, and congregate in the cities and larger towns" was a common observation.[12]

The free Negro's position in Southern towns was always precarious, occupying, as one Southerner put it, "a sort of uncertain and undefined position in our midst."[13] His color suggested servitude, but his status secured a portion of freedom. Hence he suffered many of the inhibitions of his slave brothers while enjoying some privileges denied them. His advantages over the slave were considerable. He could marry, have children, and enjoy something of a normal family life. He could own property, have the right to his earnings, and engage in a few trades forbidden the enslaved. Though the situation was never favorable to either domestic tranquillity or economic advancement, there was at least a measure of independence. And, most crucial of all, in the privacy of the home could be found a seclusion from the constant surveillance of the white world.

Free Negroes learned quickly not to count on much beyond this. "We know full well," the New Orleans *Picayune* wrote with candor, "that the pretence of any real freedom being designed or expected for these negroes is but a sham."[14] In the streets the distinction among colored people was not clear; in the courts the free were sometimes only fined while the slaves were whipped; and legislation increasingly covered all blacks with only nominal regard for status. City ordinances usually handled both categories in a single section. An 1832 Baltimore ordinance dealing with Negro discipline set forth the crucial identification: "such free negro or mulatto shall be subject to the same punishment, and be liable in every respect to the same treatment and penalty as slaves" and "be guilty of, and convicted of, any offense for which slaves are now punishable."[15]

Despite these obstacles, the free colored of every city struggled to establish a meaningful associational life. They formed congregations and erected churches, established schools and aid societies, and organized improvement projects aimed at bringing some of the better things of life to their members. . . .

To a few Southerners the presence of free Negroes created no great problem. . . .

But the common judgment went the other way. A Louisville editor in 1851 came close to the nearly universal view when he stated bluntly that "the free negro question is the most insoluble of all the social problems of the day, and stands as a practical sarcasm on all the theories of abolition and emancipation." [16] A Richmond memorial containing the signature of John Marshall elaborated the ordinary indictment. They numbered "not an eighth part of the inhabitants; yet it would be hazarding little to say that half the criminals tried in the City for the offense of larceny, are free persons of color." In addition, the petitioners said, "their idleness is proverbial; they live, few know in what way, and fewer still know where; their rate of increase far exceeds even that of the slaves, and in a higher degree that of the whites; and whatever energy can be spared from annoying both classes, appears to be expended in multiplying their own number." [17] And a New Orleans editor called the full roll when he spoke of "the absolute idleness, the thriftlessness, the laziness, the dishonesty, the drunkenness, the proneness to vagrancy and vice of the negro when free from all the restraints of servitude." [18]

The central complaint, however, had less to do with the wretchedness of free Negro life, or even with their high crime rate, than with their influence on slaves. Living amongst bondsmen, yet without masters, carrying by color the stigma of servitude, yet without its most humiliating features, shut off from white society, yet released from the confinements of slavery, the free blacks were always a disturbing factor. "They are a plague and pest in the community," the *New Orleans Daily Picayune* asserted, because they brought "the elements of mischief to the slave population." [19]

"The superior condition of the free persons of color," a memorial of Charleston citizens argued, "excites discontent among our slaves, who continually have before their eyes, persons of the same color, many of whom they have known in slavery, and with all of whom they associate on terms of equality." The slave saw these blacks "freed from the control of masters, working where they please, going whither they please, and spending money how they please." He thus became "dissatisfied" and "pants after liberty." [20] . . .

. . . Whatever the precise formulation of the argument, Southern town dwellers could agree that their free colored residents rendered control over their slaves increasingly difficult. . . .

They could also agree that there were some whites who were almost as unsettling to the system as freed blacks. These people had found a place at the edge of slavery where their economic life was enmeshed in the irregular relationships bred by the system in its urban environment. Some were grocers who sold to slaves; others ran shops which catered to a colored clientele; still others were ministers who organized Negro churches and sought to bring religion to the enslaved. Port merchants, too, could be included, since their trade brought ships with mixed crews into the harbor. Less easily identified, but also important, were whites sporadically connected with the informal life of town blacks. These interests were obviously quite different, but all developed a stake in the loose form of bondage which evolved in the cities. . . .

In the metropolis the worlds of bondage and freedom overlapped. The line between free blacks and slaves became hopelessly blurred. Even whites and blacks found their lives entangled in some corners of the institution of slavery. No matter what the law said or the system required, this layer of life expanded. Though much of it was subterranean, at points it could be easily seen. The mixed balls, the numberless grog and grocery shops, the frequent religious gatherings, and the casual acquaintances in the streets were scarcely private. Physical proximity bred a certain familiarity that most residents came to expect. . . .

What did bother townspeople, however, was the evidence that beyond these visible contacts lay a world of greater conviviality and equality. In this nether world blacks and whites mingled freely, the conventions of slavery were discarded, and the worst fears of Southerners became realized. Not only did the men find fellowship without regard to color in the tippling shops, back rooms, and secluded sheds, but the women of both races joined in. Such mixing engaged a good deal of the private conversation of white people in cities, but its public manifestations were usually found in only police reports and the major's court. . . .

There can be no doubt of the wide extent of this miscegenation. Visitors often commented on it; the newspapers complained about it; the court records teem with it. Even Governor Hammond, who defended the South in general against the charge of racial mixing, admitted its prominence in the cities. The clandestine nature of these attachments makes a more precise generalization risky, but the fear, if not the fact, of "amalgamation," "miscegenation," and "mixing," plainly increased in the decades before 1860. Few defenders, much less advocates, appeared. The public stigma and the hostility of the law made it clear why: those who practiced it did not preach it.

New Orleans, with its large population of free and enslaved blacks, had the most famous demi-world in Dixie. The celebrated masked balls and the casual acceptance of colored mistresses seemed to reflect its Spanish and French roots. Yet that explanation is too facile. The rural areas of Louisiana, some of which reflected similar origins, did not develop the same mores; and, more persuasively, other cities with quite different beginnings did. Actually what visitors noticed about New Orleans was true of urban life throughout the South.

Northern cities, too, had their disorganized elements who left a trail across police blotters, court records and poorhouse lists. There too community leaders, somewhat bewildered by the spread of undisciplined low life, sought some way to introduce a system and stability. But, important as this was to civic leaders elsewhere, in the South the problem was greatly complicated by the existence of slavery. On the one hand, the institution required a high degree of order, the careful regulation of Negro affairs, and a fixed status for bondsmen. On the other hand, the city demanded fluidity, a constant re-allocation of human resources, and a large measure of social mobility. Initially, it appeared as though slavery could provide the discipline town life seemed to need. In the long run, however, the force of urbanization loosened the restraints of bondage, smudged the distinctions of status among Negroes, and at points pierced the racial walls of Dixie's cities.

This antithesis was early felt by some municipal leaders. Since slavery was presumed to be an established part of Southern town life for any foreseeable future, none talked about incompatibility. Instead, the dominant race sought to solve it with ordinances, the orderly development of a legal hiring-out system, and a plentiful police force in case of trouble. Yet the acids of urbanization continually eroded the discipline on which bondage rested. Though the disintegration was often hard to gauge, those close to the problem knew it was happening.

To arrest the attrition and handle its consequences, Southern cities moved along three lines. One involved the sale of young male blacks into the countryside. This removed one of the most disturbing elements from the urban scene while meeting a constant demand for field hands in the cotton and cane regions. A second was the tightening of emancipation procedures to stop the accumulation of free Negroes in towns. A third was to develop racial arrangements which took into account the new situation and which embodied most of the features later identified as segregation. . . . By 1860 the percentage of free Negroes among the South's urban population had dropped considerably.

While Southern cities increasingly moved to reduce their colored population, both slave and free, they also developed a new system of racial deference more appropriate to urban life than slavery in its traditional form. As the institution of slavery encountered mounting difficulties and, as its control over the blacks weakened, another arrangement was devised which maintained great social distance within the physical proximity of town life. Increasingly public policy tried to separate the races whenever the surveillance of the master was likely to be missing. To do this, the distinction between slave and free Negro was erased; race became more important than legal status; and a pattern of segregation emerged inside the broader framework of the "peculiar institution."

In a sense this tendency was always present, though the reliance on traditional controls obscured its importance. The heart of the established system was, of course, the subordination of the slave to his owner. The wide discretion vested in the master made day-to-day discipline almost a private matter. But in the cities a public etiquette was needed to govern the relations of races when the blacks were beyond the supervision of their owners. Increasingly that etiquette required the separation of black and white without regard to legal status. Beginning in only a few areas, the arrangement spread to include the most important public aspects of life. . . .

Law and custom sanctioned the segregation of races in public places and accommodations as well as in churches and schools. To disentangle white and black in employment and housing was a different matter. Yet the significant fact is that such a separation took place increasingly often in the last few decades before the Civil War. Under the pressure of white craftsmen, Negroes were pushed out of one line of work after another. With the weakening of the reins of slavery, bondsmen found housing away from their owners and generally in areas of accumulating colored population. Both movements were far from complete, but the tendency was unmistakable.

In employment the clearest manifestation of segregation was the exclusion of blacks, slave and free, from the better jobs. A memorial of Charleston's City Council to the state legislature expressed both the difficulties and the objects of the policy. Noting that "slavery is so interwoven with the constitution of our Society that even if our interests permitted it would be impossible to eradicate it," the petitioners argued that it was "necessary to fix as far as possible the grade of employments" for slaves and "to exclude them by Legislative enactment from all others." [21] Charleston's own ordinances prohibited teaching slaves "in any mechanic or handicraft trade," though the wording was vague and its enforcement almost impossible.[22]

In Savannah the restrictions were more precise. No Negro could be apprenticed "to the trade of Carpenter, Mason, Bricklayer, Barber or any other Mechanical Art or Mystery." [23] Later, cabinetmaker, painter, blacksmith, tailor, cooper, and butcher were added to the list.[24] Georgia excluded blacks from "being mechanics or masons, from making contracts for the erection . . . or repair of buildings." [25] Though no two cities had the same categories, all tried to keep colored workers out of the higher skills. The fact that practice often belied the law simply underlined the significance of the intent.

If slaves and blacks were still found in many of the better crafts in 1860, they had been pushed out of many of the lesser-skilled jobs. In Baltimore whites took the carting and draying business from them by 1830.[26] A few years later, a visitor could report that "the Irish and other foreigners are, to a considerable extent, taking the place of colored laborers and of domestic servants." [27] In 1823 the City Council of New Orleans directed the mayor "to hire white labor for the city works, in preference to negroes." [28] Two decades later, some prominent citizens there described the extent of the attrition: "Ten years ago, say they, all the draymen of New Orleans, a numerous class, and the cabmen, were colored. Now they are nearly all white. The servants of the great hotels were formerly of the African, now they are of the European race." [29] Even in the home, the displacement occurred with the customary racial rationale. "We have all times spoken against the impropriety of having white and black servants in homes in the South," the *Richmond Enquirer* explained, "especially so in any capacity where slaves or negroes may be inclined to consider themselves on a par of equality with white servants." [30]

John S. C. Abbott, who toured the South in 1859, found this tendency pronounced everywhere. In Mobile, for instance, he was "surprised to see how effectually free labor seems to have driven slave labor from the wharves and streets." The Irish and Germans, he noted, did the outside work, while white girls moved into domestic service. When he saw New Orleans, he commented, though no doubt with exaggeration, that "hardly a colored face is to be seen on the levee, and the work is done by the Germans and the Irish. . . . Indeed, now, New Orleans and Mobile seem but little more like slave cities than do Philadelphia and New York." [31]

Though the process varied in Dixie's cities and Negroes hung on in many skills, "job busting" became a normal tactic for the growing white labor force faced with traditional colored employment practices. As the black population dropped, white newcomers moved in and took over craft after craft. Occasionally accompanied by violence and usually with official sanction, slave and free colored workers were shunted into the most menial and routine chores. In 1830 Negroes, both slave and free, had been used in a wide variety of employments; by 1860 the number of possibilities had shrunk markedly. The movement toward segregation, so noticeable in other aspects of urban life, was rapidly invading employment.

In housing the same trend was perceptible, though less advanced. The spread of the "living out" system, both in its legal and irregular form, gave slaves some choice of residence. Since the urge to leave the enclosure reflected the freedom from surveillance it entailed, slaves sought spots as removed from whites as possible. For most this meant a retreat to the outer edges of the city or beyond the municipal line altogether. There was seldom any escape from all whites, but there were parts of town with clusters of colored inhabitants. By the 'forties and 'fifties it was apparent in most places that Negroes were settling on the periphery of the cities. . . .

The movement to the periphery was increasingly common, though in some towns colored concentrations grew up more haphazardly in small enclaves or strips in out-of-the-way places. And the centers of Negro life, formal and informal, followed the people. Colored churches, especially those established after 1840, sought locations in these neighborhoods. Grocery stores and dram shops, too, settled there. Even the cemeteries were put near the living. In Savannah's case, for example, four Negro churches, three Baptist, and one Methodist, were on the west side, while another served the east side. The central city had none. Of 174 "grocers" 101 did business in the outer residential wards, West Broad alone accommodating 19.[32] In Charleston the convergence was on the northern border and the Neck beyond.

In no case did anything like full residential segregation emerge.

Few streets, much less blocks, were solidly black. Everywhere some whites occupied nearby dwellings. Still the inclination to cluster here, to concentrate there, was more marked by 1860 than in 1820. The separation apparent in other areas of life was slowly insinuated into housing.

Thus, even before slavery had been abolished, a system of segregation had grown up in the cities. Indeed, the whites thought some such arrangement was necessary if they were to sustain their traditional supremacy over the Negroes. The countryside provided enough room to give meaning to racial separation. The master could be physically quite removed from his blacks, though sharing the same plantation or farm. And together both were isolated from others. In cities these spatial relationships were quite different. Both races were thrown together; they encountered each other at every corner, they rubbed elbows at every turn; they divided up, however inequitably, the limited space of the town site. Segregation sorted people out by race, established a public etiquette for their conduct, and created social distance where there was proximity. Urban circumstances produced this system long before the destruction of slavery itself.

Of course, the complete separation of races was impossible in the city, and the practice differed from place to place. In some towns, public conveyances remained mixed; in others Negroes were not excluded from all public grounds; in still others housing continued scrambled. Yet every city developed its own arrangement expressed in the contrived separation of colored and white in countless ways. Though never total, the segregation was so extensive that Negroes were never permitted to forget their inferior position.

The rising incidence of segregation was another index of the increasing weakness of slavery in the cities. Rooted in the white's need for discipline and deference, it developed to take up the slack in the loosening system. It provided public control to replace dwindling private supervision of the master over his slave. To do this, the difference between free and enslaved Negroes had to be narrowed, depriving free blacks of part of their freedom even while permitting a wider latitude to bondsmen. To most whites, however, there seemed no alternative. The old system no longer really controlled; the walls no longer really confined; the chains no longer really held.

The decline of slavery in the cities was the central fact of race relations in the South's cities in the ante-bellum decades. It was also a fact that conditioned Negro life in subsequent generations, for it meant that, when emancipation finally did come, most of the colored population would be in the countryside rather than in cities. Accustomed only to routine tasks, imbruted by the severe limitations of plantation existence, and unused to managing their own affairs, they became free under the most difficult of circumstances.

If the Negro population in the cities had grown in the same proportion as the whites, there would have been present an invaluable pool of potential leadership, for there many blacks, even under slavery, had begun to develop the most important tools of citizenship. There they acquired some skills and learned the rudiments of reading and writing. There, too, many had commenced to manage their own affairs, and in churches they developed a capacity for organization. In short, the metropolis nourished the literacy and self-reliance needed in a free system. . . .

The full significance of the de-urbanization of the Negro under slavery was apparent only much later. Emancipation found him located primarily in the least dynamic area of American life. Capable of simple tasks, familiar only with rural routine, largely illiterate, and unused to managing his own affairs, he faced a long road to full freedom. Ultimately that road carried him to the city. Though confronted by both discrimination and segregation, he could find there the numbers and leadership which could one day spring him loose from the confinements of an earlier bondage.

NOTES

1. *Richmond Enquirer*, November 29, 1853.
2. Finch, *An Englishwoman's Experience in America*, 300.
3. Abbott, *South and North*, 112-13.
4. Walker, "Diary of a Louisiana Planter."
5. *De Bow's Review*, XXIX (1860), 615.
6. Douglass, *My Bondage*, 235.
7. Lyell, *Second Visit*, I, 209.
8. Solomon Northup, *Twelve Years a Slave; Narrative of Solomon Northup, A Citizen of New York, Etc.* (Auburn, 1853), 62.
9. Douglass, *My Bondage*, 176.
10. Abbott, *South and North*, 138-9.
11. Walker, "Diary of a Louisiana Planter."
12. Andrews, *Slavery*, 43.
13. Quoted in Everett, *Free Persons of Color in New Orleans*, 191.
14. Quoted in Everett, *Free Persons of Color in New Orleans*, 197.
15. Baltimore, Ordinances, March 14, 1832.
16. *Louisville Daily Democrat*, August 5, 1851.
17. Petition of the Colonization Society of Virginia to the Virginia State Legislature, Dec. 20, 1831, MSS., Virginia State Library, Richmond.

18. *New Orleans Bee*, April 16, 1858.

19. *New Orleans Daily Picayune*, March 8, 1856.

20. A *Documentary History of American Industrial Society*, II, 108-9.

21. Memorial of the City Council to the Legislature of South Carolina, 1826, MSS., South Carolina Archives Division.

22. Charleston, Ordinances, October 28, 1806.

23. Savannah, Minutes of the Council, October 15, 1822, MSS., City Hall, Savannah.

24. Savannah, Ordinances, November 11, 1831.

25. Quoted in Lyell, *Second Visit*, II, 81.

26. *Genius of Universal Emancipation*, January 12, 1828.

27. Andrews, *Slavery*, 73.

28. New Orleans, Proceedings, September 13, 1823.

29. Lyell, *Second Visit*, II, 125. John Milton Mackie found the same thing in Mobile; *From Cape Cod to Dixie and the Tropics* (N.Y., 1864), 158. Though the book bears a later date, this trip took place before the war.

30. *Richmond Enquirer*, August 27, 1857.

31. Abbott, *South and North*, 112, 113.

32. *Directory for the City of Savannah to Which is Added a Business Directory for 1860* (Savannah, 1860), 176-7.

• Significant differences developed, as Richard Wade has shown, between the patterns of slave life on the farms and those in the cities of the South. In the two cultures examined by Herbert S. Klein, the mixed economy of Spanish Cuba and Virginia's plantation economy, the opportunities available to Negro bondsmen differed even more strikingly. Klein's comparative analysis of these slave societies offers important insights into the divergent paths of Negro personality development in Spanish and English America.

The Slave Economies of Cuba and Virginia:
A Comparison

HERBERT S. KLEIN

INTRODUCTION

In the creation of their slave regimes, both Cuba and Virginia would be most immediately influenced by local economic forces. And although . . . Cuba would have to be highly sensitive to outside institutions jealous of their rights, its system of Negro slavery would be molded in important ways by the economic use to which it was put.

For the Negro, both slave and free, the question of his economic occupation would have a determining influence not only upon the level of social and economic power he might attain in the colonial community but in the development of his personality as well. No matter what the law did or did not create, the means of production demanded adjustments on the part of the Negro that might prove either harmful or beneficial to him, allow him room for personal development and expression, or destroy his individuality and dull his abilities. Moreover, his control over strategic economic crafts and in-

From Herbert S. Klein, *Slavery in the Americas, A Comparative Study of Cuba and Virginia* (Chicago: University of Chicago Press, 1967), pp. 127-8, 142-51, 162-5, 177-9, 182-3, 186-7, 191-2. Copyright © 1967 by the University of Chicago. Reprinted by permission.

dustries provided him with a position of potential economic power by which he might greatly influence the attitude of the master class in its dealings and attitudes toward him. Thus the economic foundations of Negro slavery fixed certain limits to which all other developments of the slave regime had to adjust.

Crucial in determining this economic role would be the place of the Negro slave within the plantation systems of these two societies. Was the Negro confined only to unskilled plantation labor? Were nonplantation skills and occupations open to him? Were these nonplantation opportunities readily available and in large supply? What role did the Negro slave and also the colored freedman play in the labor market? Did he successfully compete with white labor in nonplantation jobs and skills? Was he permitted to determine his craft and opportunities as a slave and freedman by economic criteria alone, or by noneconomic standards? Could he transfer skills learned in slavery to his free status when this occurred? These are some of the crucial questions that determined the impact of the economy on the world of Negro slavery.[1]

CUBA AND THE DIVERSIFIED ECONOMY

. . . [In] 1532 there were some 500 African slaves, and by 1535 close to 1,000 were reported to be on Cuba.[2] Throughout the rest of the century there was a steady importation of Negroes, both legal and illegal, so that by 1606 there were said to be some 20,000 on the island.[3] So quickly did they replace Indian labor in importance that as early as 1542, the procuradores of the island declared that "Here the principal property are the Negroes." [4] Thus within thirty years of his introduction into Cuba, the Negro had become a major factor in the economic and social life of the island, whereas in Virginia it would take close to a century before Negro slave labor would begin to dominate the economic scene.

The major reason for this early predominance of coloreds in the labor market was essentially due to the initial lack of heavy white migration into the island in the first two centuries of colonization. In the history of Spanish migration to the Indies in this two-hundred-year span of time, the system of white indenture was never carried into effect. The careful exclusion of large numbers of "new Christians" and (in the first years) non-Castillians, did not allow for unrestricted immigration, and those who could meet the qualifications were required to pay for their own passage.[5] Although large numbers were transported free under particular expeditions supported either by the crown or by private funds, they were primarily soldiers rather than peasants or laborers. At various times, the crown did support the migration of groups of farmers, and it always maintained a small stream of artisans to the Indies. Under Charles V and Philip II various industrious merchants and farmers from imperial countries—especially Portugal—were allowed to settle in limited numbers in the depopulated Antilles.[6] But when all these sources of white migrations are added together, they are of little significance, especially when compared to the English migrations under the indenture system whereby thousands of industrious laborers were indiscriminately allowed to cross the ocean. Without passage money of their own, countless numbers sold their labor to the colonials for a specified number of years to emigrate to America. But even if a large number of Spanish peasants and workers had wished to emigrate, the Spanish vessels of the sixteenth century were incapable of carrying such a volume of free white passengers profitably, especially under the fleet system.

The reintroduction of free trade within the empire in the eighteenth century and the tremendous growth of Cuba in the nineteenth drew in large numbers of white immigrants from the Canary Islands and the Basque countries, and thus turned the balance back to the whites; but this did not change already established patterns. The majority of migrants who came still sought the golden riches and a rapid return to their homes, and often they came with less skills than the long-established Negroes, free and slave, who inhabited the island. Although the unskilled white immigration labor competed successfully with the skilled artisans on the North American continent and succeeded in driving the skilled blacks out of numerous occupations, this did not occur in Cuba.[7] Faced by a financially prosperous free artisan class and a very skilled slave labor market, the newcomers simply adapted to the system and complemented the colored work force. No skills, as we shall see in the study of the free colored class, were pre-empted by the whites from the blacks, who in fact maintained their dominant, or proportionally greater, majority in almost all the major artisanal and labor activities on the island. The poor white immigrants in their turn, occupied many of the unskilled lower ranks, even below the free and slave blacks. The reason for this accommodation is probably due to the fact that economic considerations predominated over all others and that the immigrants neither thought to, nor would they have succeeded in, making a sharp distinction of occupational skills based on the color line, as they did in North America.

Aiding this development was the strong desire, at least in the first two centuries of colonization, of whites to give up manual labor. Driven to the Indies for economic betterment and inbred with the classic *hidalguismo* ideals of the ignobility of manual toil, large numbers of poorer white immigrants gladly deserted their skilled callings for the lure of a lifetime of living off the land. Status in Cuban society came from the possession of land, and the trades marked a man, even of the upper merchant classes, as a person of distinctly lower status.[8] Because of this hidalguismo ideal, master craftsmen gladly taught their skills to their Negro slaves, and as soon as they had accumulated enough capital, they willingly removed themselves from their occupations altogether. This left all the skilled trades open to Negro labor, first as slaves, and then quite rapidly, as freedmen. Thus when massive white peasant immigration got underway in the nineteenth century, the unskilled European peasants found the labor market already heavily controlled by the Negroes, and this control was never broken. Thus the lack of a large white immigration for the first two hundred years and the wholesale abandonment of the artisanal occupations to the Negroes, slave and free, set a pattern of unchallengable Negro power in the Cuban labor market.

Because of this the Negro came to be employed in almost every branch of industry and commerce on the island. Negroes were employed deep within the island in all the stages of cattle raising and slaughtering.[9] They were, as in almost every other Spanish colony, the principal miners, first in gold and later in the copper deposits near Santiago de Cuba.[10] In the 1540's Negroes first opened these deposits, and in 1546 a German expert was teaching, in apprenticeships lasting a year and a half, copper mining and smelting to Negro slaves belonging to the settlers.[11]

In this early period of Cuban history, however, the Negroes were most heavily concentrated in and around the major cities, where the heart of Cuban civilization lay.[12] The *estancias*, or small produce farms—which were located in the environs of all the major cities, and which supplied the urban areas with their food and the fleets of Havana with their fresh fruits and vegetables—were largely operated by the Negro, either by free colored on their own lands or by slaves working for their masters.[13] Within the towns, the Negro worked at an infinite number of nonagricultural occupations. In Havana for instance, the Negresses, both slave and free, owned and operated almost all the taverns, eating houses, and lodgings. The taverns and inns with their sale of wines and tobacco soon proved so lucrative a trade that in 1557 the cabildo prohibited Negresses from owning them, and they largely fell under the ownership of the whites.[14] The colored women had no competition as the laundresses of Havana, the domestic laborers, and the prostitutes of this, the greatest port in the New World.[15] And in time of emergency, such as in 1555, they were even employed in defense of the city.[16]

Negro males, again both slave and free, were the prime construction workers on the island. As we have seen, as early as 1515, the crown was sending in a steady stream of Negroes to be employed specifically in heavy masonry construction, and throughout the colonial period, all the massive fortifications built on the island, and especially at Havana, were built by Negro labor.[17] Nor was heavy construction the only type of creative labor performed by the Negro, for he was early employed in ship construction and repair, as well as in numerous other trades and skills essential to an urban community.

Under urban slavery, unlike a rural system, the most common method of labor distribution was through the hiring-out or renting of slave labor from the crude bozales to the most highly skilled artisans. Although crude bozal laborers were rented by their masters to third parties and usually worked in a gang labor force, the skilled Negro slave hired himself out and controlled his own income, typically paying his master a fixed sum at stated intervals.[18]

In practice this usually meant complete freedom for the slave to live where he chose and to set up his business the way he wished—renting space, making contracts, and so forth—in short to be a free artisan in all but name.

The pattern of urban slave rentals is well illustrated by the announcements of the daily press of Havana at the beginning of the nineteenth century. Typical rental notices ran as follows:

> Seek a Negro woman cook for service in a house.[19]
>
> Wish a Negro man or woman who knows how to sell any type of goods that are given to them, under the responsibility of their master or of a known person, and equally wanted, a master shoemaker who wishes to work for a private person.[20]
>
> Seek a Negro for selling, and whom his master will guarantee. . . .[21]
>
> Seek a good coachman and of good qualities. . . .[22]
>
> Wish to rent Negro field hands for one year or each six months; the master wishing to assure himself by this means of the salary of his slaves should come to casa 39. . . .[23]

Seek eight Negroes to hire, either for six months or a year, who are good for labor in the countryside, some four leagues from the city.[24]

This pattern of domestic urban growth and diversified small-farming agriculture that was established by the end of the sixteenth century would set the pattern for the Cuban economy until the twentieth century. But the initial growth of the colony in the first century of its establishment began to level off in the seventeenth century under the combined impact of the disastrous decline of the colonial fleet system and the general state of war in the Caribbean, which constantly disturbed the local and regional economy. Because of this, the internal capital of Cuba was insufficient to pay for the importation of large numbers of slaves, and by the end of the seventeenth century, the total colored population on the island probably did not exceed 40,000 persons.[25] This sluggish growth was in sharp contrast to the phenomenal importation of Negro slaves into the French and British West Indian islands, where sugar production was creating a legendary wealth. By the mid-eighteenth century, when Cuba probably had no more than 50,000 Negroes and mulattoes, tiny Barbados had 60,000 slaves, Haiti over 450,000 Negroes, and even Virginia had well over 300,000.[26]

Although the seventeenth century was one of economic depression, it nevertheless witnessed the growth of the first of the modern agricultural commercial crops—tobacco. Unlike Virginia, where tobacco would be developed as a plantation crop with intensive use of slave labor, the Cuban tobacco industry from the beginning was uniquely a small farm, individually cultivated, largely free labor crop. Spreading down the rich alluvial lands along the banks of the major rivers of the island, the tobacco planters reached deep into hitherto unexploited regions of the interior. Because of the nature of the crop land, and the pre-emption of almost all the island's territory by cattle *latifundios*, the tobacco farm, or *vega*, tended to be a small property, or *minifundio* system. A good percentage of the tobacco farmers, in fact, rented their lands either from the towns or the cattlemen and produced a relatively small crop on their natural or alluvial vegas. A large number of slaves were employed in the cultivation of tobacco, but these were scattered in small lots among numerous families, and it was often common for the poor white tobacco farmer to work alongside his slaves in the field. It also appears that some slaves even rented vegas on their own and paid their masters a fixed sum. The bulk of the workers, however, were poor whites and a fair number of free colored. Because of this labor and land pattern, the tobacco industry had a sharply democratic flavor to it.

Since tobacco growing was labor intensive and required little initial capital, it attracted poor white colonists from the Canary Islands and Spain and was the major drawing power for white immigration to the islands. Although its rapid growth at the end of the seventeenth and beginning of the eighteenth centuries seemed to promise that the industry would develop into a more capital intensive one, this did not occur. Beginning in 1717, the crown created a monopoly and fixed price structure for the product of the industry. The resulting governmental fiscal policies prevented planters from making major profits, and this worked against the large-scale introduction of slave labor. This governmental stifling of industrial growth and profitability quickly put a ceiling on the continued expansion of the industry, despite the tremendous growth of European demand. Thus, although Cuban tobacco farmers produced 8 million pounds of tobacco in 1717, at the end of the century, production was at almost the same position, being some 9 million pounds in 1788. Nevertheless, while the tobacco industry tended to level off in the eighteenth century, its position within the economy became entrenched, and it continued to maintain an important place in Cuban agriculture for the rest of the colonial period.[27]

With the new administration in Spain in the eighteenth century, the opening up of greater commercial contacts, and the important destruction of Haitian industries toward the end of the century, a whole new era of economic growth occurred in Cuba. First in importance of the new crops of the eighteenth century was coffee. Although it was introduced into Cuba in the early part of the century, coffee production did not become commercially important until the 1790's. From that date, however, its growth was phenomenal. Unlike tobacco, coffee immediately became a plantation crop. It did not require as great an initial outlay of capital as sugar production, but the pattern of plantation slave labor required major investment of capital. In this case, most of the capital seems to have been provided by French planter emīgrées from Santo Domingo who quickly made Cuba a major world producer of coffee, and for a time, an effective competitor of the infant Brazilian industry.[28] Thus production rose from 7,000 arrobas (a twenty-five pound measure) in 1790 to 900,000 in 1815,[29] with the industry at this latter date employing some 28,000 slaves.[30] But despite government protection, the industry suffered a major setback after the middle of the nineteenth century, and thereafter went into a slow but steady decline.[31]

The final major commercial crop that became of prime importance in the closing years of the eighteenth century was, of course, sugar. Sugar had been one of the first crops brought by the Spaniards to Cuba in the sixteenth century and had been steadily cultivated for the next two centuries, but it remained a relatively minor crop until the closing decades of the eighteenth century. Through the combination of the investment of foreign capital, the growth of European markets, and the disastrous decline of Haitian production, the industry began to acquire a new importance. Large numbers of slaves were now imported and heavy expenditures were made for refining machinery. Thus production by the 1780's was up to 1 million arrobas per year, by the 1790's to 2 million, and practically doubled every decade until by the 1850's the island was producing close to 30 million arrobas a year.[32]

Sugar rapidly gained a predominant influence on the foreign trade of the island, and both the economy and the institution of slavery came to be judged by the operation of the sugar plantation system. Of all forms of slave labor, the contemporary chroniclers of Cuba qualified sugar plantation labor as the worst. Since it required more time for production and harvesting than other crops—the cutting and harvesting of the cane being one of the most toilsome of occupations —sugar work was exacting and grueling. Hours were long, work harsh, *mayorales*, or overseers, extremely cruel, and mortality quite high by the island's standards. In the early days, especially, the new sugar planters tended to use only raw bozal males, to discourage family life by refusing to purchase females, and deliberately to overtax their slaves. Because of this, many later commentators, including Fernando Ortiz, tended to see Cuban slavery as an unmitigated harsh system by New World standards, at least compared to North America. But despite this belief, it should be kept in mind that sugar did not become the all-encompassing mono-production industry of Cuba until *after* the end of slavery, and that even at the height of slavery in the nineteenth century, it did not control a majority of the Negro slaves on the island.

Thus despite the fact that the sugar industry was one of the prime importers of African slaves after 1800, the overwhelming bulk of the Negroes on Cuba neither lived nor worked on the great sugar plantations during the entire period of Cuban slavery. So diversified had the Cuban economy become that despite its importance sugar employed only a minority of the slaves, even in the 1860's. For throughout the period of the rise of the new commercial export crops of coffee and sugar, there had also occurred the steady growth of such classical agricultural industries as cattle and hides, truck farming, and a host of diversified agricultural crops from a huge bee industry to cotton production. And all this was beside the steady growth of a major industrial complex in the key urban centers of the island.

Thus in 1825, when coffee was reaching its peak and sugar just beginning to take over its dominant position, Humboldt estimated the number of slaves engaged in the production of sugar at over 66,000 and in all staple crops at some 140,000, with another 45,000 or so rural slaves completely outside this staple crop production engaged in a tremendously diversified rural economy. Out of the total of about 260,000 slaves on the island at this time, 28% or over 73,000 of the slaves were located in the cities and larger towns engaged in an infinite variety of urban occupations.[33]

These estimations were fully supported by the studies of Ramón de la Sagra [,the] famous botanist and demographer[,]concerning the value and distribution of slaves in rural industry in 1830.[34] In the census of 1827, the government listed a total slave population for the island at 286,942, which meant that according to the above estimation, a good half of the slaves were not even engaged in rural agriculture but were in the cities in urban occupations, and this was completely exclusive of the large urban free colored population.[35] . . .

There were even cases of rural skilled slaves migrating to the cities and there escaping to freedom. The crown especially had this problem with its royal slave community in the copper mining town of Santiago del Cobre. Since copper production was often in suspension, the crown hired out large numbers of these slaves as daily laborers for work in the cities, both in nearby Santiago de Cuba and in Havana. Once in these towns, large numbers of these slaves escaped, set themselves up as freedmen, and to the crown's astonishment, even succeeded in having local parish priests register their children as free-born.[36]

Employed in every conceivable industry and profession in the urban centers and heavily engaged in a multitude of rural activities, from produce farming to cattle raising and bee keeping, the African Negro slave lived in a rich world of economic opportunity. Wages for skilled labor were high throughout the colonial period, and this coupled with the great demand for skills and the possibilities for private and self-employment allowed a large amount of private wealth to accumulate in the hands of slaves. From this wealth came the capital for self-purchase and for a multitude of amenities that relieved the daily burden of slavery. Even in the remotest rural areas, Catalan inkeepers kept the rural slaves well supplied with a host of products for their ready cash, including hard liquor,[37] and in the urban areas, entire sections of the town were filled with canteens and taverns that catered primarily to the monied slaves.

This abundance of economic opportunity not only provided a large reserve of private capital for slaves, but it also left them with a rich industrial heritage. The master's investment in the training and education of his slaves of course gave the master a large return on his capital, but it also left the slave endowed with assets that would last him a lifetime. All of this made for an easy transfer from slave status to free. Working in every industry as freedmen, the slaves— once emancipated or having purchased their own freedom—simply continued in the same economic occupation as before, often even in the same factories and shops.

All of this was in sharp contrast to Virginia. Here, unskilled rural labor from a plantation economy would dominate the labor market, and even for the skilled artisanal slaves, there would be heavy and, eventually, completely overpowering competition from free white workers, which would drive them out of the labor market. As for those slaves who were freed, a host of racial laws and anti-education restrictions deprived them of the opportunity to compete with white labor, to learn a skill, or often even to practice the few skills that they did acquire.

The economic heritage and opportunities of the Cuban Negro slave were thus crucially different from those of the Virginia slave. Because of this rich industrial heritage, the Cuban Negro occupied a vital place within Cuban society, which racial opposition denied him in Virginia. For even with the influx of white peasants from Europe, the Negro easily retained his economic leadership in most artisanal professions and thereby retained his extremely important place in Cuban society. Without the Negro, the island would have been deprived not only of a major part of its unskilled labor force, but of its entire complex of urban and rural skilled labor upon which the entire economic life of the community rested. In short, in the urban areas, as well as on the rural plantations, the Negro was a vital economic element of society, and this economic importance procured for him a host of privileges that even the benevolent crown could not have granted him.

VIRGINIA AND THE PLANTATION SYSTEM

The success of self-government in Virginia and the emergence of an entrenched planter leadership freed from imperial control forms the prime background for the discussion of the role of the Negro in the Virginian economy. For when the planters' attention was focused upon the establishment of the institution of Negro slavery, it was economic considerations, to the exclusion of all others, that operated most decisively upon the entire structure of statutory law and custom that made up the slave regime.

It is the history of tobacco, the mass migration of laboring whites, and the rise of the plantation system that more than anything else, determined the character of slave institutions in Virginia. These and other economic factors were the prime catalysts rather than the interests and attitudes of a distant monarchy and an all-powerful church—which in the case of Cuban slavery were of such positive importance.

Whereas Cuba sought economic stability and development through a diversified economy heavily influenced by urban organization, Virginia was overwhelmingly dominated by a rural plantation system and tobacco. With little exaggeration it has been claimed that the colonial history of Virginia is merely the story of tobacco, for it was tobacco more than any other single factor that came to dominate the Virginia scene.[88]

Throughout the years of early settlement, the need to find a commercially profitable crop had been the dominant theme. For until a commercial product of some kind was found, the colony proved a constant drain on the ever dwindling resources of the company, and the latter had to resort to all kinds of subscriptions, lotteries, and new issues of stock to survive financially.[89] From the beginning the company was forever seeking the desperately needed commodity, especially as precious metals and a northwest passage failed to appear. At first considering Virginia as a semi-tropical area, it experimented with all the crops that had proven successful in such areas previously, and hence the company's stress on silk and grapes, as well as on a host of other commodities not produced in England.[40] Yet for one reason or another, all these attempts failed, all except the attempt to grow the phenomenal tobacco leaf, which seemed to have been the first plant that successfully prospered in all of England's early New World possessions.[41] The tobacco experiments were initially carried out by the colonist John Rolfe in 1612, and within a few short years the Virginia leaf had been brought up to acceptable standards. So quickly did

Virginia leaf find a profitable market that by the end of the third decade of the seventeenth century, tobacco had achieved its position of dominance over the Virginia economy that was thereafter never seriously challenged.[42]. . .

. . . By 1700 there were 6,000 slaves reported in the colony. By 1708 the figure had risen to 12,000, and it was reported that 3,000 of these had been imported between 1705 and 1708. Within another seven years the number of slaves had almost doubled, and by 1742 there were 42,000 slaves in the colony. This figure was more than doubled in the next decade, for by the late 1750's there were well over 100,000 Negroes in Virginia. By the 1780's this figure had phenomenally doubled again, and by the first federal census of 1790, there were over 292,000 slaves in the newly created state of Virginia.[43]

Along with this tremendous increase in absolute numbers, the eighteenth century had also seen the very rapid percentage increase of the colored population. Representing 24% of the total population in 1715, the Negroes accounted for 41% of the total by 1756. [44] But this percentage growth quickly leveled out, despite the tremendous expansion of slave importations, with an equally heavy importation of free white colonists. Thus by 1790 the total was still 41% of the population, and this figure never rose higher than 43% in 1820–30 throughout the rest of the nineteenth century. In fact, the percentage actually declined, despite the growth in absolute terms of the colored class, to a low of 34% in 1860.[45]

Without question, the major occupation of the overwhelming majority of Negro slaves in the colonial period was tobacco production. Virginia had, in this period, a truly exploitive monoproduction economy, which produced little beyond the most elemental needs and devoted all its time and energy to the production of one raw material, tobacco.[46] What skilled labor was performed in this plantation-dominated economy was done largely by white artisans who had been imported in large numbers into the colony from the very first years and who continued to dominate the skilled trades right through the colonial period.[47] Thus to labor in tobacco, for which reason they had been enslaved in the first place, was the lot assigned to the mass of Virginia Negroes, and what a monotonous task it was.

The cultivation of tobacco, either orinoko or sweet-scented, involved a long, painstaking routine. The seed had to be sown in early winter, around the middle of January, in specially prepared beds of mould, while the fields themselves were broken and laid off by shallow furrows into hills some four feet apart. When the carefully prepared seedlings had reached a certain height they were taken from the mould beds, usually during or just after an April, May, or June rain, and transplanted in the fields. Once laid out in these hills, the plants needed a steady repetition of hoeings and plowings to keep them free from weeds and to keep the soil loose. Then came the even more tedious job of topping each plant when a specified number of leaves had been grown to prevent further growth; removing the suckers growing at the base of the leaf stems; and examining the leaves periodically for horn worms. When the crop began to turn yellow it was necessary to cut the stalks close to the ground, to wilt the leaves, and finally to cure them in tobacco houses. In the curing, each stalk with its leaves had to be pegged at a specified distance from its neighbor. The pegged tobacco was then air cured for a period of five to six weeks or more, and on an appropriately moist day, the leaves were stripped, made into "hands," and put into hogsheads. Often by this time a new crop was being prepared for planting, and the routine began again. What spare time was left to the Negro work gangs in this year round routine was given to clearing new fields. This was especially important and difficult since a field was planted in tobacco on an average of only once in three years, and new fields had constantly to be hacked out of the heavily forested tracts that surrounded the old fields. The gangs were also put to tending subsidiary crops, building hogsheads, mending fences, and so forth.[48]

The plantation worked primarily by Negro slaves was already in existence by the last decades of the seventeenth century. There were the Negro quarters, the work gangs, and the white overseers.[49] With a ready pool of white labor available to the planter, there was no need to rely upon the Negro for either plantation management or for work in the skilled trades. The overwhelming number of overseers were drawn from the class of newly freed white indentured servants. As a rule, they were paid a percentage of the tobacco produced, a system that the Virginians eventually found to be hard both on the land and on the Negroes. For the larger the volume the greater the overseer's return, and there was no need or desire for him to conserve anything. In spite of the obvious evils of this system, however, it was not until the 1830's that the salary scheme was finally adopted by tobacco planters.[50] . . .

Thus the Virginia field hand saw the world in a vertical hierarchy —a precise hierarchy consisting of field hands, drivers, artisans, house servants, and finally overseers and masters. Rewards, punishments, and opportunities all came from above. Although this pattern also existed for the Cuban plantation slave, there was in addition another dimension, extending horizontally, that encompassed the church, towns, local merchants, holidays, private property, and even the cimarron villages. And there was as well the awareness of the existence of a majority of coloreds, both slaves and free, who were not even bound by the rigid plantation—big house complex. For sugar estates were interspersed with coffee plantations and were surrounded in the outlying regions by cattle ranches, and near the towns were a great variety of produce farms, and everywhere along the rivers were the small tobacco farmers. Virginia on the other hand, tended to aggregate its tobacco plantations in one area, primarily because of the special soil conditions. And even when small farms were scattered among the great estates, they were farms of poor whites whose attitude, if anything, tended to support the isolation of the plantation Negroes. There were no other major occupations for the Negro, and almost two-thirds would be found on the plantations from the development of the system until 1860.

Although opportunity for the non-field hands was somewhat greater, it was not significantly different from that of the field hands. Any skills that the Negro was allowed to acquire were intimately tied up with tobacco production, and although as early as the seventeenth century records show numerous Negro mechanics, these were primarily carpenters and coopers—the trades essential for making hogsheads. That the training received by these Negroes fitted them merely for the crudest and most elemental tasks is seen from the fact that large slaveholders like Byrd and Fitzhugh continued to import English artisans at very heavy expense right through the seventeenth century, men whose skills were similar to those in which some of their own slaves had been trained.[51] Nor did the colony as a whole ever lack a white artisan group. Although the majority of them, unlike their English compatriots, devoted themselves to the production of tobacco and became planters as well as artisans, this class of free artisans survived and prospered despite the influx of cheap Negro labor.[52]

In the period between the American Revolution and the War of 1812, many plantations were temporarily forced into becoming self-sustaining economies, but the post-1812 period saw an even greater return to the simple monoproduction of a staple crop and the wholesale importation of manufactured goods for all the luxuries and many of the necessities of plantation life, including the clothes and food for the slaves themselves.[53] Thus the skilled plantation artisan, between the competition of local white artisans and the importation of manufactured goods, was left only a small area of skills, these being associated with house construction and the immediate packaging and handling of the staple crop.

In fact, only the house servants, who were associated closely with the white family's separate economic and social life, had the possibility of breaking out of the confined world of the plantation. In the big house, skills were often well rewarded, and faithful service could lead to substantial improvement in daily living. Here, too, there was the possibility for an education, for better food, clothing, shelter, and religion. Here, too, was the possibility for manumission. It is interesting to observe in all the records of manumission how often a planter on his death would free only a half-dozen or so of his several hundred slaves, and these were almost always house servants. . . .

. . . [Despite] the spread of tobacco production to several western states and the turning of many fields to corn, wheat, and other crops, Virginia was still the largest producer of tobacco in the nation right through the nineteenth century until the Civil War.[54]

The Tidewater planters, even though they had often switched to corn and wheat, still maintained the large plantation slave-labor system.[55] That the plantation system remained intact is indicated by the distribution and ownership of slaves in Virginia. By the 1770's, slavery was largely centered in the Tidewater and Piedmont regions,[56] and this pattern remained unchanged up to emancipation. If anything, the plantation system had been further entrenched as the size of the slave labor force constantly increased and the number of slave owners constantly decreased in the years between 1790 and 1860. In 1790 there were 292,627 slaves in Virginia—more than double the number of slaves in any other state of the union—and 34,026 slave owners, who represent 7.6% of the white population. In 1860, Virginia still had the largest number of slaves in the union, this time 490,865, but the number of slave owners was now 55,063, and they represented only 0.5% of the white population.[57]

This seventy-year period also showed an actual increase of the number of slaves involved in the plantation system. Thus, according to L. C. Gray, slaves were considered to be part of the plantation system if they were held in lots of ten or more under one owner.[58] By this definition, some 72% of the slaves in 1790 were thus involved in the plantation regime. In 1860 this figure had risen to close to 73%, and the median average slaveholding was 18.8 slaves. That is, approximately one-half of the slaves were held in parcels of 18.8 slaves or over! And in the tobacco regions of the Tidewater and Piedmont, median holdings were even higher. Thus in 1860 in the middle-Virginia tobacco region, the median holding of slaves was 24, and in the south central tobacco area, it was 28.[59]

All of this is in sharp contrast to the Cuban experience. Here it appears that the vast amount of slaves were held in small parcels and that no more than half of them, even in the middle decades of the nineteenth century, were held on large gang-labor plantations. In 1830, for example, only some 17% of the Cuban slave force was engaged in sugar plantation agriculture, the figure rising to only 18% in 1846, and even in 1860, a peak year for sugar production, the percentage of slaves in sugar was only some 38% and about 40% to 45% in all plantation crops.

That the plantation system was so predominant in Virginia was probably due not only to the continued dominance of commercial crops like tobacco, but also to the essential lack of urban growth and the lack of alternative economic opportunities for the use of slave labor. Without urbanization there was not only the lack of major urban industries and trades, but also of allied agriculture, particularly truck and produce farming which was an essential industry in Cuba. This is not to say that urban slavery or industrial slave labor did not exist in Virginia, but that its importance was minimal compared to the rural economy and almost negligible compared to plantation slavery. Even despite this minority position of urban and industrial slavery, Virginia was probably unique in the South in the extent of its manufacturing and the use of slaves in industry. . . .

. . . [But] the urban condition was too liberal for chattel slavery, and in almost every southern city of the nation from 1820 to 1860, slavery seriously declined both in terms of percent and often in absolute numbers. For urban slavery, which was such a recognized and accepted part of the Cuban scene, was totally incapable of surviving in the closed world of the chattel-slave plantation system of North America.[60]

Thus the prime characteristics of Virginia slavery were the dominance of the plantation system and the lack of economic diversity. Faced by the hierarchical and closed system of the plantation and largely confined to unskilled labor, the Virginia Negro was denied self-expression and creativity in every facet of his life. Opposed by white labor and denied the opportunities of an economically diversified economy, the domination of this plantation system left the majority of slaves with abilities and a level of education commensurate only with the unskilled labor of the staple crop economy. A vigorous yeomanry or artisan class was extraneous to this system and was, in fact, a serious danger to the stability and docility of the plantation worker. For the planters, the primary objective was to maintain a docile and efficient labor force. If they often grumbled about slave inefficiency, the planters nevertheless never went out of their way to change the system, to increase the slaves' skills, or to create incentives. As Frederick Law Olmstead observed in the last years of southern slavery, "I begin to suspect that the great trouble and anxiety of Southern gentlemen is—How, without quite destroying the capabilities of the Negro for any work at all, to prevent him from learning to take care of himself." [61]

NOTES

1. Of key importance in the following pages will be the discussion of the plantation, and it would be well at this point to clarify the term. Perhaps the most adequate definition of the plantation has been provided by L. C. Gray, who noted that: "the plantation was a capitalistic type of agricultural organization in which a considerable number of unfree laborers were employed under unified direction and control in the production of a staple crop." Lewis Cecil Gray, *History of Agriculture in the Southern United States to 1860* (2 vols.; Washington: Carnegie Institution, 1933), I, 302. Since the time of Gray's definition, which is perfectly applicable to the present historical analysis, social scientists have tended to broaden the definition to include all types of large-scale commercial crop agricultural systems, no matter whether the labor is free or slave, and they have tried to distinguish it from the feudal type of hacienda pattern, where production is not capitalistic in terms of management, nor in terms of producing a commercial export crop. For some of these problems, see the excellent study by the Pan American Union, *Plantation Systems of the New World* (Washington: P.A.U., Social Science Monographs, No. VII, 1959).

2. Mauro, *Portugal et l'Atlantique*, pp. 156, 160-61.

3. Irene Aloha Wright, "Rescates: With special reference to Cuba, 1599–1610," *Hispanic American Historical Review*, III (1920), 358.

4. Ortiz, *Los negros esclavos*, pp. 68-69.

5. Not only religious and territorial restrictions but a whole series of technical requirements greatly restricted immigration. See Haring, *Trade and Navigation*, pp. 102-3.

6. Silvio Zavala, "Los trabajadores antillanos en el siglo xvi," Part II, *Revista de Historia de América*, No. 3 (September, 1938), pp. 73-76. Writing of the period from 1555 to 1607 when these foreign introductions occurred, Guerra y Sánchez states that "the number of these foreigners was so reduced, that they were consequently an almost insignificant factor of the population." Guerra y Sánchez, *La nación cubana*, I, 232.

7. For an excellent survey of this problem in the southern United States see Richard C. Wade, *Slavery in the Cities, The South 1820–1860* (New York: Oxford University Press, 1964), pp. 273-75.

8. For the concept of hidalguismo see Americo Castro, *The Structure of*

Spanish History, trans. Edmund L. King (Princeton: Princeton University Press, 1954), pp. 628 ff.

9. Negro vaqueros, or cowboys, seem to have been an important group, for in 1574 when Negro slaves were prohibited from carrying arms, they were specifically exempted from this proviso. Ortiz, *Los negros esclavos*, p. 445.

10. Possibly the first Negro slave revolt on the island occurred in 1533 at the new Jacabo mines. Wright, *Early History of Cuba*, p. 151.

11. *Ibid.*, p. 206. For the history of this mining community of Santiago del Cobre (or Santiago del Pardo), see e.g. Archivo General de Indias, Sevilla, Audiencia de Santo Domingo, legs. 1627-31. [Hereafter cited as AGI.]

12. By 1606 half of the island's total population was located in and around Havana. Guerra y Sánchez, *La nación cubana*, I, 316.

13. *Ibid.*, I, 298.

14. Ortiz, *Cuban Counterpoint*, pp. 286-87. The Negresses must still have had a good deal of control over the ownership of these establishments, however, for in 1574 these prohibitions were reiterated. See Ortiz, *Los negros esclavos*, p. 445.

15. Friedlaender, *Historia económica de Cuba*, pp. 31-32.

16. Wright, *Early History of Cuba*, p. 237.

17. E.g., see *ibid.*, pp. 249, 275, 288-89.

18. Ortiz, *Los negros esclavos*, p. 312.

19. *La Cena*, October 24, 1814.

20. *Noticioso, Diario del Comercio*, October 18, 1814.

21. *Ibid.*, October 25, 1814.

22. *Ibid.*, October 28, 1814.

23. *Diario Civico*, May 21, 1814.

24. *El Observador de la isla de Cuba*, January 28, 1821. The above Havana newspapers can be found in AGI, Santo Domingo, legs. 1635, 1637.

25. For a survey of the seventeenth century economy, see Guerra y Sánchez, *La nación cubana*, I, 322-27. The first formal census in Cuba was not undertaken until 1774, and then the total colored population had risen to 75,180, or only some 50,000 in 168 years. Humboldt estimated that only 60,000 African Negroes were imported into Cuba between 1521 and 1763. Alexander von Humboldt, *The Island of Cuba*, trans. with notes by J. S. Thrasher (New York: Derby & Jackson, 1856), p. 217.

26. Ramiro Guerra y Sánchez, *Sugar and Society in the Caribbean, an Economic History of Cuban Agriculture* (New Haven: Yale University Press, 1964), p. 46.

27. Guerra y Sánchez, *La nación cubana*, II, 140-42, 170-73.

28. *Ibid.*, II, 180.

29. Friedlaender, *Historia económica*, p. 121.

30. Humboldt, *The Island of Cuba*, p. 283.

31. Note by Thrasher, *ibid.*, p. 284.

32. Jacobo de la Pezuela, *Diccionario geográfico, estadístico, histórico de la isla de Cuba* (4 vols.; Madrid: Imprenta Mellado, 1863-66), I, 62-63.

33. Humboldt, *The Island of Cuba*, pp. 242 n. 275. In 1811, *ca.* 32% were urban slaves.

34. Ramón de la Saga, *Historia económico-política y estadística de la isla de Cuba* (Havana: Imprenta de las viudas de Arazoza y Soler, 1831), p. 123.

35. *Ibid.*, p. 7 for the census of 1827.

36. AGI, Santo Domingo, leg. 358, no. 28, 1704. In a census of Santiago del Cobre (also called Santiago del Pardo) taken in 1796, it was discovered that there were 129 fugitive slaves missing out of a community of around 1,500 slaves. The average.time that these slaves had been fugitives from the community was almost 5 years. See AGI, Santo Domingo, leg. 1627, November 24, 1796.

37. D. Philalethes, *Yankee Travels*, p. 27.

38. "In no similar instance," wrote the most eminent historian of seventeenth-century Virginia, "has an agricultural product entered so deeply and extensively into the spirit and framework of any modern community." Philip Alexander Bruce, *Economic History of Virginia in the Seventeenth Century* (2 vols.; New York: Macmillan Co., 1896), II, 496.

39. Wesley Frank Craven, *The Southern Colonies in the Seventeenth Century, 1607–1689* (Baton Rouge: Louisiana State University Press, 1949), pp. 110-11, 114, 116-17, 121.

40. *Ibid.*, pp. 45-46, 108-9.

41. In the 1620's tobacco was planted by the English on the Guiana coast of South America and on the islands of St. Christopher and Barbados. Arthur Percival Newton, *The European Nations in the West Indies, 1493–1688* (London: A. & C. Black Ltd., 1933), pp. 142-43, 158. Nor was Bermuda far behind Virginia in this production. Craven, *The Southern Colonies*, p. 119.

42. Lewis Cecil Gray, *History of Agriculture in the Southern United States to 1860* (2 vols.; Washington: Carnegie Institution, 1933), I, 21-22.

43. Greene and Harrington, *American Population*, pp. 139-41, 154-55.

44. Gray, *Agriculture in the Southern U. S.*, I, 355.

45. U.S. Bureau of the Census, *Negro Population 1790–1915* (Washington: Government Printing Office, 1918), p. 51, Table 5.

46. The Virginia planter Robert Beverley wrote in 1705 of the complete lack of home manufactures of even the most elemental kind despite an abundance of natural resources: "They have their Clothing of all sorts from *England*, as Linnen, Woollen, Silk, Hats, and Leather, Yet Flax, and Hemp grow no where in the World, better than there; their sheep yield a mighty increase, and bear good Fleeces, but they shear them only to cool them. . . . The very Furrs that their Hats are made of, perhaps go first from thence; and most of their Hides lie and rot, or are made use of, only for covering dry Goods, in a leaky House. . . . Nay, they are such abominable Ill-husbands, that tho' their Country be over-run with Wood, yet they have all their Wooden Ware from *England*; their Cabinets, Chairs, Tables, Stools, Chests, Boxes, Cart-Weels, and all other things, even so much as their Bowls, and Birchen Brooms. . . ." Robert Beverley, *The History and Present State of Virginia*, ed. Louis Wright (Chapel Hill: University of North Carolina Press, 1947), p. 295.

47. Bruce, *Economic History*, II, 400-405.

48. Ulrich Bonnell Phillips, *American Negro Slavery, A Survey of the Supply, Employment, and Control of Negro Labor as determined by the Plantation Regime* (New York: D. Appleton and Co., 1929), pp. 82-83; Bruce, *Economic History*, I, 438-42. For the nineteenth-century modifications of these planting and harvesting patterns see Joseph Clarke Robert, *The*

Tobacco Kingdom, Plantation, Market, and Factory in Virginia and North Carolina, 1800–1860 (Durham: Duke University Press, 1938), chap. 3.

49. Bruce, *Economic History*, II, 106.

50. *Ibid.*, II, 47, 429-30; Robert, *Tobacco Kingdom*, p. 23.

51. Bruce, *Economic History*, II, 403, 405.

52. *Ibid.*, II, 410, 418.

53. Gray, *Agriculture in the Southern U. S.*, I, 453 ff.

54. Gray, *Agriculture in the Southern U. S.*, II, 757-58, 919-20; Robert, *Tobacco Kingdom*, chaps. 2, 8.

55. Gray, *Agriculture in the Southern U. S.*, II, 921-22. There are strong grounds for belief that aside from raising non-tobacco crops like wheat and corn, the Tidewater plantations also carried on a thriving business of slave breeding and were able successfully to maintain their economic advantage and the large plantation pattern. See Frederic Bancroft, *Slave-Trading in the Old South* (Baltimore: J. H. Furst Company, 1931), especially chap. 4; and Alfred H. Conrad and John R. Meyer, *The Economics of Slavery and Other Studies in Econometric History* (Chicago: Aldine Publishing Co., 1964), pp. 43 ff.

56. For the geographic distribution of slaves in the eighteenth century, see the population map drawn by Brown and Brown, *Virginia 1705–1786*, p. 73.

57. U. S. Bureau of the Census, *A Century of Population Growth . . . 1790–1909* (Washington: Government Printing Office, 1909), p. 135.

58. Gray, *Agriculture in the Southern U. S.*, I, 481.

59. *Ibid.*, I, 530-31.

60. Richard C. Wade, *Slavery in the Cities, The South 1820–1860* (New York: Oxford University Press, 1964), pp. 106-9, 243 ff.

61. Frederick Law Olmstead, *A Journey in the Seaboard Slave States, in the Years 1853–1854* (2 vols.; New York: G. P. Putnam's Sons, 1904), I, 64.

III: THE MASTER

• The South seemed receptive to proposals for emancipating the slaves during the Revolutionary period, when many of its leading figures, including Thomas Jefferson, publicly denounced the institution and searched for means of eliminating it. Yet even these popular Southern critics of slavery could not stimulate widespread support in the region for abolition, nor did they succeed in devising acceptable means of achieving this reform. Robert McColley examines the beliefs of Virginia slaveholders in the Revolutionary generation and points out their dilemmas in attempting to deal with the slavery question.

Slavery and the Revolutionary Generation

ROBERT MC COLLEY

The crowd of notable statesmen who represented Virginia in the early republic wrote and spoke against slavery with vigor and feeling. Their sentiments have often been cited as evidence that they were as antislavery as any Americans of their time, and that they were clear headed and secure in their belief that slavery would soon cease to exist. A close examination of the things they said about slavery, and where and when they said them, produces more complex conclusions. Virginians were most often defending slavery while denouncing it, for unlike southerners of later generations, they could command the sympathy of outsiders simply by showing the right attitudes.

During the Revolutionary War, Virginians were obliged to cooperate as closely and amicably as possible with soldiers and statesmen from the northern states and from France, almost all of whom found slavery distasteful. Again, in the two decades following the drafting of the federal constitution, Virginians were pleased to collaborate with northerners in the formation of national parties, and whether they

From Robert McColley, *Slavery and Jeffersonian Virginia* (Urbana, Ill.: University of Illinois Press, 1964), pp. 114-22, 124-5, 130-32. Reprinted by permission.

avowed Federalism or Republicanism, they were certain to meet many enemies of slavery. Further exposure to foes of slavery came from the enthusiastic support of the French Revolution given by Virginians, and from partisanship for France in her wars against Britain.

This is not to say that Virginians cynically adopted a mask of anti-slavery for the benefit of outsiders whose esteem they hoped to win. Rather, they found themselves partners in the liberal vanguard of their times, and were properly embarrassed at a stigma from which their other partners were free. Accepting with pleasure, and some-times with fervor, most of the assumptions of the Enlightenment, Virginia's leaders must necessarily denounce slavery as an evil institu-tion. From their frequent statements in this vein, these statesmen have caused their constituents to enjoy the reputation of being anti-slavery, as if the statesmen were voicing the convictions of their society and class. But if one looks closely, it appears that attacks on slavery usually occurred in the relations of Virginia with the outside world. In private correspondence, in the Congress of the United States, and in foreign capitals, Virginians typically indicted slavery whenever the subject arose. But among the class of wealthy planters whom they chiefly represented not one Virginia statesman of the Jeffersonian era ever advanced a practical proposal for the elimination of slavery, or for the systematic amelioration of the Negro's condition, with the single exception of St. George Tucker, a jurist and pedagogue. Schemes were, indeed, discussed in private. But, Tucker excepted, no politically prominent man came forward publicly to advocate the end of slavery. As there is practically no evidence to suggest that the dominant planters would have responded to such initiative, one must conclude that those leaders who genuinely hated slavery refrained from acting because they were convinced that their leadership would be rejected. Under a system of frequent elections, the Virginia statesman who came out publicly against slavery would very quickly be retired to private life.

The Virginia statesman saved himself from the charge of hypocrisy by acknowledging certain "truths" about Negroes, slavery, and society. He developed a set of logical propositions which made it natural and consistent for him to denounce slavery in principle, yet satisfy his constituents in practice that he would do nothing to injure their in-terests. Some of the axioms which were used to support these propo-sitions were reasonable enough for the times. To entertain others must have required considerable mental effort.

One of the more dubious notions was that Virginians could not be held responsible for the existence of slavery among them, because it had been forced upon their ancestors by the tyranny of the English crown. The Virginia Constitution of 1776 mentioned how the King of England, "by an inhuman use of his negative," had prevented the colony from excluding slaves.[1] Only the intervention of gentlemen from the Deep South kept Jefferson from including this count in his indictment of George III contained in the Declaration of Independence. But, of course, neither the crown nor anybody else had ever forced a Virginian to buy a single slave. For over twenty years before the Revolution the British government had prevented Virginia from barring the further introduction of slaves, but this hardly represented either renunciation of slavery on the part of Virginia or a systematic policy of the Crown to force slavery into areas where it was not wanted. By the time colonial Virginia tried to prevent slave importation, her leading planters were faced with the problem of perennial overproduction, and of course owned more than enough slaves, who were a large majority in the Tidewater area. Also, given this problem of overproduction, the value of slaves was likely to fall if slave traders were permitted to dump unlimited quantities of their merchandise into a Virginia market which had a limited capacity to absorb them. As a rule Virginians did not like to sell their slaves, at least not in the open market. But neither were they happy when the market value of their slaves declined.

Another important reason for prohibiting the importing of slaves, even in colonial days, was an apprehension of slave rebellions. If the slave population should be permitted to grow more rapidly than the white population, the danger of successful insurrection would be markedly increased. Virginians had enough imagination to foresee the possibility of living under garrison conditions, and the prospect was repugnant to them. They further felt, probably with justification, that imported slaves were likely to be less docile than those bred to their proper station in the Old Dominion.

Therefore, the ruling class of colonial Virginia tried to control the size of their slave population. The British government, on the other hand, could argue that as long as there were people in Virginia who wanted to import Negroes, they should have the right to do so. Such a policy had the advantage of keeping content the British interests in the slave trade, and those British merchants who were pleased at the abundance and low cost of Virginia tobacco. All of these complexities were kept out of mind, however, or at least out of public utterance, and Virginians after the Revolution stuck to their dogma that the evil of slavery dwelt among them because of the diabolical commercial policy of the Old Empire. Given this notion of inherited evil without inherited guilt, they often represented themselves as laboring under a burden. The wretched class of unfortunates residing among them, they claimed, depended for its mere survival on their stewardship and careful management.

Turning these unfortunates free, on the other hand, would be a disaster for both the Negroes and the whites. The former race had not the moral fiber, intelligence, and industry necessary for citizenship in the society of the latter. Hostility and jealousy were bound to result from a coequal existence within the same territory, until one race must enslave or destroy the other. On the other hand, if the races should not destroy one another in civil war, the black must eventually interbreed with the white, destroying the intelligence and beauty of the superior race. . . .

It is doubtful whether the majority of Virginians who owned slaves found it necessary to embrace the foregoing propositions. Those who were not involved in public affairs seem, in what letters and diaries they have left, to have accepted slavery as a normal feature of life, excepting the abolitionists of certain religious persuasions. Obsessions with guilt over the holding of slaves are, with the exception noted, extremely difficult to find. There were occasional anxieties, but such exist in any sphere of life. Anyway, it was bad form to dwell on the evils of slavery in public. Such ideas might reach the slaves themselves, making them unruly and discontented. This would force the masters to apply a stricter, harsher discipline. Therefore the net result of public protest against slavery would be to make the life of the slave more miserable, which was surely an effect not desired by those who deplored the evil effects of slavery in the first place.

Discussions of the evils of slavery were confined to private drawing rooms in Virginia, except for an occasional outburst in the legislature, or from an evangelical pulpit. The newspapers of the times avoided so delicate an issue, and there were no other forms of journalism practiced. . . .

With regard to slavery, Virginia statesmen were in the peculiar position of repeatedly describing an evil and then proceeding to insist that nothing could be done about it. Thus, said John Nicholas to the House of Representatives in 1797, "On inquiry . . . it would not be found the fault of the southern states that slavery was tolerated, but their misfortune; but to liberate their slaves would be to act like madmen; it would be to injure all parts of the United States as well as those who possess slaves." [2] Nor had the general government any business tampering with Virginia's slaves, or even thinking about them except in one respect. Another representative of Virginia explained this to Congress: "Mr. Lee observed that gentlemen were sent to that House to protect the rights of the people and the rights of property. That property which the people of the southern states possess consisted of slaves, and therefore Congress had no authority but to protect it, and not take measures to deprive the citizens of it. . . ." [3] This was said after a petition of free Negroes came before the House of Representatives, praying that it might consider means of bringing more people out of bondage. General Henry Lee answered, in effect, that Congress might properly act only to continue the holding of people in bondage.

John Randolph joined the debate to "hope that the conduct of the House would be so decided as to deter the petitioners," or anyone else, "from ever presenting [a petition] of a similar nature. The effects must be extremely injurious." [4] Finally, a less celebrated representative of Virginia, Samuel Goode, submitted an amendment to the House resolution denying the petition, which denounced the petitioners themselves. He argued, quite in the fashion of the southerners of the 1830's, that emancipation was a subject "from which the general government is precluded by the Constitution," and that petitions advocating it had "a tendency to create disquiet and jealousy, and ought therefore to receive the pointed disapprobation of this house." [5] As a matter of fact, southerners, including Virginians, were fully as eager to choke off antislavery petitions to Congress in the Jeffersonian era as they were in the days of Garrison and Weld. When a petition drawn by Benjamin Franklin was submitted in 1790, suggesting with characteristic mildness that Congress might consider some means of uplifting Negroes held in bondage, Congress was embroiled in a week of acrimony. Fisher Ames of Massachusetts described the scene: "The Quakers have been abused, the eastern states inveighed against, the chairman rudely charged with partiality. Language low, indecent, and profane has been used; wit equally stale and wretched has been attempted; in short we have sunk below the General Court [of Massachusetts] in the disorderly moment of a brawling nomination of a committee, or even of a country town-meeting." [6]

It was not the attitude of the representatives of slaveholders that changed between the 1790's and the 1830's, but rather the attitude of the North. In the earlier period northern Congressmen acquiesced, somewhat grudgingly, in the refusal to consider such petitions, and accepted the southern contention that they probably caused more

harm than good. Because the refusal to consider petitions was not followed by widespread public indignation and a flood of further petitions, the southerners had no cause, as they later did, to try to prevent
such petitions even being brought into the halls of Congress. . . .

In brief, the antislavery pronouncements of Virginia's statesmen
were so rarely accompanied by any positive efforts against slavery as to
cast doubt on their sincerity, and when initiative against slavery was
proposed by others they normally resisted it. This makes still more
doubtful the proposition that their constituents were agreeable to anti-
slavery sentiments. The indirect evidence available to us on the position of the Virginia planters suggests that most of them were for all
practical purposes proslavery. But even if the average planter held
views on the Negro question identical to those of Thomas Jefferson,
slavery would have remained fixed in Virginia, for the most liberal of
all Virginia statesmen was himself unable to find a practical means to
dismantle the institution he freely acknowledged as a curse. He was effectively prevented from doing so because, on the one hand, he shared
too many of the traditional southern ideas about the character and
potentialities of the Negro, and, on the other hand, he was unwilling
to risk the certain loss of political influence that outspoken opposition
to slavery must have caused.

Jefferson attained an important station in public life at a fairly early
age, and continued to command the serious attention of many Americans until his death in 1826. Over a period of six decades his hopes
about slavery changed significantly, so that the possibility and the
imminence of emancipation seemed much stronger to him at one
time than at others. In the years just following the Declaration of Independence he worked out an elaborate law for the gradual emancipation *and removal* of the Negroes of Virginia but he, along with his
colleagues in revising the laws, refrained from submitting this to the
legislature. At that time Jefferson thought that the people of Virginia
would very likely be more receptive to his scheme after the passage of
years brought an increase in liberal and humanitarian sentiment. But
the occasion never arose, and it seems clear that by the time of his
presidency, Jefferson had entirely dismissed the notion of doing anything himself in behalf of emancipation. In 1891 Moncure D. Conway, a native Virginian who had suffered immense odium by being an
abolitionist before the Civil War, ruminated in a private letter about
Jefferson's reputed opposition to slavery. "Bancroft has given him a
world-wide reputation," Conway wrote, "as having tried to pass an

antislavery act in Virginia. Never did man achieve more fame for what he did not do." [7]

Jefferson did indeed recommend in 1784 that the western territories should be closed to the introduction of slavery, and this recommendation, unlike the celebrated sixth article of the final Ordinance for the Northwest Territory, applied equally to the Southwest. As president, however, he guaranteed the protection of Spanish and French slavery in Louisiana, and helped open that territory to American slavery as well. Nor does he seem to have used his influence as president to discourage the attempt, led by William Henry Harrison, to suspend the operation of Article Six in Indiana and Illinois. Jefferson's reputation has indeed been fortunate, when one considers that he has been recognized universally as the father of exclusion in the Old Northwest, but has never been labeled as the father of slavery in Louisiana, except by a few seething Federalists in his own day, who have long since been discredited. . . .

Even in his boldest undertaking, the plan for general emancipation that was indefinitely withheld, Jefferson proposed an emancipation so gradual that it would guarantee the planters of Virginia slave labor for several generations, and the entire project was dependent on a federally subsidized removal of all free Negroes.[8] And by the time of his presidency, Jefferson was unwilling to be associated with any projects for the reduction of slavery. In 1805 Thomas Brannagan of Philadelphia wrote Jefferson asking him to subscribe to (which meant also to endorse) his poem, "Avenia; or, a Tragical Poem on the Oppression of the Human Species." With respect to this, Jefferson wrote to Dr. George Logan that he had "most carefully avoided every public act or manifestation" on the subject of slavery.[9] Jefferson continued:

> Should an occasion ever occur in which I can interpose with decisive effect, I shall certainly know, and do my duty with promptitude and zeal. But in the meantime it would only be disarming myself of influence to be taking small means. The subscription to a book on this subject is one of those little irritating measures, which, without advancing its end at all, would by lessening the confidence and good will of a description of friends composing a large body, only lessen my powers of doing them good in the other great relations in which I stand to the public.

A legion of general historians and biographers have endowed Jefferson with the most exalted reputation in American history among intellectuals. Reflecting on Jefferson's experience with and attitudes toward slavery, they have cited Jefferson's attacks on the institution with commendable thoroughness, but have been much less conscientious both in tracing his provincial views of the character and capacity of the Negro and in acknowledging the degree to which Jeffersonian politics tended to promote and extend the planting interests of the South. They have suggested that, considering his birth and upbringing in a slaveholding society, his opinions were still surprisingly liberal and in advance of his times.

It is certainly true that there were Europeans and American northerners who shared the belief that the Negro race was genetically inferior in moral and intellectual endowment, and who would fully sympathize with Jefferson's horror at the prospect of miscegenation. But from the 1770's onward there were also serious and dedicated men in Europe, the northern states, and even in Virginia who demonstrated in practice as well as in theory that the Negro slave could be educated, emancipated, and civilized. Jefferson was not ahead, but rather far behind, such public advocates of emancipation as John Jay and Alexander Hamilton of New York, Anthony Benezet and Benjamin Franklin of Philadelphia, and Robert Pleasants and Warner Mifflin of Virginia.

Yet it is certainly true that Jefferson went as far, in attacking and limiting slavery, as an elected representative of Virginia could go, while retaining the suffrage and confidence of the effective majority in that state. Like the Congress of the United States, an elected representative of Virginia was free, not to attack the property of gentlemen, but only to protect it. But Jefferson accepted the limitations of being a Virginia statesman with good grace, for he was quite as bound to slavery in his private life as he was obliged to be publicly. The labor of his slaves created and sustained the modest splendors of Monticello, and the crops they grew purchased (though they never quite covered the cost) the fine wines and books that made his life at home seem so attractive. Jefferson was not one of those southern Founding Fathers who freed his slaves. The claims of creditors would, under Virginia law, have precluded or at least postponed such an emancipation, but even without these he had so many relatives committed to the plantation way of life that such an act would have amounted to a disinheritance. George Washington, a much more acute business manager than Jefferson, and a man with no direct heirs, helped his various relations in Virginia develop fine estates in their own names, and was still able to relieve his conscience and embellish his reputation by freeing those slaves he owned in his own right. But apart from freeing a couple of typical old "faithful retainers," Jefferson was obliged by his own way of life to leave his Negroes indefinitely bound to servitude. . . .

NOTES

1. F. N. Thorpe, ed., *The Federal and State Constitutions, Colonial Charters, and Other Organic Laws* (Washington, D.C., 1909), VII, 3815.

2. *Annals of the 5th Congress*, III, 664.

3. *Annals of the 6th Congress, 2nd Session*, p. 231.

4. *Ibid.*, p. 233.

5. *Ibid.*, p. 240.

6. Quoted in John Bach McMaster, *History of the People of the United States* (New York, 1883–95), I, 579.

7. Letter to William Wirt Henry, 23 December 1891, W. W. Henry Papers, Box 2, Virginia State Library, Richmond.

8. Mary S. Locke, *Anti-Slavery in America* . . . 1619–1808 (Boston, 1901), p. 76.

9. Jefferson, *Works*, VIII, 352.

• By the 1830's, Southern support for the abolition of slavery
had generally disappeared. The growing pressures of abolitionist sentiment in the North and fears of slave insurrections
in their own states led many Southerners to begin construct-
ing an elaborate and belligerent ideological defense of Negro
slavery. The pivotal episode in the development of Southern
sectional consciousness during the 1830's concerned the tariff
question, and South Carolina led in defending Southern interests against Jackson, the federal government, and the North.
William W. Freehling describes the changing attitudes toward slavery on the part of South Carolinians in the two
transitional decades between Jeffersonian and Jacksonian
America.

Slavery and the Nullification Crisis

WILLIAM W. FREEHLING

A society reveals its deepest anxieties when it responds hysterically to
a harmless attack. The South Carolina lowcountry's morbid sensitivity
to the relatively undeveloped abolitionist crusade in the 1820's is a
case in point. The northern antislavery campaign, although slowly
gaining strength in the years before the Nullification Controversy, remained a distant threat in 1832. Yet during the prenullification decade, the Carolina tidewater was periodically in an uproar over the
slavery issue. In the 1820's lowcountry congressmen delivered fire-
eating harangues at any mention of the subject. And in the early
1830's the lowcountry gentry embraced the nullifiers' cause partly to
win constitutional protection against a nascent abolitionist crusade.
Throughout the period, the discrepancy between the abolitionists'
innocuous attack and the slaveholders' frenzied response was a measure

From William W. Freehling, "A Disturbing Institution," from *Prelude to
Civil War: The Nullification Crisis in South Carolina*, 1816–1836, pp. 49-53,
64-72, 82-6. Copyright © 1965, 1966 by William Wilhartz Freehling. Reprinted by permission of Harper & Row, Publishers.

of the guilt and fear which made Negro slavery a profoundly disturbing institution in ante bellum South Carolina.

During the years from 1820 to 1832, only the most prescient Americans realized they were witnessing the first signs of a growing crusade against slavery. In the benevolent reform empire which stretched along the eastern seaboard, idealists were more concerned with temperance and Sunday schools than with the plight of American Negroes. Those reformers who were distressed by racial problems usually soothed their consciences by joining the American Colonization Society. The society, dedicated to removing free Negroes from the United States, had at best only a tangential interest in freeing southern slaves.

However, as the twenties progressed a handful of antislavery crusaders initiated the campaign which would convulse the nation's politics in the years ahead. In 1821 Benjamin Lundy began his influential newspaper, *The Genius of Universal Emancipation*. In 1828 young William Lloyd Garrison assumed control of the Bennington (Vermont) *Journal of the Times*, wrote his first antislavery editorial, and collected over 2,000 signatures on his first antislavery petition. In 1829 David Walker, a militant free Negro, published his *Appeal*, urging slaves to revolt against their masters. Finally, on January 1, 1831, Garrison founded his bellicose newspaper, the *Liberator*. By the eve of the Nullification Controversy, the Nat Turner Revolt and its alleged connection with Garrison's writings had made the *Liberator* notorious in the nation's households.

Yet by 1832 Garrison had gained little support for his crusade. When Garrison organized the New England Anti-Slavery Society at the end of 1831, he managed to persuade only eleven disciples to sign the constitution. The founding fathers could contribute little more than their zeal; not one of them could have scraped together over $100. In the ensuing year, the Garrisonian onslaught continued to lack both funds and followers.

A more significant development of the prenullification years was the mounting evidence that the slavery issue could not be kept out of national politics. The 1820's commenced with a long congressional debate over slavery during the Missouri Controversy. Frightened by the savage emotions which the debates revealed, leading American statesmen attempted to bury the issue. But in 1824 the Ohio state legislature raised the subject again by proposing a national program of gradual emancipation. In 1826 a presidential proposal for a delegation to the Panama Congress of Spanish-American nations touched off a stormy discussion. The delegates would have to hobnob with the successful slave conspirators of San Domingo, and the United States might appear to sanction servile insurrection. In 1827 the American Colonization Society's request for congressional aid inspired another ominous dispute over slavery. It was fitting that the famed Hayne-Webster debate of 1830, with its far-ranging discussion of public issues, should focus at last on the vexing problem which the nation could not avoid.[1]

It must be emphasized again that most Americans—including most southerners—paid little heed to these nagging controversies. The slavery issue would not become a major national political problem until the gag-rule disputes of the mid-1830's. The point is that the South Carolina lowcountry was too uneasy about slavery to tolerate the slightest signs of a growing abolitionist attack. One leading Charlestonian wrote, as early as 1823, "all the engines and all the means and machines, which talent, fanaticism, false charity, fashionable humanity, or jealousy or folly can invent, are in dreadful operation and array." [2]

South Carolinians raged at the first indications of an antislavery crusade partly because they viewed emancipation with dread. Abolition conjured up grotesque specters of plunder, rape, and murder. The slave, too barbaric and degraded to adjust peaceably to freedom, seemed certain to declare race war the moment he threw off his chains. Moreover, in South Carolina alone, $80 million worth of slave property would be wiped out. Upcountry planters, like most slaveholders, could at least hope to salvage landed property from the wreck of emancipation. But tidewater gentlemen feared they would lose their huge investment in improved land as well as a fortune in slave property. Negroes would never work efficiently without bondage and the fatal swamps could never be cultivated without Negroes. "The richest, most productive land in the State, must be forever left waste," wrote Frederick Dalcho, a conservative Charlestonian. ". . . Can we reasonably be expected to submit to this state of things? Certainly not by reasonable men." [3] Abolition posed a greater *economic* threat than the abominations of the highest protective tariff.

The possibility of an abolitionist triumph was enough to make Negro slavery the most explosive issue an American Congress has ever faced. The fear of ultimate emancipation, however, pervaded the South throughout the ante bellum period, and became more intense as the abolitionist crusade grew stronger. The Carolina lowcountry's intransigence in the 1820's was more explicitly a reaction to the first stages of the conflict over slavery. The real issue in the period of transition was not so much whether slavery should be abolished but rather whether slavery could be discussed. If emancipation could unleash a race war, antislavery agitation could inspire a servile insurrection. An abolitionist attack would also force planters to defend slavery, and many of them regarded slavery as an abomination which should never be defended. The tidewater gentry had every reason to tremble at a full-scale discussion of the slavery issue; and its acute anxiety over facing the issue made the era of nullification a time of great crisis along the South Carolina coast.

In the late eighteenth century, such southerners as Thomas Jefferson and James Madison had helped to forge an American liberal philosophy which was still dogma in South Carolina during the years of the Nullification Controversy. Before the 1830's southerners often admitted that slavery had no place in a land which assumed that men had a natural right to life, liberty, and the pursuit of happiness. Moreover, they could never forget that insurrection was legitimate if men were deprived of their natural rights. The sight of a slave listening to a Fourth of July oration chilled the bravest southerner. "The celebration of the *Fourth of July*, belongs *exclusively* to the white population," wrote a leading Charlestonian. ". . . In our speeches and orations, much, and sometimes more than is politically necessary, is said about personal liberty, which Negro auditors know not how to apply, except by running the parallel with their own condition." [4]

Of course abolitionists insisted that the theory which the Fourth celebrates belongs to Negroes as well as whites. That assertion, no matter how dispassionately presented, made slaveholders consider any abolitionist tract "incendiary" if it reached the eyes of a slave. Thomas Jefferson's felicitous Declaration of Independence seemed almost as dangerous as David Walker's fiery *Appeal*.

The South Carolina tidewater, with its high proportion of slaves and its considerable number of African imports, was always more apprehensive about slave revolts than any other region in the Old South. Thus the lowcountry gentry watched the Missouri debates with considerable concern. Governor John Geddes of Charleston warned the state legislature of 1820 that "the Missouri question . . . has given rise to the expression of opinions and doctrines respecting this specie of property, which tend not only to diminish its value, but also to threaten our safety." He called for measures which would "oppose at the threshold, everything likely in its consequences to disturb our domestic tranquility." The lawmakers responded by enacting laws designed to halt the increase of free Negroes. South Carolina masters were no longer permitted to free their slaves, and colored freemen were denied the right to enter the state. The legislature also provided heavy penalties for distributing "incendiary" papers. But as South Carolinians soon discovered, these laws were in no way sufficient to keep at least some slaves from taking in deadly earnest the cardinal tenets of the white man's political dogma.[5]

The nullification crusade made many heroes. Still, the man most responsible for bringing South Carolina to the boiling point was not a great planter-politician, such as John C. Calhoun or James Hamilton, Jr., but a lowly Charleston mulatto named Denmark Vesey. The tragic slave conspiracy which Vesey inspired, although completely crushed in 1822, remained in 1832 and long thereafter a searing reminder that all was not well with slavery in South Carolina.[6] . . .

Uneasy, even in decades of calm, because of the heavy concentration of Negroes, lowcountry South Carolina faced four serious slave disturbances in the ten years preceding the Nullification Crisis. These recurrent conspiracies seemed particularly alarming because they followed on the heels of the first signs of an antislavery attack. The Denmark Vesey Conspiracy occurred two years after the Missouri congressional debates; the Nat Turner Revolt occurred less than a year after the appearance of Garrison's notorious *Liberator*. By 1832 the lowcountry gentry understandably believed that a slight growth of antislavery "fanaticism" immediately led to mounting cases of servile insurrection.

In the longer perspective of ante bellum history, the decade which began with Denmark Vesey and ended with Nat Turner emerges as the great period of slave conspiracies in South Carolina. Never before and never again did the slaves conspire so shrewdly, so widely, so often. Perhaps the rising abolitionist crusade influenced bondsmen, and perhaps they sensed their masters' uneasiness and irresolution in the face of external attack. After 1835, when slaveholders defended slavery as a "positive good" and tightened controls, slaves seldom dared to seek freedom by revolution. By 1860 South Carolinians were probably less apprehensive about servile insurrection. The famous slave conspiracies of the prenullification decade, like the exaggerated fear they helped to create, were products of the period of transition in southern history, when the beleaguered Carolinian tried to find the nerve to defend a system which he regarded as an abomination against outsiders who believed abominations should be abolished.

The grim chronicle of sabotage and conspiracy, however necessary for an understanding of slavery in South Carolina, distorts the peculiar institution. A small minority of slaves were involved in overt rebellions. Moreover, if planters sometimes regarded slaves with fear and trembling, they often viewed "their people" with kindly affection and an abiding sense of parental duty. The gay barbecues, the Christmas holidays, the homecoming celebrations, however exaggerated in the Old South's myth of plantation life, fulfilled a real need to treat one's slaves with warmth and affection. Indeed, the myth of the mellow old plantation and the dutiful, carefree Sambos who worked on it, like all utopian myths, has an important reality of its own. A society's vision of perfection reveals its most acutely frustrated desires. In the myth, southerners expressed their craving for a kindly, paternalistic slave system, without tension or punishment or violence, where master and slave lived together in rich comradeship and intuitive understanding.[7]

Even if plantation life could have approximated the utopian myth, southerners would not have rested easily. The philosophy which planters so enthusiastically celebrated on the Fourth of July would have remained a nagging moral burden. Moreover, the Carolina social code limited the value of an idyllic master-slave relationship. The drawing-room code, which insisted upon conversation between honorable equals, condemned the fawning slave, while accepting his inferiority with a smile, as a hopelessly degraded human being. Judged by the southerner's own values, a utopian plantation remained an illegitimate form of human exploitation.

Unfortunately plantation reality was rarely so sublime as the flawed utopia of the myth. Of course many southern slaves resembled the Sambo stereotype. Indulgent masters and their dutiful house servants often enjoyed a lifetime of friendship. But every plantation manager had to cope with a significant percentage of troublesome bondsmen. And the attempt to impose discipline on recalcitrant slaves frequently made managing the southern plantation a grim, ugly way of life. As one South Carolinian lamented, slaveholding subjected "the man of care and feeling to more dilemmas than perhaps any other vocation he could follow."[8]

The dilemmas of the scrupulous planter centered around the problems of discipline. As the Denmark Vesey Conspiracy demonstrated, indulged slaves could become archconspirators. And though few slaves emulated the notorious Rolla Bennett, many resisted their chains with devious sabotage and destructive laziness. When masters stopped painting their slaves as banjo-strumming Sambos or bloodthirsty savages, they presented another, equally revealing, stock portrait: the seemingly innocent but cunning laborer who could misunderstand adroitly, loiter diligently, or destroy guilefully. Indulgence and kindness, *by themselves*, could neither avoid rebellions nor produce an efficient labor force. Whipping, deprivation of privileges, and other punishments were accepted everywhere as a necessary part of plantation government. "Were *fidelity* the only security we enjoyed," exclaimed one slaveholder, ". . . deplorable indeed would be our situation. The fear of punishment is the principle to which we must and do appeal, to keep them in awe and order." [9]

Occasionally planters tried to escape from this unpleasant conclusion. In the halcyon days before the Vesey affair, many slaveholders "exulted in what they termed the progress of liberal ideas upon the subject of slavery." Planters experimented with a regime which, like the plantation of the myth, eschewed the lash and other forms of punishment, and relied on incentives, praise, and kindness to keep the slaves in order. Charleston's slaves were permitted "to assemble without the presence of a white person for . . . social intercourse or religious worship." Many bondsmen were given "the facilities of acquiring most of the comforts and many of the luxuries of improved society." Slaves were allowed "means of enlarging their minds and extending their information." But the events of 1822 proved to everyone that the peculiar institution could not endure if only humane treatment was employed. We must proceed "to govern them," Charlestonians concluded sadly, "on the only principle that can maintain slavery, the principle of fear." [10]

Still, employing the lash was distasteful to owners who liked to regard their slaves as personal friends. "We think it a misfortune," wrote William Harper, "that we should be compelled to subject to a jealous police, and to view with distrust and severity, those whom we are disposed to regard with confidence and kindness." The "misfortune," one suspects, seemed most upsetting with indulged house servants, who often had a close personal relationship with their masters, but still needed an occasional whipping. The unpleasant problems of discipline could be most clearly seen in Charleston, where personal servants formed a high percentage of the slave population and masters were forced to inflict stripes personally rather than pass the task on to plantation overseers. Few ante bellum events are more revealing than the obscure decision of the Charleston city council, in 1825, to erect a treadmill in the city workhouse, thereby relieving sensitive masters of the necessity of whipping their own people. "Such a mode of correction has long been a desideratum with many of our citizens,"

reported Robert Mills in 1826. Many slaveholders had "been often induced to pass over faults in their slaves demeriting correction, rather
than resort to coercive measures with them, who now will, without
doing violence to their feelings, be able to break their idle habits." [11]

The large slaveholder, closer to his house servants, probably found
disciplining his field hands a less disturbing business. Still, field hands
were "his people" as well as his property, and plantation management
was fraught with dilemmas. The most successful disciplinarians were
so rigid and strict that they rarely had to punish. But even such planters
went through a distressing period of frequent punishment when they
"broke in" their slaves, and they never escaped the necessity of prov-
ing to bondsmen that the system was screwed tight. "When I first
began to plant I found my people in very bad subjection," James Hammond explained to a new overseer. ". . . It required of me a year of
severity which cost me infinite pain and gained a name which I detest
of all others to subdue them. They are now entirely broken in, & . . .
it will be seldom necessary to use the lash." But overseers on his
plantation could never forgo the lash for long.[12]

Many planters could not emulate Hammond's agonized persistence;
rigorous discipline was simply too severe a strain on uneasy consciences. This—not the weather—was the crucial cause of the lazy
pace and inefficient practices on many declining plantations. Yet those
who could not bear to impose strict plantation rules and punish all
transgressions in the end whipped all the more. Spotty discipline encouraged passive resistance, devious sabotage, and—with the more
willful slaves—overt violence. James Edward Calhoun, traveling
through the lowcountry in 1826, encountered one unforgettable example of the tension which pervaded the plantation of an inconsistent
disciplinarian. James Kirk, a leading Beaufort planter, told Calhoun
that "if he lives 10 or 15 yrs. longer" his slaves would "gain ascendency
over him . . . is sensible they are gaining on him: confesses whips in
a passion & half the time unjustly. . . . Confesses scruples of conscience about slavery." [13]

In the 1820's leading South Carolinians admitted that inconsistent
disciplinarians abounded in their state. "The relaxed, sentimental,
covert abolitionist," lamented the editor of the *Southern Agriculturist*,
"first begins by spoiling his slave, next becomes severe, which is followed by running away, this again by enormous depredations . . . a
large proportion of our ablest and most intelligent slaves are annually
sent out of the State for misconduct arising from the most erroneous
notions of discipline." The editor of the *Southern Review* added:

"One great evil of the system is its tendency to produce in process of time, laxity of discipline, and consequently, disorders and poverty . . . by the excessive indulgence of careless or too scrupulous masters . . . some of the worst symptoms of the time are owing to this ill-judged, but we fear, inevitable facility and indulgence." [14]

The slaveholder's guilt was thus more than a reaction to the discrepancy between Jefferson's Declaration and southern slavery. It was also a response to the gulf between the plantation myth and the realities of bondage—a gulf evident day after day in the painful dilemmas of discipline. Planters who eschewed fear entirely and relied only on kindness invited economic bankruptcy and servile insurrection. Slaveholders who employed punishment erratically lived with periodic flareups and sometimes faced the unpleasant necessity of having to sell rebellious bondsmen. Planters who imposed discipline consistently had the least trouble in the long run, but endured the anxiety of inflicting perpetual punishment during the breaking-in period.

Of course many planters rarely worried about the morality of slavery or the dilemmas of discipline. At the other extreme, a few slaveholders, convinced that profits could be kept up only by a distasteful driving of slaves, sold out their plantations. Many others found solace in treating slaves as kindly as possible within the limits set by proper discipline. Plantation fell apart when control was based entirely on indulgence and incentives. But when punishment and fear were employed, kindness and courtesy effectively produced a more contented, efficient labor force. This, in turn, reduced the necessity to punish. As one astute observer noted, humane planters were "saved from many painful feelings at home and cared less about being traduced abroad." For many planters, however, the acts of kindness and the familial relationships were never quite enough. "I have a just partiality for all our servants from many touching recollections, & expect my residence at home made very comfortable by having them about me," remarked Hugh S. Legaré. "This circumstance is after all sometimes a great compensation for the unquestionable evils attendant upon the institution of slavery." [15]

Just as the unusually heavy concentration of slaves in tidewater Carolina intensified the lowcountry's fear of slave uprisings, so the special problems of the coastal plantation may have increased the gentry's guilt. As always, the problems centered around the malaria. Paternalistic masters felt compelled to protect their people's health. Yet planters knew that a slave thrust into the swamp was likely to become debilitated with illness and would sometimes prematurely die.

Many owners must have pushed the ugly problem out of their minds. Some salved their conscience by employing fine plantation physicians. But for others, providing excellent medical care could not compensate for subjecting the slaves to malarial fever in the first place. The planters betrayed their qualms by incessantly claiming what they knew to be false—that Negroes were immune from the diseases of the swamp. One leading slaveholder even exposed his uneasy conscience in his plantation journal. On James Hammond's Savannah River plantation, slaves were required to cut fodder in river swamps every September:

> September 23, 1833: At plantation all day nursing the sick. Some very low—High grade of bilious fever—Twenty-two on the sick list . . . September 26, 1833: Sick all better and the list reduced to 15—Pulling Fodder today in the Lower Bluff. *Fearful that it will produce more sickness.* . . . September 26, 1834: Saw Dr. Galphin who anticipates cholera here. Ordered all hands to be removed from the river . . . September 29—The cholera has driven almost everybody from the swamp. September 30—hands pulling fodder. Another case of cholera—Eleanor—very severe—It happened in my presence—Left her better—Ordered them to pull no more fodder. . . . October 3—Mr. Dawkins [the overseer] came up this evening and stated that there had been no new cases of cholera. He says he has put the hands to pulling fodder in the swamp again—*Feel uneasy about it.*[16] [Italics mine.]

Later Hammond noted that on his plantation slaves died faster than they were born. "One would think from this statement that I was a monster of inhumanity," he added. "Yet this one subject has caused me more anxiety and suffering than any other in my life." [17]

Disease-ridden swamps led planters to rely on unsupervised overseers, which raised special moral problems. Every contract between owners and overseers contained a clause binding the manager to treat Negroes with moderation and humanity. Overseers were frequently dismissed because they whipped slaves passionately or passed out medicine sparingly. Still, overseers were most often judged by their skill at raising yields. Overseers, like slave-traders, were more involved in the economic, exploitative side of slavery than the personal, paternalistic side; this is one reason they were despised. The incompetent young men who served as overseers on many tidewater plantations, and the absence of the owner's restraining word, undoubtedly increased the severity of slavery. As James Hammond summed up the matter in the midst of a famous proslavery polemic, a "leading" cause of cruelty to slaves was "the absenteeism of proprietors. Agents are always more unfeeling than owners, whether placed over West Indian or American slaves, or Irish Tenantry. We feel the evil greatly even here." [18]

Finally, the nature of absentee ownership involved tidewater gentlemen in a curious paradox. On the one hand, they were shielded from observing the unseemly side of plantation slavery during the summer months; in this sense they could ignore the dilemmas of discipline more easily than other planters. On the other hand, aristocrats who owned hundreds of slaves and often left their plantations had few memories of warm relationships with field hands to soften the exploitative aspect of slavery. They also had the detachment, time, and cultivated education to agonize over the morality of owning slaves. Elsewhere, relatively uneducated planters, personally involved day after day with building an economic empire, were less likely to stand back and question the means they were employing. One suspects that reasons like these help to explain why the Charleston aristocracy found it necessary to conduct "liberal" experiments with discipline and to build treadmills to punish slaves.

The diseases of the coastal Negro, the character of lowcountry overseers, and the nature and effects of absentee ownership *might* (for this is speculative) have intensified the guilt of the tidewater planter. Although less important than the lowcountry's particularly intense fear of slave revolts, this acute guilt may have helped to make slavery at the South Carolina tidewater so peculiarly disturbing. . . .

Thus the proslavery argument of the 1820's, although growing in strength, was still a fragmentary and qualified polemic which was not widely accepted. The few proslavery theorists made almost as little headway convincing the community that slavery was a blessing as the few Carolina abolitionists made in persuading the planters that bondage could be abolished. The huge majority of slaveholders, distressed by slavery but seeing no way out, clung stubbornly to the untenable "necessary evil" position. They did not widely discuss or accept the "positive good" thesis until *after* South Carolina adopted nullification.

The most revealing public reaction to the tensions slavery generated in the 1820's and early 1830's was neither the "necessary evil" nor the "positive good" argument but rather the attempt to repress open debate. The conviction that slavery was an abomination ran too deep to be overcome in a season, and antislavery opponents easily refuted the argument from necessity. If subjected to a barrage of criticism, conscience-stricken planters might become covert abolitionists who would fight half-heartedly for slavery's perpetuation and relax the discipline which kept their slaves in order. Moreover, public debate might increase the restlessness of. Negro slaves and would certainly magnify the apprehensions of the white community.

Thus South Carolina profoundly desired to keep the subject buried. The discovery of a copy of Walker's *Appeal*, or an issue of Garrison's *Liberator*, or a handkerchief stamped with Negroes in a state of defiance was enough to start a panic over insurrection. Charleston's newspapers avoided notice of slave conspiracies, and upcountry sheets gave only cursory details. Lowcountry editors trembled at items that approached the issue and refused to meet the matter head on. Pre-1833 editorials chanted that the evil was necessary and the subject too danerous to discuss.[19]

In 1832, when the Virginia legislature engaged in a month of searching arguments on the merits of slavery, and Thomas Ritchie's *Richmond Enquirer* doubled the danger by printing the debates, even Carolina unionists were flabbergasted. Benjamin F. Perry, a moderate, refused "to comment on a policy so unwise, and blended with so much madness and fatality"; the sober *Camden Journal* rejected an essay *against* the Virginia experiment with open discussion because "it is a subject that ought not to be agitated at all in this State." [20]

If the unionists fumed, the fire-eaters raged. In Sumter, John Hemphill urged patrols to be on the alert and denounced Ritchie as "the apostate trator, the recreant and faithless sentinel, the cringing parasite, the hollow-hearted, hypocritical advocate of Southern interests . . . who has scattered the firebrands of destruction everywhere in the South." In Washington, Duff Green proclaimed that Ritchie's heresy was "calculated to unsettle everything—the minds of masters and slaves." The *Charleston Mercury* added: "We cannot too earnestly deprecate the public discussion of such a topic. . . . The very agitation . . . is fraught with evils of the most disastrous kind." [21]

For a moment in early 1832, one Carolina editor dared to broach the forbidden subject. Young Maynard Richardson, son of the Carolina jurist and editor of the Sumterville *Southern Whig*, opened his columns "for a *liberal* and *guarded* discussion of slavery." Southerners invited northern attack, he argued, by their "own sensitiveness. We receive their objections with bitter revilings, nor do we ever deign any answer save the most unqualified contempt and abhorrence. This course augurs badly for us. It implies consciousness of a weak cause, and an unwillingness to undergo scrutiny."

Richardson printed a communication from "W. E." in the *Southern Whig* "without hesitation" because it merely discussed the "abstract question . . . upon which we . . . are . . . safest." The "W. E." essay was the type of argument which leading southerners wished neither guilty whites nor restless slaves to read. "Is it an argument," asked the correspondent, to assert that slavery is legitimate because northerners abuse their free Negroes? "Is it not rather the retort, 'You do so too'? . . . Is it an argument," inquired "W. E.," to blame slave-traders for the inception of bondage? "Or is it not rather an attempt to cover our own weakness, in yielding to seduction, by throwing the blame on the seducer?" Does the Negro's mental imbecility justify slavery? For

> the mental imbecility of the Negro is the result of our own injustice and oppression. Do we not endeavor, by every means in our power, to debase his mind? . . . And why do we act thus towards him? Is knowledge inconsistent with justice and the safety of the majority? . . . Is it an argument when he tells us, that our lands cannot bc cultivatcd without thcm? Or docs it not rather prove that we are resolved, at all hazards, on the gratification of our lust for power? [22]

John Hemphill, editor of the rival *Sumter Gazette*, spoke for a frightened community when he castigated Richardson's policy and called on the patrol for greater vigilance. Still, Hemphill refused to answer "W. E." With "a dense slave population at our own firesides," he wrote, South Carolinians would never allow anyone to "discuss the subject *here*." The value of an essay refuting "W. E." could never justify the danger involved. "Must we free ourselves," asked Hemphill's *Gazette*, "from such misrepresentation at the risk of such appalling mischief?" [23]

Maynard Richardson countered by accusing Hemphill of "the sickly sensitiveness and ridiculous squeamishness, about touching the subject of slavery which have ever been the subject of our misunderstanding abroad and of which there is not a nervous female who is not thoroughly ashamed." Yet Richardson stopped printing communications on slavery and picked a quarrel with Hemphill to cover his isolation in the community. A vituperative battle royal ensued between the two editors. Newspaper epithets soon gave way to physical violence. On an April day at Sumter Court House, Richardson, armed with a dirk, and

Hemphill, equipped with a pistol, scuffled for their honor. Other Sumterites swarmed in the street, wanting to join the brawl, and Judge Richardson plunged into the fray. Before the riot ended, the combatants were marked by bloody heads and torn clothing. And the image of the honorable judge wrestling in the dirt for the pistol comments on the eclipse of Maynard Richardson's rather noble aims and the disturbing nature of slavery in South Carolina.[24]

The Hemphill-Richardson affair was the most dramatic incident in the decade-long Carolina attempt to repress public discussion of slavery. But this policy in South Carolina could hardly be reconciled with the strategy of vigorous defense in Washington. Leading South Carolinians always believed that they must put down the smallest beginnings of a political antislavery campaign. An incessant abolitionist attack was expected to reach menacing proportions in the North and to provoke servile insurrections in the South. Yet a vigorous proslavery campaign in Congress would flounder without the enthusiastic support of southerners at home. A thoroughgoing propaganda campaign was needed to convince slaveholders to crusade for their institutions. And the incessant discussion of slavery in South Carolina seemed almost as dangerous as a growing abolitionist crusade in the North.

This irreconcilable commitment to both a strategy of militant defense in Washington and a policy of complete repression at home was the essence of South Carolina's dilemma in the 1820's. Desperately anxious to keep the distressing subject buried, the South Carolina congressmen lashed out stridently at the mildest antislavery proposals during the 1820's. And one of the crucial appeals of crusading for nullification on the tariff issue was that a weapon could be won to check the abolitionists without discussing slavery. The event would reveal that South Carolina could not escape the dilemma so painlessly. . . .

NOTES

1. The best survey of the abolitionist movement is in Louis Filler, *The Crusade Against Slavery, 1830–1860* (New York, 1960). See also Dwight L. Dumond, *Anti-Slavery: The Crusade for Freedom in America* (Ann Arbor, 1961).

2. Caroliniensis [Robert J. Turnbull and Isaac E. Holmes], *Caroliniensis on the Appeal of a British Seaman* . . . (Charleston, 1823), p. 24.

3. *Practical Considerations Founded on the Scriptures, Relative to the Slave Population of South Carolina* (Charleston, 1823), pp.7-8.

4. *Ibid.*, p. 33n.

5. Message of Nov. 27, 1820, Governors Papers, South Carolina Arch.; *Statutes at Large*, VII, 459-60.

6. Unless otherwise noted, the following account of the Vesey Conspiracy is based on the standard published sources: Lionel H. Kennedy and Thomas Parker, *An Official Report of the Trials of Sundry Negroes Charged with an Attempt to Raise an Insurrection* . . . (Charleston, 1822); [James Hamilton, Jr.], *Negro Plot. An Account of the Late Intended Insurrection Among a Portion of the Blacks in the City of Charleston, South Carolina* (Boston, 1822); *Niles Weekly Register,* XXIII (Sept. 7, 1822), 10.

For the purposes of understanding the Nullification Controversy, the most important aspect of the Vesey Conspiracy was its impact on the political behavior of the low-country gentry. I have chosen to describe the conspiracy as the South Carolinians themselves viewed it. The planters' beliefs about the affair, rather than what was objectively true, produced their intransigence in the face of abolitionists.

There remain, however, substantial doubts about whether the conspiracy was as widespread as Charlestonians believed, doubts that were expressed at the time by Governor Thomas Bennett and have been recently re-emphasized by Professor Richard Wade. Bennett believed that a serious conspiracy was afoot, but he doubted that it involved more than eighty Negroes and questioned whether it ever came close to being consummated. Wade, going a step further, seems to disbelieve in any conspiracy; the Vesey affair, he writes, "was probably never more than loose talk by aggrieved and embittered men." In my judgment, Bennett's position, but not Wade's, is consistent with all the evidence. While the terrorized community exaggerated the extent of the danger, there was, in fact, a conspiracy worth getting excited about. Since the evidence is complex and technical, I will deal with it in a separate essay. . . . For now, the important point is that Bennett's contemporaries almost universally condemned his position and repudiated his leadership. For Bennett's opinion, see his Message #2 to the state legislature, Nov. 28, 1822, Governors Papers, South Carolina Arch. For Wade's verdict, see his "The Vesey Plot: A Reconsideration," *Journal of Southern History,* XXX (May 1964), 143-61. South Carolina's reaction to Bennett is evident in the Cheves-Potter Correspondence, 1822, Cheves Papers, and *City Gazette,* Dec. 4, 5, 10, 1822.

7. The following view of South Carolina slavery is based on the plantation journals listed in the bibliographical essay. The most important sources are the Manigault Plantation Records, NC, and the James Hammond Plantation Records, 1831–55, SC. An edition of the Hammond Records, edited by the author, will be published shortly. My interpretation of slavery has been heavily influenced by Wilbur J. Cash, *The Mind of the South* (New York, 1941); Charles Grier Sellers, Jr., "The Travail of Slavery" in Sellers (ed.), *The Southerner as American* (Chapel Hill, 1960); the penetrating analysis of the dilemmas of conscientious slaveholders in Stampp, *The Peculiar Institution;* and the methodological insights of Henry Nash Smith, *Virgin Land: The American West as Symbol and Myth* (Cambridge, Mass., 1950).

8. S Ag, III (July 1830), 238.

9. *Southern Patriot,* Feb. 10, 1826.

10. Phillips (ed.), *Plantation and Frontier,* pp. 103ff.

11. SR, I (Feb. 1828), 230; Mills, *Statistics,* pp. 420-1.

12. Hammond to [John] Walker, Dec. 27, 1836, Hammond Papers, LC.

13. James Edward Calhoun Diary, entries for Jan. 25 through Feb. 1, 1826, SC.

14. S Ag, II (Dec. 1829), 575-6; SR, IV (Nov. 1829), 358. For some superb examples of the psychic stress inconsistent discipline caused, see James Holmes' compulsive attempts to convince Lucy Ruggles that he believes in slavery in Lucy Ruggles Diary, DU, and the M. L. Dorsey incident, 1824, in Pinckney Family Papers, LC.

15. W. J. Myddleton to Cheves, Sept. 8, 1821, Cheves Papers; Seabrook, *Essay on the Management of Slaves*, pp. 1-10; P. M. Butler to John M. Walker, March 18, 1837, Hammond Papers, LC; *Carolina Planter*, Apr. 1, 1840; Legaré to his mother, Jan. 26, 1835, Legaré Papers.

16. Hamilton to Dr. Furth, May 19, 1828, Miscellaneous Manuscripts Coll., New-York Historical Soc.; [Dalcho], *Practical Considerations*, p. 7; Hammond Plantation Records, SC.

17. Hammond Diary, entry for Sept. 5, 1841, LC. Two qualifications are in order: (1) Hammond was *also*, perhaps *more*, concerned about pecuniary losses from slave decreases and (2) he did not *always* blame the high death rate on the location of the plantation. The Hammond plantation was geographically in the upcountry, but the Savannah River fields gave it all the characteristics of lowcountry tracts.

18. *Carolina Planter*, Feb. 19, 1840; Sellers (ed.), *Southerner as American*, p. 60; William Harper *et al.*, *The Pro-Slavery Argument* (Philadelphia, 1853), p. 128.

19. Benjamin F. Hunt to Harrison Gray Otis, Oct. 4, 1831, Hayne to Otis, Oct. 14, 1831, Samuel Eliot Morison, *The Life and Times of Harrison Gray Otis* . . . (2 vols.; New York, 1913), II, 277-81; *Pendleton Messenger*, Oct. 5, 1831; *Camden Journal*, Apr. 21, 1832.

20. *Greenville Mountaineer*, Feb. 4, 1832; *Camden Journal*, Feb. 11, 1832.

21. *Sumter Gazette*, Apr. 28, 1832; *United States Telegraph*, Jan. 26, 1832; *Charleston Mercury*, Jan. 16, 1832.

22. March 8, 1832.

23. March 10, 1832.

24. Both papers, March and April 1832, esp. *Southern Whig*, March 15, 1832. See also *Pendleton Messenger*, May 16, 1832; *Winyaw Intelligencer*, July 16, 1831; Stephen La Coste to Miller, Apr. 20, 1832, Hemphill to Miller, Apr. 29, 1832, Chestnut-Manning-Miller Papers.

• As fears of slave revolts and of abolitionist intrigues grew
during the Jacksonian period, Southerners became increasingly concerned with protecting the security of their slave
system. Local militia units and patrols were not characteristic
only of the South during the ante-bellum period, of course,
and the tradition of vigilante-administered justice had become well established in this country even before the end of
the colonial period. Responding to the growing political
crisis over slavery in nineteenth-century America, however,
the South mobilized its white citizens through slave patrols
and constant militia duty in order to guard against the internal and external threats which it detected. John Hope Franklin describes the climate of Southern militancy.

The Militant South

JOHN HOPE FRANKLIN

"A MILITANT GENTRY"

. . . Despite the fact that the plantation sought to be self-sufficient
and that it succeeded in many respects, the maintenance of a stable
institution of slavery was so important that owners early sought the
cooperation of the entire community. This cooperation took the form
of the patrol, which became an established institution in most areas of
the South at an early date. There were many variations in its size
and organization. The South Carolina law of 1690 provided that each
patrol detachment should be composed of ten men under the captain
of a militia company. The number was reduced to five in 1721. All
white men were eligible for patrol service when the system was established. Between 1737 and 1819, however, patrol service was limited
to men of some affluence, presumably slaveholders. In the latter year

Reprinted by permission of the publishers from John Hope Franklin, *The
Militant South, 1800–1861* (Cambridge, Mass.: The Belknap Press of Harvard
University Press, 1956), pp. 72-3, 76-90. Copyright © 1956, by the President
and Fellows of Harvard College.

all white males over eighteen were made liable for patrol duty; non-slaveholders, however, were excused from duty after reaching the age of forty-five.[1] In Alabama the law of 1819 required not less than three nor more than five owners of slaves for each patrol detachment, while the Mississippi law called for four men, slaveholders or non-slave-holders, for each detachment.[2]

The duties of the patrols were similar in all places. The detachment was to ride its "beat" at night for the purpose of apprehending any and all Negroes who were not in their proper places. Alabama empowered its patrols to enter, in a peaceable manner, upon any plantation; "to enter by force, if necessary, all Negro cabins or quarters, kitchens and outhouses, and to apprehend all slaves who may there be found, not belonging to the plantation or household, without a pass from their owner or overseer or strolling from place to place, without authority."[3] There were variations in the disposition of offenders taken up by patrols. If the violators were free Negroes or runaways, they were to be taken before a justice of the peace. If they were slaves, temporarily away from their master's plantation, they were to be summarily punished by a whipping, not to exceed thirty-nine lashes.[4] There were, of course, abuses. On occasion, for example, members of the patrol whipped slaves who were legally away from their masters' premises or who were even "peaceably at home."[5]

The patrol system tended to strengthen the position of the military in the Southern community. In most instances there was a substantial connection between the patrol and the militia, either through the control of one by the other or through identity of personnel. In South Carolina the patrol system was early merged into the militia, "making it a part of the military system, and devolving upon the military authority its arrangement and maintenance." There the "Beat Company" was composed of a captain and four others of the regular militia, all of whom were to be excused from any other military service.[6] Sydnor has observed that in Mississippi the structure of the patrol was "but an adaptation of the militia to the control of slaves." In Alabama the infantry captains of the state militia completely dominated the selection of personnel for patrol duty and designated the officers.[7] Under such circumstances the patrol system was simply an arm of the military. . . .

The South's greatest nightmare was the fear of slave uprisings; and one of the most vigorous agitations of her martial spirit was evidenced whenever this fear was activated by even the slightest rumor of revolt. Fear easily and frequently mounted to uncontrollable alarm in which the conduct of some citizens could hardly be described as sober or responsible. "We regard our Negroes as JACOBINS" of the country, Edwin Clifford Holland declared. The whites should always be on their guard against them, and although there was no reason to fear any permanent effects from insurrectionary activities, the Negroes "should be watched with an eye of steady and unremitted observation . . . Let it never be forgotten, that our Negroes are freely the JACOBINS of the country; that they are the ANARCHISTS and the DOMESTIC ENEMY: the COMMON ENEMY OF CIVILIZED SOCIETY, and the BARBARIANS WHO WOULD, IF THEY COULD, BECOME THE DESTROYERS OF OUR RACE." [8]

A farmer's account of how the fear of revolts completely terrified some Alabama whites suggested to Olmsted both the extent of fear and the impact of fear upon the mind. The farmer said that when he was a boy "folks was dreadful frightened about the niggers. I remember they built pens in the woods," he continued, "where they could hide, and Christmas time they went and got into the pens, 'fraid the niggers was risin' . . . I remember the same thing where we was in South Carolina . . . we had all our things put up in bags, so we could tote 'em, if we heerd they was comin' our way." [9]

This was hardly the usual reaction to threats of slave insurrections. To be sure, such grave eventualities threw them into a veritable paroxysm of fear; but they moved swiftly to put up a defense against the foe. Committees of safety sprang into existence with little prior notice, and all available military resources were mobilized for immediate action. These were not the times to entrust the lives of the citizens to the ordinary protective agencies of civil government. If a community or a state had any effective military force, this was the time for its deployment. Military patrols and guards were alerted, and volunteer troops and the regular militia were called into service. It was a tense martial air that these groups created. For all practical purposes, moreover, even the civil law of the community tended to break down in the face of the emergency. Something akin to martial law, with its arbitrary searches and seizures and its summary trials and executions, prevailed until the danger had passed.

Instances when fears of uprisings were not followed by immediate militarization of a wide area of the Southern countryside are practically non-existent. When Gabriel attempted the revolt in Richmond in 1800, the Light Infantry Blues were called into immediate service, the public guard was organized and drilled to help avert the calamity, and Governor Monroe instructed every militia commander in the state to be ready to answer the call to duty.[10] In 1822, when Charleston was thrown into a panic by rumors of Vesey's plot, all kinds of military groups were called into service. A person unfamiliar with the problem doubtless would have thought that such extensive mobilization was for the purpose of meeting some powerful foreign foe. The Neck Rangers, the Charleston Riflemen, the Light Infantry, and the Corps of Hussars were some of the established military organizations called up. A special city guard of one hundred and fifty troops was provided for Charleston. The cry for reinforcement by federal troops was answered before the danger had completely subsided.[11] The attempted revolt of Nat Turner in 1831 brought military assistance, not only from the governor of the state, "acting with his characteristic energy," but from neighboring North Carolina counties, and from the federal government.[12] Indeed, more troops reached Southampton County than were needed or could be accommodated.[13] With artillery companies and a field piece from Fort Monroe, detachments of men from two warships, and hundreds of volunteers and militia men converging on the place, there was every suggestion of a large-scale impending battle.[14]

There was a strong show of military force not only when large-scale plots like those of Gabriel, Vesey, and Turner were uncovered, but also whenever there was any intimation of insurrection, however slight. Even a cursory glance at the accounts of insurrections and threats or rumors of insurrections reveals the role of the military.[15] The rumor of revolt in Louisiana in January 1811, caused Governor Claiborne to call out the militia: a contingent of four hundred militiamen and sixty federal troops left Baton Rouge for the reported scene of action.[16] Two years later the Virginia militia was ordered out to quell a suspected revolt in Lancaster.[17] In 1816 the South Carolina militia took summary action against a group of Negroes suspected of subversive activities.[18] The militia of Onslow County, North Carolina, was so tense during a "Negro hunt" in 1821 that its two detachments mistook each other for the Negro incendiaries and their exchange of fire caused several casualties.[19] Alabama pressed its militia into service in 1841 to search for slave outlaws and to put down rumored uprisings.[20]

Few ante-bellum years were completely free of at least rumors of slave revolts. Agitation for stronger defenses against slave depredations was almost constant, with some leaders advocating a state of continuous preparation for the dreaded day of insurrection. Governor Robert Hayne of South Carolina told the state legislature, "A state of military preparation must always be with us a state of perfect domestic security. A period of profound peace and consequent apathy may expose us to the danger of domestic insurrection."[21] A New Orleans editor called for armed vigilance, adding that "The times are at least urgent for the exercise of the most watchful vigilance over the conduct of slaves and free colored persons." [22]. . .

"DEFENDING THE CORNERSTONE"

Slavery strengthened the military tradition in the South because owners found it desirable, even necessary, to build up a fighting force to keep the slaves under control. They also felt compelled to oppose outside attacks with a militant defense. They regarded the abolitionist attack as a war on their institutions. Calhoun called it "a war of religious and political fanaticism, mingled, on the part of the leaders, with ambition and the love of notoriety." The object being "to humble and debase us in our own estimation, and that of the world in general; to blast our reputation, while they overthrow our domestic institutions." [23] As they read antislavery literature, observed the establishment of organizations dedicated to the destruction of slavery, and felt the sting of "subversive" activities like the Underground Railroad, Southerners reasoned that they were the targets of an all-out offensive war. . . .

As Garrison and his fellows forced the North to consider the danger of the ever increasing slave power, the Southern leaders asserted themselves. From dozens of pens came ardent defenses of a social structure by which they would live or die. . . . They evolved a defense of slavery that was as full of fight as a state militia called out to quell a slave uprising. Chancellor Harper, Professor Dew, Governor Hammond, Fitzhugh, and others seemed aware of the fact that, however sound or logical their proslavery arguments might be, they must infuse in them a fighting spirit. The successful defense of slavery, whether by argument or by force, depended on the development of a powerful justification based on race superiority that would bring to its support all—or almost all—white elements in the South. Thus they redefined the "facts" of history, the "teachings" of the Bible, the "principles" of economics.[24] Convinced that thought could not be free, they believed that there should be some positive modifications of the democratic principles enunciated by the founding fathers. They rejected the equalitarian teachings of Jefferson and asserted that the inequality of man was fundamental to all social organization. There were no rights that were natural or inalienable, they insisted. In his *Disquisition on Government*, Calhoun asserted that liberty was not the right of every man equally. Instead of being born free and equal, men "are born subject not only to parental authority, but to laws and institutions of the country where born, and under whose protection they draw their first breath." [25] Fiery Thomas Cooper stopped working on the South Carolina statutes long enough to observe wryly, "we talk a great deal of nonsense about the rights of man. We say that man is born free, and equal to every other man. Nothing can be more untrue: no human being ever was, now is, or ever will be born free." [26]

In the rejection of the principles of liberty and equality, political democracy was also rejected. "An unmixed democracy," said one Mississippian, "is capricious and unstable, and unless arrested by the hand of despotism, leads to anarchy . . ." There was too much talk about democracy and too little about the aristocratic tradition. "Too much liberty and equality beget a dissolute licentiousness and a contempt for law and order." Virginians and South Carolinians led the demand for a recognition of Southern honor because they were true to their ancient sentiments and "with constant pride they guard their unstained escutcheons." [27] Life, liberty, and the pursuit of happiness were not inalienable rights. Every government, South Carolina's Chancellor William Harper explained, deprives men of life and liberty for offenses against society, while "all the laws of society are intended for nothing else but to restrain men from the pursuit of happiness . . ." It followed, accordingly, that if the possession of a black skin was dangerous to society, then that society had the right to "protect itself by disfranchising the possessor of civil privileges and to continue the disability to his posterity . . ." [28]

It was left to George Fitzhugh, that shrewd professional Southerner, to crystallize and summarize Southern thinking on social organization. Free society was an abject failure, he said; and its frantic, but serious consideration of radical movements like socialism, communism, and anarchism was a clear admission of its failure. If slavery was more widely accepted, man would not need to resort to the "unnatural remedies of woman's rights, limited marriages, voluntary divorces, and free love, as proposed by the abolitionists." [29] Only in a slave society were there proper safeguards against unemployment and all the evils that follow as a country becomes densely settled and the supply of labor exceeds its demand. Fitzhugh, with a sneer at the North, observed that the "invention and use of the word Sociology in a free society and the science of which it treats, and the absence of such word and science in slave society shows that the former is afflicted with disease, the latter healthy." It was bad enough that free communities were failures, but it was intolerable that they should try to impose their impossible practices on the South. "For thirty years," he argued, "the South has been a field on which abolitionists, foreign and domestic, have carried on offensive warfare. Let us now, in turn, act on the offensive, transfer the seat of war, and invade the enemy's territory." [30]

The South's society was to rest on the inequality of men in law and economics. Social efficiency and economic success demanded organization; and organization inevitably meant the enslavement of the ignorant and unfortunate. *Slavery was a positive good.* It was regarded by James H. Hammond as "the greatest of all the great blessings which a kind providence has bestowed." It made possible the transformation of the South from a wilderness into a garden, and gave the owners the leisure in which to cultivate their minds and create a civilization rich in culture and gentility. More than that, it gave to the white man the only basis on which he could do something for a group of "hopelessly and permanently inferior" human beings.[31]

The idea of the inferiority of the Negro enjoyed wide acceptance among Southerners of all classes and was an important ingredient in the theory of society promulgated by Southern leaders. It was organized into a body of systematic thought by the scientists and social scientists of the South, out of which emerged a doctrine of racial superiority to justify any kind of control maintained over the slave. In 1826, Dr. Thomas Cooper had said that he had not the slightest doubt that Negroes were of an "inferior variety of the human species; and not capable of the same improvement as the whites"; [32] but, while a mere chemist was apparently unable to elaborate the theory, the leading physicians of the South were. Dr. S. C. Cartwright of the University of Louisiana was only one of a number of physicians who set themselves up as authorities on the ethnological inferiority of the Negro. In his view, the capacities of the Negro adult for learning were equal to those of a white infant; and the Negro could properly perform certain physiological functions only when under the control of white men. For example, Negroes "under the compulsive power of the white man . . . are made to labor or exercise, which makes the lungs perform a duty of vitalizing the blood more perfectly than is done when they are left free to indulge in idleness. It is the red, vital blood sent to the brain that liberates their mind when under the white man's control; and it is the want of a sufficiency of red, vital blood that chains their mind to ignorance and barbarism when in freedom." Because of his inferiority, liberty and republican institutions were not only unsuited to the Negro, but actually poisonous to his happiness.[33] Variations on this theme were still being played by many Southern "men of science" when Sumter was bombarded. Like racists in other parts of the world, Southerners sought support for their militant racist ideology by developing a common bond with the less privileged. The obvious basis was race, and outside the white race there was to be found no favor from God, no honor or respect from man. Indeed, those beyond the pale were the objects of scorn from the multitudes of the elect.[34] By the time that Europeans were reading Gobineau's *Inequality of Races,* Southerners were reading Cartwright's *Slavery in the Light of Ethnology.* In both cases the authors conceded "good race" to some, and withheld it from others. In admitting all whites into the pseudo-nobility of race, Cartwright won their enthusiastic support in the struggle to preserve the integrity and honor of *the* race.

While uniting the various economically divergent groups of whites, the concept of race also strengthened the ardor of most Southerners to fight for the preservation of slavery. All slaves belonged to a degraded, "inferior" race; and, by the same token, all whites, however wretched some of them might be, were superior. In a race-conscious society whites at the lowest rung could identify themselves with the most privileged and affluent of the community. Thomas R. Dew, Professor of Political Law at the College of William and Mary, made this point clear when he said that in the South "no white man feels such inferiority of rank as to be unworthy of association with those around him. Color alone is here the badge of distinction, the true mark of aristocracy, and all who are white are equal in spite of the variety of occupation." [35] De Bow asserted this even more vigorously in a widely circulated pamphlet published in 1860. At one point, he said that the non-slaveholding class was more deeply interested than any other in the maintenance of Southern institutions. He said that non-slaveholders were made up of two groups: those who desired slaves but were unable to purchase them; and those who were able but preferred to hire cheap white labor. He insisted that there was no group of whites in the South opposed to slavery. One of his principal arguments was that the non-slaveholder preserves the status of the white man "and is not regarded as an inferior or a dependent. . . . No white man at the South serves another as a body servant, to clean his boots, wait on his table, and perform the menial services of his household. His blood revolts against this, and his necessities never drive him to it. He is a companion and an equal." [36]

Southern planters paid considerable attention to the non-slaveholding element whenever its support was needed in the intersectional struggle. Their common origins, at times involving actual kinship of planters and yeomen, gave them a basis for working together in a common cause. The opportunities for social mobility, however rare, provided the dreams of yeomen. These dreams strengthened their attachment to the planter class; while the fear of competition with a large group of freed men was a nightmare. But *race*—the common membership in a superior order of beings of both planters and poorer whites—was apparently the strongest point in the argument that the enslavement of the Negro was as good for small farmers as it was for large planters. The passion of the Southern planter and politician for oratory found ample release in the program to persuade Southern whites that theirs was a glorious civilization to be defended at all costs. In the absence of active and bitter class antagonisms, it was possible for the various white groups to cooperate especially against outside attacks and in behalf of slavery.[37]

Most Southerners were not satisfied merely to have their leaders restate the theory of Southern society and argue with abolitionists in Congress and other respectable places; they wanted to give effective and tangible support to their cause. Chancellor Harper had told them that, in the South as in Athens, "every citizen should be a soldier, and qualified to discharge efficiently the duties of a soldier." [38] In *De Bow's Review* "a Virginian" advised his fellows that *"without ceasing to be free citizens, they must cultivate the virtues, the sentiments, nay, the habits and manners of soldiers."* [39] They should be ready for vigorous, militant action to protect and defend the South's institutions. James Buckingham believed that they were determined to do exactly that. In 1839, he remarked, "Here in Georgia . . . as everywhere throughout the South, slavery is a topic upon which no man, and, above all, a foreigner, can open his lips without imminent personal danger, unless it is to defend and uphold the system." He stated further that the violence of the measures taken against the few who ventured to speak in favor of abolition was such as to strike terror in others.[40]

There was no strong antislavery sentiment in the Southern states after 1830. Moreover, Northern antislavery organizations were doing little to incite the slaves to revolt or, except for sporadic underground railroad activities, to engage in other subversive activities. It was enough, however, for Southerners to believe either that abolitionists were active or that there was a possibility of their becoming active. This belief, running very strong at times, placed under suspicion everything Northern, including persons and ideas. . . .

After 1830, the South increased its vigilance over outside subversion, and pursued the elusive, at times wholly imaginary, abolitionist with an ardor born of desperation. When they could not lay hands on him they seized the incendiary publications that were the products of his "fiend-ish" mind. In the summer of 1835, overpowering the city guard, they stormed the post office in Charleston and burned a bag of abolitionist literature. According to the postmaster, this act was not perpetrated by any "ignorant or infuriated rabble." [41] In the same year, citizens of Fairfax County, Virginia, formed local vigilance committees in each militia district "to detect and bring to speedy punishment all persons circulating abolitionist literature." A correspondence committee of twenty was to keep in touch with developments in other parts of the South.[42] . . .

All over the South mob action began to replace orderly judicial procedure, as the feeling against abolitionists mounted and as South-ern views on race became crystallized. Even in North Carolina, where one citizen felt that there should be some distinction between that "civilized state and Mississippi and some other Western states," the fear of abolitionists caused many of its citizens to resort to drastic measures.[43] In 1850, two missionaries, Adam Crooks and Jesse Mc-Bride, came into the state from Ohio, ostensibly to preach to these North Carolina Methodists who had not joined the newly organized Methodist Episcopal Church, South.[44] Soon they were suspected of abolitionist activities, and McBride was convicted of distributing incen-diary publications. According to one source they were "mobed and drove out of Gulford." Ten years later a vigilance committee threatened to deal violently with one John Stafford whose crime had been to give food and shelter to Crooks and McBride during their sojourn in the state.[45] This was the kind of activity that Professor Benjamin S. Hedrick, dismissed from the University of North Carolina for his free-soil views, deprecated. Safe in New York City he asked Thomas Ruffin, Chief Justice of the North Carolina Supreme Court, to use his influ-ence "to arrest the terrorism and fanaticism" that was rampant in the South. "If the same spirit of terror, mobs, arrests and violence con-tinue," he declared, "it will not be long before civil war will rage at the South." [46]

NOTES

1. Howell M. Henry, *The Police Control of the Slave in South Carolina* (Emory, Virginia, 1914), pp. 31ff.

2. Charles S. Davis, *The Cotton Kingdom in Alabama* (Montgomery, 1939), p. 97; and Charles S. Sydnor, *Slavery in Mississippi* (New York, 1933), p. 78.

3. *The Code of Alabama* (Montgomery, 1852), p. 235.

4. *Ibid.*, p. 235 and John B. Miller, *A Collection of the Militia Laws of the United States and South Carolina* (Columbia, 1817), pp. 71ff.

5. Henry, *Police Control*, p. 40.

6. *Ibid.*, p. 32.

7. Sydnor, *Slavery in Mississippi*, p. 78; and Davis, *Cotton Kingdom in Alabama*, p. 97.

8. Edwin Clifford Holland, *A Refutation of the Calumnies Circulated Against the Southern and Western States Respecting the Institution and Existence of Slavery Among Them* (Charleston, 1822), pp. 61, 82.

9. Olmsted, *Back Country*, p. 203.

10. William Asbury Christian, *Richmond, Her Past and Present* (Richmond, 1912), p. 53; Herbert Aptheker, *American Negro Slave Revolts* (New York, 1943), pp. 218ff; and George Morgan, *The Life of James Monroe* (Boston, 1921), p. 228.

11. Theodore D. Jervey, *Robert Y. Hayne and His Times* (New York, 1909), pp. 131-132; Aptheker, *Slave Revolts*, pp. 273ff; and Henry, *Police Control*, pp. 152-153.

12. *Nashville Republican*, September 10, 1831.

13. *Norfolk Herald*, August 21, 1831, reprinted in *Nashville Republican*, September 10, 1831.

14. Frederick T. Wilson, *Federal Aid in Domestic Disturbances, 1787–1903* (Washington, 1903), pp. 56, 261-263.

15. In *American Negro Slave Revolts*, Aptheker calls attention to many instances in which military forces were used in connection with slave uprisings.

16. Charles Gayarré, *History of Louisiana* (New Orleans, 1903), IV, 267-268.

17. Aptheker, *Slave Revolts*, p. 255.

18. Harvey T. Cook, *The Life and Legacy of David Rogerson Williams* (New York, 1916), p. 130.

19. Guion G. Johnson, *Ante-Bellum North Carolina* (Chapel Hill, 1937), pp. 514-515.

20. Aptheker, *Slave Revolts*, p. 335.

21. *Journal of the Legislature of South Carolina for the Year 1833*, p. 6.

22. *Daily Picayune*, December 24, 1856.

23. John C. Calhoun, *The Works of John C. Calhoun* (New York, 1854), I, 483-484.

24. *Southern Literary Messenger*, XXIII (October 1856), 247.

25. Calhoun, *Works*, II, 58-59.

26. Jenkins, *Pro-slavery Thought*, p. 125.

27. Quoted in Edward Ingle, *Southern Sidelights* (New York, 1896), p. 31.

28. William Harper, *The Pro-slavery Argument* (Philadelphia, 1853), p. 11.

29. George Fitzhugh, *Cannibals All! or Slaves Without Masters* (Richmond, 1857), pp. 97-98.

30. George Fitzhugh, *Sociology for the South; or The Failure of Free Society* (Richmond, 1854), p. 222.

31. *Selections From the Letters and Speeches of the Hon. James H. Hammond of South Carolina* (New York, 1866), p. 34.

32. Thomas Cooper to Mahlon Dickerson, March 16, 1826, in "Letters of Dr. Thomas Cooper, 1825-1832," *American Historical Review*, VI (July, 1901), 729. The idea of Negro inferiority was believed by some Northerners,

but it neither was as widespread in that section nor did it constitute a whole body of thought as it did in the South.

33. S. C. Cartwright, "Diseases and Peculiarities of the Negro," *The Industrial Resources, etc., of the Southern and Western States* (New Orleans, 1853), II, 316.

34. See Alfred Vagts, *A History of Militarism* (New York, 1937), pp. 165, 479.

35. Thomas R. Dew, *Review of the Debate in the Virginia Legislature of 1831 and 1832* (Richmond, 1832), pp. 112-113.

36. J. D. B. De Bow, *The Interest in Slavery of the Southern Non-Slaveholder* (Charleston, 1860), pp. 3, 5, 8-10.

37. For discussions of inter-class harmony in the South see Frank L. Owsley, *Plain Folk of the Old South* (Baton Rouge, 1949), pp. 133-134; and Paul H. Buck, "Poor Whites of the Ante-Bellum South," *American Historical Review,* XXXI (October 1925), 41, 51-52.

38. Harper, *Pro-slavery Argument,* p. 80.

39. "The Black Race in North America," *De Bow's Review,* XX (February 1856), 209. (Italics in original.)

40. Buckingham, *Slave States,* I, 183.

41. Alfred Huger to Amos Kendall, July 30, 1855, in Theodore D. Jervey, *Robert Y. Hayne,* pp. 379-380.

42. Eaton, "Mob Violence," p. 358.

43. David W. Stone to Thomas Ruffin, May 3, 1842, in J. G. de Roulhac Hamilton, editor, *The Papers of Thomas Ruffin* (Raleigh, 1918), II, 206.

44. For a detailed account of the experiences of Crooks and McBride, see Eaton, *Freedom of Thought,* pp. 138-139.

45. John Stafford to Thomas Ruffin, January 24, 1860, in Hamilton, *Papers of Thomas Ruffin,* II, 65-67.

46. Benjamin S. Hedrick to Thomas Ruffin, January 16, 1860, in *Papers of Thomas Ruffin,* III, 64-65.

● *The slaveholder was also an American, a democrat, and a believer in libertarian principles. For many Southerners it proved difficult to resolve the contradiction between assuming the beneficence of slavery yet maintaining a democratic creed on other matters. Charles Sellers describes the dilemma posed for the white South by this conflict of ideologies.*

The Travail of Slavery

CHARLES GRIER SELLERS, JR.

The American experience knows no greater tragedy than the Old South's twistings and turnings on the rack of slavery. Others suffered more from the "peculiar institution," but only the suffering of white Southerners fits the classic formula for tragedy. Like no other Americans before or since, the white men of the ante-bellum South drove toward catastrophe by doing conscious violence to their truest selves. No picture of the Old South as a section confident and united in its dedication to a neo-feudal social order, and no explanation of the Civil War as a conflict between "two civilizations," can encompass the complexity and pathos of the ante-bellum reality. No analysis that misses the inner turmoil of the ante-bellum Southerner can do justice to the central tragedy of the southern experience.*

The key to the tragedy of southern history is the paradox of the slaveholding South's devotion to "liberty." Whenever and wherever Southerners sought to invoke their highest social values—in schoolboy declamations, histories, Fourth of July orations, toasts, or newspaper editorials—"liberty" was the incantation that sprang most frequently and most fervently from their lips and pens. "The love of liberty had taken deep root in the minds of carolinians [sic] long before the

Charles Grier Sellers, Jr., "The Travail of Slavery," from Sellers (ed.), *The Southerner as American* (Chapel Hill: University of North Carolina Press, 1960), 40-71. Reprinted by permission .

* My interpretation of the Old South draws heavily on the brilliant insights of Wilbur J. Cash in *The Mind of the South* (New York, 1941), and also on Clement Eaton's *Freedom of Thought in the Old South* (Durham, 1940).

172

revolution," explained South Carolina's historian David Ramsay in 1809. The "similarity of state and condition" produced by the early settlers' struggle to subdue the wilderness had "inculcated the equality of rights" and "taught them the rights of man." [1]

The Revolutionary struggle made this implicit colonial liberalism explicit and tied it to patriotic pride in the new American Union. From this time on, for Southerners as for other Americans, liberty was the end for which the Union existed, while the Union was the instrument by which liberty was to be extended to all mankind. Thus the Fourth of July, the birthday of both liberty and Union, became the occasion for renewing the liberal idealism and the patriotic nationalism which united Americans of all sections at the highest levels of political conviction. "The Declaration of Independence, and the Constitution of the United States—Liberty and Union, now and forever, one and inseparable," ran a Virginian's toast on July 4, 1850. The same sentiment and almost the same phrases might have been heard in any part of the South in any year of the ante-bellum period.[2]

Now "liberty" can mean many things, but the Old South persistently used the word in the universalist sense of the eighteenth-century Enlightenment. At Richmond in 1826 John Tyler eulogized Jefferson as "the devoted friend of man," who "had studied his rights in the great volume of nature, and saw with rapture the era near at hand, when those rights should be proclaimed, and the world aroused from the slumber of centuries." Jefferson's fame would not be confined to Americans, said Tyler, for his Declaration of Independence would be known wherever "man, so long the victim of oppression, awakes from the sleep of ages and bursts his chains." The conservative, slaveholding Tyler would soon be indicted by northern writers as a leader of the "slave power conspiracy" against human freedom; yet in 1826 he welcomed the day "when the fires of liberty shall be kindled on every hill and shall blaze in every valley," to proclaim that "the mass of mankind have not been born with saddles on their backs, nor a favored few booted and spurred to ride them. . . ." [3]

Although a massive reaction against liberalism is supposed to have seized the southern mind in the following decades, the Nullifiers of the thirties and the radical southern sectionalists of the forties and fifties did not ignore or reject the Revolutionary tradition of liberty so much as they transformed it, substituting for the old emphasis on the natural rights of all men a new emphasis on the rights and autonomy of communities. It was ironic that these slaveholding defenders of liberty against the tyranny of northern domination had to place themselves in the tradition of '76 at all, and the irony was heightened by their failure to escape altogether its universalist implications. Even that fire-eater of fire-eaters, Robert Barnwell Rhett, declaimed on "liberty" so constantly and so indiscriminately that John Quincy Adams could call him "a compound of wild democracy and iron bound slavery." [4]

Indeed the older nationalist-universalist conception of liberty remained very much alive in the South, and Southerners frequently used it to rebuke the radical sectionalists. Denouncing nullification in 1834, a Savannah newspaper vehemently declared that Georgians would never join in this assault on America's Revolutionary heritage. "No!" said the editor, "the light of the 4th of July will stream across their path, to remind them that liberty was not won in a day. . . ." Even a Calhounite could proudly assure an Independence Day audience in Virginia a few years later that American principles were destined "to work an entire revolution in the face of human affairs" and "to elevate the great mass of mankind." In NorthCarolina in the forties, citizens continued to toast "The Principles of the American Revolution —Destined to revolutionize the civilized world"; and editors rejoiced that the Fourth sent rays of light "far, far into the dark spots of oppressed distant lands." In Charleston itself a leading newspaper proclaimed that Americans were "the peculiar people, chosen of the Lord, to keep the vestal flame of liberty, as a light unto the feet and a lamp unto the path of the benighted nations, who yet slumber or groan under the bondage of tyranny." [5]   Throughout the ante-bellum period the South's invocation of liberty was reinforced by its fervent devotion to the Union. "America shall reach a height beyond the ken of mortals," exclaimed a Charleston orator in the 1820's; and through the following decades Southerners continued to exult with other Americans over their country's unique advantages and brilliant destiny. The Old South's Americanism sometimes had a surprisingly modern ring, as when a conservative Georgia newspaper called on "True Patriots" to join the Whigs in defending the "American Way" against the "Red Republicanism" of the Democratic party. Even that bellwether of radical Southernism, De Bow's Review, printed article after article proclaiming the glorious destiny of the United States.[6]

To the very eve of the Civil War the Fourth of July remained a widely observed festival of liberty and union in the South. By 1854, a hard-pressed orator was complaining that there was nothing fresh left to say: "The Stars and Stripes have been so vehemently flourished above admiring crowds of patriotic citizens that there is hardly a rhetorical shred left of them. . . . The very Union would almost be dissolved by eulogizing it at such a melting temperature." The rising tide of sectional antagonism did somewhat dampen Independence Day enthusiasm in the late fifties, but even after the Civil War began, one southern editor saw "no reason why the birth of liberty should be permitted to pass unheeded wherever liberty has votaries. . . . The accursed Yankees are welcome to the exclusive use of their 'Doodle' but let the South hold on tenaciously to Washington's March and Washington's Principles and on every recurring anniversary of the promulgation of the Declaration, reassert the great principles of Liberty." [7]

What are we to make of these slaveholding champions of liberty? Was the ante-bellum Southerner history's most hypocritical casuist? Or were these passionate apostrophes to the liberty of distant peoples a disguised protest against, or perhaps an escape from, the South's daily betrayal of its liberal self? Southerners were at least subconsciously aware of the "detestable paradox" of "our every-day sentiments of liberty" while holding human beings in slavery, and many Southerners had made it painfully explicit in the early days of the republic.[8]

A Virginian was amazed that "a people who have declared 'That all men are by nature equally free and independent' and have made this declaration the first article in the foundation of their government, should in defiance of so sacred a truth, recognized by themselves in so solemn a manner, and on so important an occasion, tolerate a practice incompatible therewith." Similarly, in neighboring Maryland, a leading politician expressed his astonishment that the people of the Old Free State "do not blush at the very name of Freedom." Was not Maryland, asked William Pinkney, "at once the fair temple of freedom, and the abominable nursery of slaves; the school for patriots, and the foster-mother of petty despots; the asserter of human rights, and the patron of wanton oppression?" "It will not do," he insisted, "thus to talk like philosophers, and act like unrelenting tyrants; to be perpetually sermonizing it with liberty for our text and actual oppression for our commentary." [9]

Still another leading Marylander pointed out that America's Revolutionary struggle had been "grounded upon the *preservation of those rights* to which God and nature entitled *us* not in *particular*, but in common with *all the rest of mankind*." The retention of slavery, declared Luther Martin in 1788, was "a solemn mockery of, and insult to, that God whose protection we had then implored, and could not fail to hold us up to detestation, and render us contemptible to every true friend of liberty in the world." During the Revolution said Martin "when our liberties were at stake we warmly felt for the common rights of men." [10]

Martin did not exaggerate the inclusiveness of the liberal idealism that had accompanied the Revolutionary War in the southern states. Many of the Revolutionary county committees had denounced slavery, and Virginia's Revolutionary convention of 1774 had declared its abolition to be "the greatest object of desire in those colonies where it was unhappily introduced in their infant state." The implications of universalist liberalism for slavery were recognized most clearly, perhaps, by the Georgia county committee which resolved early in 1775 "to show the world that we are not influenced by any contracted motives, but a general philanthropy for all mankind, of whatever climate, language, or complexion," by using its best endeavors to elminate "the unnatural practice of slavery." [11]

It is well known that the South's great statesmen of the Revolutionary generation almost unanimously condemned slavery as incompatible with the nation's liberal principles. Though these elder statesmen proved incapable of solving the problem, Thomas Jefferson consoled himself with the thought that it could safely be left to the "young men, grown up, and growing up," who "have sucked in the principles of liberty, as it were, with their mother's milk." [12] Such young men did indeed grow up, and they kept most Southerners openly apologetic about slavery for fifty years following the Declaration of Independence.

When, in the mid-thirties, John C. Calhoun declared on the floor of the Senate that slavery was "a good—a great good," one of Jefferson's protégés and former law students was there to denounce "the obsolete and revolting theory of human rights and human society by which, of late, the institution of domestic slavery had been sustained and justified by some of its advocates in a portion of the South." Slavery was "a misfortune and an evil in all circumstances," said Virginia's Senator William C. Rives, and he would never "deny, as has been done by this new school, the natural freedom and equality of man; to contend that slavery is a positive good." He would never "attack the great principles which lie at the foundation of our political system," or "revert to the dogmas of Sir Robert Filmer, exploded a century and a half ago by the immortal works of Sidney and Locke." [13] *

* Almost as significant as Rives' own position is the fact that he touched Calhoun at a tender point when he associated him with the anti-libertarian Filmer. The South Carolinian "utterly denied that his doctrines had any thing to do with the tenets of Sir Robert Filmer, which he abhorred." "So far from holding with the dogmas of that writer, he had been the known and open advocate of freedom from the beginning." Calhoun was reported as saying. "Nor was there any thing in the doctrines he held in the slightest degree inconsistent with the highest and purest principles of freedom."

Though open anti-slavery utterances grew infrequent after the 1830's, the generation which was to dominate southern life in the forties and fifties had already come to maturity with values absorbed from the afterglow of Revolutionary liberalism. On the eve of the Civil War *De Bow's Review* was to complain that during these earlier years, "when probably a majority of even our own people regarded the existence of slavery among us as a blot on our fair name . . . our youth [were allowed] to peruse, even in their tender years, works in which slavery was denounced as an unmitigated evil." [14] Some of these youngsters had drawn some vigorous conclusions. "How contradictory" was slavery to every principle of "a republican Government where liberty is the boast and pride of its free citizens," exclaimed the son of a slaveholding family in South Carolina. Similarly a fifteen-year-old Tennessee boy called slavery "a foul, a deadly blot . . . in a nation boasting of the republicanism of her principles" and owing allegiance to "the sacred rights of man." [15]

A whole generation cannot transform its most fundamental values by a mere effort of will. Though Southerners tended during the latter part of the ante-bellum period to restrict their publicly voiced libertarian hopes to "oppressed distant lands," the old liberal misgivings about slavery did not die. Instead they burrowed beneath the surface of the southern mind, where they kept gnawing away the shaky foundations on which Southerners sought to rebuild their morale and self-confidence as a slaveholding people.

Occasionally the doubts were exposed, as in 1857, when Congressman L. D. Evans of Texas lashed out at the general repudiation of liberalism to which some defenders of slavery had been driven. The doctrine of human inequality and subordination might do for the dark ages of tyranny, he declared, "but emanating from the lips of a Virginia professor, or a statesman of Carolina, it startles the ear, and shocks the moral sense of a republican patriot." But Evans only illustrated the hopelessness of the southern dilemma by his tortured argument for transforming slavery into a kind of serfdom which would somehow preserve the slave's "natural equality," while gradually evolving into a state of "perfect equality." [16]

The same year a Charleston magazine admitted that "We are perpetually aiming to square the maxims of an inpracticable philosophy with the practice which nature and circumstances force upon us." Yet on the very eve of war, few Southerners were ready to resolve the dilemma by agreeing with the writer that "the [liberal] philosophy of the North is a dead letter to us." [17]

If the Southerner had been embarrassed by his devotion to liberty and Union alone, he would have had less trouble easing his mind on the subject of slavery. But as a Virginia legislator exclaimed in 1832, "This, sir, is a Christian community." Southerners "read in their Bibles, 'Do unto all men as you would have them do unto you'; and this golden rule and slavery are hard to reconcile." [18] During those early decades of the nineteenth century, when the South was confessing the evils of slavery, it had been swept by a wave of evangelical orthodoxy. Though the wave crested about the time some Southerners, including some clergymen, began speaking of slavery as a positive good, it does not follow that the evangelical reaction against the eighteenth century's religious ideas contributed significantly to the reaction against the eighteenth century's liberalism with regard to slavery.

On the contrary, the evangelical denominations had strong anti-slavery tendencies. Methodists, Quakers, and Baptists nurtured an extensive abolitionist movement in the upper South during the twenties, when the rest of the country was largely indifferent to the slavery question; and the Presbyterians were still denouncing slavery in Kentucky a decade later. It would be closer to the truth to suggest that as Southerners wrestled with their consciences over slavery, they may have gained a first-hand experience with the concepts of sin and evil that made them peculiarly susceptible to Christian orthodoxy. At any rate, as late as 1849, a pro-slavery professor at the University of Alabama complained to Calhoun that no one had yet published a satisfactory defense of slavery in the light of New Testament teachings. The "many religious people at the South who have strong misgivings on this head," he warned, constituted a greater threat to the peculiar institution than the northern abolitionists.[19]

Even the irreligious found it hard to resist the claims of simple humanity or to deny that slaves, as one Southerner put it, "have hearts and feelings like other men." And those who were proof against the appeals to Revolutionary liberalism, Christianity, and humanity, still faced the arguments of Southerners in each succeeding generation that slavery was disastrous to the whites. Jefferson's famous lament that the slaveholder's child, "nursed, educated, and daily exercised in tyranny . . . must be a prodigy who can retain his manners and morals undepraved," was frequently echoed. George Mason's lament that slavery discouraged manufactures, caused the poor to despise labor, and prevented economic development, found many seconders in Virginia's slavery debate of 1831–32 and received elaborate statistical support from Hinton Rowan Helper in the fifties. The seldom mentioned but apparently widespread practice of miscegenation was an especially heavy cross for the women of the South. "Under slavery we live surrounded by prostitutes," wrote one woman bitterly. ". . . Any lady is ready to tell you who is the father of all the mulatto children in everybody's household but her own. . . . My disgust sometimes is boiling over." [20]

It is essential to understand that the public declarations of Southerners never revealed the full impact of all these anti-slavery influences on the southern mind. Fear of provoking slave insurrections had restrained free discussion of slavery even in the Revolutionary South, and an uneasy society exerted steadily mounting pressure against anti-slavery utterances thereafter. Only when Nat Turner's bloody uprising of 1831 shocked Southerners into open debate over the peculiar institution did the curtain of restraint part sufficiently to reveal the intensity of their misgivings. Thomas Ritchie's influential Richmond *Enquirer* caught the mood of that historic moment when it quoted a South Carolinian as exclaiming, "We may shut our eyes and avert our faces, if we please, but there it is, the dark and growing evil at our doors; and meet the question we must, at no distant day. . . . What is to be done? Oh! my God, I do not know, but something must be done." [21]

Many were ready to say what had to be done, especially a brilliant galaxy of the liberty-loving young Virginians on whom the dying Jefferson had pinned his hopes. "I will not rest until slavery is abolished in Virginia," vowed Governor John Floyd; and during the winter of 1831–32 a deeply earnest Virginia legislature was wrapped in the Old South's only free and full debate over slavery. Not a voice was raised to justify human servitude in the abstract, while a score of Virginians attacked the peculiar institution with arguments made deadly by the South's endemic liberalism and Christianity. Two years later a Tennessee constitutional convention showed a tender conscience on slavery by admitting that "to prove it to be an evil is an easy task." Yet in both states proposals for gradual emancipation were defeated.[22]

The outcome was no surprise to the editor of the Nashville *Republican*. Few would question the moral evil of slavery, he had written back in 1825, "but then the assent to a proposition is not always followed by acting in uniformity to its spirit." Too many Southerners believed, perhaps from "the exercise of an interested casuistry," that nature had ordained the Negro to slavery by giving him a peculiar capacity for labor under the southern sun. Furthermore, southern white men would have to "be convinced that to labor personally is a more agreeable, and desirable occupation, than to command, & superintend the labor of others." Consequently, "as long as slavery is conceived to advance the pecuniary interests of individuals, they will be slow to relish, and reluctant to encourage, any plan for its abolition. They will quiet their consciences with the reflection that it was entailed upon us —that it has grown up with the institutions of the country—and that the establishment of a new order of things would be attended with great difficulty, and might be perilous." [23]

Thus when Nat Turner frightened Southerners into facing squarely the tragic ambiguity of their society, they found the price for resolving it too high. The individual planter's economic stake in slavery was a stubborn and perhaps insurmountable obstacle to change; and even Jefferson's nerve had failed at the task of reconstituting the South's social system to assimilate a host of Negro freedmen.

The whole South sensed that a fateful choice had been made. Slowly and reluctantly Southerners faced the fact that, if slavery were to be retained, things could not go on as before. The slaves were restive, a powerful anti-slavery sentiment was sweeping the western world, and southern minds were not yet nerved for a severe struggle in defense of the peculiar institution to which they were now committed. The South could no longer ease its conscience with hopes for the eventual disappearance of slavery, or tolerate such hopes in any of its people. "It is not enough for them to believe that slavery has been entailed upon us by our forefathers," proclaimed Calhoun's national newspaper organ. "We must satisfy the consciences, we must allay the fears of our own people. We must satisfy them that slavery is of itself right—that it is not a sin against God—that it not an evil, moral or political. . . . In this way, and this way only, can we prepare our own people to defend their institutions." [24] So southern leaders of the Calhoun school began trying to convince themselves and others that slavery was a "positive good," white southern legislatures abridged freedom of speech and press, made manumission difficult or impossible, and imposed tighter restrictions on both slaves and free Negroes. The Great Reaction was under way.

Yet the Great Reaction, for all its formidable façade and terrible consequences, was a fraud. Slavery simply could not be blended with liberalism and Christianity, while liberalism and Christianity were too deeply rooted in the southern mind to be torn up overnight. Forced to smother and distort their most fundamental convictions by the decision to maintain slavery, and goaded by criticism based on these same convictions, Southerners of the generation before the Civil War suffered the most painful loss of social morale and identity that any large group of Americans has ever experienced.

The surface unanimity enforced on the South in the forties and fifties by the Great Reaction concealed a persistent hostility to slavery. It is true that large numbers of the most deeply committed anti-slavery men left the South. They were usually men of strong religious conviction, such as Levi Coffin, the North Carolina Quaker who moved to Indiana to become the chief traffic manager of the Underground Railroad, or Will Breckinridge, the Kentucky Presbyterian who declared "I care little where I go—so that I may only get where every man I see is as free as myself." In fact the national banner of political anti-slavery was carried in the forties by the former Alabama slaveholder, James G. Birney, who had rejected slavery for the same reasons that bothered many other Southerners—because it was "inconsistent with the Great Truth that all men are created equal, . . . as well as the great rule of benevolence delivered to us by the Savior Himself that in all things whatsoever ye would that men should do unto you do ye even so to them." [25]

Many zealous anti-slavery men remained in the South, however, to raise their voices wherever the Great Reaction relaxed its grip. If this almost never happened in the lower South, a dissenter in western Virginia could exult in 1848 that "anti-slavery papers and anti-slavery orators are scattering far and wide the seeds of freedom, and an immense number of persons are uttering vaticinations in contemplation of a day of emancipation"; while the reckless courage of Cassius Clay and his allies kept the anti-slavery cause alive in Kentucky. "The contention of planter politicians that the South had achieved social and political unity," concludes the ablest student of the peculiar institution, "appears, then, to have been the sheerest of wishful thinking." [26]

Far more significant than outright anti-slavery opinion was the persistent disquietude over slavery among the many white Southerners who found the new pro-slavery dogmas hard to swallow. The official southern view held that slaveholders "never inquire into the propriety of the matter, . . . they see their neighbors buying slaves, and they buy them . . . leaving to others to discuss the right and justice of the thing." In moments of unusual candor, however, the pro-slavery propagandists admitted the prevalence of misgivings. Calhoun's chief editorial spokesman thought, the principal danger of northern abolitionism was its influence upon "the consciences and fears of the slave-holders themselves." Through "the insinuation of their dangerous heresies into our schools, our pulpits, and our domestic circles," Duff Green warned, the abolitionists might succeed in "alarming the consciences of the weak and feeble, and diffusing among our own people a morbid sensitivity on the question of slavery." [27]

Slavery's apologists were particularly irritated by the numerous instances "in which the superstitious weakness of dying men . . . induces them, in their last moments, to emancipate their slaves." Every manumission was an assault on the peculiar institution and a testimony to the tenacity with which older values resisted the pro-slavery dogmas. "Let our women and old men, and persons of weak and infirm minds, be disabused of the false . . . notion that slavery is sinful, and that they will peril their souls if they do not disinherit their offspring by emancipating their slaves!" complained a Charleston editor in the fifties. It was high time masters "put aside all care or thought what Northern people say about them." [28]

Yet the manumissions went on, despite mounting legal obstacles. The census reported more than 3,000 for 1860, or one manumission for every 1,309 slaves, which was double the number reported ten years before. If this figure seems small, it should be remembered that these manumissions were accomplished against "almost insuperable obstacles"—not only southern laws prohibiting manumission or making it extremely difficult, but also northern laws barring freed Negroes. The evidence indicates that there would have been many more manumissions if the laws had been more lenient, and if masters had not feared that the freed Negroes would be victimized. [29]

The explanations advanced by men freeing their slaves illustrate the disturbing influence of liberalism and Christianity in the minds of many slaveholders. A Virginia will affirmed the testator's belief "that slavery in all its forms . . . is inconsistent with republican principles, that it is a violation of our bill of rights, which declared, *that all men are by nature equally free*; and above all, that it is repugnant to the spirit of the gospel, which enjoins universal love and benevolence." A North Carolinian listed four reasons for freeing his slaves: (1) "Agreeably to the rights of man, every human being, be his colour what it may, is entitled to freedom"; (2) "My conscience, the great criterion, condemns me for keeping them in slavery") (3) "The golden rule directs us to do unto every human creature, as we would wish to be done unto"; and (4) "I wish to die with a clear conscience, that I may not be ashamed to appear before my master in a future World." In Tennessee, one man freed his slave woman because he wanted her to "Enjoy Liberty and the birthright of all Mankind." Another not only believed "it to be the duty of a Christian to deal with his fellow man in a state of bondage with humanity and kindness," but also feared that his own "happiness *hereafter*" depended on the disposition he made of his slaves. Still another, after ordering two slaves freed, hoped that "no one will offer to undo what my conscience tole me was my duty," and that "my children will consider it so and folow the futsteps of their father and keep now [no] slaves longer than they pay for their raising and expenses." [30]

But conscience was a problem for many more Southerners than those who actually freed their slaves, as the pro-slavery philosophers were compelled to recognize. "I am perfectly aware that slavery is repugnant to the *natural* emotions of men," confessed William J. Grayson on the eve of the Civil War. James H. Hammond was one of many who sought to quiet the troublesome southern conscience by picturing slavery as an eleemosynary institution, maintained at considerable cost by generous slaveholders. Southerners must content themselves, said Hammond, with "the consoling reflection, that what is lost to us is gained to humanity." Grayson, on the other hand, despaired of quieting conscience and concluded grimly that conscience itself must be discredited. "I take the stand on the position that our natural feelings are unsafe guides for us to follow in the social relations." [31]

But a host of Southerners, perhaps including Grayson and Hammond, could neither satisfy nor ignore their consciences. One troubled master confided to his wife, "I sometimes think my feelings unfit me for a slaveholder." A North Carolina planter told his son that he could not discipline his slaves properly, believing that slavery was a violation of "the natural rights of a being who is as much entitled to the enjoyment of liberty as myself." In the rich Mississippi Delta country, where many of the largest slaveholders remained loyal to the Union in 1861, one man had long sought "some means . . . to rid us of slavery, because I never had any great fondness for the institution although I had been the owner of slaves from my youth up." Another Mississippi slaveholder was "always an abolitionist at heart," but "did not know how to set them free without wretchedness to them, and utter ruin to myself." Still another "owned slaves & concluded if I was merciful & humane to them I might just as well own them as other Persons . . . [but] I had an instinctive horror of the institution." How many masters held such opinions privately can never be known, but observers at the close of the Civil War noted a surprisingly general feeling of relief over the destruction of slavery. An upcountry South Carolinian certainly spoke for many Southerners when he said, "I am glad the thing is done away with; it was more plague than pleasure, more loss than profit."

The nub of the Southerner's ambivalent attitude toward slavery was his inability to regard the slave consistently as either person or property. Slaves "were a species of property that differed from all others," James K. Polk declared as a freshman congressman, "they were rational; they were human beings." [33] The slaves indeterminate status was writ large in the ambiguity of the whole structure of southern society. A sociologist has analyzed the institutional features of slavery as lying along a "rationality-traditionalism range," whose polar points were mutually contradictory. At one pole lay the economic view. Since slavery was a labor system employed in a highly competitive market economy, a minimum of rational efficiency was necessarily prescribed for economic survival. This called for a "sheerly economic" view of slavery, one which regarded the slave as property, which gave the master unlimited control over the slave's person, which evaluated the treatment of slaves wholly in terms of economic efficiency, which structured the slaves situation so that his self-interest in escaping the lash became his sole motivation to obedience, which sanctioned the domestic slave trade and demanded resumption of the foreign slave trade as essential mechanisms for supplying and redistributing labor, and which dismissed moral considerations as both destructive of the labor supply and irrelevant. Though the plantation system tended during the latter part of the slavery period to approach the ideal type of a purely commercial economic organization, especially with the geographical shift to the new lands of the Southwest, few if any Southerners ever fully accepted this "sheerly economic" view of slavery.

At the other pole lay a "traditional" or "familial" view, which regarded the slave more as person than property and idealized "the patriarchial organization of plantation life and the maintenance of the family estate and family slaves at all costs." Both the "sheerly economic" and the "familial" views of slavery were sanctioned by southern society; economics and logic drove Southerners toward the former, while sentiment, liberalism, and Christianity dragged them in the other direction. [34]

This fundamental ambivalence was most clearly apparent in the law of slavery. Early colonial law had justified the enslavement of Negroes on the ground that they were heathens, so that the conversion of slaves to Christianity raised a serious problem. Though the Negro was continued in bondage, the older conviction that conversion and slave status were incompatible died hard, as was demonstrated by the successive enactments required to establish the new legal definition of slavery on the basis of the Negro's race rather than his heathenism. Even then problems remained. Not all Negroes were slaves, and the South could never bring itself to reduce free Negroes to bondage. Moreover the slave's admission to the privilege of salvation inevitably identified him as a person. But slavery could not be viewed as a legal relationship between legal persons; in strict logic it had to be a chattel arrangement that left the slave no legal personality.

Was the slave a person or merely property in the eyes of the law? This question southern legislatures and courts never settled. He could not legally marry, own property, sue or be sued, testify, or make contracts; yet he was legally responsible for crimes he committed, and others were responsible for crimes committed against him. The ambiguity was most striking in the case of a slave guilty of murder; as a person he was responsible and could be executed; but he was also property, and if the state took his life, his owner had to be compensated. "The slave is put on trial as a *human being*," declared a harrassed court in one such case. "Is it not inconsistent, in the progress of the trial, to treat him as property, like . . . a horse, in the value of which the owner has a pecuniary interest which makes him incompetent as a witness?" [35]

The Southerner's resistance to the legal logic of making slavery a simple property arrangement is amply illustrated in court decisions. "A slave is not in the condition of a horse," said a Tennessee judge. "He has mental capacities, and an immortal principle in his nature." The laws did not "extinguish his high-born nature nor deprive him of many rights which are inherent in men." Similarly a Mississippi court declared that it would be "a stigma upon the character of the State" if a slave could be murdered "without subjecting the offender to the highest penalty known to the criminal jurisprudence of the country. Has the slave no rights, because he is deprived of his freedom? He is still a human being, and possesses all those rights of which he is not deprived by the positive provision of the law." [36]

The anguish induced by the legal logic of slavery was expressed most clearly in a North Carolina decision. Recognizing the objectives of slavery to be "the profit of the master, his security and the public safety," and recognizing the slave to be "doomed in his own person, and his posterity, to live without knowledge, and without the capacity to make any thing his own, and to toil that another may reap the fruits," the court concluded that, "Such services can only be expected from one . . . who surrenders his will in implicit obedience to that of another. . . . The power of the master must be absolute." The judge felt "as deeply as any man can" the harshness of this proposition. "As a principle of moral rights, every person in his retirement must repudiate it.

. . . It constitutes the curse of slavery to both the bond and the free portions of our population. But it is inherent in the relation of masters and slaves." [37]

The slave's indeterminate status was not just a legal problem, but a daily personal problem for every master. "It is difficult to handle simply as property, a creature possessing human passions and human feelings," observed Frederick Law Olmstead, "while, on the other hand, the absolute necessity of dealing with property as a thing, greatly embarrasses a man in any attempt to treat it as a person." Absentee owners and the masters of large, commercially rationalized plantations might regard their field hands as economic units, but few of them could avoid personalizing their relationships with house servants in a way that undercut the sheerly economic conception of the peculiar institution. The majority of slaveholders, moreover, were farmers who lived and worked closely with their slaves, and such masters, according to D. R. Hundley, "seem to exercise but few of the rights of ownership over their human chattels, making so little distinction between master and man, that their Negroes [are] . . . in all things treated more like equals than slaves." [38]

The personalized master-slave relationship was a direct threat to the peculiar institution, for slavery's stability as an economic institution depended upon the Negro's acceptance of the caste line between himself and the white man. Sociologists tell us that such caste systems as India's were stabilized by the fact that "those goals and value-attitudes which were legitimate for the dominant caste had no implications concerning their legitimacy for the subordinate caste." In the South, however, where the values of the dominant caste produced personalized master-slave relationships, and where Negroes could view manumission as the crucial product of personalization, members of the subordinate caste learned to regard the value system and goals of the dominant caste as at least partly valid for themselves. The presence of free Negroes in southern society meant that the caste line did not coincide completely with the color line, and the overlap made liberty a legitimate goal even for the slave. Thus the slave's passion for freedom, manifested in countless escapes and insurrection plots, was not "lit up in his soul by the hand of Deity," as a Virginia legislator thought, but was implanted by the white man's own inability to draw the caste line rigidly.[39]

Though Southerners could guard against the dangers of personalization in the abstract, as when legislatures prohibited manumission, the individual master, face to face with his human property, found it harder to behave in accordance with the sheerly economic view of slavery.

Economic efficiency demanded "the painful exercise of undue and tyrannical authority," observed a North Carolina planter; and the famous ex-slave Frederick Douglass testified that kind treatment increased rather than diminished the slave's desire for freedom. Consequently humanity and the profit motive were forever struggling against each other in the master's mind. While the profit motive frequently won out, humanity had its victories too. "I would be content with much less . . . cotton if less cruelty was exercised," said a disturbed planter in Mississippi. "I fear I am near an abolition[i]st." Most often, perhaps, the master's humanitarian and economic impulses fought to a draw, leaving him continually troubled and frustrated in the management of his slaves. Slaveholding, concluded one master, subjected "the man of care and feeling to more dilemmas than any other vocation he could follow." [40]

Certainly southern opinion condemned thoroughgoing economic rationality in the treatment of slaves. This was most apparent in the low social status accorded to slave traders and overseers, when by normal southern canons of prestige their intimate relation with the peculiar institution and their control over large numbers of slaves should have given them a relatively high rank. Both groups were absolutely essential to the slavery system, and both bore a purely economic relation to it. The overseer, who was judged primarily by the profits he wrung out of slave labor, typified the sheerly exploitative aspects of slavery; while the slave trader, who presided over the forcible disruption of families and the distribution of slaves as marketable commodities, was the most conspicuous affront to the familial conception of the peculiar institution. These men certainly developed a cynical attitude toward the human property they controlled, but they did not uniformly exhibit the dishonesty, greed, vulgarity, and general immorality that southern opinion ascribed to them. By thus stereotyping these exemplars of the sheerly economic aspects of slavery, southern society created scapegoats on whom it could discharge the guilt feelings arising from the necessity of treating human beings as property.[41]

These guilt feelings seem to have increased during the final years of the ante-bellum period, as slavery approximated the sheerly economic pattern on more and more plantations. Never had Southerners regaled themselves and others so insistently with the myth of the happy slave. A European traveler met few slaveholders who could "openly and honestly look the thing in the face. They wind and turn about in all sorts of ways, and make use of every argument . . . to convince me that the slaves are the happiest people in the world, and do not wish to be placed in any other condition." At the same time there developed a strong movement to extend and implement the paternalistic-personalistic pattern. Some states amended their slave codes to prescribe minimum standards of treatment, and there was agitation for more fundamental reforms—legalization of slave marriages, protection against disruption of slave families, and encouragement of Negro education.[42]

Especially significant was the crusade for religious instruction of slaves. "We feel that the souls of our slaves are a solemn trust, and we shall strive to present them faultless and complete before the presence of God," declared that high priest of southern Presbyterianism, Dr. James Henley Thornwell. The argument for religious instruction was also a justification for slavery, and the only one that effected any kind of real accommodation between the peculiar institution and the white Southerner's innate disposition to regard the slave as a human being. It was precisely for this reason that the religious interpretation of slavery quieted more southern qualms than any other facet of the pro-slavery argument. "However the world may judge us in connection with our institution of slavery," said Georgia's Bishop Stephen Elliott, "we conscientiously believe it to be a great missionary institution—one arranged by God, as he arranges all the moral and religious influences of the world so that the good may be brought out of the seeming evil, and a blessing wrung out of every form of the curse."

Yet the religious argument was ultimately subversive of slavery. By giving the slave's status as person precedence over his status as property, and by taking as its mission the elevation of the slave as a human being, the movement for religious instruction necessarily called into question the inherent beneficence and permanence of the institution. Dr. Thornwell resolutely argued that slavery could end only in heaven, because only there could the sin that produced it end; meanwhile the Christian's duty was to mitigate its evils. Bishop Elliott, on the other hand, believed that by giving the slaves religious instruction "we are elevating them in every generation" here on earth, and he spoke for many another southern churchman when he conceded that this implied ultimately some change in the slaves' worldly status. Thus, by the close of the slavery era, the religious defense of the institution was bringing the South back toward its old colonial doubts about the validity of continued bondage for converted men and women.[43]

Nowhere, in fact, was the South's painful inner conflict over slavery more evident than in the elaborate body of theory by which it tried to prove (mainly to itself) the beneficence of its peculiar social system.

"It has not been more than . . . thirty years since the abolition of slavery was seriously debated in the legislature of Virginia," observed the *Southern Literary Messenger* on the eve of the Civil War. "Now, on the contrary . . . the whole Southern mind with an unparalleled unanimity regards the institution of slavery as righteous and just, ordained of God, and to be perpetuated by Man." Yet the stridency with which southern unanimity was ceaselessly proclaimed stands in suggestive contrast to the private views of many Southerners. "To expect men to agree that Slavery is a blessing, social, moral, and political," wrote a North Carolina Congressman to his wife, "when many of those who have all their lives been accustomed to it . . . believe exactly the reverse, is absurd." Even the fire-eaters confessed privately that outside South Carolina most slaveholders were "mere negro-drivers believing themselves wrong and only holding on to their negroes as something to make money out of." South Carolinians themselves had "retrograded," wrote Robert W. Barnwell in 1844, "and must soon fall into the same category." [44]

Close examination of the superficially impressive pro-slavery philosophy reveals, as Louis Hartz has brilliantly demonstrated, a "mass of agonies and contradictions in the dream world of southern thought." The peculiar institution could be squared theoretically with either the slave's humanity or democratic liberalism for whites, but not with both. Thus the necessity for justifying slavery, coupled with the white South's inability to escape its inherited liberalism or to deny the common humanity it shared with its Negro slaves, inspired "a mixture of pain and wide hyperbole." [45]

Recognizing that the religious argument by itself was a threat to the peculiar institution, one school of pro-slavery philosophers sought to preserve both slavery and the slave's humanity by sacrificing democratic liberalism and falling back to a neo-feudal insistence on the necessity of subordination and inequality in society. "Subordination rules supreme in heaven and must rule supreme on earth," asserted Bishop Elliott, and he did not attempt to disguise the repudiation of democratic liberalism that followed from this principle. Carried away by Revolutionary fervor, Southerners along with other Americans had "declared war against all authority and against all form"; they had pronounced all men equal and man capable of self-government. "Two greater falsehoods could not have been announced," Elliott insisted, "because the one struck at the whole constitution of civil society as it had ever existed, and because the other denied the fall and corruption of man." [46]

George Fitzhugh, the most logical and impressive of the pro-slavery philosophers and the leading exponent of southern neo-feudalism, would have preserved the humanity of the Negroes but denied freedom to the white masses by making both subject to the same serf-like subordination. Only thus could men be saved from the frightful corruption and turbulence of "free society." But southern planters were too much bourgeois capitalists and southern farmers were too much Jacksonian democrats to entertain the neo-feudalists' vituperation at "free society." "Soon counties, neighborhoods, or even individuals will be setting up castles," commented a sarcastic Alabamian.[47] Fitzhugh and his fellow intellectuals might talk all they pleased about reducing the masses, white and black, to serfdom, but practical politicians and publicists knew better than to fly so directly in the face of the South's liberal bias.

At the hands of men like James H. Hammond, therefore, neo-feudalism became a racial "mud-sill" theory, which divided society along the color line, relegating Negroes to bondage and reserving democratic liberalism for white men only. In the late forties a school of southern ethnologists arose to declare the Negro a distinct and permanently inferior species; and by 1854 Mississippi's Senator Albert G. Brown could invite Northerners to his state "to see the specimen of that equality spoken of by Jefferson in the Declaration of Independence." Nowhere else in the Union, said Brown, was there such an exemplification of Jefferson's beautiful sentiment. "In the South all men are equal. I mean of course, white men; negroes are not men, within the meaning of the Declaration." [48]

The racist argument was attacked with surprising vehemence by both religionists and feudalists. At least one Southerner went far beyond most northern abolitionists in asserting that "the African is endowed with faculties as lofty, with perceptions as quick, with sensibilities as acute, and with natures as susceptible of improvement, as we are, who boast a fairer skin." Indeed, said this Virginian, if Negroes were "operated upon by the same ennobling impulses, stimulated by the same generous motives, and favored by the same adventitious circumstances, they would, as a mass, reach as high an elevation in the scale of moral refinement, and attain as great distinction on the broad theatre of intellectual achievement, as ourselves." [49]

While few Southerners would go as far as this, the religionists did maintain stoutly "that the African race is capable of considerable advance." Religious instruction of slaves would have been pointless without some such assumption, but the churchmen objected more fundamentally to the racist argument because it robbed the slave of his essential humanity. The feudalists, too, rejected the idea of racial inferiority, with Fitzhugh arguing that "it encourages and incites brutal masters to treat negroes, not as weak, ignorant and dependent brethren, but as wicked beasts, without the pale of humanity." The Negro was essential to the web of reciprocal duties and affections between superiors and subordinates that was supposed to knit the idyllic neo-feudal world together. "The Southerner is the negro's friend, his only friend," said Fitzhugh. "Let no intermeddling abolitionist, no refined philosophy dissolve this friendship." [50]

The debate between the religionists and feudalists, on the one hand, and the racists, on the other, defined the Old South's central dilemma. The first two championed personalism and the familial view of the peculiar institution. The religionists were willing to question the beneficence and permanence of slavery in order to assert the slave's humanity; and the feudalists were willing to surrender democratic liberalism in order to retain a personalized system of servitude. The racists, on the other hand, denied the slave's full human status in order to reconcile slavery with democratic liberalism for whites. The South's ingrained liberalism and Christianity, in short, were continually thwarting the logic-impelled effort to develop a fully rationalized, sheerly economic conception of slavery, warranted by the racist argument.

It was this inner conflict which produced the South's belligerent dogmatism in the recurrent crises of the fifties. The whole massive proslavery polemic had the unreal ring of logic pushed far beyond conviction. "I assure you, Sir," Fitzhigh confessed in a private letter, "I see great evils in Slavery, but in a controversial work I ought not to admit them." [51] If the South's best minds resolutely quashed their doubts, it is small wonder that crisis-tossed editors and politicians took refuge in positive and extreme positions.

The final open collision between the two contradictory tendencies in the South's thinking about slavery came on the very eve of the Civil War, when some Southerners relentlessly pursued the logic of slavery's beneficence to the conclusion that the foreign slave trade should be reopened. "I would sweep from the statute-book every interference with slavery," shouted a fire-eating South Carolina congressman. "I would repeal the law declaring the slave trade piracy; I would withdraw our slave squadron from the coast of Africa; and I would leave slavery unintervened against, wherever the power of the country stretches." [52]

Despite the lip service paid to the "positive good" doctrine, majority southern opinion was deeply shocked by its logical extension to sanction the foreign slave trade. Few Southerners were willing "to roll back the tide of civilization and christianity of the nineteenth century, and restore the barbarism of the dark ages," declared a Georgia newspaper, and churchmen denounced the proposal with special vehemence. Even one of its original advocates turned against it when he witnessed the suffering of the Negroes aboard a captured slave ship. This "practical, fair evidence of its effects has cured me forever," confessed D. H. Hamilton. "I wish that everyone in South Carolina, who is in favor of re-opening of the Slave-trade, could have seen what I have been compelled to witness . . . It seems to me that I can never forget it." [53] This was the agony of the pro-slavery South under the shadow of Civil War.

How, then, did the fundamentally liberal, Christian, American South ever become an "aggressive slavocracy"?* How did it bring itself to flaunt an aristocratic social philosophy? To break up the American Union? To wage war for the purpose of holding four million human beings in a bondage that violated their humanity? The answer is that Southerners did not and could not rationally and deliberately choose slavery and its fruits over the values it warred against. Rather it was the very conflict of values, rendered intolerable by constant criticism premised on values Southerners shared, which drove them to seek a violent resolution.

Social psychologists observe that such value conflicts—especially when they give rise to the kind of institutional instability revealed by the ambiguities of southern slavery—make a society "suggestible," or ready to follow the advocates of irrational and aggressive action.† Thus

* The viewpoint of the present essay is not to be confused with the interpretation of the Civil War in terms of a "slave power conspiracy." Chauncey S. Boucher has demonstrated convincingly that the South was incapable of the kind of concerted action necessary for conspiracy. "*In Re* That Aggressive Slavocracy," *Mississippi Valley Historical Review*, VIII (June-September, 1921), 13-79. He is less persuasive, however, in demonstrating the equal inappropriateness of the designation "aggressive slavocracy." Boucher does admit (p. 30) that many Southerners "took a stand which may perhaps best be termed 'aggressively defensive.' " This is not too far from the attitude of the present essay, especially in view of Boucher's tantalizing suggestion (p. 70) that when Southerners talked of slavery as a divinely ordained institution, they were in the position of "saying a thing and being conscious while saying it that the thing is not true . . . but a position forced upon them by necessity of circumstances for their own immediate protection."

† Hadley Cantril, *The Psychology of Social Movements* (New York, 1941), 61-64. The social sciences have much to contribute to southern historical

it was fateful that the Old South developed an unusually able minority of fire-eating sectionalists, who labored zealously, from the 1830's on, to unite the South behind radical measures in defense of slavery. Though a majority of Southerners remained profoundly distrustful of these extremists throughout the ante-bellum period, their unceasing agitation stea lily aggravated the South's tensions and heightened its underlying suggestibility. By egging the South on to ever more extreme demands, the Calhouns, Rhetts, and Yanceys provoked violent northern reactions, which could then be used to whip the South's passions still higher. At length, in 1860, capitalizing on intrigues for the Democratic presidential nomination, the fire-eaters managed to split the Democratic party, thus insuring the election of a Republican President and paving the way for secession.

Inflammatory agitation and revolutionary tactics succeeded only

---

scholarship; in fact, the essential key to understanding the Old South seems to lie in the area of social psychology. Though Harry Elmer Barnes asserted as much nearly forty years ago, scholarly efforts in this direction have hardly moved beyond the naïve enthusiasm of Barnes' suggestion that "southern chivalry" was "a collective compensation for sexual looseness, racial intermixture, and the maltreatment of the Negro."—"Psychology and History: Some Reasons for Predicting Their More Active Cooperation in the Future," *American Journal of Psychology*, XXX (October, 1919), 374. A psychologist has interpreted southern behavior in terms of defense mechanism, rationalization, and projection.— D. A. Hartman, "The Psychological Point of View in History: Some Phases of the Slavery Struggle," *Journal of Abnormal Psychology and Social Psychology*, XVII (October-December, 1922), 261-73. A psychoanalyst has traced the white South's treatment of the Negro to the general insecurities of Western man uprooted by industrialism, and to an unconscious sexual fascination with the Negro as "a symbol which gives a secret gratification to those who are inhibited and crippled in their instinctual satisfaction."—Helen V. McLean, "Psychodynamic Factors in Racial Relations," *Annals of the American Academy of Political and Social Science*, CCLIV (March, 1946), 159-66. And a sociologist has sought to explain the South in terms of a concept of "social neurosis."— Read Bain, "Man Is the Measure," *Sociometry: A Journal of Inter-Personal Relations*, VI (November, 1943), 460-64.

These efforts, while suggestive, seem hardly more systematic and considerably less cautious than the historian's unsophisticated, commonsense way of trying to assess psychological factors. Yet Hadley Cantril's *Psychology of Social Movements* has demonstrated that the infant discipline of social psychology can, even in its present primitive state, furnish the historian with extremely useful concepts. Historians of the Old South have special reason for pressing their problems on their brethren in social psychology, while the social psychologists may find in historical data a challenging area for developing and testing hypotheses. Especially rewarding to both historians and social scientists would be a collaborative study of ante-bellum southern radicalism and its perculiar locus, South Carolina.

because Southerners had finally passed the point of rational self-control. The almost pathological violence of their reactions to northern criticism indicated that their misgivings about their moral position on slavery had become literally intolerable under the mounting abolitionist attack. "The South has been moved to resistance chiefly . . . by the popular dogma in the free states that slavery is a crime in the sight of GOD," said a New Orleans editor in the secession crisis. "The South, in the eyes of the North, is degraded and unworthy, because of the institution of servitude." [54]

Superimposed on this fundamental moral anxiety was another potent emotion, fear. John Brown's raid in October, 1859, created the most intense terror of slave insurrection that the South had ever experienced; and in this atmosphere of dread the final crisis of 1860–61 occurred. The press warned that the South was "slumbering over a volcano, whose smoldering fires, may at any quiet starry midnight, blacken the social sky with the smoke of desolation and death." Southerners believed their land to be overrun by abolitionist emissaries, who were "tampering with our slaves, and furnishing them with arms and poisons to accomplish their hellish designs." Lynch law was proclaimed, and vigilance committees sprang up to deal with anyone suspected of abolitionist sentiments. A Mississippian reported the hanging of twenty-three such suspects in three weeks, while the British consul at Charleston described the situation as "a reign of terror." [55]

Under these circumstances a large part of the southern white population approached the crisis of the Union in a state of near-hysteria. One man thought that "the minds of the people are aroused to a pitch of excitement probably unparalleled in the history of our country." "The desire of some for change," reported a despairing Virginian, "the greed of many for excitement, and the longing of more for anarchy and confusion, seems to have unthroned the reason of men, and left them at the mercy of passion and madness." [56]

Just as important as the hysteria which affected some Southerners was the paralysis of will, the despair, the sense of helplessness, which the excitement created in their more conservative fellows. Denying that the southern people really wanted to dissolve the Union, a Georgia editor saw them as being "dragged on, blindfolded, to the consummation of the horrid act." A "moral pestilence" had "swept over the South," said a prominent North Carolinian, "dethroning reason, & paralyzing the efforts of the best Union men of the country." But even some who decried the hysteria felt that "no community can exist & prosper when this sense of insecurity prevails," and concluded that almost any alternative was preferable to the strain of these recurrent crises. It was this conviction, more than anything else, which caused moderate men to give way to the bold and confident radicals.[57]

From the circumstances of the secession elections—the small turn-outs, the revolutionary tactics of the fire-eaters, the disproportionate weighting of the results in favor of plantation areas, the coercive conditions under which the upper South voted, and the hysteria that prevailed everywhere—it can hardly be said that a majority of the South's white people deliberately chose to dissolve the Union in 1861. A member of South Carolina's secession convention frankly admitted that "the common people" did not understand what was at stake. "But whoever waited for the common people when a great movement was to be made?" he asked. "We must make the move and force them to follow. That is the way of all revolutions and all great achievements." [58]

The leaders made the move, and the people followed, but with what underlying misgivings the sequel only too plainly demonstrated. The first flush of enthusiasm was rapidly supplanted by an apathy and a growing disaffection which historians have identified as major factors in the Confederacy's failure. During the dark winter of 1864–65, North Carolina's Governor Zebulon Vance commented on the supineness with which the southern population received the invading Sherman. It was evidence, said Vance, of what he had "always believed, that *the great popular heart* is not now, and never has been in this war! It was a revolution of the *Politicians*, not the *People*." [59]

And when the cause was lost, Southerners abandoned it with an alacrity which underscored the reluctance of their original commitment. It was left for a leading ex-fire-eater to explain why they returned to the Union of their fathers with so little hesitation. Standing before the Joint Congressional Committee on Reconstruction in 1866, James D. B. De Bow attested in all sincerity the South's willingness to fight once again for the flag of the Union. "The southern people," he said, "are Americans, republicans." [60] Yet it is idle to wonder whether secession represented the deliberate choice of a majority of white Southern-ers, or to speculate about the outcome of a hypothetical referendum, free from ambiguity, coercion, and hysteria. Decisions like the one that faced the South in 1860–61 are never reached in any such ideal way. And even had the South decided for the Union, its and the nation's problem would have remained unsolved, and a violent resolution would only have been postponed. Slavery was doomed by the march of history and by the nature of Southerners themselves, but so deeply had it involved them in its contradictions that they could neither deal with it rationally nor longer endure the tensions and anxieties it generated. Under these circumstances the Civil War or something very like it was unavoidable. It was also salutary, for only the transaction at Appomattox could have freed the South's people—both Negro and white—to move again toward the realization of their essential natures as Southerners, liberals, Christians, and Americans.

NOTES

1. David Ramsay, *The History of South-Carolina, from Its First Settlement in 1670, to the Year 1808* (2 vols., Charleston, 1809), II, 384.

2. Fletcher M. Green, "Listen to the Eagle Scream: One Hundred Years of the Fourth of July in North Carolina (1776–1876)," *North Carolina Historical Review,* XXXI (July, October, 1954), 36, 534.

3. *A Selection of Eulogies Pronounced in the Several States, in Honor of Those Illustrious Patriots and Statesmen, John Adams and Thomas Jefferson* (Hartford, 1826), 6-7. For an indication of the currency of similar sentiments, see Green, "Listen to the Eagle Screem," *N. C. Hist. Rev.,* XXXI, 303, 305, 548.

4. Laura A. White, *Robert Barnwell Rhett, Father of Secession* (New York, 1931), 50-52; Merle Curti, *The Roots of American Loyalty* (New York, 1946), 137-38, 153-54.

5. Curti, *American Loyalty,* 68, 154; R. M. T. Hunter, *An Address Delivered before the Society of Alumnia of the University of Virginia . . . on the 4th of July, 1839* (Charlottesville, 1839), 4.

6. Curti, *American Loyalty,* 41, 43, 61, 72, 102-3, 152; Horace Montgomery, *Cracker Parties* (Baton Rouge, 1950), 3.

7. Green, "Listen to the Eagle Scream," *N. C. Hist. Rev.,* XXXI, 314, 319-20, 534-36.

8. Daniel R. Goodloe, *The Southern Platform: or, Manual of Southern Sentiment on the Subject of Slavery* (Boston, 1858), 91.

9. William S. Jenkins, *Pro-Slavery Thought in the Old South* (Chapel Hill, 1935), 37-38.

10. Goodloe, *Southern Platform,* 94.

11. *Ibid.,* 3-5.

12. Hinton Rowan Helper, *The Impending Crisis of the South: How to Meet It* (New York, 1860), 197.

13. *Register of Debates,* 24th Cong., 2nd Sess., 719-23.

14. Russell B. Nye, *Fettered Freedom: Civil Liberties and the Slavery Controversy, 1830–1860* (East Lansing, Mich., 1949), 72.

15. Lillian A. Kibler, *Benjamin F. Perry, South Carolina Unionist* (Durham, 1946), 31; Pulaski *Tennessee Beacon and Farmers Advocate,* June 16, 1832.

16. W. G. Bean, "Anti-Jeffersonianism in the Ante-Bellum South," *North Carolina Historical Review,* XII (April, 1935), 111.

17. John Hope Franklin, *The Militant South, 1800– 1861* (Cambridge, 1956), 222.

18. Goodloe, *Southern Platform*, 49.

19. E. Mitchell to John C. Calhoun, February 5, 1849, John C. Calhoun Papers (Clemson College Library).

20. Goodloe, *Southern Platform*, 49; Helper, *Impending Crisis*, 195, 208-9; John J. Flournoy, *An Essay on the Origin, Habits, &c. of the African Race . . .* (New York, 1835), 25; Kenneth M. Stampp, *The Peculiar Institution: Slavery in the Ante-Bellum South* (New York, 1956), 356.

21. Joseph C. Robert, *The Road from Monticello: A Study of the Virginia Slavery Debate of 1832* (Durham, 1941), 17-18, and *passim*.

22. Charles H. Ambler, *The Life and Diary of John Floyd* (Richmond, 1918), 172; Jenkins, *Pro-Slavery Thought*, 88n.

23. Nashville *Republican*, October 22, 1825.

24. Washington *United States Telegraph*, December 5, 1835.

25. Walter B. Posey, "The Slavery Question in the Presbyterian Church in the Old Southwest," *Journal of Southern History*, XV (August, 1943), 319; Betty Fladeland, *James Gillespie Birney: Slaveholder to Abolitionist* (Ithaca, 1955), 83.

26. Kenneth M. Stampp, "The Fate of the Southern Antislavery Movement," *Journal of Negro History*, XXVIII (January, 1943), 20, 22, and *passim*.

27. Stampp, *Peculiar Institution*, 422-23; Washington *United States Telegraph*, December 5, 1835.

28. Stampp, *Peculiar Institution*, 234, 423.

29. Clement Eaton, *Freedom of Thought in the Old South* (2nd edn., New York, 1951), xxi-xiii; J. Merton England, "The Free Negro in Ante-Bellum Tennessee," *Journal of Southern History*, IX (February, 1943), 44-45. Cf. Stampp, *Peculiar Institution*, 234-35.

30. Eaton, *Freedom of Thought*, 18-19; Stampp, *Peculiar Institution*, 235-36; England, "Free Negro," *Jour. Southern Hist.*, IX, 43-44.

31. Jenkins, *Pro-Slavery Thought*, 236; Stampp, *Peculiar Institution*, 383.

32. Stampp, *Peculiar Institution*, 424; Eaton, *Freedom of Thought*, 19; Frank W. Klingberg, *The Southern Claims Commission* (Berkeley and Los Angeles, 1955), 11, 108; J. W. De Forest, "Chivalrous and Semi-Chivalrous Southrons," *Harper's New Monthly Magazine*, XXVIII (January, February, 1869), 200.

33. *Register of Debates*, 19th Cong., 1st Sess., 1649.

34. Wilbert E. Moore, "Slavery, Abolition, and the Ethical Valuation of the Individual: A Study of the Relations between Ideas and Institutions" (Ph.D. dissertation, Harvard University, 1940), 193-212.

35. Wilbert E. Moore, "Slave Law and the Social Structure," *Journal of Negro History*, XXVI (April, 1941), 171-202.

36. Stampp, *Peculiar Institution*, 217; Helper, *Impending Crisis*, 223-24.

37. Moore, "Slavery and Ethical Valuation," Ph.D. Dissertation (Harvard), 187-88.

38. Stampp, *Peculiar Institution*, 193; D. R. Hundley, *Social Relations in Our Southern States* (New York, 1860), 193.

39. Moore, "Slavery and Ethical Valuation," 233-35; Wilbert E. Moore and Robin M. Williams, "Stratification in the Ante-Bellum South," *American Sociological Review*, VII (June, 1942), 348-51; Robert, *Road from Monticello*, 103.

40. Stampp, *Peculiar Institution*, 89-90, 141, 191.

41. Moore, "Slavery and Ethical Valuation," 194-95; Moore and Williams, "Stratification," 345-46.

42. Stampp, *Peculiar Institution*, 423; Herbert Aptheker, *American Negro Slave Revolts* (New York, 1943), 59-60.

43. Jenkins, *Pro-Slavery Thought*, 214-18.

44. Jay B. Hubbell, "Literary Nationalism in the Old South," in David K. Jackson, ed., *American Studies in Honor of William Kenneth Boyd* (Durham, 1940), 183n.; David Outlaw to Mrs. David Outlaw, July [28], 1848, David Outlaw Papers (Southern Historical Collection, University of North Carolina); Robert W. Barnwell to Robert Barnwell Rhett, November 1, 1844, Robert Barnwell Rhett Papers (Southern Historical Collection, University of North Carolina).

45. Louis Hartz, *The Liberal Tradition in America: An Interpretation of American Political Thought since the Revolution* (New York, 1955), 145-200.

46. Jenkins, *Pro-Slavery Thought*, 239-40.

47. Ollinger Crenshaw, *The Slave States in the Presidential Election of 1860* (Baltimore, 1945), 253.

48. *Congressional Globe*, 33rd Cong., 1st Sess., Appendix, 230.

49. Goodloe, *Southern Platform*, 93.

50. Jenkins, *Pro-Slavery Thought*, 281; Harvey Wish, *George Fitzhugh: Propagandist of the Old South* (Baton Rouge, 1943), 111.

51. Wish, *Fitzhugh*, 111.

52. Harold S. Schultz, *Nationalism and Sectionalism in South Carolina, 1852–1860: A Study of the Movement for Southern Independence* (Durham, 1950), 182.

53. Stampp, *Peculiar Institution*, 278; Schultz, *Nationalism and Sectionalism*, 158-59.

54. Dwight L. Dumond, ed., *Southern Editorials on Secession* (New York, 1931), 315-16.

55. Crenshaw, *Slave States*, 100, 103, 106; Laura A. White, "The South in the 1850's as Seen by British Consuls," *Journal of Southern History*, I (February, 1935), 44.

56. Crenshaw, *Slave States*, 111; Robert C. Gunderson, "William C. Rives and the 'Old Gentlemen's Convention,'" *Journal of Southern History*, XXII (November, 1956), 460.

57. Crenshaw, *Slave States*, 111n., 237; Klingberg, *Southern Claims Commission*, 13. Cf. Cantril, *Psychology of Social Movements*, 61.

58. White, *Rhett*, 177n.

59. Klingberg, *Southern Claims Commission*, 138.

60. *Report of the Joint Committee on Reconstruction, at the First Session, Thirty-Ninth Congress* (Washington, 1866), 133.

• One of the most important questions confronting historians of slavery, as we noted in the Introduction, concerns the comparative treatment of bondsmen in North and South America. Both Frank Tannenbaum and Stanley M. Elkins have argued that slaves possessed legal, religious, and even economic status in Latin America unlike the more stringent conditions they faced in the United States. David Brion Davis challenges the Tannenbaum-Elkins argument in the following selection, which evaluates the work of Spanish and Portuguese scholars on the daily practices and customs of slavery in Latin America. The student might compare Davis's views with Herbert Klein's discussion of slave cultures in Cuba and Virginia.

Patterns of Slavery in the Americas

DAVID BRION DAVIS

Was antislavery, then, a direct outgrowth of slavery itself? We have maintained that the concept of man as a material possession has always led to contradictions in law and custom. In the ancient world these contradictions did not give rise to abolitionism; but in the historical development of American slavery there were deep strains that made the institution a source of dissonance and discontent. Even men whose interests were closely tied to the system expressed occasional misgivings over mounting debts and economic decay, the rising proportion of Negroes to whites, the haunting threat of insurrection, the failure to infuse masters and slaves with a spirit of Christian love, and the growing discrepancy between American servitude and European ideals of liberty. It remains to be asked whether the evolution of colonial laws and customs provided a basis for believing that the worst evils of slavery could be gradually eliminated through wise legislation, or for concluding that slavery by its very nature was beyond reform.

From David Brion Davis, *The Problem of Slavery in Western Culture* (Ithaca: Cornell University Press, 1966), pp. 223-43. Copyright © 1966 by Cornell University. Used by permission of Cornell University Press.

Such a question poses many problems. As a result of differences in economy, social and political institutions, and the ratio of Negroes to whites, the actual status and condition of colonial slaves varied considerably from one region to another. Yet no slave colony had a monopoly on either kindness or cruelty. Slave codes were often enacted with a view to quieting local fears or appeasing a church or government. Travelers were sometimes biased or quick to generalize from a few fleeting impressions. Since we still seriously lack a thorough comparative study of Negro slavery in the various colonies, we must be content with fragmentary evidence and with extremely tentative conclusions. There would seem to be some basis, however, for questioning two assumptions which have been widely accepted by modern historians.

The first is that Negro slavery in the British colonies and Southern United States was of a nearly uniform severity, the slave being legally deprived of all rights of person, property, and family, and subjected to the will of his owner and the police power of the state, which barred his way to education, free movement, or emancipation. The second assumption is that the French, and especially the Spanish and Portuguese, were far more liberal in their treatment of slaves, whom they considered as human beings who had merely lost a portion of their external freedom. Untainted by racial prejudice and free from the pressures of a fluid, capitalistic economy, these easygoing colonists are supposed to have protected the human rights of the slave and to have facilitated his manumission. Some historians have simply held that slavery in North America was much harsher than that in Latin America, but Stanley M. Elkins has argued more persuasively that the great contrast was not in the bondsman's physical well-being but in the recognition of his basic humanity.[1] As a methodological device, this distinction has obvious merit, since a master might look upon his slaves as sub-human animals and still provide them with comfortable maintenance. On the other hand, it would be unrealistic to draw too sharp a line between moral status and physical treatment. It is difficult to see how a society could have much respect for the value of slaves as human personalities if it sanctioned their torture and mutilation, the selling of their small children, the unmitigated exploitation of their labor, and the drastic shortening of their lives through overwork and inadequate nourishment. While a few isolated instances of sadistic cruelty would reveal little about the legal or moral status of slaves, we should not exclude physical treatment when it is part of a pattern of systematic oppression which is fully sanctioned by the laws and custom of a society. We shall find, however, that there is other evidence than physical treatment for challenging the assumption that Latin Americans were more sensitive than Anglo-Americans to the essential humanity of their slaves.

This assumption has important implications for a history of antislavery thought. If servitude under the Spanish and Portuguese was generally mild and humane, and if the institution itself tended to promote a gradual achievement of freedom, then we should not be surprised by the fact that antislavery agitation began in Britain and British America. The peculiar severities of British colonial slavery would appear to have arisen from local economic or social conditions, and we should have reason to suspect that antislavery movements were a direct response to an unprecedented evil. And while the extremes of both slavery and antislavery could be explained by the absence of a stable social structure, we could conclude that the Anglo-American reformer might well have looked to Latin America for a rational model. By gradually imposing the institutional protections of Latin American slavery on the formless and unregulated slavery of the north, he might have removed the evils from a necessary system of labor. But if the contrast between slavery in the various American colonies was not so clear-cut as has generally been supposed, we are left with a different set of implications. It would be likely that the appearance of antislavery agitation was less a direct response to a unique evil than a result of particular cultural and religious developments in the English-speaking world. And if both the evils of slavery and the attempts to ameliorate them were fairly pervasive throughout the Americas, we should look more skeptically at programs for slow and gradual reform. We should expect to find general emancipation often associated with revolutions and civil wars, as was the case in Saint Domingue, the United States, and several of the Spanish colonies, or with political upheaval and the fall of a government, as in Brazil.[2]

A word of explanation is in order regarding the chronological range of selected examples and illustrations. If we are to judge the influence of traditional Catholic culture, the crucial period in Latin American slavery is the early colonial era, before the full impact of the Enlightenment, the American and French Revolutions, and the wars of independence. But when we test the assumption that slavery in the British colonies and Southern United States was of a monolithic character, unmitigated by any recognition of the Negro's rights of personality, it is appropriate to select examples from the nineteenth century, when laws and customs had hardened to form a self-contained system of values and precedents. If some of the ameliorative elements we usually associate with Latin American slavery were common in North America, even at a time when bondage had grown more formalized and severe, then we should have less reason to suppose that the basic evils of the institution could have been eliminated by mere palliative reforms.

ii

By the late eighteenth century most travelers agreed that in Brazil and the Spanish colonies the condition of slaves was considerably better than in British America.[3] Any comparison must consider Negro slavery as a system of forced labor, of social organization, and of class and racial discipline. Numerous accounts from the late eighteenth and nineteenth centuries tell us that the Latin American slave enjoyed frequent hours of leisure and was seldom subjected to the factory-like regimentation that characterized the capitalistic plantations of the north; that he faced no legal bars to marriage, education, or eventual freedom; that he was legally protected from cruelty and oppression, and was not stigmatized on account of his race. This relative felicity has quite plausibly been attributed to a culture that de-emphasized the pursuit of private profit, to the Catholic Church's insistence on the slave's right to marry and worship, and to what Gilberto Freyre has termed the "miscibility" of the Portuguese, which submerged sensitivity to racial difference in a frank acceptance of sexual desire.[4]

No doubt there is much truth in even the idyllic picture of the Brazilian "Big House," where slaves and freemen pray and loaf together, and where masters shrug their shoulders at account books and prefer to frolic with slave girls in shaded hammocks. But we should not forget that West Indian and North American planters were fond of idealizing their own "Big Houses" as patriarchal manors, of portraying their Negroes as carefree and indolent, and of proudly displaying humane slave laws which they knew to be unenforceable. Their propaganda, which was supported by travelers' accounts and which long seemed persuasive to many Northerners and Englishmen, has largely been discredited by numerous critical studies based on a wealth of surviving evidence. Many of the records of Brazilian slavery were destroyed in the 1890's, in a fit of abolitionist enthusiasm, and the subject has never received the careful scrutiny it deserves.[5] Only in recent years have such historians as Octávio Ianni, Fernando Henrique Cardoso, Jaime Jaramillo Uribe, and C. R. Boxer begun to challenge the stereotyped images of mild servitude and racial harmony.

There is little reason to doubt that slavery in Latin America, compared with that in North America, was less subject to the pressures of competitive capitalism and was closer to a system of patriarchal rights and semifeudalistic services. But after granting this, we must recognize the inadequacy of thinking in terms of idealized models of patriarchal and capitalistic societies. Presumably, an exploitive, capitalistic form of servitude could not exist within a patriarchal society. The lord of a manor, unike the entrepreneur who might play the role of lord of a manor, would be incapable of treating men as mere units of labor in a speculative enterprise. But neither would he think of exploring new lands, discovering gold mines, or developing new plantations for the production of sugar and coffee. It is perhaps significant that accounts of Latin American slavery often picture the relaxed life on sugar plantations after their decline in economic importance, and ignore conditions that prevailed during the Brazilian sugar boom of the seventeenth century, the mining boom of the early eighteenth century, and the coffee boom of the nineteen century. Similarly, Southern apologists tended to overlook the human effects of high-pressure argiculture in the Southwest, and focus their attention on the easygoing and semipatriarchal societies of tidewater Maryland and Virginia. Eugene D. Genovese has recently suggested that while the North American slave system was stimulated and exploited by the capitalist world market, it retained many precapitalistic features, such as a lack of innovation, restricted markets, and low productivity of labor, and actually gravitated toward an uneconomical paternalism that was basically antithetical to capitalistic values.

Although a particular instance of oppression or well-being can always be dismissed as an exception, it is important to know what range of variation a system permitted. If an exploitive, capitalistic form of servitude was at times common in Brazil and Spanish America, and if North Americans conformed at times to a paternalistic model and openly acknowledged the humanity of their slaves, it may be that differences between slavery in Latin America and the United States were no greater than regional or temporal differences within the countries themselves. And such a conclusion would lead us to suspect that Negro bondage was a single phenomenon, or *Gestalt*, whose variations were less significant than underlying patterns of unity.

Simon Gray, a Natchez river boatman, provides us with an example of the flexibility of the North American slave system. During the 1850's, most Southern states tightened their laws and to all appearances erected an impassable barrier between the worlds of slave and freeman. But the intent of legislators was often offset by powerful forces of economic interest and personality. Simon Gray was an intelligent slave whose superior abilities were recognized by both his master and the lumber company which hired his services. In the 1850's this lowly slave became the captain of a flatboat on the Mississippi, supervising and paying wages to a crew that included white men. In defiance of law, Gray was permitted to carry firearms, to travel freely on his own, to build and run sawmills, and to conduct commercial transactions as his company's agent. Entrusted with large sums of money for business purposes, Gray also drew a regular salary, rented a house where his family lived in privacy, and took a vacation to Hot Springs, Arkansas, when his health declined. Although there is evidence that in Southern industry and commerce such privileges were not as uncommon as has been assumed, we may be sure that Simon Gray was a very exceptional slave.[6] He might well have been less exceptional in Cuba or Brazil. The essential point, however, is that regardless of restrictive laws, the Southern slave system had room for a few Simon Grays. The flatboat captain could not have acted as he did if the society had demanded a rigorous enforcement of the law.

By the time Simon Gray was beginning to enjoy relative freedom, Portugal and Brazil were the only civilized nations that openly resisted attempts to suppress the African slave trade. It has been estimated that by 1853 Britain had paid Portugal some £2,850,965 in bribes intended to stop a commerce whose horrors had multiplied as a result of efforts to escape detection and capture. But despite British bribes and seizures, the trade continued, and was countenanced by the society which has been most praised for its humane treatment of slaves. One of the boats captured by the British, in 1842, was a tiny vessel of eighteen tons, whose crew consisted of six Portuguese. Between decks, in a space only eighteen inches high, they had intended to stow two hundred and fifty African children of about seven years of age.[7] Suspicion of Britain's motives probably prevented more outspoken attacks on a trade that outraged most of the civilized world. But the fact remains that Brazilian society not only permitted the slave trade to continue for nearly half a century after it had been outlawed by Britain and the United States, but provided a flourishing market for Negroes fresh from Africa. During the 1830's Brazil imported more than 400,000 slaves; in the single year of 1848 the nation absorbed some sixty thousand more. That the reception of these newcomers was not so humane as might be imagined is suggested by a law of 1869, six years after Lincoln's Emancipation Proclamation, which forbade the separate sale of husband and wife, or of children under fifteen. Not long before, even children under ten had been separated from their parents and sent to the coffee plantations of the south.[8]

These examples are intended only to illustrate the range of variation that could occur in any slave society, and hence the difficulties in comparing the relative severity of slave systems. Barbados and Jamaica were notorious for their harsh laws and regimentation, but occasional proprietors like Josiah Steele or Matthew Lewis succeeded in creating model plantations where Negroes were accorded most of the privileges of white servants. John Stedman, who provided Europe with ghastly pictures of the cruelty of Dutch masters in Surinam, also maintained that humanity and gentleness coexisted with the worst barbarity. The well-being of any group of slaves was subject to many variables. It seems certain that the few Negroes in eighteenth-century Québec lived a freer and richer life than hundreds of thousands of slaves in nineteenth-century Brazil and Cuba, despite the fact that the latter were technically guarded by certain legal protections, and the former were defined as chattels completely subject to their owner's authority. Islands like Dominica and Saint Lucia, which were disorganized by war and a transfer from one nation to another, had few social resources for restraining the unscrupulous master or curbing slave resistance. In the newly developed lands of captured or ceded colonies, such as Berbice, Demerara, Trinidad, and Louisiana, there were few effective checks on the speculative planter bent on reaping maximum profit in the shortest possible time. And whereas the North American slave frequently lived in a land of peace and plentiful food, his West-Indian brother was the first to feel the pinch of famine when war cut off essential supplies, or when his master was burdened by debt and declining profits. On the small tobacco farms of colonial Virginia and Maryland the physical condition of slaves was surely better than in the mines of Minas Gerais or on the great plantations of Bahia, where a Capuchin missionary was told in 1682 that a Negro who endured for seven years was considered to have lived very long.[9]

North American planters were fond of comparing the fertility of their own slaves with the high mortality and low birth rate of those in the West Indies and Latin America, and of concluding that theirs was the milder and more humane system. Such reasoning failed to take account of the low proportion of female slaves in the West Indies, the communicable diseases transmitted by the African trade, and the high incidence of tetanus and other maladies that were particularly lethal to infants in the Caribbean. No doubt differences in sanitation and nutrition, rather than in physical treatment, explain the fact that while Brazil and the United States each entered the nineteenth century with about a million slaves, and subsequent importations into Brazil were three times greater than those into the United States, by the Civil War there were nearly four million slaves in the United States and only one and one-half million in Brazil.[10] But after all such allowances are made, it still seems probable that planters in Brazil and the West Indies, who were totally dependent on fresh supplies of labor from Africa, were less sensitive than North Americans to the value of human life. When a slave's life expectancy was a few years at most, and when each slave could easily be replaced, there was little incentive to improve conditions or limit hours of work. According to both C. R. Boxer and Celso Furtado, Brazilian sugar planters took a short-term view of their labor needs, and accepted the axiom, which spread to the British Caribbean, that it was good economy to work one's slaves to death and then purchase more. In colonial Brazil, Jesuit priests felt it necessary to admonish overseers not to kick pregnant women in the stomach or beat them with clubs, since this brought a considerable loss in slave property.[11]

But what of the benevolent laws of Latin America which allowed a slave to marry, to seek relief from a cruel master, and even to purchase his own freedom? It must be confessed that on this crucial subject historians have been overly quick to believe what travelers passed on from conversations with slaveholders, and to make glowing generalizations on the basis of one-sided evidence.

Much has been made of the fact that the Spanish model law, *las Siete Partidas*, recognized freedom as man's natural state, and granted the slave certain legal protections. But the argument loses some of its point when we learn that the same principles were accepted in North American law, and that *las Siete Partidas* not only made the person and possessions of the bondsman totally subject to his master's will, but even gave owners the right to kill their slaves in certain circumstances.[12] Some of the early Spanish and Portuguese legislation protecting Indians has erroneously been thought to have extended to Negroes as well. In actuality, the first laws pertaining to Negroes in such colonies as Chile, Panama, and New Granada were designed to prohibit them from carrying arms, from moving about at night, and above all, from fraternizing with Indians.[13] It is true that in the late seventeenth and early eighteenth centuries the Portuguese crown issued edicts intended to prevent the gross mistreatment of Negro slaves. But as C. R. Boxer has pointed out, Brazilian law was a chaotic

tangle of Manueline and Filipine codes, encrusted by numerous decrees which often contradicted one another, and which were interpreted by lawyers and magistrates notorious for their dishonesty. Even
if this had not been true, slaves were dispersed over immense areas
where there were few towns and where justice was administered by
local magnates whose power lay in land and slaves. It is not surprising
that in one of the few recorded cases of the Portuguese crown interven-
ing to investigate the torture of a slave, nothing was done to the
accused owner. This revisionist view receives support from Jaime
Jaramillo Uribe's conclusion that the judical system of New Granada
was so ineffective that even the reform legislation of the late eighteenth century did little to change the oppressive life of Negro
slaves.[14]

In theory, of course, the Portuguese or Spanish slave possessed an
immortal soul that entitled him to respect as a human personality. But
though perfunctorily baptized in Angola or on the Guinea coast, he
was appraised and sold like any merchandise upon his arrival in America. Often slaves were herded in mass, stark naked, into large warehouses where they were examined and marketed like animals. As late
as the mid-nineteenth century the spread of disease among newly
arrived Negroes who were crowded into the warehouses of Rio de
Janeiro brought widespread fears of epidemic. The Spanish, who
ordinarily sold horses and cows individually, purchased Negroes in lots,
or *piezas de Indias*, which were sorted according to age and size. There
is abundant evidence that Brazilians were little troubled by the separation of Negro families; in the 1850's coffee planters in the rich
Parahyba Valley thought nothing of selling their own illegitimate
children to passing traders. Despite protests from priests and governors, it was also common practice for Brazilians to purchase attractive
girls who could profitably be let out as prostitutes.[15]

In Brazil, as in other slave societies, there were apparently authentic
reports of bondsmen being boiled alive, roasted in furnaces, or subjected to other fiendish punishments. More significant than such extreme cases of sadism is the evidence that planters who were successful
and were accepted as social leaders equipped their estates with the
chambers and instruments of torture; that it was common custom to
punish a recalcitrant slave with *novenas*, which meant that he would
be tied down and flogged for nine to thirteen consecutive nights, his
cuts sometimes being teased with a razor and rubbed with salt and
urine. In the mid-eighteenth century, Manuel Ribeiro Rocha attacked
the Brazilian "rural theology" which allowed masters to welcome their

new slaves with a vicious whipping, to work them in the fields without rest, and to inflict one hundred or more lashes without cause. A century later planters in the Parahyba Valley taught their sons that Negroes were not true men but inferior beings who could only be controlled by continued punishment; and some of the clergy maintained that Africans were the condemned sons of Cain. This widespread conviction of racial inferiority justified a regime of hatred and brutality in which the slave had no right of appeal and even fatal beatings went unpunished.[16]

Obviously much depended on regional differences in economy and social tradition. The recent studies of the extreme southern provinces of Brazil by Octávio Ianni and Fernando Cardoso reveal a picture of harsh chattel slavery and racial prejudice which stands in marked contrast to the familiar images of benign servitude in the north. During the last third of the eighteenth century the southern states developed a capitalistic economy which was initially stimulated by the export of wheat but which came to rely heavily on the production of jerked beef. Whether engaged in agriculture, stock raising, or the processing of meat or leather, the slaveholding capitalists were bent on maximizing production for commercial profit. Because the economy rested on slave labor and because physical labor was largely associated with the African race, Negroes and mulattoes were regarded as mere instruments of production, wholly lacking in human personality. According to Ianni, the slave was a totally alienated being; able to express himself only through the intermediary of his owner, he was under the complete dominion of a master class which rigidly controlled his movements and held power over his life and death. Though kind and paternalistic masters were to be found in Paraná, Santa Catarina, and Rio Grande do Sul, as elsewhere in the Americas, the overriding fact is that the ideology and judicial framework of southern Brazil were geared to the maintenance of an exploitive system of labor, to the preservation of public security, and to the perpetuation of power in the hands of a wl ite ruling caste. At every point the Negro was forced to shape his behavior in accordance with the actions and expectations of the white man.[17]

Conditions were undoubtedly better in the cities, where protective laws were more often enforced and where Negroes had at least a chance of acquiring money that could purchase freedom. But in colonial Cartagena, Negro slaves were subject to the most repressive police regulations, and to punishments which ranged from death to the cutting off of hands, ears, or the penis. In Marina the city councilors demanded in 1755 that the right to purchase freedom be withdrawn and that slaves who tried to escape be crippled for life. While both proposals aroused the indignation of the viceroy at Bahia, they indicate the state of mind of a master class which, in Minas Gerais, posted the heads of fugitive slaves along the roadsides. And men who accepted such brutality as a necessary part of life could not always be expected to abandon their fields or shut down their sugar mills on thirty-five religious holidays, in addition to fifty-two Sundays.[18] It was not an idyllic, semifeudal servitude that made colonial Braxil widely known as "the hell for Negroes," and as a place where their lives would be "nasty, brutish, and short"; or that drove countless bondsmen to suicide or revolt, and reduced others to a state of psychic shock, of flat apathy and depression, which was common enough in Brazil to acquire the special name of *banzo*.[19]

In the second half of the eighteenth century Spain and Portugal, like Britain and France, became intensely concerned with the reform of imperial administration. Severe losses in the Seven Years' War forced Spain to re-examine her colonial policy and to consider the best means for increasing the labor force, especially in Cuba. Ideas derived in part from the French Enlightenment encouraged statesmen to centralize administration, draft vast systems of law, and experiment with plans for social and economic progress. In Portugal, the Marquis de Pombal initiated colonial reforms that included a tightening of administration and the enactment of laws for the protection of slaves and the greater equalization of races. It is important to note, however, that Pombal's legislation affirming the civil rights of Indian and Asiatic subjects did not, in the words of C. R. Boxer, extend "in anything like the same measure to persons of Negro blood." And even in Asia there was such racial prejudice among the Portuguese that colonists long resisted the decrees, though they dreaded Pombal's dictatorial methods and usually carried out his orders without delay.[20]

Inspired by French ideals and administrative techniques, Charles III of Spain also supported a series of enlightened reforms that were intended to increase the force of reason and humanity in the Spanish Empire. Since Spain intended to stock Cuba with prodigious numbers of new slaves, and since the existing laws were a confused patchwork of ancient statutes and ordinances, it was obviously essential to follow the example of Colbert, and construct a code that would ensure a profitable use of labor without wholly subverting the cardinal precepts of religion and morality. Because the *Real Cédula* was drafted in 1789 and bore the influence of the Enlightenment as well as of

Spanish-Catholic tradition, it was an improvement over the *Code Noir* of 1685. Most notably, it included provisions for registering and keeping records of slaves, and machinery for securing information and punishing masters who denied their slaves adequate food or religious instruction. In 1784 a royal edict had also prohibited the branding of Negroes, a protection which had been given to Indians long before. But in spite of laws and traditions in the Spanish colonies that permitted slaves to buy their own freedom, the *Real Cédula* was silent on the subject of manumission. And it not only ruled that every slave was to work from dawn to dusk, but made clear that his employment should be confined to agriculture alone.[21] There are many indications, moreover, that Spanish planters paid little attention to the law. Certainly the Negro slaves who revolted in Venezuela in 1795 did not think their grievances could be expressed through appeals to kindly priests and judges.[22] Without minimizing the importance of the *Real Cédula* as an advance in humane legislation, one may observe that by 1789 there were far more enlightened proposals being discussed in Britain, France, and the United States, and that even British and American slaveholders were suggesting reforms that went beyond the Spanish law.

Furthermore, to round out one's picture of Spanish attitudes toward slavery it is well to look at other colonial slave codes, such as the one written for Santo Domingo in 1785, which claimed to be in accordance with a recent royal ordinance. The chief purposes of this detailed code were to reinvigorate a declining economy, to prevent insurrection, to put an end to the growing idleness, pride, and thievery of Negroes, and to preserve a clear-cut division between the white race and "las clases ínfimas." Since slaves were regarded as indispensable instruments for the public welfare, their owners were obliged to provide adequate food and clothing. Yet slaves were incapable of acting in their own behalf in court, and could acquire no property except for the benefit and by the permission of their masters. All Negroes, whether slave or free, were barred from public and religious elementary schools; their movements and employment were placed under the strictest regulations; they were required at all times to be submissive and respectful to all white persons, and to treat each one like a master. Any Negro or mulatto who contradicted a white man, or who spoke in a loud or haughty voice, was to be severly whipped. The penalties increased for raising a hand against a white person, but diminished in accordance with the lightness of the offender's skin. The stigma of slavish origin extended even to occupation and dress: Negroes were not to deprive white men of jobs by working in artisan trades, nor were they to wear fine clothes, gold, or precious jewels.[23]

There is evidence that, beginning in the late eighteenth century, Negro bondage became milder and better regulated in certain parts of Latin America. In such areas as New Granada the very survival of the institution was jeopardized by the revolutionary example of Saint Domingue, the outbreak of rebellions and continuing raids by fugitive *cimarrons*, the uncertainty of the African trade in the face of war and British humanitarianism, and the unsettling effects of war on markets and credit. The tumultuous period from the French Revolution to the Spanish American wars for independence brought abrupt changes in economic and political interests which often favored the Negro slave. But even Cuba, which had a long tradition of encouraging man-umissions, was the scene of gross cruelty and heavy slave mortality through much of the nineteenth century; and critics of the regime, like the reformer José Antonio Saco, were either silenced or banished from the island.[24]

In 1823, when the Britsh government pledged itself to the amelio-ration and eventual eradication of colonial slavery, José Bonifácio de Andrada hoped to persuade his fellow Brazilians that the success of their independence and new constitution depended on making a simi-lar commitment. Although Portugal, he charged, was guilty of the initial sin, "we tyrannize over our slaves and reduce them to the state of brutish animals, and they, in return, initiate us in their immorality and teach us all their vices." Calling on Brazil to follow the lead of Wilberforce and Buxton, José Bonifácio's words approached the vio-lence of a Garrison: "Riches, and more riches, do our pseudo-states-men cry out, and their call is reechoed by the buyers and sellers of human flesh, by our ecclesiastical blood hounds, by our magistrates." His proposals included the abolition of the African trade, the creation of special councils for the protection of bondsmen, the encouragement of marriage and religious instruction, and the transfer to a new master of any slave who could prove he had been the victim of cruelty or injustice. While we have been told that these moderate provisions were always characteristic of Brazilian slavery, they received no hearing after the General Constituent Assembly was dissolved and José Boni-fácio was arrested and banished. His proposal that the sale of slaves be registered so that a price could be fixed for the eventual purchase of freedom was not guaranteed by statute until 1871, although judges in some areas often enforced such a rule.[25]

In conclusion, it would appear that the image of the warmly human

Big House must be balanced by a counterimage of the brutal society of the coffee barons, who even in the 1870's and 1880's governed a world in which there were no gradations between slavery and freedom. In their deep-rooted racial prejudice, their military-like discipline, their bitter resistance to any restrictions on a slaveowner's will, their constant fear of insurrection, and their hostility toward meaningful religious instruction of their Negroes, these planters were hardly superior to their brothers in Mississippi. Even with the approach of inevitable emancipation, they made no effort to prepare their slaves for freedom. It was in the face of this "slave power" that the Brazilian abolitionists resorted to the familiar demands for "immediate" and "unconditional" emancipation, and modeled themselves on the champions of British and American reform. Joaquim Nabuco, the great leader of the Brazilian antislavery movement, adopted the pen name of "Garrison." [26]

With the exception of legal barriers to manumission, . . . the salient traits of North American slavery were to be found among the Spanish and Portuguese. Notwithstanding variations within every colony as a result of environment, economic conditions, social institutions, and the personality of owners, the Negro was everywhere a mobile and transferable possession whose labor and well-being were controlled by another man. Any comparison of slavery in North and South America should take account of the fact that Brazil alone had an area and variety comparable to all British America, and that the privileged artisans, porters, and domestic servants of colonial Brazilian cities can be compared only with their counterparts in New York and Philadelphia. Similarly, conditions in nineteenth-century Alabama and Mississippi must be held against those in the interior coffee-growing areas of south-central Brazil. Given the lack of detailed statistical information, we can only conclude that the subject is too complex and the evidence too contradictory for us to assume that the treatment of slaves was substantially better in Latin America than in the British colonies, taken as a whole.

NOTES

1. Stanley M. Elkins, *Slavery: A Problem in American Institutional and Intellectual Life* (Chicago, 1959), pp. 27-80. It is not my purpose to question all of Elkins's highly imaginative insights, or to attempt to prove that differences in religion, economy, and social structure had no bearing on the institution of Negro slavery. My aim is simply to show that the importance of such national and cultural differences has been exaggerated, and that all American slave-

holding colonies shared certain central assumptions and problems. I do not believe that the modern historian can escape what Elkins terms the moral "coercions" of the great nineteenth-century controversies by portraying both American slavery and antislavery as the pathological results of "the dynamics of unopposed capitalism." It should be noted that Elkins borrowed much of his conceptual framework from Frank Tannenbaum's enormously influential *Slave and Citizen: The Negro in the Americas* (New York, 1947). Though Tannenbaum was one of the first historians to emphasize the importance of Negro slavery in the overall development of the Americas, it seems to me that his comparison of Latin and Anglo-American slavery suffers from three basic weaknesses. First, he assumes that North American law, unlike that of Latin America, refused to recognize the slave as a moral personality. But this is an error, as we shall see. Second, he ignores the fact that the "classical" view of slavery, as embodied in Latin culture, drew as much from Plato and Aristotle as from Cicero and Seneca. Nineteenth-century Brazilian reformers, such as José Bonifácio, found it necessary to counter their opponents' use of classical authorities by arguing that Greeks and Romans had been ignorant of divine religion, and that, in any event, slavery in antiquity had not been so severe as that in Brazil, where racial and cultural differences deprived the bondsman of opportunities for equality (José Bonifácio de Andrada e Silva, *Memoir Addressed to the General, Constituent and Legislative Assembly of the Empire of Brazil* . . . [tr. by William Walton, London, 1826], pp. 20-22). As in Roman and North American law, the slave in Latin America was conceived at once as a chattel or instrument, and as a man with a soul. Third, Tannenbaum seems to think of Negro slavery in Latin America as a relatively unchanging institution, and assumes that certain humane laws of the late eighteenth and nineteenth centuries were typical of bondage in all Latin America throughout its long history. Even more questionable is his assumption that the admirable laws of European governments were obeyed by colonial slaveholders. For a thoughtful discussion of the Tannenbaum-Elkins thesis, see Sidney Mintz's long review of Elkins's book in *American Anthropologist*, LXIII (June, 1951), 579-87. An article which appeared after this chapter was written, and which presents a similar thesis, is Arnold A. Sio, "Interpretations of Slavery: The Slave Status in the Americas," *Comparative Studies in Society and History*, VII (April, 1965), 289-308.

2. The violence of the American Civil War has led some historians to assume that other nations abolished Negro slavery without bitter conflict. Yet even in Brazil, where Dom Pedro II strove consciously to avoid the bloody course taken by the United States, there was a radical abolitionist movement, an underground railroad, and sectional cleavage; the stormy conflict played an important part in bringing the downfall of the monarchy (see especially, Percy A. Martin, "Slavery and Abolition in Brazil," *Hispanic American Historical Review*, XIII [May, 1933], 151-96). British planters in the Caribbean frequently threatened secession, and finally submitted to the superior force of the British government only because they were too weak, economically and politically, to resist. They might have acted differently, as did the planters of Saint Domingue during the French Revolution, if Britain had moved to abolish slavery at the time of their greatest power.

3. Sir Harry Johnston, *The Negro in the New World* (New York, 1910), pp. 42-47, 87-94; Henry Koster, *Travels in Brazil* (London, 1816), pp. 385-86, 390,

444; Mary M. Williams, "The Treatment of Negro Slaves in the Brazilian Empire; a Comparison with the United States," *Journal of Negro History*, XV (1930), 313-36; Donald Pierson, *Negroes in Brazil* (Chicago, 1942), pp. 45-46; H. B. Alexander, "Brazilian and United States Slavery Compared," *Journal of Negro History*, VII (1922), 349-64; Gilberto Freyre, *The Masters and the Slaves: A Study in the Development of Brazilian Civilization* (tr. by Samuel Putnam, New York, 1946), pp. 7-11, 40-41, 369 ff and *passim*; Tannenbaum, *Slave and Citizen*, pp. 56, 100-5. An occasional traveler, such as Alexander Marjoribanks, observed that if Brazilian slaves were as well treated as those in the United States, there would have been no need to rely so heavily on the African trade as an answer to slave mortality (*Travels in South and North America* [London, 1853], p. 60). Freyre, Johnston, and Pierson have balanced a generally favorable picture of Latin American slavery with references to extreme cruelty and suffering.

4. Freyre, *Masters and Slaves*, pp. 7-11, and *passim*. But Freyre also maintains that the sexual relations of masters and slaves were authoritarian in character, and often led to sadistic cruelty.

5. Arthur Ramos, *The Negro in Brazil* (tr. by Richard Pattee, Washington, 1951), pp. 19-20.

6. John H. Moore, "Simon Gray, Riverman: A Slave Who was Almost Free," *Mississippi Valley Historical Review*, XLIX (Dec., 1962), 472-84.

7. Christopher Lloyd, *The Navy and the Slave Trade; the Suppression of the African Slave Trade in the Nineteenth Century* (London, 1949), pp. 34, 45. The United States showed laxness in suppressing the African trade, and American ships and capital helped to supply slaves to the chief nineteenth-century markets, Cuba and Brazil. But this laxness was quite a different thing from the open approval of the slave trade by Brazilians. And a recent study which takes a more favorable view of American attempts to suppress the slave trade points out that between 1837 and 1862 American ships captured at least 107 slavers (Peter Duignan and Clarence Clendenen, *The United States and the African Slave Trade*, 1619-1862 [n.p. (Stanford University), 1963], p. 54).

8. Octávio Tarquinio de Sousa, *História dos fundadores do Império do Brasil* (Rio de Janeiro, 1957-58), IX, 74; Stanley J. Stein, *Vassouras: A Brazilian Coffee County*, 1850-1900 (Cambridge, Mass., 1957), p. 20; Williams, "Treatment of Negro Slaves in the Brazilian Empire," p. 325. Not only did laws protecting the unity of slave families come surprisingly late, but they were for the most part unenforceable. See Stein, *Vassouras*, pp. 155-59; Martin, "Slavery and Abolition in Brazil," *passim*.

9. Lowell Joseph Ragatz, *The Fall of the Planter Class in the British Caribbean*, 1763-1833 (New York, 1928), pp. 66-67, 70-71; John Gabriel Stedman, *Narrative of a Five Years' Expedition, Against the Revolted Negroes of Surinam . . .* (London, 1796), I, 201-7; Marcel Trudel, *L'Esclavage au Canada française; histoire et conditions de l'esclavage* (Québec, 1960), pp. 160-92, 232-56; C. R. Boxer, *The Golden Age of Brazil, 1695-1750: Growing Pains of a Colonial Society* (Berkeley, 1962), p. 174; *Acts of the Assembly, Passed in the Charibbee Leeward Islands from 1690, to 1730* (London, 1732), *passim*; W. L. Burn, *Emancipation and Apprenticeship in the British West Indies* (London, 1937), pp. 64-70. Jean F. Dauxion-Lavaysse, who had traveled widely in the Spanish, French, and British colonies, said that the slaves on Sir William Young's model plantation at Saint Vincent were treated better than any he

had seen (*A Statistical, Commercial, and Political Description of Venezuela, Trinidad, Margarita, and Tobago* [tr. by E. Blaquière, London, 1820], p. 390).

10. Gaston Martin, *Histoire de l'esclavage dans les colonies françaises* (Paris, 1948), pp. 124-35; Ragatz, *Fall of Planter Class*, pp. 34-35; Frank W. Pitman, "Slavery on British West India Plantations in the Eighteenth Century," *Journal of Negro History*, XI (Oct., 1962), 610-17; Celso Furtado, *The Economic Growth of Brazil; a Survey from Colonial to Modern Times* (Berkeley, 1963), pp. 127-28. There is a certain irony in the fact that proslavery Southerners like Thomas R. R. Cobb accepted the conventional antislavery view of the West Indies. In contrast with the cruelty, impersonality, and depotism of the islands, North American masters and slaves worked side by side in clearing forests, building new homes, and hunting game; consequently, there developed a sense of cooperation and mutual sympathy which was unknown in the Caribbean, or so Cobb claimed in his *Inquiry into the Law of Negro Slavery* (Savannah, 1858), pp. clvii-clix.

11. Furtado, *Economic Growth of Brazil*, pp. 51, n. 129; C. R. Boxer, *Race Relations in the Portuguese Colonial Empire, 1415–1825* (Oxford, 1963), p. 101; Boxer, *Golden Age of Brazil*, pp. 7-9; Maurilio de Gouveia, *História da escravidão* (Rio de Janeiro, 1955), p. 68. In 1823 José Bonifácio noted that while Brazil had been importing some 40,000 slaves a year, the increase in the total slave population was hardly perceptible. Like British and North American reformers of a generation earlier, he was confident that the abolition of the trade would force masters to take better care of their human property (*Memoir Addressed to the General, Constituent and Legislative Assembly*, pp. 26-28).

12. *Las Siete Partidas de Rey don Alfonso el Sabio . . .* (Madrid, 1807), III, 117-28. Even Elsa V. Goveia exaggerates the liberality of Spanish law, although she rightly emphasizes the importance of an authoritarian government in checking the worst inclinations of slaveholding colonists. In the British West Indies, where the colonists long had a relatively free hand in framing their own laws, slaves were for a time deprived of virtually any legal protection. But given the loopholes and ambiguities in the Spanish law, one suspects that any difference in actual protection was more a result of differences in administrative machinery than in legal traditions (see Goveia, "The West Indian Slave Laws of the Eighteenth Century," *Revista de ciencias sociales*, IV [Mar., 1960], 75-105).

13. Rollando Mellafe, *La introducción de la esclavitud negra en Chile: tráfico y rutas* (Santiago de Chile, 1959), pp. 76-82; Richard Konetzke (ed.), *Colección de documentos para la historia de la formación social de Hispanoamérica, 1493–1810* (Madrid, 1962), II, 280, 427-28; Magnus Mörner, "Los esfuerzos realizados por la Corona para separar negrese indies en Hispano-américa durante el siglo XVI" (unpublished paper); Jaime Jaramillo Uribe, "Esclavos y señores en la sociedad colombiana del siglo XVIII," *Anuario colombiano de historia social y de la cultura*, I (Bogotá 1963), 5, 21.

14. Boxer, *Race Relations in Portuguese Colonial Empire*, p. 103; Gouveia, *História da escravidão*, p. 69; Boxer, *Golden Age of Brazil*, pp. 7, 138-39, 306-7; Uribe, "Esclavos y señores en la sociedad colombiana," pp. 22-25. In 1710 the king of Spain, hearing of the extremely cruel treatment of slaves in Peru and New Spain, issued orders allowing the governors to intervene and sell slaves who had been abused to kinder masters (Konetzke [ed.], *Colecció de documentos*, III, pt. 1, 113-14).

15. Boxer, *Golden Age of Brazil*, pp. 2-7, 138, 165; Robert Southey, *History of Brazil* (London, 1817–22), II, 644, 674-75; Georges Scelle, *La traite négrière aux Indes de Castille: contrats et traités d'assiento* (Paris, 1906), I, 504-5; Stein, *Vassouras*, pp. 64, 156-59.

16. Boxer, *Golden Age of Brazil*, pp. 8-9, 45-47; Williams, "Treatment of Negro Slaves in the Brazilian Empire," p. 326; Ramos, *Negro in Brazil*, pp. 34-36; Koster, *Travels in Brazil*, pp. 429, 444-55; Boxer, *Race Relations in Portuguese Colonial Empire*, pp. 27, 101, 112; Tarquinio de Sousa, *História dos fundadores do Império do Brasil*, IX, 70; Stein, *Vassouras*, pp. 132-39.

17. Octávio Ianni, *As metamorfoses do escravo* (São Paulo, 1962), pp. 82, 134-49, 282-85; Fernando Henrique Cardoso, *Capitalismo e escravidão no Brasil meridional* (São Paulo, 1962), pp. 35-81, 133-67, 310-13; Cardoso and Ianni, *Côr e mobilidade social em Florianópolis: aspectos das relações entre negros e brancos numa comunidade do Brasil meridional* (São Paulo, 1960), pp. 125-35.

18. Southey, *History of Brazil*, III, 780-84; Uribe, "Esclavos y señores en la sociedad colombiana," pp. 21-23; Boxer, *Golden Age of Brazil*, pp. 171-72. According to Boxer, in Brazil's "Golden Age" slaves on sugar plantations were worked around the clock when the mills were grinding cane, and some planters successfully evaded the rules against work on Sundays and religious holidays (*Golden Age of Brazil*, p. 7). In the nineteenth century, slaves worked on Sundays and saints' days in the Parahyba Valley (Stein, *Vassouras*, p. 75). Obviously there was more incentive to observe such rules when there were fewer pressures to maximize production. But the laws of many British colonies prohibited Sunday work and provided for religious holidays. Edward Long claimed that Jamaican slaves enjoyed about eighty-six days of leisure a year, counting Sundays and Saturday afternoons. The Jamaican slave code of 1816 prohibited Sunday work and ruled that at least twenty-six extra days a year should be given to slaves to cultivate their own gardens. There is evidence, however, that these regulations were disregarded, especially during crop time ([Edward Long], *The History of Jamaica; or, General Survey of the Antient and Modern State of that Island . . .* [London, 1774], II, 491; *Slave Law of Jamaica: with Proceedings and Documents Relative Thereto* [London, 1828], pp. 2, 63-65, 145-58; Burn, *Emancipation and Apprenticeship*, pp. 44-45).

19. Boxer, *Golden Age of Brazil*, pp. 7-9; Boxer, *Race Relations in Portuguese Colonial Empire*, p. 101; Stein, *Vassouras*, pp. 139-41; Pierson, *Negroes in Brazil*, pp. 3-7; Ramos, *Negro in Brazil*, p. 36. It is interesting to note that, according to Elkins, slavery in the United States was so severe and absolute that it molded the Negro's character into a submissive, childlike "Sambo," whose traits resembled those of the victims of Nazi concentration camps. Elkins could find no "sambos" in Latin America, and concludes that the character type was unique to the United States (*Slavery*, pp. 81-139). Without debating the merits of this intriguing thesis, we should point out that one source of "Sambo," which Elkins ignores, can be found in eighteenth-century English literature. . . . [This] fictional stereotype suited the tastes of a sentimental age. In actuality, ship captains and planters of various nationalities agreed that when Negroes were subjected to the harshest treatment, their usual responses were revolt, suicide, flight, or a sullen withdrawal and mental depression. The state which the Portuguese described as *banzo* was clearly the result of severe shock which altered the entire personality.

20. Raúl Carrancá y Trujillo, "El estatuto jurídico de los esclavos en las postrimerías de la colonización española," in *Revista de historia de América* (México, D.F.), No. 3 (Sept., 1938), 28-33; Agostinho Marques Perdigão Malheiro, *A escravidão no Brasil; ensaio historico-juridico-social* (Rio de Janeiro, 1866–67), part iii, pp. 32, 89-129; James Ferguson King, "The Evolution of the Free Slave Trade Principle in Spanish Colonial Administration," *Hispanic American Historical Review*, XXII (Feb., 1942), 34-56; Boxer, *Race Relations in Portuguese Colonial Empire*, pp. 73-74, 98-100. In 1761 Portugal prohibited the introduction of Negro slaves and ruled that all slaves brought to Portugal, the Azores, or Madeira would be emancipated. This law has sometimes been interpreted as humanitarian in motive and has been credited with having abolished slavery in metropolitan Portugal. According to Charles Verlinden, however, slavery remained legal in Portugal, and such legislation was an answer to the protests of free laborers against slave competition. A law of 1773 which provided for the emancipation of imported slaves also prohibited the importation of free colored laborers from Brazil, and in some ways resembled a French law of 1777 excluding all Negroes (see José Antonio Saco, *Historia de la esclavitud desde los tiempos mas remotos hasta nuestros dias* [2nd ed., Habana, 1936-45], III, 345; Charles Verlinden, *I'Esclavage dans l'Europe médiévale; tome premier: Péninsule Ibérique, France* [Brugge, 1955], p. 839; Boxer, *Race Relations in Portuguese Colonial Empire*, p. 100).

21. The text of the *Real Cédula* is in Carrancá, "Estatuto jurídico de los esclavos," pp. 51-59; for a detailed discussion of the law, see pp. 34-49.

22. Uribe, "Esclavos y señores en la sociedad colombiana," pp. 22-35, 42 ff; Federico Brito Figueroa, *Las insurrecciónes de los esclavos negros en la sociedad colonial Venezolana* (Caracas, 1910), pp. xii-xiii, 15-17, 41-42.

23. Konetzke (ed.), *Colección de documentos*, III, 553-73. If a Negro raised his hand against a white man, the penalty was one hundred lashes and two years in jail. . . .

24. Uribe, "Esclavos y señores en la sociedad colombiana," pp. 21-25; 42-51; Figueroa, *Las insurrecciónes de los esclavos negros*, pp. 41-42; Goveia, "West Indian Slave Laws," p. 79; Friedrich Heinrich Alexander von Humboldt, *The Island of Cuba* (tr. by J. S. Thrasher, New York, 1856), pp. 211-28, and *passim*; Hubert H. S. Aimes, "Coartación: A Spanish Institution for the Advancement of Slaves into Freedom," *Yale Review*, XVII (Feb., 1909), 421; Augustin Cochin, *The Results of Slavery* (tr. by Mary L. Booth, Boston, 1863), pp. 159-85.

25. José Bonifácio de Andrada, *Memoir Addressed to the General Constituent and Legislative Assembly*, pp. 14-23, 38-53; José Bonifácio de Andrada, *O patriarcha da independencia* (São Paulo, 1939), pp. 288-316; Tarquinio de Sousa, *História dos fundadores do Império do Brasil*, I, 129-30, 247-49; IX, 71-72. The English translator of José Bonifácio's address wrote a preface presenting a more favorable view of Brazilian slavery; but this was in line with British antislavery doctrine, which held that British slavery was much worse than that in either Latin America or the United States, José Bonifácio, on the other hand, said his reforms had been drawn from Danish, Spanish, and Mosaic legislation, and clearly thought Brazil was lagging behind the more enlightened nations. He was particularly harsh on the clergy, whom he accused of oppressing slaves for profit and sexual gratification.

26. Stein, *Vassouras*, pp. 67, 132-45, 155-60, 196-99, 290; Ianni, *As meta-*

morfoses do escravo, pp. 144-49; Cardoso, *Capitalismo e escravidao no Brasil meridional,* pp. 133-67; Carolina Nabuco, *The Life of Joaquim Nabuco* (tr. and ed. by Ronald Hilton, Stanford, 1950), pp. 108-13. One complex question which we cannot begin to consider is whether the survival of African cultural patterns in Brazil was the result of a less rigorous system of slavery. It seems possible that this persistence of culture was partly a product of heavy slave mortality and a continuing reliance on the African trade. By 1850 most slaves in the United States were removed by many generations from their African origins; this was certainly not the case in Brazil.

IV: THE SYSTEM

• *Kenneth M. Stampp's essay in the* American Historical Review *developed the basic lines of disagreement between older perspectives on slavery, embodied in the writings of historians such as Ulrich B. Phillips, and modern approaches to the subject.*

The Historian and Southern Negro Slavery

KENNETH M. STAMPP

A survey of the literature dealing with southern Negro slavery reveals one fundamental problem that still remains unresolved. This is the problem of the biased historian. It is, of course, a universal historical problem—one that is not likely to be resolved as long as historians themselves are divided into scientific and so-called "subjectivist-presentist-relativist" schools.[1] These schools seem to agree that historians ought to strive for a maximum of intellectual detachment and ought not to engage in special pleading and pamphleteering. But whether they are entitled to pass moral judgments, whether they can overcome the subjective influences of their own backgrounds and environments, are still debatable questions—at least they are questions which are still being debated. Yet it must be said that so far as Negro slavery is concerned we are still waiting for the first scientific and completely objective study of the institution which is based upon no assumptions whose validity cannot be thoroughly proved. And as long as historians must select their evidence from a great mass of sources, as long as they attempt to organize and interpret their findings, the prospects are not very encouraging.

This does not mean that everyone who has written about slavery has had the *same* bias, or that some have not been more flagrantly biased than others, or more skillful than others in the use of the subtle innuendo. It most certainly does not imply that further efforts toward a

From Kenneth M. Stampp, "The Historian and Southern Negro Slavery," *American Historical Review*, LVII (April 1952), pp. 613-24. Reprinted by permission.

clearer understanding of slavery are futile, or that we are not enormously indebted to the many scholars who have already engaged in research in this field. No student could begin to understand the complexities of the slave system without being thoroughly familiar with the findings and varying points of view of such historians as Ulrich B. Phillips, Herbert Aptheker, Lewis C. Gray, John Hope Franklin, Avery Craven, Carter G. Woodson, Frederick Bancroft, Charles S. Sydnor, John Spencer Bassett, and many others.

Among these scholars, the late Professor Phillips has unquestionably made the largest single contribution to our present understanding of southern slavery. It may be that his most durable monument will be the vast amount of new source material which he uncovered But Phillips was also an unusually able and prolific writer. Measured only crudely in terms of sheer bulk, his numerous books and articles are impressive.[2] That, taken together with his substantial compilations of fresh factual information, his rare ability to combine scholarship with a fine literary style, and his point of view for which there has been a persistent affinity, explains the deep impression he has made. One needs only to sample the textbooks and monographic literature to appreciate the great influence of Professor Phillips' interpretations and methodology. A historian who recently attempted to evaluate Phillips' investigations of the slave-plantation system arrived at this conclusion: "So thorough was his work that, granted the same purpose, the same materials, and the same methods, his treatment . . . is unlikely to be altered in fundamental respects." [3]

"There is, however," this historian hastened to add, "nothing inevitable about his point of view or his technique." Rather, he contended that "a materially different version" would emerge when scholars with different points of view and different techniques subjected the slave system to a similarly intensive study.[4] Indeed, he might have noted that a "materially different version" is already emerging. For the most notable additions to the bibliography of slavery during the past three decades have been those which have in some way altered Phillips' classic exposition of the slave regime. This revisionism is the product of new information discovered in both old and new sources, of new research techniques, and, to be sure, of different points of view and different assumptions. In recent years the subject has become less and less an emotional issue between scholarly descendants of the northern abolitionists and of the southern proslavery school. It may only be a sign of the effeteness of the new generation of scholars, but there is a tendency among them to recognize that it is at least conceivable that a colleague on the other side of the Mason and Dixon line could write something significant about slavery. For the new light that is constantly being shed upon the Old South's "peculiar institution" we are indebted to historians of both southern and northern origins— and of both the Negro and white races.

One of these revisionists has raised some searching questions about Phillips' methodology. Professor Richard Hofstadter has discovered a serious flaw in Phillips' sampling technique, which caused him to examine slavery and slaveholders on "types of plantations that were not at all representative of the common slaveholding unit." Phillips made considerable use of the case-study method, and he relied heavily upon the kinds of manuscript records kept primarily by the more substantial planters. Therefore, Hofstadter concludes, "Insofar . . . as Phillips drew his picture of the Old South from plantations of more than 100 slaves [as he usually did], he was sampling about 10% of all the slaves and less than 1% of all the slaveholders." [5] The lesser planters and small slaveholding farmers, who were far more typical, rarely kept diaries and formal records; hence they received considerably less attention from Phillips. The danger in generalizing about the whole regime from an unrepresentative sample is obvious enough.

Getting information about the slaves and masters on the smaller holdings is difficult, but it is nevertheless essential for a comprehensive understanding of the slave system. Professor Frank L. Owsley has already demonstrated the value of county records, court records, and census returns for this purpose.[6] Phillips made only limited use of the evidence gathered by contemporary travelers, especially by Frederick Law Olmsted in whom he had little confidence. The traveler in the South who viewed slavery with an entirely open mind was rare indeed, but it does not necessarily follow that the only accurate reporters among them were those who viewed it sympathetically.

How the picture of slavery will be modified when life on the small plantations and farms has been adequately studied cannot be predicted with as much assurance as some may think. The evidence now available suggests conflicting tendencies. On these units there was very little absentee ownership, the proverbially harsh overseer was less frequently employed, and contacts between masters and slaves were often more numerous and intimate. Undoubtedly in many cases these conditions tended to make the treatment of the Negroes less harsh and the system less rigid. But it is also necessary to consider other tendencies, as well as the probability that the human factor makes generalization risky. Sometimes the material needs of the slaves were provided for more adequately on the larger plantations than they were on the smaller ones. Sometimes the lower educational and cultural level and the insecure social status of the small slaveholders had an unfavorable effect upon their racial attitudes. There are enough cases in the court records to make it clear that members of this group were, on occasion, capable of extreme cruelty toward their slaves. Nor can the factor of economic competition be overlooked. The lesser planters who were ambitious to rise in the social scale were, to phrase it cautiously, exposed to the temptation not to indulge their slaves while seeking their fortunes in competition with the larger planters. To be sure, as Lewis C. Gray points out, many of these small slaveholders lived in relatively isolated areas where the competitive factor was less urgent.[7] But there is still a need for further investigation of these small slaveholders before generalizations about conditions among their slaves will cease to be highly speculative.

A tendency toward loose and glib generalizing is, in fact, one of the chief faults of the classic portrayal of the slave regime—and, incidentally, of some of its critics as well. This is true of descriptions of how the slaves were treated: how long and hard they were worked, how severely they were punished, how well they were fed, housed, and clothed, and how carefully they were attended during illness. It may be that some historians have attached an undue significance to these questions, for there are important philosophical implications in the evaluation of slavery in terms of such mundane matters as what went into the slave's stomach. In any event, the evidence hardly warrants the sweeping pictures of uniform physical comfort or uniform physical misery that are sometimes drawn. The only generalization that can be made with relative confidence is that some masters were harsh and frugal, others were mild and generous, and the rest ran the whole gamut in between. And even this generalization may need qualification, for it is altogether likely that the same master could have been harsh and frugal on some occasions and mild and generous on others. Some men became increasingly mellow and others increasingly irascible with advancing years. Some masters were more generous, or less frugal, in times of economic prosperity than they were in times of economic depression. The treatment of the slaves probably varied with the state of the master's health, with the vicissitudes of his domestic relations, and with the immediate or subsequent impact of alcoholic beverages upon his personality. It would also be logical to suspect—and there is evidence that this was the case—that masters did not treat all their slaves alike, that, being human, they developed personal animosities for some and personal affections for others. The care of slaves under the supervision of overseers might change from year to year as one overseer replaced another in the normally rapid turnover. In short, the human factor introduced a variable that defied generalization.

This same human factor complicates the question of how the Negroes reacted to their bondage. The generalization that the great majority of Negroes were contented as slaves has never been proved, and in the classic picture it was premised on the assumption that certain racial traits caused them to adapt to the system with peculiar ease. If freedom was so far beyond their comprehension, it was a little remarkable that freedom was the very reward considered most suitable for a slave who rendered some extraordinary service to his master or to the state. It is well known that many slaves took advantage of opportunities to purchase their freedom. Resistance by running away and by the damaging of crops and tools occurred frequently enough to cause Dr. Samuel Cartwright of Louisiana to conclude that these acts were the symptoms of exotic diseases peculiar to Negroes.[8] Though there is no way to discover precisely how much of the property damage was deliberate, and how much was merely the by-product of indifference and carelessness, the distinction is perhaps inconsequential. Finally, there were individual acts of violence against masters and overseers, and cases of conspiracy and rebellion. If the significance of these cases has been overstated by Herbert Aptheker,[9] it has been understated by many of his predecessors.

This is not to deny that among the slaves only a minority of undeterminable size fought the system by these various devices. It is simply to give proper emphasis to the fact that such a minority did exist. In all probability it consisted primarily of individuals of exceptional daring, or intelligence, or individuality. Such individuals constitute a minority in all societies.

That the majority of Negroes seemed to submit to their bondage proves neither their special fitness for it nor their contentment with it. It merely proves that men *can* be enslaved when they are kept illiterate, when communication is restricted, and when the instruments of violence are monopolized by the state and the master class.[10] In the light of twentieth-century experience, when white men have also been forced to submit to tyranny and virtual slavery, it would appear to be a little preposterous to generalize about the peculiarities of Negroes in this respect. In both cases the majority has acquiesced. In neither case does it necessarily follow that they have reveled in their bondage.

To be sure, there were plenty of opportunists among the Negroes who played the role assigned to them, acted the clown, and curried the favor of their masters in order to win the maximum rewards within the system, sometimes even at the expense of their fellow slaves. There were others who, in the very human search for personal recognition within their limited social orbit, salvaged what prestige they could from the high sales prices attached to them, or from the high social status of their masters.[11] Nor is it necessary to deny that many slaves sang and danced, enjoyed their holidays, and were adaptable enough to find a measure of happiness in their daily lives. It is enough to note that all of this still proves nothing, except that it is altogether likely that Negroes behaved much as people of other races would have behaved under similar circumstances.

In describing these various types of slave behavior historians must always weigh carefully, or at least recognize, the moral implications and value judgments implicit in the adjectives they use. How, for example, does one distinguish a "good" Negro from a "bad" Negro in the slave regime? Was the "good" Negro the one who was courteous and loyal to his master, and who did his work faithfully and cheerfully? Or was the "good" Negro the defiant one who has sometimes been called "insolent" or "surly" or "unruly"? Was the "brighter" side of slavery to be found in the bonds of love and loyalty that developed between some household servants and some of the more genteel and gentle masters? Or was it to be found among those slaves who would not submit, who fought back, ran away, faked illness, loafed, sabotaged, and never ceased longing for freedom in spite of the heavy odds against them? In short, just what *are* the proper ethical standards for identifying undesirable or even criminal behavior among slaves? There is no answer that is not based upon subjective factors, and the question therefore may not be within the province of "objective" historians. But in that case historians must also avoid the use of morally weighted adjectives when they write about slavery.

The general subject of slave behavior suggests a method of studying the institution which revisionists need to exploit more fully. For proper balance and perspective slavery must be viewed through the eyes of the Negro as well as through the eyes of the white master.[12] This is obviously a difficult task, for slaves rarely wrote letters or kept diaries.[13] But significant clues can be found in scattered sources. The autobiographies and recollections of fugitive slaves and freedmen have value when used with the caution required of all such sources. Slaves were interviewed by a few travelers in the ante-bellum South, and ex-slaves by a few historians in the post-Civil War period; [14] but unfortunately the interviewing was never done systematically until the attempt of the Federal Writers Project in the 1930's.[15] The mind of the slave can also be studied through his external behavior as it is described in plantation manuscripts, court records, and newspaper files. For example, there is undoubtedly some psychological significance in the high frequency of stuttering and of what was loosely called a "downcast look" among the slaves identified in the advertisements for fugitives.[16] Finally, the historian might find clues to the mental processes of the slaves in the many recent sociological and anthropological studies of the American Negro. The impact of nineteenth-century slavery and of twentieth-century prejudice and discrimination upon the Negro's thought and behavior patterns have some significant similarities.[17]

This kind of perspective is not to be found in the Phillips version of slavery, for he began with a basic assumption which gave a different direction to his writings. That he failed to view the institution through the eyes of the Negro, that he emphasized its mild and humorous side and minimized its grosser aspects, was the result of his belief—implicit always and stated explicitly more than once—in the inherent inferiority of the Negro race. The slaves, he wrote, were "by racial quality" "submissive," "light-hearted," "amiable," "ingratiating," and "imitative." Removing the Negro from Africa to America, he added, "had little more effect upon his temperament than upon his complexion." Hence "the progress of the generality [of slaves] was restricted by the fact of their being negroes." [18] Having isolated and identified these "racial qualities," Phillips conclusions about slavery followed logically enough.

It is clear in every line Phillips wrote that he felt no animus toward the Negroes. Far from it. He looked upon them with feelings of genuine kindliness and affection. But hearing as he did the still-faintly-ringing laughter of the simple plantation Negroes, the songs sung in their melodious voices, Phillips was unable to take them seriously. Instead he viewed them as lovable, "serio-comic" figures who provided not only a labor supply of sorts but also much of the plantation's social charm. Thus slavery was hardly an institution that could have weighed heavily upon them.

Now, it is probably true that the historian who criticizes slavery per se reveals a subjective bias, or at least certain assumptions he cannot prove. The sociological argument of George Fitzhugh that slavery is a positive good, not only for the laboring man but for society in general, cannot be conclusively refuted with scientific precision. Those who disagree with Fitzhugh can only argue from certain unproved premises and optimistic convictions about the so-called "rights" and "dignity" of labor and the potentialities of free men in a democratic society. And the historian may run into all sorts of difficulties when he deals with such subjective matters.

But to assume that the *Negro* was peculiarly suited for slavery because of certain inherent racial traits is quite another matter. This involves not primarily a subjective bias but ignorance of, or disregard for, the overwhelming evidence to the contrary. Much of this evidence was already available to Phillips, though it must be noted that he grew up at a time when the imperialist doctrine of the "white man's burden" and the writings of such men as John Fiske and John W. Burgess were giving added strength to the belief in Anglo-Saxon superiority. Nor should he be blamed for failing to anticipate the findings of biologists, psychologists, anthropologists, and sociologists subsequent to the publication of his volume *American Negro Slavery* in 1918. It may be significant that he presented his own point of view with considerably more restraint in his *Life and Labor in the Old South* which appeared a decade later.

Nevertheless, it is this point of view which both dates and outdates the Phillips version of slavery. No historian of the institution can be taken seriously any longer unless he begins with the knowledge that there is no valid evidence that the Negro race is innately inferior to the white, and that there is growing evidence that both races have approximately the same potentialities.[19] He must also take into account the equally important fact that there are tremendous variations in the capacities and personalities of individuals within each race, and that it is therefore impossible to make valid generalizations about races as such.

An awareness of these facts is forcing the revisionists to discard much of the folklore about Negroes that found a support in the classic portrayal of slavery. Take, for example, the idea that the primitive Negroes brought to America could only adapt to the culture of the civilized white man in the course of many generations of gradual growth. Phillips saw the plantation as "a school constantly training and controlling pupils who were in a backward state of civilization. . . . On the whole the plantations were the best schools yet invented for the mass training of that sort of inert and backward people which the bulk of the American negroes represented." [20]

This idea would seem to imply that the Negroes could only be civilized through a slow evolutionary process, during which they would gradually acquire and transmit to their descendants the white man's patterns of social behavior. In actual fact the first generation of Negroes born in the English colonies in the seventeenth century was as capable of learning these patterns of social behavior—for they were things that were learned, not inherited—and of growing up and living as free men as was the generation alive in 1865. Indeed many of the Negroes of this Civil War generation were *still* unprepared for freedom; and that fact reveals the basic flaw in the whole Phillips concept. It does not show that the plantation school had not had sufficient time to complete its work but rather that it was capable of doing little more than training succeeding generations of slaves. After two centuries of slavery most Negroes had to learn how to live as free men by *starting* to live as free men. The plantation school may have had some limited success as a vocational institution, but in the field of the social sciences it was almost a total failure.

Other discredited aspects of the mythology of slavery can be mentioned only briefly. Revisionists no longer attempt to explain the origin of the institution with a doctrine of "climatic determinism." Since white men did and still do labor long and hard in cotton and tobacco fields there is little point in tracing southern slavery to the generative powers of southern heat.[21] Nor does it appear that the health of Negroes in the fever-infested rice swamps was as flourishing as it has sometimes been described.[22] And the fact that unfree labor alone made possible the rise of the plantation system proves neither the "necessity" nor the "inevitability" of slavery. For there was nothing inevitable about the plantation. Without this supply of unfree labor southern agriculture would probably have given less emphasis to the production of staples, and the small-farm unit would have prevailed. But the South would not have remained a wilderness. Moreover, Negroes *might* have been brought to America as servants rather than slaves (as the first ones were). Thus, like the white servants, many of them might have become landowning farmers in the period when land was abundant and cheap.

Slavery, then, was the inevitable product of neither the weather nor some irresistible force in the South's economic evolution. Slaves were used in southern agriculture because men sought greater returns than they could obtain from their own labor alone. It was a man-made institution. It was inevitable only insofar as everything that has happened in history was inevitable, not in terms of immutable or naturalistic laws.

And finally, the revisionists have brought some of the classic conclusions about the economics of slavery under serious scrutiny. Was it really a profitable institution? Although Thomas R. Dew and some other proslavery writers argued that it was and that it would have been abolished had it not been, there has been a persistent tendency, dating back to ante-bellum times, to minimize the question of profits and to emphasize other factors. It was not that slavery was profitable—indeed many contended that it was actually unprofitable for most slaveholders —but rather it was the race question or the masters' feeling of responsibility for the Negroes that explained its preservation. This was also the conclusion of Professor Phillips who believed that, except on the rich and fresh lands of the Southwest, slavery had nearly ceased to be profitable by 1860.[23]

But in recent years there has been much disagreement with this conclusion. Lewis C. Gray, Thomas P. Govan, Robert R. Russel, and Robert Worthington Smith have found evidence that slavery continued to be profitable for the slaveholders as a class down to the very outbreak of the Civil War.[24] Frequently the average money investment in the plantation labor force has been exaggerated; depreciation on this investment has been figured as a cost when the slaves were actually increasing in both numbers and value; and faulty accounting methods have resulted in listing interest on the slave investment as an operational expense. Too often profits have been measured exclusively in terms of staple production, and the value of the natural increase of slaves, of the food they produced for the master and his family, and of the personal services they rendered have been ignored. Many of the debt-burdened planters provided evidence not of the unprofitability of slavery but of their tendency to disregard the middle-class virtue of thrift and to live beyond their means. Nor does slavery appear to be primarily responsible for the crude agricultural methods or for the soil exhaustion that occurred in the South.[25]

Rarely has a group engaged in agriculture earned the returns and achieved the high social status enjoyed by the southern slaveholding class. Certainly no colonial or nineteenth-century farmer could have hoped to reap such fruits from his own labor. The fact that some planters made fortunes while others failed, that the profits were painfully low in times of economic depression, merely demonstrates that the slave-plantation system had many striking similarities to the factory system based on private capitalist production. Is one to generalize about the profits of industrial capitalism from the fortunes accumulated by some, or from the failures suffered by thousands of others?

From the high returns in periods of prosperity, or from the low returns in periods of depression? And what is to be made of the oft-repeated argument that the planters got nowhere because "they bought lands and slaves wherewith to grow cotton, and with the proceeds ever bought more slaves to make more cotton"? [26] If this is the essence of economic futility, then one must also pity the late Andrew Carnegie who built a mill wherewith to make steel, and with the proceeds ever built more mills to make more steel. The economist would not agree that either Carnegie or the planters were in a vicious circle, for they were simply enlarging their capital holdings by reinvesting their surplus profits.

The revisionists still agree that slavery, in the long run, had some unfavorable economic consequences for the South as a whole, especially for the nonslaveholding whites.[27] And some historian may yet point out that slavery was not very profitable for the Negroes. At least he may question the baffling generalization that the southern whites were more enslaved by Negro slavery than were the Negro slaves.[28] For in the final analysis, it was the Negro who had the most to gain from emancipation.

Abolitionists have suffered severely at the hands of historians during the past generation. They have been roundly condemned for their distortions and exaggerations. But are historians really being "objective" when they combine warm sympathy for the slaveholders' point of view with cold contempt for those who looked upon the enslavement of four million American Negroes as the most shocking social evil of their day? Perhaps historians need to be told what James Russell Lowell once told the South: "It is time . . . [to] learn . . . that the difficulty of the Slavery question is slavery itself—nothing more, nothing less." [29] It may be that the most important fact that the historian will ever uncover about the South's "peculiar institution" is that slavery, at its best, was still slavery, and that certain dangers were inherent in a master-slave relationship even among normal men.

NOTES

1. Chester McArthur Destler, "Some Observations on Contemporary Historical Thought," *American Historical Review*, LV (April, 1950), 503-29.

2. Phillips's findings and conclusions can be studied most conveniently in *American Negro Slavery* (New York, 1918), and in *Life and Labor in the Old South* (Boston, 1929).

3. Richard Hofstadter, "U. B. Phillips and the Plantation Legend," *Journal of Negro History*, XXIX (April, 1944), 124.

4. *Ibid.*, pp. 122, 124.

5. *Ibid.*, pp. 109-19.

6. Frank L. and Harriet C. Owsley, "The Economic Basis of Society in the Late Ante-Bellum South," *Journal of Southern History*, VI (February, 1940), 24-45. Much information about the treatment of slaves on the small plantations and farms can be found in Helen T. Caterall, ed., *Judicial Cases concerning American Slavery and the Negro* (5 vols., New York, 1926-37).

7. Lewis C. Gray, *History of Agriculture in the Southern United States to 1860* (Washington, 1933), I, 518, 556-57.

8. Raymond A. and Alice H. Bauer, "Day to Day Resistance to Slavery," *Jour. Negro Hist.*, XXVII (October, 1942), 388-419. For references to some of Dr. Cartwright's unique views see Felice Swados, "Negro Health on the Ante Bellum Plantations," *Bulletin of the History of Medicine*, X (October, 1941), 462.

9. Herbert Aptheker, *American Negro Slave Revolts* (New York, 1943). Many acts of violence by individual slaves are recorded in Caterall, *passim*.

10. The techniques of Negro enslavement are described in Aptheker, pp. 53-78.

11. Historians who failed to grasp the psychological significance of such slave behavior have sometimes drawn some unjustifiable inferences from it, for example, that Negroes were naturally docile and felt no personal humiliation because of their inferior status.

12. John Hope Franklin makes a brief attempt to accomplish this in *From Slavery to Freedom* (New York, 1948), pp. 204-12.

13. *Cf.* Carter G. Woodson, ed., *The Mind of the Negro as Reflected in Letters Written during the Crisis, 1800–1860* (Washington, 1926).

14. See, for example, Harrison A. Trexler, *Slavery in Missouri, 1804–1865* (Baltimore, 1914), *passim*.

15. Selections from these interviews are published in Benjamin A. Botkin, ed., *Lay My Burden Down* (Chicago, 1945).

16. The present writer was impressed by this while searching through thousands of advertisements for fugitive slaves in various southern newspapers.

17. Especially suggestive is Robert L. Sutherland, *Color, Class, and Personality* (Washington, 1942).

18. *American Negro Slavery*, pp. 291-92, 339, 341-42.

19. For a summary of the evidence and literature on this subject see Gunnar Myrdal, *An American Dilemma: The Negro Problem and Modern Democracy* (New York, 1944), esp. chap. VI, including the footnotes to this chapter, pp. 1212-18.

20. *American Negro Slavery*, pp. 342-43.

21. Oscar and Mary F. Handlin, "Origins of the Southern Labor System," *William and Mary Quarterly*, VII (April, 1950), 199.

22. Swados, pp. 460-72; J. H. Easterby, ed., *The South Carolina Rice Plantation as Revealed in the Papers of Robert F. W. Allston* (Chicago, 1945), p. 30; Bennett H. Wall, "Medical Care of Ebenezer Pettigrew's Slaves," *Mississippi Valley Historical Review*, XXXVII (December, 1950), 451-70.

23. *American Negro Slavery*, pp. 391-92.

24. Lewis C. Gray, "Economic Efficiency and Competitive Advantage of Slavery under the Plantation System," *Agricultural History*, IV (April, 1930), 31-47; Thomas P. Govan, "Was Plantation Slavery Profitable?" *Jour. Southern*

Hist., VIII (November, 1942), 513-35; Robert R. Russel, "The General Effects of Slavery upon Southern Economic Progress," *ibid.*, IV (February, 1938), 34-54; Robert Worthington Smith, "Was Slavery Unprofitable in the Ante-Bellum South?" *Agric. Hist.*, XX (January, 1946), 62-64.

25. Gray, *History of Agriculture*, I, 447-48, 470; Avery O. Craven, *The Repressible Conflict*, 1830–1861 (Baton Rouge, 1939), chaps. I, II.

26. Phillips, *American Negro Slavery*, pp. 395-98.

27. Gray, *History of Agriculture*, II, 940-42.

28. "In a real sense the whites were more enslaved by the institution than the blacks." James G. Randall, *The Civil War and Reconstruction* (Boston, 1937), p. 73. "As for Sambo . . . there is some reason to believe that he suffered less than any other class in the South from its 'peculiar institution.' " Samuel Eliot Morison and Henry Steele Commager, *The Growth of the American Republic* (4th ed.; New York, 1950), I, 537.

29. [James Russell Lowell], "The Question of the Hour," *Atlantic Monthly*, VII (1861), 120-21.

• The following selection presents Stanley M. Elkins's influential analysis of the mechanisms used by American slaveholders to produce infantile behavior among their Negro bondsmen. It also discusses his controversial concentration-camp analogy. The student should remember that Elkins is attempting only to describe the "Sambo"-like characteristics which he associates with role-playing expected of American Negro slaves; he is not in any sense expressing his approval of the concept, whatever its validity as an explanation of slave personality.

Slavery and Negro Personality

STANLEY M. ELKINS

PERSONALITY TYPES AND STEREOTYPES

. . . It will be assumed that there were elements in the very structure of the plantation system—its "closed" character—that could sustain infantilism as a normal feature of behavior. These elements, having less to do with "cruelty" per se than simply with the sanctions of authority, were effective and pervasive enough to require that such infantilism be characterized as something much more basic than mere "accommodations." It will be assumed that the sanctions of the system were in themselves sufficient to produce a recognizable personality type.[1]

It should be understood that to identify a social type in this sense is still to generalize on a fairly crude level—and to insist for a limited purpose on the legitimacy of such generalizing is by no means to deny that, on more refined levels, a great profusion of individual types might have been observed in slave society. Nor need it be claimed that the "Sambo" type, even in the relatively crude sense employed here, was a

From Stanley M. Elkins, *Slavery, A Problem in American Institutional and Intellectual Life* (Chicago: University of Chicago Press, 1959), pp. 86-9, 115-39. Reprinted by permission of the University of Chicago Press. Copyright © 1959 by The University of Chicago Press.

universal type. It was, however, a plantation type, and a plantation existence embraced well over half the slave population.[2] Two kinds of material will be used in the effort to picture the mechanisms whereby this adjustment to absolute power—an adjustment whose end product included infantile features of behavior—may have been effected. One is drawn from the theoretical knowledge presently available in social psychology, and the other, in the form of an analogy, is derived from some of the data that have come out of the German concentration camps. It is recognized in most theory that social behavior is regulated in some general way by adjustment to symbols of authority—however diversely "authority" may be defined either in theory or in culture itself—and that such adjustment is closely related to the very formation of personality. A corollary would be, of course, that the more diverse those symbols of authority may be, the greater is the permissible variety of adjustment to them—and the wider the margin of individuality, consequently, in the development of the self. The question here has to do with the wideness or narrowness of that margin on the antebellum plantation.

The other body of material, involving an experience undergone by several million men and women in the concentration camps of our own time, contains certain items of relevance to the problem here being considered. The experience was analogous to that of slavery and was one in which wide-scale instances of infantilization were observed. The material is sufficiently detailed, and sufficiently documented by men who not only took part in the experience itself but who were versed in the use of psychological theory for analyzing it, that the advantages of drawing upon such data for purposes of analogy seem to outweigh the possible risks.

The introduction of this second body of material must to a certain extent govern the theoretical strategy itself. It has been recognized both implicitly and explicitly that the psychic impact and effects of the concentraion-camp exprience were not anticipated in existing theory and that consequently such theory would require some major supplementation.[3] It might be added, parenthetically, that almost any published discussion of this modern Inferno, no matter how learned, demonstrates how "theory," operating at such a level of shared human experience, tends to shed much of its technical trappings and to take on an almost literary quality. The experience showed, in any event, that infantile personality features could be induced in a relatively short time among large numbers of adult human beings coming from very diverse backgrounds. The particular strain which was thus placed upon prior theory consisted in the need to make room not only for the cultural and environmental sanctions that sustain personality (which in a sense Freudian theory already had) but also for a virtually unanticipated problem: actual change in the personality of masses of adults. It forced a reappraisal and new appreciation of how completely and effectively prior cultural sanctions for behavior and personality could be detached to make way for new and different sanctions, and of how adjustments could be made by individuals to a species of authority vastly different from any previously known. The revelation for theory was the process of detachment.

These cues, accordingly, will guide the argument on Negro slavery. Several million people were detached with a peculiar effectiveness from a great variety of cultural backgrounds in Africa—a detachment operating with infinitely more effectiveness upon those brought to North America than upon those who came to Latin America. It was achieved partly by the shock experience inherent in the very mode of procurement but more specifically by the type of authority-system to which they were introduced and to which they had to adjust for physical and psychic survival. The new adjustment, to absolute power in a closed system, involved infantilization, and the detachment was so complete that little trace of prior (and thus alternative) cultural sanctions for behavior and personality remained for the descendants of the first generation. For them, adjustment to clear and omnipresent authority could be more or less automatic—as much so, or as little, as it is for anyone whose adjustment to a social system begins at birth and to whom that system represents normality. We do not know how generally a full adjustment was made by the first generation of fresh slaves from Africa. But we do know—from a modern experience—that such an adjustment is possible, not only within the same generation but within two or three years. This proved possible for people in a full state of complex civilization, for men and women who were not black and not savages. . . .

THREE THEORIES OF PERSONALITY

The immense revelation for psychology in the concentration-camp literature has been the discovery of how elements of dramatic personality change could be brought about in masses of individuals. And yet it is not proper that the crude fact of "change" alone should dominate the conceptual image with which one emerges from this problem. "Change" per se, change that does not go beyond itself, is productive of nothing; it leaves only destruction, shock, and howling bedlam behind it unless some future basis of stability and order lies waiting to guarantee it and give it reality. So it is with the human psyche, which is apparently capable of making terms with a state other than liberty as we know it. The very dramatic features of the process just described may upset the nicety of this point. There is the related danger, moreover, of unduly stressing the individual psychology of the problem at the expense of its social psychology.

These hazards might be minimized by maintaining a conceptual distinction between two phases of the group experience. The process of detachment from prior standards of behavior and value is one of them, and is doubtless the more striking, but there must be another one. That such detachment can, by extension, involve the whole scope of an individual's culture is an implication for which the vocabulary of individual psychology was caught somewhat unawares. Fluctuations in the state of the individual psyche could formerly be dealt with, or so it seemed, while taking for granted the more or less static nature of social organization, and with a minimum of reference to its features. That such organization might itself become an important variable was therefore a possibility not highly developed in theory, focused as theory was upon individual case histories to the invariable minimization of social and cultural setting. The other phase of the experience should be considered as the "stability" side of the problem, that phase which stabilized what the "shock" phase only opened the way for. This was essentially a process of adjustment to a standard of social normality, though in this case a drastic readjustment and compressed within a very short time—a process which under typical conditions of individual and group existence is supposed to begin at birth and last a lifetime and be transmitted in many and diffuse ways from generation to generation. The adjustment is assumed to be slow and organic, and it normally is. Its numerous aspects extend much beyond psychology; those aspects have in the past been treated at great leisure within the rich provinces not only of psychology but of history, sociology, and literature as well. What rearrangement and compression of those provinces may be needed to accommodate a mass experience that not only involved profound individual shock but also required rapid assimilation to a drastically different form of social organization, can hardly be known. But perhaps the most conservative beginning may be made with existing psychological theory.

The theoretical system whose terminology was orthodox for most of the Europeans who have written about the camps was that of Freud. It was necessary for them to do a certain amount of improvising, since the scheme's existing framework provided only the narrowest leeway for dealing with such radical concepts as out-and-out change in personality. This was due to two kinds of limitations which the Freudian vocabulary places upon the notion of the "self." One is that the superego—that part of the self involved in social relationships, social values, expectations of others, and so on—is conceived as only a small and highly refined part of the "total" self. The other is the assumption that the content and character of the superego is laid down in childhood and undergoes relatively little basic alteration thereafter.[4] Yet a Freudian diagnosis of the concentration-camp inmate—whose social self, or superego, did appear to change and who seemed basically changed thereby—is, given these limitations, still possible. Elie Cohen, whose analysis is the most thorough of these, specifically states that "the superego acquired new values in a concentration camp."[5] The old values, according to Dr. Cohen, were first silenced by the shocks which produced "acute depersonalization" (the subject-object split: "It is not the real 'me' who is undergoing this"), and by the powerful drives of hunger and survival. Old values, thus set aside, could be replaced by new ones. It was a process made possible by "infantile regression"—regression to a previous condition of childlike dependency in which parental prohibitions once more became all-powerful and in which parental judgments might once more be internalized. In this way a new "father-image," personified in the SS guard, came into being. That the prisoner's identification with the SS could be so positive is explained by still another mechanism: the principle of "identification with the aggressor." "A child," as Anna Freud writes, "interjects some characteristic of an anxiety-object and so assimilates an anxiety-experience which he has just undergone. . . . By impersonating the aggressor, assuming his attributes or imitating his aggression, the child transforms himself from the person threatened into the person who makes the threat."[6] In short, the child's only "defense" in the presence of a cruel, all-powerful father is the psychic defense of identification.

Now one could, still retaining the Freudian language, represent all this in somewhat less cumbersome terms by a slight modification of the metaphor. It could simply be said that under great stress the superego, like a bucket, is violently emptied of content and acquires, in a radically changed setting, new content. It would thus not be necessary to postulate a literal "regression" to childhood in order for this to occur. Something of the sort is suggested by Leo Alexander. "The psychiatrist stands in amazement," he writes, "before the thoroughness and completeness with which this perversion of essential superego values was accomplished in adults . . . [and] it may be that the decisive importance of childhood and youth in the formation of [these] values may have been overrated by psychiatrists in a society in which allegiance to these values in normal adult life was taken too much for granted because of the stability, religiousness, legality, and security of the 19th Century and early 20th Century society." [7]

A second theoretical scheme is better prepared for crisis and more closely geared to social environment than the Freudian adaptation indicated above, and it may consequently be more suitable for accommodating not only the concentration-camp experience but also the more general problem of plantation slave personality. This is the "interpersonal theory" developed by the late Harry Stack Sullivan. One may view this body of work as the response to a peculiarly American set of needs. The system of Freud, so aptly designed for a European society the stability of whose institutional and status relationships could always to a large extent be taken for granted, turns out to be less clearly adapted to the culture of the United States. The American psychiatrist has had to deal with individuals in a culture where the diffuse, shifting, and often uncertain quality of such relationships has always been more pronounced than in Europe. He has come to appreciate the extent to which these relationships actually support the individual's psychic balance—the full extent, that is, to which the self is "social" in its nature. Thus a psychology whose terms are flexible enough to permit altering social relationships to make actual differences in character structure would be a psychology especially promising for dealing with the present problem. [8]

Sullivan's great contribution was to offer a concept whereby the really critical determinants of personality might be isolated for purposes of observation. Out of the hopelessly immense totality of "influences" which in one way or another go to make up the personality, or "self," Sullivan designated one—the estimations and expectations of others—as the one promising to unlock the most secrets. He then made a second elimination: the *majority* of "others" in one's existence may for theoretical purposes be neglected; what counts is who the *significant* others are. Here, "significant others" [9] may be understood very crudely to mean those individuals who hold, or seem to hold, the keys to security in one's own personal situation, whatever its nature. Now as to the psychic processes whereby these "significant others" become an actual part of the personality, it may be said that the very sense of "self" first emerges in connection with anxiety about the attitudes of the most important persons in one's life (initially, the mother, father, and their surrogates—persons of more or less absolute authority), and automatic attempts are set in motion to adjust to these attitudes. In this way their approval, their disapproval, their estimates and appraisals, and indeed a whole range of their expectations become as it were internalized, and are reflected in one's very character. Of course as one "grows up," one acquires more and more significant others whose attitudes are diffuse and may indeed compete, and thus "significance," in Sullivan's sense, becomes subtler and less easy to define. The personality exfoliates; it takes on traits of distinction and, as we say, "individuality." The impact of particular significant others is less dramatic than in early life. But the pattern is a continuing one; new significant others do still appear, and theoretically it is conceivable that even in mature life the personality might be visibly affected by the arrival of such a one—supposing that this new significant other were vested with sufficient authority and power. In any event there are possibilities for fluidity and actual change inherent in this concept which earlier schemes have lacked.

The purest form of the process is to be observed in the development of children, not so much because of their "immaturity" as such (though their plasticity is great and the imprint of early experience goes deep), but rather because for them there are fewer significant others. For this reason—because the pattern is simpler and more easily controlled—much of Sullivan's attention was devoted to what happens in childhood. In any case let us say that unlike the adult, the child, being drastically limited in the selection of significant others, must operate in a "closed system."

Such are the elements which make for order and balance in the normal self: "significant others" plus "anxiety" in a special sense—conceived with not simply disruptive but also guiding, warning functions.[10] The structure of "interpersonal" theory thus has considerable room in it for conceptions of guided change—change for either beneficent or malevolent ends. One technique for managing such change would of course be the orthodox one of psychoanalysis; another, the actual changing of significant others.[11] Patrick Mullahy, a leading exponent of Sullivan, believes that in group therapy much is possible along these lines.[12] A demonic test of the whole hypothesis is available in the concentration camp.

Consider the camp prisoner—not the one who fell by the wayside but the one who was eventually to survive; consider the ways in which he was forced to adjust to the one significant other which he now had —the SS guard, who held absolute dominion over every aspect of his life. The very shock of his introduction was perfectly designed to dramatize this fact; he was brutally maltreated ("as by a cruel father"); the shadow of resistance would bring instant death. Daily life in the camp, with its fear and tensions, taught over and over the lesson of absolute power. It prepared the personality for a drastic shift in standards. It crushed whatever anxieties might have been drawn from prior standards; such standards had become meaningless. It focused the prisoner's attention constantly on the moods, attitudes, and standards of the only man who mattered. A truly childlike situation was thus created: utter and abject dependency on one, or on a rigidly limited few, significant others. All the conditions which in normal life would give the individual leeway—which allowed him to defend himself against a new and hostile significant other, no matter how powerful—were absent in the camp. No competition of significant others was possible; the prisoner's comrades for practical purposes were helpless to assist him.[13] He had no degree of independence, no lines to the outside, in any matter. Everything, every vital concern, focused on the SS: food, warmth, security, freedom from pain, all depended on the omnipotent significant other, all had to be worked out within the closed system. Nowhere was there a shred of privacy; everything one did was subject to SS supervision. The pressure was never absent. It is thus no wonder that the prisoners should become "as children." It is no wonder that their obedience became unquestioning, that they did not revolt, that they could not "hate" their masters. Their masters' attitudes had become *internalized* as a part of their very selves; those attitudes and standards now dominated all others that they had. They had, indeed, been "changed."

There still exists a third conceptual framework within which these phenomena may be considered. It is to be found in the growing field of "role psychology." This psychology is not at all incompatible with interpersonal theory; the two might easily be fitted into the same system.[14] But it might be strategically desirable, for several reasons, to segregate them for purposes of discussion. One such reason is the extraordinary degree to which role psychology shifts the focus of attention upon the individual's cultural and institutional environment rather than upon his "self." At the same time it gives us a manageable concept—that of "role"—for mediating between the two. As a mechanism, the role enables us to isolate the unique contribution of culture and institutions toward maintaining the psychic balance of the individual. In it, we see formalized for the individual a range of choices in models of behavior and expression, each with its particular style, quality, and attributes. The relationship between the "role" and the "self," though not yet clear, is intimate; it is at least possible at certain levels of inquiry to look upon the individual as the variable and upon the roles extended him as the stable factor.[15] We thus have a potentially durable link between individual psychology and the study of culture. It might even be said, inasmuch as its key term is directly borrowed from the theater, that role psychology offers in workable form the long-awaited connection—apparently missed by Ernest Jones in his *Hamlet* study—between the insights of the classical dramatists and those of the contemporary social theorist.[16] But be that as it may, for our present problem, the concentration camp, it suggests the most flexible account of how the ex-prisoners may have succeeded in resuming their places in normal life.

Let us note certain of the leading terms.[17] A "social role" is definable in its simplest sense as the behavior expected of persons specifically located in specific social groups.[18] A distinction is kept between "expectations" and "behavior;" the expectations of a role (embodied in the "script") theoretically exist in advance and are defined by the organization, the institution, or by society at large. Behavior (the "performance") refers to the manner in which the role is played. Another distinction involves roles which are "pervasive" and those which are "limited." A pervasive role is extensive in scope ("female citizen") and not only influences but also sets bounds upon the other sorts of roles available to the individual ("mother," "nurse," but not "husband," "soldier"); a limited role ("purchaser," "patient") is transitory and intermittent. A further concept is that of "role clarity." Some roles are more specifically defined than others; their impact upon performance (and, indeed, upon the personality of the performer) depends on the clarity of their definition. Finally, it is asserted that those roles which carry with them the clearest and most automatic rewards and punishments are those which will be (as it were) most "artistically" played.

What sorts of things might this explain? It might illuminate the process whereby the child develops his personality in terms not only of the roles which his parents offer him but of those which he "picks up" elsewhere and tries on. It could show how society, in its coercive character, lays down patterns of behavior with which it expects the individual to comply. It suggests the way in which society, now turning its benevolent face to the individual, tenders him alternatives and defines for him the style appropriate to their fulfilment. It provides us with a further term for the definition of personality itself: there appears an extent to which we can say that personality is actually made up of the roles which the individual plays.[19] And here, once more assuming "change" to be possible, we have in certain ways the least cumbersome terms for plotting its course.

The application of the model to the concentration camp should be simple and obvious. What was expected of the man entering the rôle of camp prisoner was laid down for him upon arrival:

> Here you are not in a penitentiary or prison but in a place of instruction. Order and discipline are here the highest law. If you ever want to see freedom again, you must submit to a severe training. . . . But woe to those who do not obey our iron discipline. Our methods are thorough! Here there is no compromise and no mercy. The slightest resistance will be ruthlessly suppressed. Here we sweep with an iron broom! [20]

Expectation and performance must coincide exactly; the lines were to be read literally; the missing of a single cue meant extinction. The role was pervasive; it vetoed any other role and smashed all prior ones. "Role clarity"—the clarity here was blinding; its definition was burned into the prisoner by every detail of his existence:

> In normal life the adult enjoys a certain measure of independence; within the limits set by society he has a considerable measure of liberty. Nobody orders him when and what to eat, where to take up his residence or what to wear, neither to take his rest on Sunday nor when to have his bath, nor when to go to bed. He is not beaten during his work, he need not ask permission to go to the W.C., he is not continually kept on the run, he does not feel that the work he is doing is silly or childish, he is not confined behind barbed wire, he is not counted twice a day or more, he is not left unprotected against the actions of his fellow citizens, he looks after his family and the education of his children.
>
> How altogether different was the life of the concentration-camp prisoner! What to do during each part of the day was arranged for him, and decisions were made about him from which there was no appeal. He was impotent and suffered from bedwetting, and because of his chronic diarrhea he soiled his underwear. . . . The dependence of the prisoner on the SS . . . may be compared to the dependence of children on their parents. . . .[21]

The impact of this role, coinciding as it does in a hundred ways with that of the child, has already been observed. Its rewards were brutally simple—life rather than death; its punishments were automatic. By the survivors it was—it had to be—a role *well played*.

Nor was it simple, upon liberation, to shed the role. Many of the inmates, to be sure, did have prior roles which they could resume, former significant others to whom they might reorient themselves, a repressed superego which might once more be resurrected. To this extent they were not "lost souls." But to the extent that their entire personalities, their total selves, had been involved in this experience, to the extent that old arrangements had been disrupted, that society itself had been overturned while they had been away, a "return" was fraught with innumerable obstacles.[22]

It is hoped that the very hideousness of a special example of slavery has not disqualified it as a test for certain features of a far milder and more benevolent form of slavery. But it should still be possible to say, with regard to the individuals who lived as slaves within the respective systems, that just as on one level there is every difference between a wretched childhood and a carefree one, there are, for other purposes, limited features which the one may be said to have shared with the other.

Both were closed systems from which all standards based on prior connections had been effectively detached. A working adjustment to either system required a childlike conformity, a limited choice of "significant others." Cruelty per se cannot be considered the primary key to this; of far greater importance was the simple "closedness" of the system, in which all lines of authority descended from the master and in which alternative social bases that might have supported alternative standards were systematically suppressed.[23] The individual, consequently, for his very psychic security, had to picture his master in some way as the "good father," [24] even when, as in the concentration camp, it made no sense at all.[25] But why should it not have made sense for many a simple plantation Negro whose master did exhibit, in all the ways that could be expected, the features of the good father who was really "good"? If the concentration camp could produce in two or three years the results that it did, one wonders how much more pervasive must have been those attitudes, expectations, and values which had, certainly, their benevolent side and which were accepted and transmitted over generations.

For the Negro child, in particular, the plantation offered no really satisfactory father-image other than the master. The "real" father was virtually without authority over his child, since discipline, parental responsibility, and control of rewards and punishments all rested in other hands; the slave father could not even protect the mother of his children except by appealing directly to the master. Indeed, the mother's own role loomed far larger for the slave child than did that of the father. She controlled those few activities—household care, preparation of food, and rearing of children—that were left to the slave family. For that matter, the very etiquette of plantation life removed even the honorific attributes of fatherhood from the Negro male, who was addressed as "boy"—until, when the vigorous years of his prime were past, he was allowed to assume the title of "uncle."

From the master's viewpoint, slaves had been defined in law as property, and the master's power over his property must be absolute. But then this property was still human property. These slaves might never be quite as human as *he* was, but still there were certain standards that could be laid down for their behavior: obedience, fidelity, humility, docility, cheerfulness, and so on. Industry and diligence would of course be demanded, but a final element in the master's situation would undoubtedly qualify that expectation. Absolute power for him meant absolute dependency for the slave—the dependency not of the developing child but of the perpetual child. For the master, the role most aptly fitting such a relationship would naturally be that of the father. As a father he could be either harsh or kind, as he chose, but as a *wise* father he would have, we may suspect, a sense of the limits of his situation. He must be ready to cope with *all* the qualities of the child, exasperating as well as ingratiating. He might conceivably have to expect in this child—besides his loyalty, docility, humility, cheerfulness, and (under supervision) his diligence—such additional qualities as irresponsibility, playfulness, silliness, laziness, and quite possibly) tendencies to lying and stealing. Should the entire prediction prove accurate, the result would be something resembling "Sambo."

The social and psychological sanctions of role-playing may in the last analysis prove to be the most satisfactory of the several approaches to Sambo, for, without doubt, of all the roles in American life that of Sambo was by far the most pervasive. The outlines of the role might be sketched in by crude necessity, but what of the finer shades? The sanctions against overstepping it were bleak enough,[26] but the rewards —the sweet applause, as it were, for performing it with sincerity and feeling—were something to be appreciated on quite another level. The law, untuned to the deeper harmonies, could command the player to be present for the occasion, and the whip might even warn against his missing the grosser cues, but could those things really insure the performance that melted all hearts? Yet there was many and many a performance, and the audiences (whose standards were high) appear to have been for the most part well pleased. They were actually viewing their own masterpiece. Much labor had been lavished upon this chef d'oeuvre, the most genial resources of Southern society had been available for the work; touch after touch had been applied throughout the years, and the result—embodied not in the unfeeling law but in the richest layers of Southern lore—had been the product of an exquisitely rounded collective creativity. And indeed, in a sense that somehow transcended the merely ironic, it was a labor of love. "I love the simple and unadulterated slave, with his geniality, his mirth, his swagger, and his nonsense," wrote Edward Pollard. "I love to look upon his countenance shining with content and grease; I love to study his affectionate heart; I love to mark that peculiarity in him, which beneath all his buffoonery exhibits him as a creature of the tenderest sensibilities, mingling his joys and his sorrows with those of his master's home."[27] Love, even on those terms, was surely no inconsequential reward.

But what were the terms? The Negro was to be a child forever. "The Negro . . . in his true nature, is always a boy, let him be ever so old. . . ." [28] "He is . . . a dependent upon the white race; dependent for guidance and direction even to the procurement of his most indispensable necessaries. Apart from this protection he has the helplessness of a child—without foresight, without faculty of contrivance, without thrift of any kind." [29] Not only was he a child; he was a happy child. Few Southern writers failed to describe with obvious fondness the bubbling gaiety of a plantation holiday or the perpetual good humor that seemed to mark the Negro character, the good humor of an everlasting childhood.

The role, of course, must have been rather harder for the earliest generations of slaves to learn. "Accommodation," according to John Dollard, "involves the renunciation of protest or aggression against undesirable conditions of life and the organization of the character so that protest does not appear, but acceptance does. It may come to pass in the end that the unwelcome force is idealized, that one identifies with it and takes it into the personality; it sometimes even happens that what is at first resented and feared is finally loved." [30]

Might the process, on the other hand, be reversed? It is hard to imagine its being reversed overnight. The same role might still be played in the years after slavery—we are told that it was [31] —and yet it was played to more vulgar audiences with cruder standards, who paid much less for what they saw. The lines might be repeated more and more mechanically, with less and less conviction; the incentives to perfection could become hazy and blurred, and the excellent old piece could degenerate over time into low farce. There could come a point, conceivably, with the old zest gone, that it was no longer worth the candle. The day might come at last when it dawned on a man's full waking consciousness that he had really grown up, that he was, after all, only playing a part.

MECHANISMS OF RESISTANCE TO ABSOLUTE POWER

One might say a great deal more than has been said here about mass behavior and mass manifestations of personality, and the picture would still amount to little more than a grotesque cartoon of humanity were not some recognition given to the ineffable difference made in any social system by men and women possessing what is recognized, anywhere and at any time, simply as character. With that, one arrives at something too qualitatively fine to come very much within the crude categories of the present discussion; but although it is impossible to generalize with any proper justice about the incidence of "character" in its moral, irreducible, individual sense, it may still be possible to conclude with a note or two on the social conditions, the breadth or narrowness of their compass, within which character can find expression.

Why should it be, turning once more to Latin America, that there one finds no Sambo, no social tradition, that is, in which slaves were defined by virtually complete consensus as children incapable of being trusted with the full privileges of freedom and adulthood? There, the system surely had its brutalities. The slaves arriving there from Africa had also undergone the capture, the sale, the Middle Passage. They too had been uprooted from a prior culture, from a life very different from the one in which they now found themselves. There, however, the system was not closed.

Here again the concentration camp, paradoxically enough, can be instructive. There were in the camps a very small minority of the survivors who had undergone an experience different in crucial ways from that of the others, an experience which protected them from the full impact of the closed system. These people, mainly by virtue of wretched little jobs in the camp administration which offered them a minute measure of privilege, were able to carry on "underground" activities. In a practical sense the actual operations of such "undergrounds" as were possible may seem to us unheroic and limited; stealing blankets; "organizing" a few bandages, a little medicine, from the camp hospital; black market arrangements with a guard for a bit of extra food and protection for oneself and one's comrades; the circulation of news; and other such apparently trifling activities. But for the psychological balance of those involved, such activities were vital; they made possible a fundamentally different adjustment to the camp. To a prisoner so engaged, there were others who mattered, who gave real point to his existence—the SS was no longer the *only* one. Conversely, the role of the child was not the only one he played. He could take initiative; he could give as well as receive protection; he did things which had meaning in adult terms. He had, in short, alternative roles; this was a fact which made such a prisoner's transition from his old life to that of the camp less agonizing and destructive; those very prisoners, moreover, appear to have been the ones who could, upon liberation, resume normal lives most easily. It is, in fact, these people—not those of the ranks—who have described the camps to us.[32]

It was just such a difference—indeed, a much greater one—that separated the typical slave in Latin America from the typical slave in the United States. Though he too had experienced the Middle Passage, he was entering a society where alternatives were significantly more diverse than those awaiting his kinsman in North America. Concerned in some sense with his status were distinct and at certain points competing institutions. This involved multiple and often competing "significant others." His master was, of course, clearly the chief one—but not the only one. There could, in fact, be a considerable number: the friar who boarded his ship to examine his conscience, the confessor; the priest who made the rounds and who might report irregularities in treatment to the *procurador*; the zealous Jesuit quick to resent a master's intrusion upon such sacred matters as marriage and worship (a resentment of no small consequence to the master); the local magistrate, with his eye on the king's official protector of slaves, who would find himself in trouble were the laws too widely evaded; the king's informer who received one-third of the fines. For the slave the result was a certain latitude; the lines did not all converge on one man; the slave's personality, accordingly, did not have to focus on a single role. He was, true enough primarily a slave. Yet he might in fact perform multiple roles. He could be a husband and a father (for the American slave these roles had virtually no meaning); open to him also were such activities as artisan, peddler, petty merchant, truck gardener (the law reserved to him the necessary time and a share of the proceeds, but such arrangements were against the law for Sambo); he could be a communicant in the church, a member of a religious fraternity [33] (roles guaranteed by the most powerful institution in Latin America—comparable privileges in the American South depended on a master's pleasure). These roles were all legitimized and protected *outside* the plantation; they offered a diversity of channels for the development of personality. Not only did the individual have multiple roles open to him as a slave, but the very nature of these roles made possible a certain range of aspirations should he some day become free. He could have a fantasy-life not limited to catfish and watermelons; it was within his conception to become a priest, an independent farmer, a successful merchant, a military of-ficer.[34] The slave could actually—to an extent quite unthinkable in the United States—conceive of himself *as a rebel*. Bloody slave revolts, actual wars, took place in Latin America; nothing on this order occurred in the United States.[35] But even without a rebellion, society here had a network of customary arrangements, rooted in antiquity, which made possible at many points a smooth transition of status from slave to free and which provided much social space for the exfoliation of individual character.

To the typical slave on the ante-bellum plantation in the United States, society of course offered no such alternatives. But that is hardly to say that something of an "underground"—something rather more, indeed, than an underground—could not exist in Southern slave so-ciety. And there were those in it who hardly fitted the picture of "Sambo."

The American slave system, compared with that of Latin America, was closed and circumscribed, but, like all social systems, its arrange-ments were less perfect in practice than they appeared to be in theory. It was possible for significant numbers of slaves, in varying degrees, to escape the full impact of the system and its coercions upon personality. The house servant, the urban mechanic, the slave who arranged his own employment and paid his master a stipulated sum each week, were all figuratively members of the "underground." Even among those work-ing on large plantations, the skilled craftsman or the responsible slave foreman had a measure of independence not shared by his simpler brethren. Even the single slave family owned by a small farmer had a status much closer to that of house servants than to that of plantation labor gang. For all such people there was a margin of space denied to the majority; the system's authority-structure claimed their bodies but not quite their souls.

Out of such groups an individual as complex and as highly developed as William Johnson, the Natchez barber, might emerge. Johnson's diary reveals a personality that one recognizes instantly as a type—but a type whose values came from a sector of society very different from that which formed Sambo. Johnson is the young man on the make, the ambitious free-enterpriser of American legend. He began life as a slave, was manumitted at the age of eleven, and rose from a poor apprentice barber to become one of the wealthiest and most influential Negroes in ante-bellum Mississippi. He was respected by white and black alike, and counted among his friends some of the leading public men of the state.[36]

It is of great interest to note that although the danger of slave revolts (like Communist conspiracies in our own day) was much overrated by touchy Southerners; the revolts that actually did occur were in no instance planned by plantation laborers but rather by Negroes whose qualities of leadership were developed well outside the full coercions of the plantation authority-system. Gabriel, who led the revolt of 1800, was a blacksmith who lived a few miles outside Richmond; Denmark Vesey, leading spirit of the 1822 plot at Charleston, was a freed Negro artisan who had been born in Africa and served several years aboard a slavetrading vessel; and Nat Turner, the Virginia slave who fomented the massacre of 1831, was a literate preacher of recognized intelligence. Of the plots that have been convincingly substantiated (whether they came to anything or not), the majority originated in urban centers.[37]

For a time during Reconstruction, a Negro elite of sorts did emerge in the South. Many of its members were Northern Negroes, but the Southern ex-slaves who also comprised it seem in general to have emerged from the categories just indicated. Vernon Wharton, writing of Mississippi, says:

> A large portion of the minor Negro leaders were preachers, lawyers, or teachers from the free states or from Canada. Their education and their independent attitude gained for them immediate favor and leadership. Of the natives who became their rivals, the majority had been urban slaves, blacksmiths, carpenters, clerks, or waiters in hotels and boarding houses; a few of them had been favored body-servants of affluent whites.[38]

The William Johnsons and Denmark Veseys have been accorded, though belatedly, their due honor. They are, indeed, all too easily identified, thanks to the system that enabled them as individuals to be so conspicuous and so exceptional and, as members of a group, so few.

NOTES

1. The line between "accommodation" (as conscious hypocrisy) and behavior inextricable from basic personality, though the line certainly exists, is

anything but a clear and simple matter of choice. There is reason to think that the one grades into the other, and vice versa, with considerable subtlety. In this connection, the most satisfactory theoretical mediating term between deliberate role-playing and "natural" role-playing might be found in role-psychology.

2. Although the majority of Southern slaveholders were not planters, the majority of slaves were owned by a planter minority. "Considerably more than half of them lived on plantation units of more than twenty slaves, and one-fourth lived on units of more than fifty. That the majority of slaves belonged to members of the planter class, and not to those who operated small farms with a single slave family, is a fact of crucial importance concerning the nature of bondage in the ante-bellum South." Stampp, *Peculiar Institution*, p. 31.

3. See esp. below, . . . n. 7.

4. "For just as the ego is a modified portion of the id as a result of contact with the outer world, the super-ego represents a modified portion of the ego, formed through experiences absorbed from the parents, especially from the father. The super-ego is the highest evolution attainable by man, and consists of a precipitate of all prohibitions and inhibitions, all the rules of conduct which are impressed on the child by his parents and by parental substitutes. The feeling of *conscience* depends altogether on the development of the super-ego." A. A. Brill, Introduction to *The Basic Writings of Sigmund Freud* (New York: Modern Library, 1938), pp. 12-13. "Its relation to the ego is not exhausted by the precept: 'You *ought to be* such and such (like your father); it also comprises the prohibition: 'You *must not be* such and such (like your father); that is, you may not do all that he does; many things are his prerogative.'" Sigmund Freud, *The Ego and the Id* (London: Hogarth Press, 1947), pp. 44-45. ". . . and here we have that higher nature, in this ego-ideal or super-ego, the representative of our relation to our parents. When we were little children we knew these higher natures, we admired them and feared them; and later we took them into ourselves." *Ibid.*, p. 47. "As a child grows up, the office of father is carried on by masters and by others in authority; the power of their injunctions and prohibitions remains vested in the ego-ideal and continues, in the form of conscience, to exercise the censorship of morals. The tension between the demands of conscience and the actual attainments of the ego is experienced as a sense of guilt. Social feelings rest on the foundation of identification with others, on the basis of an ego-ideal in common with them." *Ibid.*, p. 49.

5. *Human Behavior*, p. 136.

6. Anna Freud, *The Ego and the Mechanisms of Defence* (London: Hogarth Press, 1948), p. 121. "In some illustrative case reports, Clara Thompson stresses the vicious circle put in motion by this defense-mechanism. The stronger the need for identification, the more a person loses himself in his omnipotent enemy—the more helpless he becomes. The more helpless he feels, the stronger the identification, and—we may add—the more likely it is that he tries even to surpass the aggressiveness of his aggressor. This may explain the almost unbelievable phenomenon that prisoner-superiors sometimes acted more brutally than did members of the SS. . . Identification with the aggressor represented the final stage of passive adaptation. It was a means of defense of a rather paradoxical nature: survival through surrender; protection against the fear of the enemy—by becoming part of him; overcoming helplessness—by re-

gressing to childish dependence." Bluhm, "How Did They Survive?" pp. 24-25.

7. Leo Alexander, "War Crimes: Their Social-Psychological Aspects," *American Journal of Psychiatry*, CV (September, 1948), 173. "The super-ego structure is . . . in peril whenever these established guiding forces weaken or are in the process of being undermined, shifted, or perverted, and becomes itself open to undermining, shifting, or perversion even in adult life—a fact which is probably more important than we have been aware of heretofore." *Ibid.*, p. 175.

8. My use of Sullivan here does not imply a willingness to regard his work as a "refutation" to that of Freud, or even as an adequate substitute for it in all other situations. It lacks the imaginative scope which in Freud makes possible so great a range of cultural connections; in it we miss Freud's effort to deal as scientifically as possible with an infinite array of psychological and cultural phenomena; the fragmentary nature of Sullivan's work, its limited scope, its cloudy presentation, all present us with obstacles not to be surmounted overnight. This might well change as his ideas are elaborated and refined. But meanwhile it would be too much to ask that all connections be broken with the staggering amount of work already done on Freudian models.

9. Sullivan refined this concept from the earlier notion of the "generalized other" formulated by George Herbert Mead. "The organized community or social group [Mead wrote] which gives to the individual his unity of self may be called 'the generalized other.' The attitude of the generalized other is the attitude of the whole community. Thus, for example, in the case of such a social group as a ball team, the team is the generalized other in so far as it enters—as an organized process or social activity—into the experience of any one of the individual members of it." George H. Mead, *Mind, Self and Society: From the Standpoint of a Social Behaviorist* (Chicago: University of Chicago Press, 1934), p. 154.

10. The technical term, in Sullivan's terminology, for the mechanism represented by these two elements functioning in combination, is the individual's "self-dynamism." David Riesman has refined this concept; he has, with his "inner-directed, other-directed" polarity, considered the possibility of different kinds of "self-dynamisms." The self-dynamism which functions with reference to specific aims and which is formed and set early in life is characterized as the "gyroscope." On the other hand the self-dynamism which must function in a cultural situation of constantly shifting significant others and which must constantly adjust to them is pictured as the "radar." See *The Lonely Crowd, passim*. The principles summarized in this and the preceding paragraphs are to be found most clearly set forth in Harry Stack Sullivan, *Conceptions of Modern Psychiatry* (Washington: William Alanson White Psychiatric Foundation, 1945). Sullivan's relationship to the general development of theory is assessed in Patrick Mullahy, *Oedipus Myth and Complex: A Review of Psychoanalytic Theory* (New York: Hermitage House, 1948).

11. Actually, one of the chief functions of psychoanalysis as it has been practiced from the beginning is simply given more explicit recognition here. The psychiatrist who helps the patient exhibit to himself attitudes and feelings systematically repressed—or "selectively ignored"—becomes in the process a new and trusted significant other.

12. "Indeed . . . when the whole Sullivanian conception of the effect of significant others upon the origin and stability of self-conceptions is pushed

farther, really revolutionary vistas of guided personality emerge. If the maintenance of certain characteristic patterns of interpersonal behavior depends upon
their support by significant others, then to alter the composition of any person's
community of significant others is the most direct and drastic way of altering
his 'personality.' This can be done. Indeed, it is being done, with impressive
results, by the many types of therapeutic groups, or quasi-families of significant
new others, which have come up in the past few years." Patrick Mullahy (ed.),
The Contributions of Harry Stack Sullivan (New York: Hermitage House,
1952), p. 193.

13. It should be noted that there were certain important exceptions. . . .

14. An outstanding instance of authorities who are exponents of both is
of that of H. H. Gerth and C. Wright Mills, whose study *Character and Social
Structure* ranges very widely in both interpersonal theory and role psychology
and uses them interchangeably.

15. Conceptually, the purest illustration of this notion might be seen in such
an analogy as the following. Sarah Bernhardt, playing in *Phèdre*, enacted a role
which had not altered since it was set down by Racine two centuries before
her time, and she was neither the first woman who spoke those lines, nor was
she the last. Nor, indeed, was *Phèdre* her only triumph. Such was Bernhardt's
genius, such was her infinite plasticity, that she moved from immutable role to
immutable role in the classic drama, making of each, as critic and theatergoer
alike agreed, a masterpiece. Now Bernhardt herself is gone, yet the lines remain, waiting to be transfigured by some new genius.

16. In the resources of dramatic literature a variety of insights may await the
"social scientist" equipped with both the imagination and the conceptual tools
for exploiting them, and the emergence of role-psychology may represent the
most promising step yet taken in this direction. A previous area of contact has
been in the realm of Freudian psychology, but this has never been a very
natural or comfortable meeting ground for either the analyst or the literary
critic. For example, in Shakespeare's *Hamlet* there is the problem, both
psychological and dramatic, of Hamlet's inability to kill his uncle. Dr. Ernest
Jones (in *Hamlet and Oedipus*) reduces all the play's tensions to a single
Freudian complex. It should be at once more "scientific" and more "literary,"
however, to consider the problem in terms of role-conflict (Hamlet as prince,
son, nephew, lover, etc., has multiple roles which keep getting in the way of
one another). Francis Fergusson, though he uses other terminology, in effect
does this in his *Ideal of a Theater.*

17. In this paragraph I duplicate and paraphrase material from Eugene and
Ruth Hartley, *Fundamentals of Social Psychology* (New York: Knopf, 1952),
chap. xvi. See also David C. McClelland, *Personality* (New York: Sloane,
1951), pp. 289-332. Both these books are, strictly speaking, "texts," but this
point could be misleading, inasmuch as the whole subject is one not normally
studied at an "elementary" level anywhere. At the same time a highly successful effort has been made in each of these works to formulate the role concept
with clarity and simplicity, and this makes their formulations peculiarly relevant
to the empirical facts of the present problem. It may be that the very simplicity
of the roles in both the plantation and concentration-camp settings accounts
for this coincidence. Another reason why I am inclined to put a special premium
on simplicity here is my conviction that the role concept has a range of
"literary" overtones, potentially exploitable in realms other than psychology.

For a recent general statement, see Theodore R. Sarbin, "Role Theory," *Handbook of Social Psychology*, I, 223-58.

18. Hartley, *Fundamentals of Social Psychology*, p. 485.

19. "Personality development is not exclusively a matter of socialization. Rather, it represents the organism's more or less integrated way of adapting to *all* the influences that come its way—both inner and outer influences, both social and nonsocial ones. Social influences, however, are essential to human personality, and socialization accounts for a very great deal of personality development.

"From this point of view it would not be surprising to find that many personality disturbances represent some sort of breakdown or reversal of the socialization process." Theodore M. Newcomb, *Social Psychology* (New York: Dryden Press, 1950), p. 475.

20. Quoted in Leon Szalet, *Experiment "E"* (New York: Didier, 1945), p. 138.

21. Cohen, *Human Behavior*, pp. 173-74.

22. Theodore Newcomb is the only non-Freudian coming to my attention who has considered the concentration camp in the terms of social psychology. He draws analogies between the ex-inmates' problems of readjustment and those of returning prisoners of war. "With the return of large numbers of British prisoners of war . . . from German and Japanese camps, toward the end of World War II, it soon became apparent that thousands of them were having serious difficulties of readjustment. It was first assumed that they were victims of war neuroses. But this assumption had to be abandoned when it was discovered that their symptoms were in most cases not those of the commonly recognized neuroses. Most of the men having difficulty, moreover, did not have the kinds of personalities which would have predisposed them to neurotic disorders. Psychiatrists then began to wonder whether their disturbances represented only a temporary phase of the men's return to civilian life. But the difficulties were neither temporary nor 'self-correcting.' 'Even when men had been back for 18 months or even longer, serious and persistent difficulties were reported in something like one-third of the men.' . . . All in all . . . the authors were led to the conclusion that the returning war prisoner's troubles did not lie entirely within himself. They represented the strains and stresses of becoming *resocialized* in a culture which was not only different from what it had been but was radically different from that to which the men had become accustomed during their years of capture." "When a deliberate attempt is made to change the personality, as in psychotherapy, success brings with it changes in role patterns. When the role perscriptions are changed—as for . . . concentration-camp inmates—personality changes also occur. When forcible changes in role prescriptions are removed, the degree to which the previous personality is 'resumed' depends upon the degree to which the individual finds it possible to resume his earlier role patterns." Newcomb, *Social Psychology*, pp. 476-77, 482.

Social workers faced with the task of rehabilitating former concentration-camp prisoners rapidly discovered that sympathy and understanding were not enough. The normal superego values of many of the prisoners had been so thoroughly smashed that adult standards of behavior for them were quite out of the question. Their behavior, indeed, was often most childlike. They made extreme demands, based not on actual physical needs but rather on the fear that they might be left out, or that others might receive more than they. Those who regained their equilibrium most quickly were the ones who were able to begin new lives in social environments that provided clear limits, precise standards, steady goals, and specific roles to play. Adjustment was not easy, however, even for the most fortunate. On the collective farms of Israel, for example, it was understood that former concentration-camp inmates would be "unable to control their greed for food" for a number of months. During that time, concern for their neighbors' sensibilities was more than one could expect. Paul Friedman, "The Road Back for the DP's" *Commentary*, VI (December, 1948), 502-10; Eva Rosenfeld, "Institutional Change in Israeli Collectives" (Ph.D. diss., Columbia University, 1952), p. 278.

23. The experience of American prisoners taken by the Chinese during the Korean War seems to indicate that profound changes in behavior and values, if not in basic personality itself, can be effected without the use of physical torture or extreme deprivation. The Chinese were able to get large numbers of Americans to act as informers and to co-operate in numerous ways in the effort to indoctrinate all the prisoners with Communist propaganda. The technique contained two key elements. One was that all formal and informal authority structures within the group were systematically destroyed; this was done by isolating officers, non-commissioned officers, and any enlisted men who gave indications of leadership capacities. The other element involved the continual emphasizing of the captors' power and influence by judicious manipulation of petty rewards and punishments and by subtle hints of the greater rewards and more severe punishments (repatriation or non-repatriation) that rested with the pleasure of those in authority. See Edgar H. Schein, "Some Observations on Chinese Methods of Handling Prisoners of War," *Public Opinion Quarterly*, XX (Spring, 1956), 321-27.

24. In a system as tightly closed as the plantation or the concentration camp, the slave's or prisoner's position of absolute dependency virtually compels him to see the authority-figure as somehow really "good." Indeed, all the evil in his life may flow from this man—but then so also must everything of any value. Here is the seat of the only "good" he knows, and to maintain his psychic balance he must persuade himself that the good is in some way dominant. A threat to this illusion is thus in a real sense a threat to his very existence. It is a common experience among social workers dealing with neglected and maltreated children to have a child desperately insist on his love for a cruel and brutal parent and beg that he be allowed to remain with that parent. The most dramatic feature of this situation is the cruelty which it involves, but the mechanism which inspires the devotion is not the cruelty of the parent but rather the abnormal dependency of the child. A classic example of this mechanism in operation may be seen in the case of Varvara Petrovna, mother of Ivan Turgenev. Mme Turgenev "ruled over her serfs with a rod of iron." She demanded utter obedience and total submission. The slightest infraction of her rules brought the most severe punishment: "A maid who did not offer her a cup of tea in the proper manner was sent off to some remote village and perhaps separated from her family forever; gardeners who failed to prevent the plucking of a tulip in one of the flower beds before the house were ordered to be flogged; a servant whom she suspected of a mutinous disposition was sent off to Siberia." Her family and her most devoted servants were treated in much the same manner. "Indeed," wrote Varvara Zhitova, the

adopted daughter of Mme Turgenev, "those who loved her and were most devoted to her suffered most of all." Yet in spite of her brutality she was adored by the very people she tyrannized. David Magarshack describes how once when thrashing her eldest son she nearly fainted with sadistic excitement, whereupon "little Nicholas, forgetting his punishment, bawled at the top of his voice: 'Water! Water for mummy!'" Mme Zhitova, who knew Mme Turgenev's cruelty intimately and was herself the constant victim of her tyranny, wrote: "In spite of this, I loved her passionately, and when I was, though rarely, separated from her, I felt lonely and unhappy." Even Mme Turgenev's maid Agatha, whose children were sent to another village, when still infants so that Agatha might devote all her time to her mistress, could say years later, "Yes, she caused me much grief. I suffered much from her, but all the same I loved her! She was a real lady!" V. Zhitova, *The Turgenev Family*, trans. A. S. Mills (London: Havill Press, 1954), p. 25; David Magarshack, *Turgenev: A Life* (New York: Grove, 1954), pp. 14, 16, 22.

25. Bruno Bettelheim tells us of the fantastic efforts of the old prisoners to believe in the benevolence of the officers of the SS. "They insisted that these officers [hid] behind their rough surface a feeling of justice and propriety; he, or they, were supposed to be genuinely interested in the prisoners and even trying, in a small way, to help them. Since nothing of these supposed feelings and efforts ever became apparent, it was explained that he hid them so effectively because otherwise he would not be able to help the prisoners. The eagerness of these prisoners to find reasons for their claims was pitiful. A whole legend was woven around the fact that of two officers inspecting a barrack one had cleaned his shoes from mud before entering. He probably did it automatically, but it was interpreted as a rebuff of the other officer and a clear demonstration of how he felt about the concentration camp." Bettelheim, "Individual and Mass Behavior," p. 451.

26. Professor Stampp, in a chapter called "To Make Them Stand in Fear," describes the planter's resources for dealing with a recalcitrant slave. *Peculiar Institution*, pp. 141-91.

27. Edward A. Pollard, *Black Diamonds Gathered in the Darkey Homes of the South* (New York: Pudney & Russel, 1859), p. 58.

28. *Ibid.*, p. viii.

29. John Pendleton Kennedy, *Swallow Barn* (Philadelphia: Carey & Lea, 1832).

30. John Dollard, *Caste and Class in a Southern Town* (2nd ed.; New York: Harper, 1949), p. 255. The lore of "accommodation," taken just in itself, is very rich and is, needless to say, morally very complex. It suggests a delicate psychological balance. On the one hand, as the Dollard citation above implies, accommodation is fraught with dangers for the personalities of those who engage in it. On the other hand, as Bruno Bettelheim has reminded me, this involves a principle that goes well beyond American Negro society and is to be found deeply imbedded in European traditions: the principle of how the powerless can manipuate the powerful through aggressive stupidity, literal-mindedness, servile fawning, and irresponsibility. In this sense the immovably stupid "Good Soldier Schweik" and the fawning Negro in Richard Wright's *Black Boy* who allowed the white man to kick him for a quarter partake of the same tradition. Each has a technique whereby he can in a real sense exploit his powerful superiors, feel contempt for them, and suffer in the process no

great damage to his own pride. Jewish lore, as is well known, teems with this sort of thing. There was much of it also in the traditional relationships between peasants and nobles in central Europe.

Still, all this required the existence of some sort of alternative forces for moral and psychological orientation. The problem of the Negro in slavery times involved the virtual absence of such forces. It was with the end of slavery, presumably, that they would first begin to present themselves in generally usable form—a man's neighbors, the Loyal Leagues, white politicians, and so on. It would be in these circumstances that the essentially intermediate technique of accommodation could be used as a protective device beneath which a more independent personality might develop.

31. Even Negro officeholders during Reconstruction, according to Francis B. Simkins, "were known to observe carefully the etiquette of the Southern caste system." "New Viewpoints of Southern Reconstruction," *Journal of Southern History*, V (February, 1939), 52.

32. Virtually all the ex-prisoners whose writing I have made use of were men and women who had certain privileges (as clerks, physicians, and the like) in the camps. Many of the same persons were also active in the "underground" and could offer some measure of leadership and support for others. That is to say, both the objectivity necessary for making useful observations and the latitude enabling one to exercise some leadership were made possible by a certain degree of protection not available to the rank and file.

I should add, however, that a notable exception was the case of Bruno Bettelheim, who throughout the period of his detention had no privileged position of any kind which could afford him what I am calling an "alternative role" to play. And yet I do not think that it would be stretching the point too far to insist that he did in fact have such a role, one which was literally self-created: that of the scientific observer. In him, the scientist's objectivity, his feeling for clinical detail and sense of personal detachment, amounted virtually to a passion. It would not be fair, however, to expect such a degree of personal autonomy as this in other cases, except for a very few. I am told, for instance, that the behavior of many members of this "underground" toward their fellow prisoners was itself by no means above moral reproach. The depths to which the system could corrupt a man, it must be remembered, were profound.

33. See Tannenbaum, *Slave and Citizen*, pp. 64-65.

34. *Ibid.*, pp. 4 ff., 56-57, 90-93; see also Johnston, *Negro in the New World*, p. 90.

35. Compared with the countless uprisings of the Brazilian Negroes, the slave revolts in our own country appear rather desperate and futile. Only three emerge as worthy of any note, and their seriousness—even when described by a sympathetic historian like Herbert Aptheker—depends largely on the supposed plans of the rebels rather than on the things they actually did. The best organized of such "revolts," those of Vesey and Gabriel, were easily suppressed, while the most dramatic of them—the Nat Turner Rebellion—was characterized by little more than aimless butchery. The Brazilian revolts, on the other hand, were marked by imagination and a sense of direction, and they often involved large-scale military operations. One is impressed both by their scope and their variety. They range from the legendary Palmares Republic of the seventeenth century (a Negro state organized by escaped slaves and successfully defended for over fifty years), to the bloody revolts of the Moslem Negroes of Bahia

which, between 1807 and 1835, five times paralyzed a substantial portion of Brazil. Many such wars were launched from the *quilombos* (fortified villages built deep in the jungles by escaped slaves to defend themselves from re-capture); there were also the popular rebellions in which th Negroes of an entire area would take part. One is immediately struck by the heroic stature of the Negro leaders: no allowances of any sort need be made for them; they are impressive from any point of view. Arthur Ramos has described a number of them, including Zambi, a fabulous figure of the Palmares Republic; Luiza Mahin, mother of the Negro poet Luiz Gama and "one of the most outstand-leaders of the 1835 insurrection"; and Manoel Francisco dos Anjos Fereira, whose followers in the *Balaiada* (a movement which drew its name from "Baliao," his own nickname) held the *entire province of* Maranhão for three years. Their brilliance, gallantry, and warlike accomplishments give to their histories an almost legendary quality. On the other hand, one could not begin to think of Nat Turner in such a connection. See Ramos, *The Negro in Brazil*, pp. 24-53; Herbert Aptheker, *American Negro Slave Revolts* (New York: Columbia University, 1943, *passim*.

36. See William R. Hogan and Edwin A. Davis (eds.), *William Johnson's Natchez: The Ante-Bellum Diary of a Free Negro* (Baton Rouge: Louisiana State University Press, 1951), esp. pp. 1-64.

37. Aptheker, *American Negro Slave Revolts*, pp. 220, 268-69, 295-96, and *passim*.

38. Vernon L. Wharton, *The Negro in Mississippi, 1865–1890* (Chapel Hill: University of North Carolina Press, 1942), p. 164.

• Harold D. Woodman summarizes and assesses a century's historical literature on the still unresolved question of slavery's unprofitability. The student might keep in mind an underlying corollary of the argument. Some historians have assumed that since slavery had become unprofitable by the late antebellum period, means might have been found for its elimination short of armed sectional conflict. This viewpoint is identified particularly with historians who have defended Negro slavery as an institution of social control. On the other hand, if slavery continued to remain reasonably profitable throughout its existence, the South would have had no economic motive for abandoning it and, as David Brion Davis observed, "no country thought of abolishing the slave trade until its economic value had considerably declined." The argument over the profitability of slavery, therefore, is closely tied to another unresolved historical dispute over the Civil War's inevitability as a means of eliminating the institution.

The Profitability of Slavery

HAROLD D. WOODMAN

Abolitionists and their proslavery antagonists in the ante bellum period argued hotly over the profitability of slavery. Since the Civil War, historians and economists have continued the argument, less acrimoniously but no less vehemently. In part, solution of the problem of the profitability of slavery has been blocked by a lack of agreement as to how the problem is to be defined. Either implicitly or—as is more often the case—explicitly, contemporaries and modern scholars alike have begun their discussion of the profitability of slavery by posing the question: Profitable for whom? For the slave? For the slaveowner? For

From Harold D. Woodman, "The Profitability of Slavery: A Historical Perennial," *Journal of Southern History*, XXIX (August 1963), 303-25. Copyright © 1963 by the Southern Historical Association. Reprinted by permission of the Managing Editor.

the South as a section? For the American economy as a whole? Answers to the general question, of course, depend upon how the question is posed. As a result, conflicting conclusions often reflect differing definitions of the problem as well as different solutions. What seem to be clashing opinions often do not clash at all but pass each other in the obscurity created by a lack of an agreed-upon definition of the problem.

When a writer answers the question, "Profitable for whom?" by limiting himself to the planter or slaveholder, he is dealing with the question of profitability in terms of a business or industry. He is concerned with such questions as: Did the planters make money? Did *all* planters make money? Did planters make as much on their investment in slaves as they would have made had they invested elsewhere? Staple production with slave labor is regarded as a business enterprise much as automobile manufacture is seen as a business enterprise today. Profitability relates only to the success or failure of slave production as a business and ignores the broader questions of the effect of this type of enterprise on the economy as a whole.

If, on the other hand, a writer answers the question, "Profitable for whom?" by discussing the effect of slavery on the South, he is treating slavery as an economic system rather than as a business enterprise. The issue of profits earned by individual planters is subordinated to the larger problems of economic growth, capital accumulation, and the effect of slavery on the general population.

Debate over the years has ranged on both aspects of the topic, with most writers emphasizing one or the other aspect and an occasional writer dealing with both. Despite the many contributions which have been made—and are still being made—historians and economists have not been able to reach a consensus on this vexing problem. The debate rages undiminished and, except for greater subtlety of method and sophistication of presentation, often rests today on substantially the same ground that it did a hundred years ago.

If we trace the development of this continuing controversy through the works of its most able participants, we can discern some reasons for the lack of substantial progress in solving the problem and suggest certain lines of approach which may lead to a more satisfactory solution.

Dispute on the profitability of slavery in the ante bellum period was confined almost solely to the question of slavery as a system rather than a business. This is not surprising. Proslavery writers could hardly be expected to defend the peculiar institution on the ground that it made the planters rich. In the face of obvious Southern economic backwardness and poverty, such a position would be tantamount to an argument for abolition in the eyes of anyone other than the favored planters. On the other hand, the antislavery or abolitionist group would have a weak argument indeed if they confined it to the contention that slaveowners made a profit. The right to make a profit was uniformly accepted in the United States, and to point out that planters made a profit by using slave labor was no indictment of them. The nature of the situation, then, led prewar commentators to deal with slavery primarily as an economic and social system rather than as a form of business enterprise and to argue its merits on the basis of its effects on the well-being of the whole population.

This did not mean, however, that the contenders clashed directly. Specific arguments seldom met with specific rebuttal. Rather, the antislavery group picked out those aspects of the question they felt most damaging and most to be condemned; defenders answered by pointing to what they considered to be the beneficial features of the peculiar institution. The antagonists, of course, were directly involved. Their aim was most often not to convince their opponents by scholarly argument but to attack or defend slavery within the larger context of the sectional controversy.

The essence of the antislavery economic argument was that the slave system caused Southern economic backwardness. The words of Hinton Rowan Helper, the North Carolina white farmer, summarize this position and at the same time show the intense feeling which the argument generated in the ante bellum South:

> . . . the causes which have impeded the progress and prosperity of the South, which have dwindled our commerce, and other similar pursuits, into the most contemptible insignificance; sunk a large majority of our people in galling poverty and ignorance, rendered a small minority conceited and tyrannical, and driven the rest away from their homes; entailed upon us a humiliating dependence on the Free States; disgraced us in the recesses of our own souls, and brought us under reproach in the eyes of all civilized and enlightened nations—may all be traced to one common source, and there find solution in the most hateful and horrible word, that was ever incorporated into the vocabulary of human economy—*Slavery!* [1]

The burden of Helper's argument was that even in the area of the South's touted superiority, agriculture, the North was far ahead. Using figures from the 1850 census, Helper argued that the value of agricultural products in the free states exceeded that of the slave states and that the value of real and personal property in the free states topped that of the slave states (when the value of slaves was excluded). Helper adduced figures for commercial and industrial development which told the same story. His contention that slavery was the cause of this economic inequality came from a process of elimination rather than from a direct analysis of the operation of the slave system. At the close of the eighteenth century the South stood in an equal or superior position to the North in all aspects of economic development. Since then the South had fallen further and further behind. Wherein lay the differences between North and South which could account for this? Slavery, obviously, was the culprit.[2]

The Kentucky editor, Cassius M. Clay, regularly condemned slavery in his newspaper, the Lexington *True American*. Slavery, he argued, was economically destructive. Because it degraded labor, whites refused to do physical work, thereby fostering idleness. Those who would work were faced by the competition of slave labor, and their wages never exceeded the subsistence level which was the pay accorded slaves. When whites did not work and slaves were kept ignorant, skill or excellence could not develop. In addition, slave labor was economically expensive for the South because capital was tied up or frozen in the form of labor:

> The twelve hundred millions of capital invested in slaves is a dead loss to the South; the North getting the same number of laborers, doing double the work, for the interest on the money; and sometimes by partnerships, or joint operations, or when men work on their own account, without any interest being expended for labor.[3]

Finally, slavery hindered the development of a home market for local industry and thereby retarded economic development:

> Lawyers, merchants, mechanics, laborers, who are your consumers; Robert Wickliffe's two hundred slaves? How many clients do you find, how many goods do you sell, how many hats, coats, saddles, and trunks, do you make for these two hundred slaves? Does Mr. Wickliffe lay out as much for himself and his two hundred slaves, as two hundred freemen do . . . ? Under the free system the towns would grow and furnish a home market to the farmers, which in turn would employ more labor; which would consume the manufactures of the towns; and we could then find our business continually increasing, so that our children might settle down among us and make industrious, honest citizens.[4]

Clay's arguments, written in the 1840's, attempted to *explain* the economic consequences of the slave system rather than to *describe* them as did Helper a decade later. Clay's three main points—slavery degrades labor and keeps it ignorant, thereby hindering the development of skills; slavery freezes capital in the form of labor, thereby making it unavailable for other enterprises; slavery limits the home market—were recurring themes in the economic attack on slavery. A pamphlet by Daniel Reaves Goodloe, written about the same time that Clay's articles appeared, raised the same arguments.[5] George Tucker, in a general economic treatise written a decade earlier, gave major stress to the problem of idleness which he felt was a result of the degradation of labor induced by slavery.[6]

The most detailed economic indictment of the slave system in the ante bellum period—published just after the outbreak of the war—was made by a British economist. J. E. Cairnes stressed the detrimental effects of slavery as a form of labor and as a form of capital. The weaknesses of slave labor, he maintained, stemmed from three characteristics: "It is given reluctantly; it is unskillful; it is wanting in versatility." Soil exhaustion necessarily followed from the use of such labor. Scientific agriculture was impossible; slaves who worked reluctantly and in ignorance were incapable of learning and applying new farming techniques. Only the best lands, therefore, were used and, losing their fertility, were left desolate.[7]

Slave labor also hindered industrial and commercial development, Cairnes continued. Slaves were kept in ignorance and were thus unable to cope with machinery. If educated and brought to the cities as industrial workers, the danger of their combining to better their conditions or of their engaging in insurrection was increased. Commerce likewise was impossible. The dangers of mutiny on the high seas or of desertion in free ports would deter slaveowners from using their property in this work.

Cairnes agreed with Clay and Goodloe that slave capital was economically expensive because it involved a larger capital outlay than free labor. Available capital was tied up in slaves and therefore unavailable for manufacturing and commerce. As manufacturing and commerce were important sources for the accumulation of capital, the lack of these enterprises hindered accumulation in the South. This completed a vicious circle, accentuating the shortage of capital and making non-agricultural pursuits even more difficult to begin.[8]

Ante bellum defenders of slavery, for the most part, did not meet these economic criticisms head on. Except for those who charged that

Helper manipulated his figures to produce the desired result,[9] upholders of slavery shifted the ground of controversy.

Slavery was defended as an economic good because it transformed ignorant and inferior African savages into productive workers. "There is nothing but slavery which can destroy those habits of indolence and sloth, and eradicate the character of improvidence and carelessness, which mark the independent savage," wrote Thomas R. Dew.[10] Another defender, Albert Taylor Bledsoe, after his sketch of the horrors of life in Africa, concluded that "No fact is plainer than that the blacks have been elevated and improved by their servitude in this country. We cannot possibly conceive, indeed, how Divine Providence could have placed them in a better school of correction." [11] William J. Grayson versified the same argument:

> Instructed thus, and in the only school
> Barbarians ever know—a master's rule,
> The Negro learns each civilising art
> That softens and subdues the savage heart,
> Assumes the tone of those with whom he lives,
> Acquires the habit that refinement gives,
> And slowly learns, but surely, while a slave,
> The lessons that his country never gave.
>
> . . . .
>
> No better mode can human wits discern,
> No happier system wealth or virtue find,
> To tame and elevate the Negro mind.[12]

Thus slavery was not only an economic good but a social and humanitarian blessing as well.

Slavery, according to its defenders, was economically beneficial in other ways. It was said to mitigate the class conflict which existed in every society.[13] "It is impossible to place labor and capital in harmonious or friendly relations, except by the means of slavery, which identifies their interests," George Fitzhugh wrote.[14] His *Cannibals All!* also stressed the well-being of the slave. Because capital and labor were united in the slave he was better cared for and suffered none of the privations visited upon the wage slave of the North for whom freedom was a condition of dubious value. Grayson employed his heroic couplets to make this point:

> It bound to daily labor while he lives,
> His is the daily bread that labor gives;
> Guarded from want, from beggary secure,

He never feels what hireling crowds endure,
Nor knows like them in hopeless want to crave,
For wife and child, the comforts of the slave,
Or the sad thought that, when about to die,
He leaves them to the cold world's charity,
And sees them slowly seek the poor-house door—
The last, vile, hated refuge of the poor.[15]

Proslavery writers, virtually ignoring the view of slavery as economically debilitating to the South, argued instead that it strengthened the nation's economy.[16] They pointed to the products of slave labor, tracing their importance to the country as a whole. Upon slavery and slave labor, in fact, rested the economic well-being of the nation and the world. David Christy, writing that slavery was not "a self-sustaining system, independently remunerative," contended that "it attains its importance to the nation and to the world, by standing as an agency, intermediate, between the grain growing states and our foreign commerce." Taking the products of the North, slavery "metamorphoses them into cotton, that they may bear export." To the world it supplied cotton for manufacture into cloth and clothing, stimulating commerce and industry. For the United States it provided the largest cash exports (cotton and tobacco); it comprised a market for manufactured goods, supplied food and other groceries, and helped to pay for foreign imports.[17] Northern profits depended upon Southern wealth, argued Thomas Kettell in 1860; the North, therefore, should do everything in its power to keep the South, with its peculiar institution, in the Union.[18]

Whatever advantages did accrue to the South came, ironically, to those who did not own slaves, according to the editor J. D. B. De Bow. Not only did the nonslaveowning merchants benefit from slavery because they handled the goods produced by slave labor, but the white worker in the South also benefited. He had status by virtue of being a white man; he was not forced to work in unhealthy shops as was his white brother in the North; and most important of all, he had the opportunity of becoming a slaveholder and by so doing relieving himself and his wife of drudgery in the fields.[19]

Although ante bellum disputants thus came to opposite conclusions regarding the profitability of the slave system, not all of their arguments were mutually exclusive. This observation is most clearly illustrated by the manner in which Ulrich B. Phillips, reexamining the question in the twentieth century, was able to incorporate a large part of both ends of the argument into his economic analysis of the slave system. He accepted many of the conclusions of slavery's defenders while at the same time maintaining that the slave system was detrimental to the economic development of the South. He was able to unite the two points of view by clearly differentiating between the plantation system and slavery. At the same time he considered another factor in his discussion, that of slavery as a business enterprise.

While slavery existed, for the most part, within the plantation system, the two, Phillips maintained, were not inseparable. Indeed, the plantation regime "was less dependent upon slavery than slavery was upon it." The plantation system was a means of organizing labor; slavery, on the other hand, was a means of capitalizing labor.

The plantation system had definite advantages both economic and social. By routinizing labor, dividing different tasks rationally, and instituting strict supervision, while at the same time caring for the health of the workers (slaves), the plantation made for efficient methods of production.[20] Such methods were required because of the crude labor used. In effectively organizing ignorant and savage labor into efficient production it was economically advantageous; and "in giving industrial education to the laboring population, in promoting certain moral virtues, and in spreading the amenities" it was socially advantageous. The plantation was "a school constantly training and controlling pupils who were in a backward state of civilization." [21]

But the ante bellum plantation system hampered the economic development of the South. Its weakness stemmed less from its role as an organizer of labor and more from its close tie-in with slavery as an economic system. If the plantation was a school, the slave system prevented the apt students from ever being graduated. Laborers whose abilities transcended crude field work were yet harnessed to it and could not establish themselves as independent farmers. Unskilled labor was what was required and planters found it economically wasteful to train many skilled laborers despite any ability they might exhibit.[22]

Slavery, then, was harmful to the South because it prevented full utilization of the potential skills and abilities in the labor force. But the detrimental effects of slavery went deeper than this, according to Phillips. The central economic disadvantage of slavery was that it required that the entire life's labor of the worker be capitalized. Under a free labor system, wages are paid as work is done, and income from the sale of products can be used to pay future wage bills as they arise. The planter, however, was forced to buy his labor; that is, his wage bill became a long-term capital investment. Thus the slave system absorbed available capital. "Individual profits, as fast as made, went into the purchase of labor, and not into modern implements or land improvements." [23]

Because capital tended to be absorbed by the slave system, its availability was at a premium and planters were forced to look to outside sources for credit: "Circulating capital was at once converted into fixed capital; while for their annual supplies of food, implements, and luxuries the planters continued to rely upon their credit with the local merchants, and the local merchants to rely upon their credit with northern merchants and bankers." The result was a continuous economic loss as capital was drained from the South.[24]

The capital shortage stunted Southern economic development by hindering diversification in the economy, thereby keeping the South dependent upon the North. While Ohio benefited New York by becoming a market and a supplier of food and raw materials, Alabama had no such reciprocal relationship with Virginia or South Carolina. On the contrary, the Southwest competed with the Southeast to the detriment of the older regions because it could produce cotton more cheaply on the better lands and because increased production and labor needs drove the prices of slaves up. Economic benefits accrued to the North where manufactured goods and services had to be purchased; the Southeast was prevented from opening mills because all available capital was absorbed in slaves.[25]

Phillips introduced another dimension to this discussion of the economics of slavery—the question of the profitability of slavery to the individual slaveholder.[26] Matching the continual public loss as capital left the South was the private loss in the form of interest payments on borrowed capital. Profits were absorbed by the need to capitalize labor, a situation which was greatly aggravated in the 1850's when prices of slaves skyrocketed. As a result, Phillips declared, by the end of the 1850's only those plantations on the best lands, under the most efficient supervision, could make a profit for their owners.[27]

For Phillips, then, the plantation system was often economically beneficial to the South.[28] Its weakness stemmed from the fact that it was inextricably bound to slavery. It was slavery as an economic system which hindered and warped Southern development and kept the South backward in the prewar period. And it was slavery which made staple production in the ante bellum period an unprofitable enterprise for all but the most favorably situated planters. Phillips concluded that slavery was "an obstacle to all progress." He had to explain the continued existence of a personally and socially unprofitable system on noneconomic grounds. Slavery, he wrote, was initially introduced as a means of labor control and at first had proved to be profitable. As the number of slaves continued to rise, slavery became essential as an instrument of race control. It became the means to police an inferior race, to keep the Negroes' "savage instincts from breaking forth, and to utilize them in civilized industry." For the moment private gain and social gain were united. But as time went on the question of race control became most important—and an end to be attained only "at the expense of private and public wealth and of progress." [29]

Phillips' work was immensely influential. In the 1920's and 1930's a series of state studies were published which tended to support his conclusions. Perhaps because they were local studies and not concerned with overall Southern development, these monographs have major emphasis to slavery as a form of business enterprise rather than as an economic system. The question posed was simply whether the planters made money on their investment in slaves. Rosser Howard Taylor, basing his conclusions on the testimony of travelers and on extant plantation records, concluded that in North Carolina "slaveholding was not generally profitable." [30] Relph B. Flanders, in his study of Georgia slavery, found that although some planters were able to amass a fortune, many others made but a marginal living. He found much evidence showing that ante bellum Georgia planters bemoaned the unprofitability of the peculiar institution.[31] Slavery in Mississippi was investigated by Charles S. Sydnor. He found that free labor was much cheaper than slave and would have been more profitable for the planter to use. A thirty-slave plantation required a $40,000 investment, while if free labor had been used only $10,000 would have been needed. The greater the capital investment, he concluded, the greater the interest costs which had to be charged against profits. Furthermore, the large investment in labor the slaveowner was forced to make "added nothing to the productivity of the soil or to the betterment of the farm equipment," and it was doubtful whether the increased efficiency gained by slavery justified the "enlarged investment of capital." After calculating the costs of production on a typical fifty-slave Mississippi plantation, Sydnor concluded that profits were low. Only by spending the interest and other hidden charges (interest on capital invested in slaves, depreciation of slave property, land, and equipment) and by not calculating their own wages as supervisors of the business could planters seem to make a profit. A similar situation prevailed in Alabama, according to the historian of the cotton kingdom in that state, Charles S. Davis. Even with cotton selling at eight cents per pound, production by slave labor "was a fair business and nothing more." While some planters did make a great deal of money, "for the great majority the planting profession meant only a living." [32]

Further support for Phillips' views came from an influential article by Charles W. Ramsdell in 1929. Ramsdell maintained that slavery could be profitable only on the very best lands and since these lands, by the late 1850's, had been almost completely settled, slavery would have gradually become more and more decadent until, finally, economic causes would have required emancipation. He pointed out that high cotton prices of the 1850's could not last and, in fact, had already shown evidence of decline by 1860. As good lands were taken up and cotton prices declined, slave prices would drop also and Eastern states would no longer have the Western slave market in which to dispose profitably of excess slaves. In the meantime, with no new land available, more slaves would be on hand than could be used. Owners of large slave forces would find the expense of maintaining them too high to make cotton production by slave labor profitable. Slaves would become an economic handicap and slaveowners would look for a way to free their slaves and thereby relieve themselves of the burden of supporting them. [33]

While Phillips and his followers were amassing a formidable array of economic reasoning and statistical data to prove that slavery was unprofitable both as an economic system (because of its effects on the South) and as a business enterprise (because slaveowners made little profit), other historians were challenging this thesis on all levels. Some sought to show that Southern backwardness was not the fault of slavery; others stoutly maintained that planters on the whole made very substantial profits. The beginnings of this anti-Phillips or revisionist school can be traced back as far as the first decade of the twentieth century, but most of the revisionist work was done in the period beginning in the 1930's. It is this school which seems to be most active at the present time; nevertheless, there are still strong adherents to the traditional point of view.

The Mississippi planter and historian, Alfred Holt Stone, writing in the first decade of the century, relied heavily on Phillips but came to different conclusions. Stone's central argument was that it was the Negro and not slavery which retarded the ante bellum South. The Negro, according to Stone, was an inferior beging incapable of advancing whether free or slave: "The negro was a negro before he was a slave and he remained a negro after he became free. I recall no sound economic argument against slave negro labor per se . . . which is not today equally as sound against free negro labor per se." Had white free labor been used in Southern production, the foundation of Southern economic life would have been sounder. Some form of the plantation system would have undoubtedly developed, "but it would have been based upon free white labor, and would have served as a great training school for the production of small farmers." [34] The innate inferiority of Negroes prevented them from reaching this level.

But the most telling of the earlier blows struck in the revisionist cause were works of Robert R. Russel and Lewis C. Gray written in the 1930's. Neither sought to reverse completely Phillips' point of view, but both aimed at changing the emphasis of his analysis.

Russel made no effort to deny that the ante bellum Southern economy was backward; he did deny, however, that slavery was responsible. Rather, the South was hamstrung by its "climate, topography, natural resources, location with respect to the North and to Europe, means of transportation, and character of the white population." [35] The fact that population in the North was less dispersed led to more concentrated markets for Northern manufacturers and lessened the problems of transportation to and from these markets. Household manufacture was more firmly entrenched in the Northeast from the start, and, as Northwestern agricultural regions opened up, Easterners were forced to leave the countryside—they were no longer able to compete—and were thus available as operatives in industry. In the South, the profitability of staple agriculture and the fact that slaves "were certainly not as well adapted to mechanical employments as to agriculture" prevented the development of this same pattern. The central weakness in the South was not simply that slave labor was used but that it was primarily an area of commercial agriculture. Planters lived on further earnings and borrowed from Northern and British sources, thereby incurring an expense which limited the amount of capital accumulation in the region. Overproduction of the staples forced prices down and cut into profits and, therefore, into savings. But these were phenomena of agricultural production and had little to do with the use of slave labor. Furthermore, the argument that slavery absorbed Southern capital was incorrect: "Slavery did not absorb Southern capital in any direct sense; it affected the distribution of capital within the section. The mere capitalization of the anticipated labor of a particular class did not destroy or diminish any other kind of property." [36]

The central element in Lewis C. Gray's revisionist argument was that slavery was a highly profitable form of business enterprise. Slave labor, when used for staple production, would always supplant free labor because it was cheaper and more efficient. The employer of slave labor had a guaranteed labor supply; women as well as men could be used in the fields; child labor could be used extensively; labor troubles such as strikes and lockouts were unknown. The slaveowner could appropriate every bit of surplus created by the slave over and above bare subsistence. Thus, slaveowners had to give their slaves only just enough to keep them alive; wage laborers could not offer their services for less.[37] The high prices of slaves in the 1850's, Gray wrote, reflected accurately the profitability of such labor, and it was profitability that accounted for its continued use.[38]

Although Gray disputed the contention that all of the South's ills could be traced to slavery, he did argue that the "ultimate influence" of slavery "upon the economic well-being of the South was pernicious." Slavery was most profitable on the richest and most favorably situated lands; other lands were left to the free population which lived at a subsistence level. This free population provided a very small market and exerted little pressure for the construction of roads, canals, schools, and other necessary social improvements. Because slavery was profitable, all available capital that was accumulated went into expansion of staple production using slave labor and, hence, was unavailable to industry or trade. The South remained, therefore, "a predominantly agricultural country" and was "consequently subject to the disadvantages characteristic" of such an economy. The fundamental disadvantage was the slow accumulation of local capital which further intensified the problems of expansion, diversification, and economic growth. "Hence," he concluded, "we have the near-paradox of an economic institution competitively effective under certain conditions, but essentially regressive in its influence on the socio-economic evolution of the section where it prevailed." [39]

The work of Gray and Russel opened up a double-barreled assult on the Phillips point of view. Russel had questioned the allegation that slavery was the main cause of Southern backwardness, and Gray had disputed the contention that slaveowning was not a profitable business enterprise. Further revisionist work proceeded along these two lines, although most of the succeeding work gave major emphasis to the problem of slavery as a business rather than as an economic system.

Thomas P. Govan subjected the bookkeeping methods used by Phillips and his followers to critical scrutiny. The central problem in determining profitability, according to Govan, was simply to decide whether planters made money on their investment. He criticized the work of Phillips, Sydnor, Flanders, and others on two counts: They failed to consider all possible sources of profit in making their calculations, and they considered as an expense an item which should have been considered as part of the profit. Services received from household slaves, food and other provisions grown on the plantation and used by the owner, and the increase in the value of land and slaves must all be considered as part of profit; yet, Govan charged, these items were ignored in figuring income. Furthermore, interest on investment, which Sydnor and others listed as an expense, was, in reality, a profit item. According to the classical economists, profit is made up of interest on investment, payment for supervision, and payment for risk. Accountants usually do not separate the first and last of these, but they do include them in the profit column. When these adjustments in bookkeeping methods are made, Govan concluded, slaveownership emerges as a highly profitable business.[40]

The bookkeeping problem was approached somewhat differently by Robert Worthington Smith. It is a mistake, he insisted, to consider capital investment on the basis of current prices on slaves. While slave prices were extremely high in the 1850's, it would be incorrect to use the appreciated value of slaves owned from an earlier period (or those born and raised on the plantation) as the capital investment in figuring profit. If, Smith concluded, profit is calculated upon the "capital actually invested in slaves" rather than upon current prices, "a very good return seems to have been paid to the majority of owners." [41]

The most all-inclusive revisionist work on the question of American slavery is Kenneth M. Stampp's *The Peculiar Institution*, published in 1956. Disagreeing with Phillips about almost every aspect of slavery in the United States, Stampp differed with him, too, over the economics of slavery. But while Phillips gave major emphasis to the problem of slavery as an economic system, Stampp was mainly concerned with slavery as a business: ". . . allowing for the risks of a laissez-faire economy, did the average ante-bellum slaveholder, over the years, earn a reasonably satisfactory return from his investment?" [42] Stampp's answer was unequivocal: "On both large and small estates, none but the most hopelessly inefficient masters failed to profit from the ownership of slaves." Slave labor was cheaper and could be more fully exploited; this made up for any loss due to inefficiency. Capital invested in slaves was not an added expense but merely a payment in advance for work which would be performed over a period of years. Hidden sources of profit, such as food produced on the plantation, sale of excess slaves, natural increase of slaves, appreciation of land values because of improvements—all, when added to the income from the sale of the staple, served to increase profits.[43] Stampp concluded that there is no evidence that slavery was decadent, no evidence that it would soon have died had not the war brought it to an abrupt end.[44]

Two Harvard economists added their voices to the chorus of revisionist argument in a paper published in 1958. Their purpose, declared Alfred H. Conrad and John R. Meyer, was to take the argument over profitability out of the realm of accounting and instead, measure profitability according to economic concepts.[45] They constructed an economic model of a Southern cotton plantation for the years 1830 to 1860 and then computed the return on investment on the basis of a Keynesian capital-value formula.[46] Their calculations showed that returns on cotton production varied from 2.2 per cent on low-yield land to 13.0 per cent on very fertile land, with returns of 4½ to 8 per cent encompassing "the majority of ante bellum cotton operations." Profits on the raising and selling of slaves were considered separately. Their calculations for this part of the slave industry showed returns varying from 7.1 per cent to 8.1 per cent depending on the number of children produced. These figures, the authors maintained, showed not only that profits were made in slaveowning, but that this form of investment was as good as an investment elsewhere in the economy. This was true throughout the South and not only on the best lands. Where lands were good, profits came from the raising and selling of slaves.[47]

Up to this point Conrad and Meyer centered their argument on the question of slavery as a business. They then turned to the broader question of slavery and its effect on the South. Slavery, they concluded, did not hamper Southern economic growth. Available capital was not used for industrialization and diversification simply because it could be more profitably used in agricultural production. The economic problems of the South were the product of an agricultural community and not a result of the existence of slavery.[48]

Two recent works, in dealing with the question of profitability, show the influence of Conrad and Meyer's findings. Stanley M. Elkins in his study of slavery wrote that the economists, by dropping accounting methods and substituting "the economic . . . concept of profit" have made a "conceptual breakthrough" on the question of profitability. Paul W. Gates, in his discussion of slavery in *The Farmer's Age*, leaned heavily on Conrad and Meyer's analysis in concluding that slavery was profitable.[49] It is clear, however, that Conrad and Meyer's work will not find universal acceptance. It was almost immediately challenged, briefly but cogently, by Douglas F. Dowd.[50]

More recently another economist, Robert Evans, Jr., has published his findings on the question of profitability. Assuming a classical market, he calculated returns on investments in slave capital on the basis of profits earned through the hiring out of slaves during the three decades before the Civil War. He found that the rate of return on slaves varied from 9.5 per cent to 18.5 per cent, figures which were usually higher than those which could be earned in possible alternate areas of investment.[51]

Almost all the writers whose work has been discussed in these pages, whether economists or historians, have, to one degree or another, influenced the conclusions of writers of more general works, who show some of the same diversity of opinion as do the specialists.[52]

It would be folly to assume that this vexing question will ever be resolved to everyone's satisfaction. In part, the difficulty in arriving at a satisfactory solution stems from varying definitions of the problem. Contemporaries argued vociferously, but they were arguing about two very different things. They could agree that slavery had to be considered in its relation to the Southern economy, but there was no agreement as to the particular issues this consideration involved. Ulrich B. Phillips in his analysis gave major stress to slavery as an economic system, but he also introduced what to him apparently was a secondary question, the profitability of slavery as a business enterprise. It was this question which his followers, and the revisionists as well, have emphasized down to our own day.[53] Thus, a subtle shift in emphasis has taken place through the years in the discussion of slavery's profitability, a shift which is obvious if one compares not the conclusions but the central problem posed by Phillips early in the century with that considered by Conrad and Meyer several decades later.

Some light at least could be shed on the problem if there could be agreement as to what the pboblem is. In reality, two distinct topics have been discussed over the years, and they are not necessarily related. At least, their relationship has to be proved before they can be considered related. Even if every slaveowner were able to realize a twenty-five per cent return on his investment, it does not necessarily follow that slavery as a system was economically profitable. The real question is neither one of bookkeeping nor one of economic profit. It is a problem of economic history.

To deal with the question of slavery as an economic system, one must clearly distinguish those elements in the Southern economy which existed because of slavery and those which were unrelated to slavery. Those who argue that Southern backwardness arose, for the most part, because the South was primarily agricultural must first show that this would have been true whether or not the institution of slavery existed. Conversely, those who argue that slavery prevented diversification must prove (1) that economic diversification did take place in nonslave agricultural areas and (2) that it was slavery and not other factors which prevented diversified investment in the South. Furthermore, if slavery is to be called the cause of any given phenomenon in the Southern economy, the exact dynamics of the influence of slavery must be shown. It is not enough to juxtapose the results with the existence of slavery to establish a causal relationship. A final methodological question must be posed: Can the economics of slavery be discussed adequately in purely economic terms?

Some work has already been done along the lines suggested here. Two decades ago Fabien Linden considered the effect of slavery on the development of manufacturing in the prewar South. Treating slavery as a political and social as well as an economic institution, Linden traced the dynamics of the opposition to a move to establish widespread manufacturing establishments in the South in the 1840's.[54] More recently Eugene D. Genovese has, in a similar manner, investigated the problem of slavery in relation to the home market in the ante bellum South.[55]

A different line of approach has been taken by Douglas Dowd, who made a comparative analysis of economic development in the South and West. Further work in this direction, including comparisons with underdeveloped countries, might yield significant results. Dowd also suggested ways in which the economic question had to be broadened: "The nature and extent of resources are of course meaningless apart from the social context within which they exist." [56]

Certainly new lines of thought and research can be explored. If scholars are mindful of the complexities of the question of profitability, and cognizant of the nature of the work already accomplished, we can expect the writings of the future to increase our knowledge of the South and its peculiar institution. The prospect is of more than academic interest. Not only could further work in this field deepen our understanding of nineteenth-century American economic history. It might also give valuable insights into the dynamics of economic growth and development.

NOTES

1. Hinton Rowan Helper, *The Impending Crisis of the South* . . . (New York, 1859), 25.
2. *Ibid.*, 1-25, 33, 39, 66, 69, 72, 81, 283-86, esp.

3. Cassius Marcellus Clay, Writings, Horace Greely, ed. (New York, 1848), 204-205, 224.

4. Ibid., 227, also 346-47.

5. [Daniel Reaves Goodloe], Inquiry into the Causes Which Have Retarded the Accumulation of Wealth and Increase of Population in the Southern States: In Which the Question of Slavery Is Considered in a Politico-Economical Point of View (Washington, 1846), passim. Goodloe added that the degradation of labor served to keep immigrants away from the South, thus depriving the section of the skills and capital which new arrivals brought to the North.

6. George Tucker, The Laws of Wages, Profits, and Rent, Investigated (Philadelphia, 1837), 46-48. Tucker argued that as the number of slaves increased, the cost of raising them would be greater than the gain from their use, and emancipation would result. Ibid., 49.

7. J. E. Cairnes, The Slave Power: Its Character, Career, and Probable Designs: Being an Attempt to Explain the Real Issues Involved in the American Contest (2nd ed., London, 1863), 44, 54-56, 81.

8. Ibid., 70-72, 74-75.

9. See Samuel M. Wolfe, Helper's Impending Crisis Dissected (Philadelphia, 1860); Elias Peissner, The American Question in Its National Aspect, Being Also an Incidental Reply to Mr. H. R. Helper's "Compendium of the Impending Crisis of the South" (New York, 1861). Obviously in response to Helper were two other works, Thomas Prentice Kettell, Southern Wealth and Northern Profits . . . (New York, 1860) and J. B. D. De Bow, The Interest in Slavery of the Southern Non-Slaveholder (Charleston, 1860). While Kettell presented figures which would dispute Helper, his main point was not to contend with Helper. De Bow was attempting to argue against Helper's contention that nonslaveholders were dupes of the planters. These two works will be discussed below.

10. Thomas R. Dew, Review of the Debate in the Virginia Legislature, 1831–32, as reprinted in The Pro-Slavery Argument . . . (Charleston, 1852), 328. Chancellor William Harper echoed these sentiments but in a more general way. Slavery, he wrote, is the only road to civilization. "If any thing can be predicated as universally true of uncultivated man, it is that he will not labor beyond what is absolutely necessary to maintain his existence . . . . The coercion of slavery alone is adequate to form man to habits of labor . . . . Since the existence of man upon the earth, with no exception whatever, either of ancient or modern times, every society which has attained civilization, had advanced to it through this process." Harper, "Slavery in the Light of Social Ethics," in E. N. Elliott (ed.), Cotton Is King, and Pro-Slavery Arguments (Augusta, Ga., 1860), 551-52.

11. Albert Taylor Bledsoe, "Liberty and Slavery; or, Slavery in the Light of Moral and Political Philosophy," ibid., 413-16.

12. William J. Grayson, The Hireling and the Slave . . . (Charleston, 1856), 34-35. See also [Stephen Colwell], The South: A Letter from a Friend in the North, with Special Reference to the Effects of Disunion upon Slavery (Philadelphia, 1856), 14.

13. "It is the order of nature and of God, that the being of superior faculties and knowledge, and therefore of superior power, should control and dispose of those who are inferior. It is as much in the order of nature, that men should

enslave each other, as that other animals should prey upon each other." Harper, "Slavery in the Light of Social Ethics," 559-60.

14. George Fitzhugh, *Cannibals All! or, Slaves Without Masters* (Richmond, 1857), 48. Governor James Henry Hammond of South Carolina, while admitting that economically speaking "slavery presents some difficulties" and that it was more expensive than free labor, nevertheless concluded that it was economically beneficial. There was no overpopulation in the South, he argued, no group of men so hungry that they would work for next to nothing. He concluded self-righteously, "We must, therefore, content ourselves with our dear labor, under the consoling reflection that what is lost to us, is gained to humanity; and that, inasmuch as our slave costs use more than your free man costs you, by so much is he better off." Hammond, "Slavery in the Light of Political Science," in Elliott (ed.), *Cotton Is King*, 646-47.

15. Grayson, *The Hireling and the Slave*, 43-44.

16. Southern backwardness could not be ignored. The tariff, rather than slavery, was frequently pointed to as the cause. See Thomas Dew, *Review of the Debate*, 486. J. D. B. De Bow, in *De Bow's Review*, regularly called for the introduction of manufacturing in the South and the establishment of direct trade to Europe to solve the section's economic problems.

17. David Christy, *Cotton Is King . . .* (New York, 1856), 78-82, 163.

18. Kettell, *Southern Wealth and Northern Profits, passim.*

19. De Bow, *The Interest in Slavery of the Southern Non-Slaveholder.*

20. Ulrich B. Phillips, "The Decadence of the Plantation System," American Academy of Political and Social Science, *Annals*, XXXV (January 1910), 37-38, and "The Origin and Growth of the Southern Black Belts," *American Historical Review*, XI (July 1906), 803-804.

21. Phillips, "Decadence," 39; Ulrich B. Phillips, *American Negro Slavery* (New York, 1918), 291, 313-14, 342.

22. *Ibid.*, 343; Phillips, "Decadence," 40.

23. Ulrich B. Phillips, "The Economic Cost of Slaveholding in the Cotton Belt," *Political Science Quarterly*, XX (June 1905), 271-72; Phillips, *American Negro Slavery*, 395-96.

24. Phillips, "Economic Cost," 272; Phillips, *American Negro Slavery*, 397, 399.

25. Phillips, "Decadence," 39; Phillips, *American Negro Slavery*, 396.

26. This was not the first time this aspect of the problem was raised. Complaints by ante bellum planters that they made little money were common, and newspapers (especially during a crisis period) carried notices of sheriffs' sales of lands and slaves lost by planters. Slavery itself was seldom seen as the root cause of such difficulties. Low cotton prices, the closing of the slave trade, the tariff, the machinations of the middlemen, and other such factors were usually adduced as the reasons for poor return with slave labor. Antislavery disputants sometimes touched on the question also, but the emphasis was on the detrimental effects on the South in general. "Slavery *is* profitable to the few," Daniel Goodloe wrote to Frederick Law Olmsted, "because it is simply a privilege of robbing the many." Frederick Law Olmsted, *The Cotton Kingdom*, Arthur M. Schlesinger, ed. (New York, 1953), xxix.

27. Phillips, "Economic Cost," 271, 274; Phillips, *American Negro Slavery*, 391-92.

28. Writing soon after the turn of the century, Phillips concluded that the

continued backwardness of the South was due to the *absence* of the old plantation system. The problem of ignorant labor remained, Phillips argued, and its
utilization is small-scale farming (through small landowning, tenantry, renting,
or sharecropping) was inefficient. Restore the order, the discipline, the direction, and the large-scale methods which characterized the ante bellum plantation, and the South, relieved of the burden of slavery, would prosper. All of
the advantages of the ante bellum situation would be present with none of the
disadvantages associated with slavery. Ulrich B. Phillips, "The Economics of
the Plantation," *South Atlantic Quartely*, II (July 1903), 231-36; Phillips,
"Decadence," 40-41; Ulrich B. Phillips, "Conservatism and Progress in the
Cotton Belt," *South Atlantic Quarterly*, III (January 1904), 1-10; Ulrich B.
Phillips, "Plantations with Slave Labor and Free," *American Historical Review*,
XXX (July 1925), 738-53.

29. Phillips, "Economic Cost," 259, 275. See also his "The Slave Labor
Problem in the Charleston District," *Political Science Quarterly*, XXII (September 1907), 416-39, and "The Central Theme of Southern History," *American Historical Review*, XXXIV (October 1928), 30-43. In a more expansive
mood, Phillips found the slave system socially useful for its benefits in building
Southern character: ". . . In the large it was less a business than a life; it
made fewer fortunes than it made men." *American Negro Slavery*, 401.

30. Rosser Howard Taylor, *Slaveholding in North Carolina, an Economic
View* (Chapel Hill, 1926), 94-98.

31. Ralph Betts Flanders, *Plantation Slavery in Georgia* (Chapel Hill
1933), 221-30. As Phillips had done earlier, Flanders found the continued
existence of a largely unprofitable business to be explained by noneconomic
factors. The planters, he wrote, confused the plantation system, slavery, and the
race question. "This confusion made it difficult for anti-slavery critics to
understand the tenacity with which slave-owners clung to a social and economic
system they despised, and which seemed to them unprofitable." *Ibid.* 231.

32. Charles Sackett Sydnor, *Slavery in Mississippi* (New York, 1933), 196-
200; Charles S. Davis, *The Cotton Kingdom in Alabama* (Montgomery, 1939),
180. In a brief analysis of the economics of slavery during the last decade before the Civil War, James D. Hill concluded that the business of production
by slave labor was in general unprofitable. Many planters, he admitted, became
rich, "but these cases were more than likely due to peculiar advantages in location, fertility of soil or individual administrative ability; on the whole, in spite
of slavery rather than because of it." Hill, "Some Economic Aspects of Slavery,
1850–1860," *South Atlantic Quarterly*, XXVI (April 1927), 161-77.

33. Charles W. Ramsdell, "The Natural Limits of Slavery Expansion,"
Mississippi Valley Historical Review, XVI (September 1929), 151-71. Ramsdell's conclusion, of course, was that slavery would have disappeared within a
generation, and therefore the Civil War had been unnecessary.

34. Alfred Holt Stone, "Some Problems of Southern Economic History,"
American Historical Review, XII (July 1908), 791; Alfred Holt Stone, "The
Negro and Agricultural Development," American Academy of Political and
Social Science, *Annals*, XXXV (January 1910), 13.

35. Robert R. Russel, "The General Effects of Slavery upon Southern
Economic Progress," *Journal of Southern History*, IV (February 1938), 54.

36. *Ibid.*, 47-52. See also Robert R. Russel, "The Effects of Slavery upon
Nonslaveholders in the Ante-Bellum South," *Agricultural History*, XV (April

1941), 112-26 and *Economic Aspects of Southern Sectionalism* 1861 (Urbana, 1924), 55-64.

37. Lewis Cecil Gray, *History of Agriculture in the Southern United States to 1860* (2 vols., Washington and New York, 1933–1941), I, 448, 462, 470-74. Gray disputed the contention that the planter's need to buy his labor supply was an added expense when figured in terms of the entire life of the slave: "When capitalization was accurately effected, the series of successive incomes as they became available actually were equivalent to interest and replacement; for interest and replacement would have been allowed for in the relatively low value that the owner paid for the services of the slave, capitalized on a terminable basis." In other words, Gray was arguing that the alleged extra cost in the form of interest and depreciation on the slave as a form of capital investment was not an extra cost at all but was a surplus which could be appropriated by the planter by virtue of his ownership of the slave over the entire period of his life. *Ibid.*, 473-74.

38. *Ibid.*, 488, 476-77; II, 933-34, 939.

39. *Ibid.*, 933-34, 940-42.

40. Thomas P. Govan, "Was Plantation Slavery Profitable?" *Journal of Southern History*, VIII (November 1942), 513-35.

41. Robert Worthington Smith, "Was Slavery Unprofitable in the Ante-Bellum South?" *Agricultural History*, XX (January 1946), 62-64.

42. Kenneth M. Stampp, *The Peculiar Institution* (New York, 1956), 390. Stampp denied that slavery kept the planters in debt. This problem arose from poor management and extravagance, a product, not of slavery, but of "the southern culture that required these etxravagances." *Ibid.*, 391. The charge that slavery absorbed capital and retarded industrialization was also false, according to Stampp: "It is doubtful . . . that slavery in any decisive way retarded the industrialization of the South. After the African slave trade was legally closed, the southern labor system absorbed little new capital that might have gone into commerce or industry . . . . The domestic slave trade involved no further investment; it merely involved thet transfer of a portion of the existing one between individuals and regions." *Ibid.*, 397. Another historian, George R. Woolfolk, in a study attacking what he called the Helper-Phillips thesis, argued that slavery did not freeze great wealth in slaves. On the contrary, he wrote, slave capital was easily converted into liquid capital because of the great facility with which slaves could be sold. Woolfolk, "Cotton Capitalism and Slave Labor in Texas," *Southwestern Social Science Quarterly*, XXXVII (June 1956), 43-52.

43. Stampp, *Peculiar Institution*, 400-11, 414. It is clear that Stampp relies heavily on Gray, Govan, and Smith. His footnotes give recognition of his debt to these earlier revisionist scholars.

44. ". . . If the slave-holder's economic self-interest alone were to be consulted, the institution should have been preserved. Nor is there any reason to assume that masters would have found it economically desirable to emancipate their slaves in the foreseeable future." *Ibid.*, 417-18.

45. Alfred H. Conrad and John R. Meyer, "The Economics of Slavery in the Ante Bellum South," *Journal of Political Economy*, LXVI (April 1958), 96.

46. "Investment returns are properly computed by using the capital-value formula $y = x_t/(1 + r)^t$, where y is the cost of the investment, x_t is realized

return t years hence, and r is the internal rate of return of what Keynes called the marginal efficiency of capital . . . . The criterion for a profitable investment is that the marginal efficiency exceeds the interest rate (in the Keynesian terminology)." *Ibid.*, 98. The authors calculated the longevity of slaves (assuming on the basis of available figures that a 20-year old field hand had a 30-year life expectancy), the cost of investment (average cost of slaves, land, equipment, and average annual maintenance costs over the period, 1830–1860), the annual average yield per hand, and the average annual price for cotton. Using 6 per cent as the rate of return slaveowners could earn in other investments outside of slavery, the authors applied these figures to the formula and solved for r. *Ibid.*, 99-107.

47. *Ibid.*, 106-107, 109-14, 120-22. Their explanation of how figures were calculated (and the assumptions they were forced to make in the absence of adequate figures) may be found on pp. 106 108.

48. *Ibid.*, 119-20. A brief article by John E. Moes suggested that the capitalization of labor "does of itself most probably have a detrimental effect on economic growth." But, Moes wrote, this is a problem only when a society "is dependent upon its own capital resources." Such was not the case in the South, for the section was able to import large amounts of capital, a situation which would tend to overcome the detrimental effects of slavery on economic growth. He concluded by questioning the generally accepted assertion that "investment (and development) in the Ante Bellum [South] lagged behind that of the North." John E. Moes, "The Absorption of Capital in Slave Labor in the Ante-Bellum South and Economic Growth," *American Journal of Economics and Sociology*, XX (October 1961), 535-41.

49. Stanley M. Elkins, *Slavery* (Chicago, 1959), 234; Paul W. Gates, *The Farmer's Age: Agriculture, 1815–1860* (New York, 1960), 154-55. Gates also cited as his sources the work of Gray and Stampp, but his argument parallels most closely that of Conrad and Meyer.

50. Douglas F. Dowd, "The Economics of Slavery in the Ante Bellum South: A Comment," *Journal of Political Economy*, LXVI (October 1958), 440-42.

51. Robert Evans, Jr., "The Economics of American Negro Slavery, 1830–1860," in National Bureau of Economic Research, *Aspects of Labor Economics* (Princeton, 1962), 185-243. Evans indicated that he used "the net rent received by owners of slaves when they rented them out as the estimate of the income earned by the capital good" (p. 191) and assumed "that the hired slave labor market was classical rather than Keynesian in character . . ." (p. 194n). Evans' method and his approach to the problem were immediately attacked by a historian (Thomas P. Govan) and an economist (John E. Moes). See "Comments" by these scholars, *ibid.*, 243-56. Govan wrote that he agreed with Evans' conclusion but added that the economist's evidence had "little relevance to this conclusion" (p. 243).

52. Avery Craven questioned whether slavery could be blamed for Southern backwardness. Southern values and ideals rather than slavery accounted for a lack of diversified economic life in the ante bellum South. "The South often deliberately chose rural backwardness." Avery Craven, *The Coming of the Civil War* (New York, 1942), 90-91. Allan Nevins came to exactly opposite colclusions. The South did not choose rural backwardness, according to Nevins; it was forced upon the section by the institution of slavery, which "discouraged

industrialism," kept immigrants from the region, discredited "the labor of the white artisan," and "tied the South to a slovenly and wasteful staple-crop system." Allan Nevins, *Ordeal of the Union* (2 vols., New York, 1947), I, 493-94. Two prominent Southern historians, Francis Butler Simkins and Clement Eaton, tend to straddle the fence in their textbooks. They recognize that the slave system was in many ways disadvantageous to the Southern economy, but they do not put the entire blame for Southern backwardness on the peculiar institution. Climate, improvidence, and, most important, the fact that the South was primarily agricultural must share the blame with slavery, according to these two. Simkins, *A History of the South* (New York, 1953), 129-32; Eaton, *A History of the Old South* (New York, 1949), 273-78. Economic historians seem to be more united in their opinions. Louis M. Hacker argued that only those few planters on the very best land could make money; most could not. Hacker, *The Triumph of American Capitalism* (New York, 1940), 317-21. The authors of current popular economic histories agree in general with this and also agree that slavery was responsible for retarding Southern economic development. Ernest L. Bogart and Donald L. Kemmerer, *Economic History of the American People* (New York, 1947), 386-410; Edward C. Kirkland, *A History of American Economic Life* (New York, 1951), 170-73; Herman E. Kroos, *American Economic Development* (Englewood Cliffs, N. J., 1956), 129-32; Gilbert C. Fite and Jim E. Reese, *An Economic History of the United States* (Boston, 1959), 164-65.

53. The works of Russel and, in part, Gray are the most noteworthy exceptions to this.

54. Fabien Linden, "Repercussions of Manufacturing in the Ante Bellum South," *North Carolina Historical Review*, XVII (October 1940), 313-31.

55. Eugene D. Genovese, "The Significance of the Slave Plantation for Southern Economic Development," *Journal of Southern History*, XXVIII (November 1962), 422-37.

56. Douglas F. Dowd, "A Comparative Analysis of Economic Development in the American West and South," *Journal of Economic History*, XVI (December 1956), 558-74.

• The twain have met. The socialist and the paternalist have joined in evincing a fondness for social cohesion and in an antipathy for the fragmented and individualistic liberty of bourgeois capitalism. It is striking but not surprising, therefore, that the most forceful reassertion of Ulrich Phillips's view of the South as a distinct semifeudal subculture within ante-bellum America should come from a Marxist historian. Eugene D. Genovese's essays on "the political economy of slavery" combine Phillips's notion of an anticapitalistic, patriarchal slave civilization with Charles Beard's view that because of this uniqueness, the Civil War represented an inevitable clash of cultures moving daily further apart. As Genovese restates the Beardian argument, "slave civilization could not forever coexist with an increasingly hostile, powerful, and aggressive Northern capitalism," Genovese's article develops these perspectives on the slave South.

The Slave South: An Interpretation

EUGENE D. GENOVESE

THE PROBLEM

Two interpretations of antebellum Southern society have, for some years, contended in a perplexing and unreal battle. The first considers the Old South an agrarian society fighting against the enroachments of industrial capitalism; the second considers the slave plantation merely a form of capitalist enterprise and suggests that the differences between Northern and Southern capitalism were more apparent than real. These two views, which one would think contradictory, are sometimes combined in the thesis that the agrarian nature of planter capitalism, for some reason, made coexistence with industrial capitalism difficult. None of these interpretations is convincing. Slavery and the rule of a

From Eugene D. Genovese, "The Slave South: An Interpretation," *Science & Society*, XXV (December 1961), 320-37. Reprinted by permission.

special type of agrarians, the planters, characterized Southern society, which despite superficial resemblances to Northern was anti-bourgeois in structure and outlook.[1]

The first view cannot explain why some agrarian societies give rise to industrialization and some do not. A prosperous agricultural hinterland has generally served as a basis for industrial development by providing a home market for manufacturers and a source of capital accumulation; and the prosperity of farmers has largely depended on the rise of industrial centers as markets for foodstuffs. In a capitalist society, agriculture is one industry among many, and its conflict with manufacturing is one of many competitive rivalries. There must have been something unusual about an agriculture that generated violent opposition to the agrarian West as well as to the industrial Northeast.

The second view, which is the more widely held, stresses that the plantation system produced for a distant market, responded to supply and demand, invested capital in land and slaves, and operated with funds borrowed from banks and factors. This, the more serious of the two interpretations, cannot begin to explain the origins of the conflict with the North and is intrinsically unsatisfactory. The reply to it will be the burden of this article.

SLAVERY AND THE EXPANSION OF CAPITALISM

The proponents of the idea of "planter capitalism" draw heavily, wittingly or not, on Lewis C. Gray's theory of the genesis of the plantation system. Gray defines the plantation as a "capitalistic type of agricultural organization in which a considerable number of unfree laborers were employed under a unified direction and control in the production of a staple corp." [2] The plantation system is here considered inseparably linked with the international development of capitalism. Gray notes the plantation's need for large outlays of capital, its strong tendency toward specialization in a single crop, and its commercialism; and he argues that these are features that appeared with the industrial revolution.

In modern times the plantation often arose under bourgeois auspices to provide industry with cheap raw materials, but the consequences were not always harmonious with bourgeois society. Colonial expansion produced three diverse patterns: (1) the capitalists of the advanced country simply invested in colonial land—as illustrated by the recent practice of the United Fruit Company in the Caribbean; (2) the colonial planters were largely subservient to the advanced country—as illustrated by the British West Indies early in the nineteenth century; and

(3) the planters were able to win independence and build a society under their own direction—as illustrated by the Southern United States.

In alliance with the North, the planter-dominated South broke away from England, and political conditions in the new republic allowed it considerable freedom for self-development. The plantation society that had begun as an appendage of British capitalism ended as a powerful, largely autonomous, aristocratic civilization, although it was tied to the capitalistic world by bonds of commodity production. The essential element in this distinct civilization was the planter domination made possible by the command of slave labor. Slavery provided the basis for a special Southern economic and social life, special problems and tensions, and special laws of development.

THE RATIONALITY AND IRRATIONALITY OF SLAVE SOCIETY

Slave economies manifest irrational tendencies that inhibit economic development and endanger social stability. Max Weber, for one, has noted four important irrational features.[3] First, the master cannot adjust the size of his labor force in accordance with business fluctuations. In particular, efficiency cannot readily be achieved through the manipulation of the labor force if sentiment, custom, or community pressure makes separation of families difficult. Secondly, the capital outlay is much greater and riskier for slave labor than for free.[4] Thirdly, the domination of a planter class increases the risk of political influence in the market. Fourthly, the sources of cheap slave labor are usually exhausted rather quickly, and beyond a certain point, costs become excessively burdensome. Weber's remarks could be extended. For example, planters have little opportunity to select specifically trained workers for special tasks as they arise.

There are other telling aspects of this economic irrationality. Under capitalism the pressure of the competitive struggle and the bourgeois spirit of accumulation direct the greater part of profits back into production. The competitive side of Southern slavery produced a similar result but one that was modified by the pronounced tendency to heavy consumption. Economic historians and sociologists have long noted the high propensity to consume among landed aristocracies. No doubt this difference is one of degree, and the greater part of slavery's profits also find their way back into production; but the method of reinvestment in the two systems is substantially different. Under capitalism profits are largely directed into an expansion of plant and equipment, not labor; in a word, economic progress is qualitative. In slave societies, for economic reasons as well as for those of social prestige, reinvestment of funds takes place along the same lines as the original investment—in land and slaves; that is, economic progress is quantitative.

In the South this weakness was fatal for the slaveholding planters. They found themselves engaged in a growing conflict with Northern farmers and businessmen over tariffs, homesteads, internal improvements, and the decisive question of the balance of political power in the Union. The slow pace of their economic progress, in contrast to the long strides of the North, threatened to undermine their political parity and result in a Southern defeat on all major issues of the day. The qualitative leaps in the Northern economy were manifested in a rapidly increasing population, an expanding productive plant, and growing political, ideological, and social boldness. The South's voice grew shriller and harsher as it contemplated the impending disaster and sought solace in complaints of Northern aggression and exploitation.

Just as Southern slavery directed reinvestment along a path that led to economic stagnation, so too did it limit the volume of capital accumulated for investment of any kind. We need not reopen the tedious argument about which came first the plantation, the one-crop system, or slavery. It should be clear that while slavery existed, the South had to be bound to a plantation system and an agricultural economy based on a few crops. The resultant dependence on Northern and British markets and on outside credit facilities and the inevitably mounting middleman's charges are well known. Perhaps less obvious was the capital drain occasioned by the importation of industrial goods. While the home market was retarded, Southern manufacturers had a difficult time producing in sufficient quantities to keep costs and prices at levels competitive with Northerners. The attendant dependence on Northern and British imports intensified the outward flow of badly needed funds.

Yet, many of the elements of irrationality were irrational only from a bourgeois standpoint. The high propensity to consume luxuries, for example, has always been functional (i.e., socially if not economically rational) in aristocratic societies, for it has provided the ruling class with the façade necessary to overawe the middle and lower classes. We may speak of the slave system's irrationality only in a strictly economic sense and then only to indicate the inability of the South to compete with Northern capitalism on the latter's grounds. The planters, fighting for political power in an essentially capitalist Union, had to do just that.

BOURGEOIS AND PSEUDO-BOURGEOIS FEATURES OF THE SLAVE ECONOMY

The slave economy had close relations with, and was in a sense exploited by, the capitalist world market; consequently, slavery developed many ostensibly capitalist features, such as banking, commerce, and credit. These features were not *per se* capitalist and played a different role in the South than in the North. Capitalism has absorbed and even encouraged many kinds of precapitalist social systems serfdom, slavery, oriental state enterprises, and others. It has introduced credit, finance, banking, and similar institutions where they did not previously exist. It is pointless to suggest that therefore nineteenth-century India or twentieth-century Saudi Arabia are to be classified as capitalist countries. Our task is to analyze a few of the more important bourgeois and pseudo-bourgeois features and, in particular, to review the barriers to industrialization, for only by so doing can we appreciate the peculiar qualities of the slave economy.[5]

The defenders of the "planter capitalism" thesis have noted the extensive commercial links between the plantation and the world market and the modest commercial bourgeoisie in the South and have concluded that there is no good reason to predicate an antagonism between cotton producers and cotton merchants. However valid as a reply to the naïve arguments of the proponents of the agrarianism-versus-industrialism thesis, this criticism has unjustifiably been twisted to suggest that the presence of commercial activity proves the presence of capitalism.[6] Many precapitalist economic systems had well developed commercial relations, but if every commercial society is to be considered "capitalist," the word loses all meaning. In general, commercial classes have supported the existing system of production. As Maurice Dobb observes, their fortunes are bound up with those of the dominant producers, and merchants are more likely to seek an extension of their middlemen's profit than to try to reshape the economic order.[7]

In the Old South extensive and complicated commercial relations with the world market permitted the growth of a small commercial bourgeoisie. The resulting fortunes flowed into slaveholding, which offered prestige and was economically and politically secure in a planter-dominated society. Independent merchants found their business dependent on the patronage of the slaveholders. The merchants either became planters themselves or assumed a servile attitude toward the planters. The commercial bourgeoisie, such as it was, was tied to the slaveholding interest, had little desire or opportunity to invest capital in industrial expansion, and adopted the prevailing aristocratic attitudes.

The Southern industrialists were in an analogous situation, although one that was potentially subversive of the political power and ideological unity of the planters. Since the Southern countryside was dominated by large planters and slaves, the home market was retarded. The Southern yeomanry, unlike the Western, lacked the purchasing power to sustain rapid industrial development.[8] The planters spent much of their money abroad for luxuries. The plantation market consisted primarily of the demand for cheap slave clothing and cheap agricultural implements for use or misuse by the slaves. Southern industrialism needed a sweeping agrarian revolution to provide it with cheap labor and a substantial rural market, but the Southern industrialists were dependent on the existing, limited, plantation market. Leading industrialists like William Gregg and Daniel Pratt were plantation-oriented and proslavery. They could hardly have been otherwise.

The banking system of the South serves as an excellent illustration of an ostensibly capitalist institution that worked to augment the power of the planters and retard the development of the bourgeoisie. Southern banks functioned much as did those which the British introduced into Latin America, India, and Egypt during the nineteenth century. Although the British banks fostered dependence on British capital, they did not directly and willingly generate internal capitalist development. They were not sources of industrial capital but "large-scale clearing houses of mercantile finance vying in their interest charges with the local usurers." [9]

The difference between the banking practices of the South and those of the West reflects the difference between slavery and agrarian capitalism. In the West, as in the Northeast, banks and credit facilities promoted a vigorous economic expansion. During the period of irresponsible Western banking (1830–1844) credit was extended liberally for industrial development as well as for land purchases and internal improvements. Manufacturers and merchants dominated the boards of directors of Western banks, and landowners played a minor role. Undoubtedly, many urban businessmen speculated in land and were particularly interested in underwriting agricultural exports; but they gave attention to building up agricultural processing industries and urban enterprises, which guaranteed the region a many-sided economy.[10]

The slave states paid considerable attention to the development of a conservative, stable banking system, which could guarantee the movement of staple crops and the extension of credit to the planters. Southern banks were primarily designed to lend the planters money for outlays that were economically feasible and socially acceptable in a slave society: the movement of crops, the purchase of land and slaves, and little else.

Whenever easy credit policies were pursued in the South, the damage done outweighed the advantages of increased production. This imbalance probably did not occur in the West, for easy credit made possible agricultural and industrial expansion of a diverse nature and, despite acute crises, established a firm basis for long-range prosperity. Easy credit in the South led to expansion of cotton production with concomitant overproduction and low prices simultaneously, it increased the price of slaves.

Planters wanted their banks only to facilitate cotton shipments and maintain sound money. They purchased large quantities of foodstuffs from the West and, since they shipped little in return, had to pay in bank notes. For five years following the New Orleans bank failures of 1837, the city's bank notes were at a discount of from ten to twenty-five per cent. This condition could not be allowed to recur. Sound banking and sound money became the cries of the planters as a class.

Southern banking tied the planters to the banks but, more important, tied the bankers to the plantations. The banks often found it necessary to add prominent planters to their boards of directors and were, in any case, closely supervised by the planter-dominated state legislatures. In this relationship the bankers could not emerge as a middle-class counterweight to the planters but could only serve as their auxiliaries.[11]

The proponents of the "planter capitalism" thesis describe the planters and their society as bourgeois. Although this description is confusing and can serve no useful purpose, let us grant it for the moment. We are then confronted with a bourgeois society that impedes the development of every normal feature of capitalism; but when we realize that the planters were not bourgeois and that their society represented the antithesis of capitalism, these difficulties disappear. The fact of slaveownership is central to our problem. The seemingly formal question of whether the owners of the means of production command labor or purchase the labor power of free workers contains in itself the entire content of Southern life. All the essential features of Southern particularity and of Southern backwardness can be traced to the relationship of master to slave.

THE BARRIERS TO INDUSTRIALIZATION

If the planters were losing their economic and political cold war with the Northern bourgeoisie, the failure of the South to develop sufficient industry was the most striking immediate cause. Its inability to develop adequate manufactures is usually attributed to the inefficiency of the labor force. No doubt, slaves did not easily adjust to industrial employment, and the indirect effects of the slave system impeded the employment of whites. Slaves were used effectively in hemp, tobacco, iron, and cotton factories but only under socially dangerous conditions. They were given a wide variety of privileges and elevated to an elite status. Planters generally appreciated the potentially subversive quality of these arrangements and were hostile to their extension.

There were other, and perhaps more important, impediments to industrialization. Slavery concentrated economic and political power in the hands of a slaveholding class hostile to industrialism. The planters feared a strong urban bourgeoisie, which might make common cause with its Northern counterpart. They feared a white urban working class of unpredictable social tendencies. In general, they distrusted the city and saw in it something incongruous with their local power and status arrangements. The planters were unwilling to assume a heavy tax burden to assist manufacturers, and as the South fell further and further behind the North in industrial development, increasing state aid was required to help industry offset the Northerners' advantages of scale, efficiency, credit relations, and business reputation.

Slavery led to the rapid concentration of land and wealth and prevented the expansion of a Southern home market. Instead of providing a basis for industrial growth, the Southern countryside, economically dominated by a few large estates, provided only a limited market for industry. Data on the cotton textile factories almost always reveal that Southern producers aimed at supplying slaves with the cheapest and coarsest kind of cotton goods. Even so, local industry had to compete with Northern firms, which sometimes shipped direct and sometimes established Southern branches.

William Gregg, the South's foremost industrialist, was aware of the modest proportions of the Southern market and warned manufacturers against trying to produce exclusively for their local areas. His own company at Graniteville, South Carolina, produced fine cotton goods that sold much better in the North than in the South. Gregg was an unusually able man, and his success in selling to the North was a personal triumph. When he had to evaluate the general situation confronting Southern manufacturers, he asserted that he was willing to stake his reputation on their ability to compete with Northerners in the production of *"coarse cotton fabrics."* [13]

Some Southern businessmen, especially those in the border states, did good business in the North. Louisville tobacco and hemp manufacturers sold much of their output in Ohio. Some producers of iron and agricultural implements sold in nearby Northern cities. This kind of business was precarious. As Northern competitors arose and the market shrank, Southern producers had to rely on the narrow and undependable Southern market. [14] Well before 1840 iron manufacturing establishments in the Northwest provided local farmers with excellent markets for grain, vegetables, molasses, and work animals. During the ante-bellum period, and after, the grain growers of America found their market at home. America's rapid industrial development offered farmers a magnificently expanding urban market, and not until much later did they come to depend to any important extent on exports.

To a small degree the South benefited in this way. By 1840 the tobacco manufacturing industry began to absorb more tobacco than was being exported, and the South's few industrial centers provided markets for local grain and vegetable growers. Since the South could not undertake a general industrialization, few urban centers arose to provide substantial markets for farmers and planters. Apart from Baltimore and New Orleans, the slave states had no large cities, and few reached the size of 15,000. Southern grain growers, except for those close to the cities of the free states, had to be content with the market offered by planters who preferred to specialize in cotton or sugar and buy foodstuffs. This market was limited by the restricted rations of the slaves and was further narrowed by limited transportation. It did not pay the planters to appropriate state funds to build a transportation system into the back country, and any measure to increase the economic strength of the back-country farmers was politically dangerous to the aristocracy of the Black Belt. The farmers of the back country remained isolated, self-sufficient, and politically, economically, and socially backward. Those grain-growing farmers who could compete with producers in the Upper South and Northwest for the plantation market were in the Black belt itself. Since the planters did not have to buy from these local producers, the economic relationship greatly strengthened the political hand of the planters.

THE GENERAL FEATURES OF SOUTHERN AGRICULTURE

The South's greatest economic weakness was the low productivity of its labor force. [15] The slaves worked indifferently. They could be made to work reasonably well under close supervision in the cotton fields, but the cost of supervising them in more than one or two operations at a time was prohibitive. Without significant technological progress productivity could not be raised substantially, and slavery prevented such progress. Of greatest relevance, the impediments to technological progress damaged Southern agriculture, for improved implements and machines were largely responsible for the dramatic increases in crop yields per acre in Northern states during the nineteenth century.

Although slavery and the plantation system led to agricultural methods that depleted the soil, the frontier methods of the free states yielded similar results; but slavery forced the South into continued dependence upon exploitative methods after the frontier had been pushed further west and prevented reclamation of wornout lands. The plantations were much too large to be fertilized easily. Lack of markets and poor care of animals by slaves made it impossible to accumulate sufficient manure. The low level of capital accumulation made the purchase of adequate quantities of commercial fertilizer unthinkable. Proper crop rotation could not be practiced, for the pressure of the credit system kept most available land in cotton, and the labor force could not easily be assigned to the required tasks without prohibitive costs of supervision. The general inefficiency of labor thwarted most attempts at improvement of agricultural methods.[16]

The South, unable to feed itself, was caught in a series of dilemmas in its attempts to increase production of nonstaple crops and to improve its livestock. An inefficient labor force and the backward business practices of its ruling planter aristocracy were among the greatest difficulties. When planters did succeed in raising their own food, they also succeeded in depriving local livestock raisers and grain growers of whatever market they had. The stock raisers of the back country could not market their produce in the North because of the high costs of transportation.

The planters had little capital with which to buy improved breeds and could not guarantee the care necessary to make such investments worthwhile. Stock raisers too lacked the capital, and if they could get it, the investments would have been foolhardy without adequate urban markets.

Thoughtful Southerners, deeply distressed by the condition of their agriculture, made a determined effort to remedy it. In Maryland and Virginia significant progress was made in crop diversification and livestock improvement, but this progress was contingent on the sale of surplus slaves to the Black Belt. These sales provided an income that offset agricultural losses and made possible investments in fertilizers, equipment, and livestock. The concomitant reduction in the size of the slave force facilitated the problem of supervision and increased labor productivity and versatility. Even, so, the income from slave sales remained an important part of the gross income of the planters of the Upper South. In other words, the reform was incomplete and could not free agriculture from the destructive effects of the continued reliance on slave labor.

The reform process had several contradictions, the most important of which was the dependence on slave sales. Surplus slaves could be sold only while gang-labor methods continued to be used in other areas. By the 1850's the deficiencies of slavery that had forced innovations in the Upper South were felt in the Lower South. Increasingly, planters in the Lower South were exploring the possibilities of reform. If the deterioration of agriculture in the Cotton Belt had proceeded much further, the planters would have had to stop buying the slaves of Maryland and Virginia. They would have had to look for markets for their own surplus slaves. Without the acquisition of fresh cotton lands there could be no general reform of Southern agriculture. The entire Southern economy was moving steadily into an insoluble crisis.

THE IDEOLOGY OF THE MASTER CLASS

The planters commanded Southern politics and set the tone of social life. Theirs was an aristocratic, antibourgeois spirit with values and mores that emphasized family and status, had its code of honor, aspired to luxury, leisure and accomplishment. In the planters' community paternalism was the standard of human relationships, and politics and statecraft were the duties and responsibilities of gentlemen. The gentleman was expected to live for politics and not, like the bourgeois politician, off politics.

The planter typically recoiled at the notions that profit is the goal of life; that the approach to production and exchange should be internally rational and uncomplicated by social values; that thrift and hard work are the great virtues; and that the test of the wholesomeness of a community is the vigor with which its citizens expand the economy.

The planter was certainly no less acquisitive than the bourgeois, but an acquisitive spirit is compatible with values antithetical to capitalism. The aristocratic spirit of the planters absorbed acquisitiveness and directed it into channels that were socially desirable to a slave society: the accumulation of land and slaves and the achievement of military and political honors. Whereas in the North people were impelled by the lure of business and money for their own sake, in the South specific forms of property carried with them the badges of honor, prestige, and power. Even the rough parvenu planters of the Southwestern frontier—the "southern Yankees"—strove to accumulate wealth in the modes acceptable to plantation society. Only in their crudeness and naked avarice did they differ from the Virginia gentlemen. That is, they were a generation removed from the refinement that follows successful primitive accumulation.

The basis of the planter's position and power was his slaveownership. It measured his affluence, marked his status, and supplied leisure for social graces and aristocratic duties. The older New England bourgeoisie, in its own way, struck an aristocratic pose, but its wealth was rooted in commercial and industrial enterprises that were being pushed into the background by the newer heavy industries arising in the West, where bourgeois upstarts took advantage of the newer, more lucrative ventures like the iron industry. In the South few such opportunities were opening. The parvenu differed from the established planter only in being cruder and perhaps sharper in his business dealings. The road to power was via the plantation. The older aristocracy kept its leadership or made room for men in the same enterprises.

Many travelers commented on the difference in material conditions from one side of the Ohio River to the other, but the difference in sentiment was seen most clearly by de Tocqueville. Writing before the slavery issue had inflamed the nation, he remarked that slavery was attacking the Union "indirectly in its manners." The Ohioan "was tormented by the desire of wealth," and would turn to any kind of enterprise or endeavor to make a fortune. The Kentuckian coveted wealth "much less than pleasure or excitement," and money had "lost a portion of its value in his eyes." [17]

Achille Murat joined de Tocqueville in admiration for Southern ways. Compared with Northerners, Southerners were found to be more impulsive, frank, clever, charming, generous, and liberal.[18] The planters paid a price for these advantages. As one Southerner put it, the North led the South in almost everything because the Yankees had quiet perseverance over the long haul, whereas the Southerners had talent and brilliance but no taste for sustained labor. Southern projects came with a flash and died just as suddenly.[19] Despite such criticisms from within the ranks, the leaders of the Old South clung to their ideals, their faults, and their conviction of superiority. Farmers, said Edmund Ruffin, could not expect to achieve a cultural level above that of the "boors who reap rich harvests from the fat soil of Belgium." In the Northern states, he added with some justification, a farmer could rarely achieve the ease, culture, intellect, and refinement that slavery made possible.[20] The prevailing attitude of the aristocratic South toward itself and its Northern rival was ably summed up by William Henry Holcombe of Natchez: "The Northerner loves to make money, the Southerner to spend it." [21]

At their best Southern ideals constituted a rejection of the crass, vulgar, inhumane elements of capitalist society. The planter simply could not accept the idea that the cash nexus was a permissible basis for human relations. Even the vulgar parvenu of the Southwest embraced the plantation myth and refused to make a virtue of necessity by glorifying the competitive side of slavery as civilization's highest achievement. The planters did identify their own ideals with the essence of civilization, and given their sense of honor, were prepared to defend them at any cost.

This civilization and its ideals were profoundly antinational in a double sense. The plantation was virtually the only market for the small nonstaple-producing farmers and was the center of necessary services for the small cotton growers; thus, the paternalism of the planters toward their slaves was reinforced by a semi-paternal relationship between the planters and their neighbors. The planters were, in truth, the closest thing to feudal lords imaginable in a nineteenth-century bourgeois republic. The planters' protestations of love for the Union were not so much a desire to use the Union to protect slave property as a strong commitment to localism as the highest form of liberty. They genuinely loved the Union so long as it alone among the great states of the world recognized that localism had a wide variety of rights. The Southerners' source of pride was not the Union as such, nor the nonexistent Southern nation; it was the plantation, which they raised to a political principle.[22]

THE GENERAL CRISIS OF THE SLAVE SOUTH

The South's slave civilization could not forever coexist with an increasingly hostile, powerful, and aggressive Northern capitalism. On the one hand, the special economic conditions arising from the dependence on slave labor bound the South, in the colonial manner, to the world capitalist market. The concentration of landholding and slaveholding prevented the rise of a prosperous yeomanry and of urban centers. The inability to build urban centers, in turn, restricted the market for agricultural produce, weakened the rural producers, and dimmed hopes for agricultural diversification. On the other hand, the same concentration of wealth, the isolated, rural nature of the plantation system, the special social psychology engendered the slaveownership, and the political opportunity presented by the separation from England, converged to give the South considerable political and social independence. This independence was primarily the contribution of the slaveholding class, and especially of the planters. Slavery, while it bound the South economically, granted it the privilege of developing an aristocratic tradition, a disciplined and cohesive ruling class, and a mythology of its own.

Aristocratic tradition and ideology intensified the South's attachment to economic backwardness. Paternalism and the habit of command made the slaveholders tough stock determined to defend their Southern heritage. The more economically debilitating their way of life, the more they clung to it. It was this side of things—the political hegemony and aristocratic ideology of the ruling class—rather than economic factors that prevented the South from relinquishing slavery voluntarily.

As the free states stepped up their industrialization and as the westward movement assumed its remarkable momentum, the South's economic and political allies in the North were steadily isolated. Years of abolitionist and free soil agitation bore fruit as the South's opposition to homestead legislation, tariffs and the like clashed more and more dangerously with Northern needs. To protect their institutions and to try to lessen their economic bondage the slaveholders slid into violent collision with Northern interests and sentiments. The economic deficiencies of slavery threatened to undermine the planters' wealth and power. Such relief measures as cheap labor and more land for slave states (reopening the slave trade and territorial expansion) conflicted with Northern material needs, aspirations, and morality.[23] The planters faced a steady deterioration of their political and social power. Even if the relative prosperity of the 1850's had continued indefinitely, the slave states would have been at the mercy of the free, for the South could not compete with the capitalist North in population growth, capital accumulation, and economic development. Any economic slump threatened to bring with it an internal political disaster, for the planters could not rely on their middle and lower classes to remain permanently loyal.[24]

When we understand that the slave South was neither a strange form of capitalism nor an indefinable agrarianism but a special civilization built on the relationship of master to slave, the root of its conflict with the North is exposed. The internal contradictions in the South and the external conflict with the North placed the slaveholders hopelessly on the defensive with little to look forward to except slow strangulation. The only hope was a bold stroke to complete their political independence and to use it to provide an expansionist solution for their economic and social problems. The ideology and social psychology of the proud planter class made surrender or resignation to gradual defeat unthinkable, for its entire civilization was at stake.

NOTES

1. For a succinct statement of the first view see Frank L. Owsley, "The Irrepressible Conflict." In Twelve Southerners, *I'll Take My Stand* (New York, 1930), p. 74. One of the clearest statements of the second position is that of Thomas P. Govan, "Was the Old South Different?" *Journal of Southern History*, XXI (Nov., 1955), p. 448.

2. *History of Agriculture in the Southern United States to 1860* (2 Vols.; Gloucester, 1958), I, p. 302.

3. *The Theory of Social and Economic Organization* (New York, 1947), pp. 276 ff. The term "rational" is used in its strictly economic sense to indicate that production is proceeding in accordance with the most advanced methods to maximize profits.

4. This simple observation has come under curious attack. Kenneth M. Stampp, for example, insists that the cost of purchasing a slave forms the equivalent of the free worker's wage bill. The *Peculiar Institution* (New York, 1956), pp. 403 ff. That equivalent, however, is to be found only in the cost of maintaining the slave through the year. The initial outlay is the equivalent of part of the capitalist's investment in fixed capital and constitutes what U. B. Phillips called the "over-capitalization" of labor under slavery. Surely, the cost of maintaining a slave is only a small part of the free worker's wage bill; but the difference in their productivity is probably much greater than the difference in their cost

5. This colonial dependence on the British and Northern markets was not ended when slavery ended. Share-cropping and tenantry produced similar results. Moreover, slavery at least offered the South a measure of political independence under planter hegemony. Since abolition occurred under Northern guns and under the program of a victorious, predatory, outside bourgeoise, instead of under internal bourgeois auspices, the colonial bondage of the economy was preserved, but the South political independence was lost.

6. Govan, *op. cit.*, p. 448.

7. *Studies in the Development of Capitalism* (New York, 1947), pp. 17 f; cf., Gunnar Myrdal, *Rich Lands and Poor* (New York, 1957), pp. 52 ff.

8. Twenty years ago an attempt was made by Frank L. Owsley and his students to prove that the Southern yeomanry was prosperous and strong. See *Plain folk of the Old South* (Baton Rouge, 1949). This view was convincingly refuted by Fabian Linden, "Economic Democracy in the Slave South: An Appraisal of some Recent Views," *Journal of Negro History*, XXI (Jan., 1946), pp. 140-89. Cf., Eugene D. Genovese, "The Limits of Agrarian Reform in the

Slave South," unpublished doctoral dissertation, Columbia University, 1959, pp. 117-21.

9. Paul A. Baran, *The Political Economy of Growth* (New York, 1957), p. 194.

10. The best introduction to this period of Western banking is the unpublished doctoral dissertation of Carter H. Golembe, "State Banks and the Economic Development of the West, 1830–1844." Columbia University, 1952, esp. pp. 10, 82-91. Cf. also Bray Hammond, "Long and Short Term Credit in Earl American Banking," *Quarterly Journal of Economics*, XLIX (Nov., 1934), esp. p. 87.

11. The bankers of the free states were also closely allied with the dominant producers, but society and economy took on a bourgeois quality provided by the rising industrialists, the urban middle classes, and the farmers who were increasingly dependent on urban markets. The expansion of credit, which in the West financed mining, manufacturing, transport, agricultural diversification, and the numerous branches of a capitalist economy, in the South bolstered the economic position of the planters, prevented the rise of alternative industries, and guaranteed the extension and consolidation of the plantation system.

12. Slavery impeded white immigration by presenting Europeans with an aristocratic, caste-ridden society that scarcely disguised its contempt for the working classes. The economic opportunities in the North were, in most respects, far greater. When white labor was used in Southern factories, it was not always superior to urban slave labor. The incentives offered by the Northern economic and social system were largely missing; opportunities for acquiring skills were fewer; and in general, productivity was much lower than in the North.

13. William Gregg, *Essays on Domestic Industry* (first published 1845; Graniteville, S. C., 1941), p. 4. Original emphasis.

14. Consider the experience of locomotive, paper, and cotton manufacturers as reported in: Carrol H. Quenzel, "The Manufacture of Locomotives and Cars in Alexandria in the 1850's," *Virginia Magazine of History and Biography*, LXII (April, 1954), pp. 182 ff.; Ernest M. Lander, Jr., "Paper Manufacturing in South Carolina Before the Civil War," *North Carolina Historical Review*, XXIX (April, 1952), pp. 225 ff.; Adelaide L. Fries, "One Hundred Years of Textiles in Salem," *North Carolina Historical Review*, XXVII (Jan., 1950), p. 13.

15. Contemporary evidence points overwhelmingly to the conclusion that the productivity of slave labor was low. For a discussion of the relevant problems see my "Limits of Agrarian Reform in the Slave South," *loc. cit.*, chapters I and II. Extract measurement of slave productivity is not possible, for the data necessary for the calculations are not available. Nevertheless, from time to time someone tries to measure it anyway. Algie Simons and Lewis C. Gray made unsuccessful attempts earlier in the century, and recently, two Harvard economists, Alfred H. Conrad and John R. Meyers, rediscovered their method (apparently without knowing it) and presented an elaborate and thoroughly useless paper: "The Economics of Slavery in the Ante-Bellum South," *Journal of Political Economy*, LXVI (April, 1958), pp. 95-130. This is not the place to subject their views to detailed criticism, but one or two observations may suffice. They measure productivity by dividing the cotton crop by the number of slaves within certain age limits. To begin with, I think they use the wrong

age and price data, but let that pass. There are two troubles right at the start. This method assumes that the proportion of the cotton crop raised by white farmers in 1830, 1840, 1850, etc., was constant. There is not a shred of evidence for this; it is doubtful, and it cannot be verified. Secondly, it is well known that when cotton prices fell, some slaves were diverted to nonstaple production. Thus, the assumption that in any two years the same proportion of slave force worked in the cotton fields is simply wrong. In addition, the authors use a great many statistical tricks, such as "rounding off" figures. In one key instance rounding off makes a 4 per cent increase look like a 20 per cent increase. But these matters must be pursued elsewhere and at another time.

16. For a more detailed treatment of the problem of soil exhaustion see Eugene D. Genovese, "Cotton, Slavery and Soil Exhaustion in the Old South," *Cotton History Review*, II (Jan., 1961), p. 3-17; for a more extensive treatment of the attempts of the South to improve its agriculture in general see my "Limits of Agrarian Reform in the Slave South," *loc. cit.*

17. *Democracy in America* (2 Vols.; New York, 1948), I, p. 395.

18. *America and the Americans* (Buffalo, 1851), pp. 19, 75.

19. J. W. D. in the *Southern Eclectic*, II (Sept., 1853), pp. 63-66.

20. *Address to the Virginia State Agricultural Society* (Richmond, 1853), p. 9.

21. Diary dated Aug. 25, 1855 but apparently written later. MS in the University of North Carolina Southern Historical Collection, Chapel Hill.

22. No genuine Southern nationalism was possible, for the bonds of commodity production did not link every part of the region with every other part. Each state's transportation system was designed to connect the Cotton Belt with the export centers. The back country was largely closed, and the typically capitalist road-railroad network was missing even in the Cotton Belt.

23. These measures were opposed by powerful sections of the planter class itself for reasons that cannot be discussed here. The independence of the South would only have brought the latent intra-class antagonisms to the surface.

24. The loyalty of these classes was real enough but unstable. For our present purposes let us merely note that Lincoln's election and federal patronage would—if Southern fears were justified—have led to the formation of an anti-planter party in the South.

• Robert Starobin examines the patterns of race relations among Negro and white industrial workers in the Old South. He finds a surprising amount of relaxed and amicable contact between the races, and he discusses the factors which encouraged this accommodation in industries using mixed labor forces.

Race Relations in Old South Industries

ROBERT STAROBIN

Of people, we've of every hue.
Some white, red, yaller, *black and blue*:
Others with dirt, so covered well,
What color they, I could not tell.

Poet "Billy" describing Auraria, Georgia, gold miners in its *Western Herald*, April 9, 1833, quoted in E. M. Coulter, *Auraria* (Atkens, 1956).

Though the economy of the ante-bellum South was predominantly agricultural, it is also true that industrialization was beginning. As early as the 1790's, the processing of agricultural staples, the extraction of ores, turpentine, and timber, and the manufacture of tobacco, hemp, iron, and textiles were important Southern industries. By 1861, transportation facilities, such as turnpikes, canals, steamboats, and railroads, had already been built; and the slave states accounted for more thn 15 per cent of the capital invested in the nation's industry.[1]

Slavery was crucial to the industrialization of the South, since most industrial enterprises employed slave labor almost exclusively. In the 1850's, for example, about 200,000 bondsmen—or about 5 per cent of the total slave population—worked in industry. Most industrial slaves were young boys and prime males, but many were women and chil-

From Robert Starobin, "Race Relations in Old South Industries." Unpublished manuscript. Reprinted by permission of the author.

dren. About four-fifths of all industrial slaves were owned by industrial enterpreneurs; the rest were hired by the month or year.[2] Only about 20 per cent of the 70,000 urban slaves living in the Old South's leading cities were employed in industries. The typical industrial slave therefore lived in a rural, plantation, or small-town setting, where most industry was located, not in a large city.[3] By the Civil War, the trend toward industrializing the South on the basis of slave labor was long underway.

Though most Old South industrial enterprises employed slave labor exclusively, a few of them successfully employed both whites and slaves at the same factory, mine, or transportation project. In short, some enterprises were "integrated." At such establishments, to a striking extent, whites often worked along side of, or in close physical proximity to, slaves who were working at similar tasks.

To be sure, even at integrated industrial enterprises, slaves were sometimes assigned to all-black work gangs, segregated into non-white areas of factories, or supervised by white overseers and artisans. Discrimination against slaves and unequal working conditions were common. Prejudice and the proslavery argument helped to make some white workers personally antagonistic toward bondsmen. Competition for jobs created racial hostility between native white craftsmen, immigrant laborers, and Negro slaves. Nevertheless, historians have exaggerated the extent of these antagonisms, for many white and black workers labored together harmoniously.[4]

Moreover, the very nature of slavery necessitated some interracial association if white men were to oversee the lives of bondsmen closely for the maintenance of social order. Slavery thus created its own peculiar patterns of personal toleration and physical intimacy between the races.

Integrated work forces were especially common in Southern extractive industries such as lumbering, salt boiling, and mining.[5] Integration at mines resulted partly from the employment of skilled British miners, but mainly because common laborers of both races frequently dug side by side. "A most motley appearance of whites, Indians, half-breeds and negroes, boys of fourteen and old men of seventy—and indeed their occupations appeared to be as various as their complexions, comprising diggers [and] sawyers," observed a visitor to Georgia's Chestatee gold mines in 1830. The most interesting integrated coal mine, however, was Virginia's Midlothian Company, which employed (and publicly advertised for) slaves, free Negroes, and "many white laborers." A visitor observing the Midlothian's two hundred miners, "made up of Americans, English, Scotch, free blacks, and slaves," concluded that, "though politically and naturally there is a difference in these operatives, yet every tub here stands on its own bottom." [6]

Upper South transportation enterprises commonly utilized integrated work forces. Several black and several white chainmen and axemen surveyed a North Carolina railroad, while more than a dozen slaves, twenty free Negroes, and thirty whites together quarried rock for a nearby line. White and slave firemen and engineers together operated trains on several Virginia railroads, whose repair shops were also staffed by slave artisans working side by side with white mechanics.[7] Slave boatmen, quarriers, and carpenters labored together with white workmen on the James River Canal; both races jointly repaired Kentucky's public waterways, as well as at least one of its turnpikes. "A motley crew [of] Negro, Indian & white men" manned an Arkansas steamboat, according to one traveler; five whites and three Negroes together piloted a Baltimore harborboat.[8]

Deep South transportation enterprises sometimes employed integrated work forces. In South Carolina, for instance, sixteen slaves and five whites together quarried at the Blue Ridge Railroad's "18 Mile Creek Work," while twenty-five slaves and fourteen white's constructed a nearby line. The Greenville and Columbia Railroad's slave firemen assisted its white engineers, while brakemen—free and slave—together operated Mississippi Central equipment.[9] Negro deckhands complemented Irish firemen on one Mississippi steamer; however, a Mobile steamer employed Irish deckhands and Negro firemen. Four whites and seven slaves together manned a Savannah dredgeboat; six Louisiana pilotboats had sixteen slaves working with thirty-five whites.[10]

Some tobacco factories, hemp factories, and brick works, as well as woodworking enterprises, used integrated work forces, even though such industries usually employed slave labor almost exclusively.[11] According to one visitor, "a due admixture of whites and blacks assemble[d] together" to process tobacco in one room of a Louisville tobacco factory; "niggers and whites re-pick[ed] the fibres out more carefully" in another compartment; while "swarthy descendants of Ham" turned the screw press in still another room. Slave hirelings and whites, including several "Dutchmen," together worked a Louisville hemp factory; nine other Germans and six hired slaves jointly manufactured bricks in Texas. For twenty years, a dozen whites and slaves together built ships at a Gulf Coast yard; native whites, slaves, and "imported tutors" fabricated furniture in South Carolina.[12]

Slaves and whites were sometimes integrated at Southern iron works. Twenty free Pennsylvanians assisted forty local bondsmen at a Kentucky furnace; sixty-eight whites and fifty slaves worked a Virginia forge; and, in 1861, eighteen blacks and about fifteen whites chopped wood at a nearby furnace.[13] Slaves comprised almost half the work force at the famous Tredegar Iron Works in Richmond, but the greatest extent of integration occurred at Tennessee's Cumberland River iron works, where in the 1850's almost four thousand whites and slaves together operated nineteen furnaces, nine forges, and two rolling mills.[14]

About a dozen Southern textile mills successfully used integrated work forces. Some textile factories totally integrated the two races; others worked whites and blacks either in separate rooms or at different tasks. Half of a Tennessee textile factory's 120 hands were free and half were slaves; a North Carolina mill employed both white girls and slave girls. At a Georgia factory twenty-five whites worked with an equal number of slaves; at a South Carolina mill many slaves worked with five poor white apprentices.[15] A Kentucky woolen mill complemented one hundred whites with a score of slaves. In Camden, South Carolina, two-thirds of the famous DeKalb cotton mill's ninety-three hands were whites and one-third slaves. The same state's Vaucluse company combined thirty whites with twenty bondsmen, who reportedly were "equally apt and skilful in every department, except the weaving." An Alabama cotton mill added one slave family to its all-white labor force; by 1858, it was reported that "negro labor is much employed by them." [16]

Integrated textile factories so fascinated the British traveler James Silk Buckingham that he visited a Richmond, Virginia, factory, where one hundred whites and 150 slaves together were busily weaving and spinning. Buckingham also saw whites and blacks working "indiscriminately together" at another textile factory near Charlottesville, while near Athens, Georgia, he observed three cotton factories:

> In each of them there are employed from 80 to 100 persons, and about an equal number of white and black. In one of them, the blacks are the property of the mill-owners, but in the other two they are the slaves of planters, hired out at monthly wages to work in the factory. There is no difficulty among them on account of colour, the white girls working in the same room and at the same loom with the black girls; and boys of each colour,

as well as men and women, working together without apparent repugnance or objection. This is only one among the many proofs I had witnessed of the fact, that the prejudice of colour is not nearly so strong in the South as in the North. . . .[17]

Integration was, of course, far from complete in ante-bellum Southern industries; racial antagonisms attested to that. Segregation of Negroes, for example, was common, but it resulted less from public legislation than from ingrained personal prejudices, the desire to avoid hostilities, or slaveowners' fears that whites would corrupt, harm, or agitate their Negroes.[18] Wagoners—black and white—often slept overnight at the same taverns on the National Road, for example, even though, according to one historian, "a separate table was invariably provided for the colored wagoners, a custom in thorough accord with the public sentiment of the time, and seemingly agreeable to the colored wagoners themselves." "So far as convenient they [the Negroes] were kept at work separately from the white hands; and they were also messed separately," observed a passenger on an Alabama steamer which hired slave and Irish crewmen at the same wage-rates. According to the foreman of a Louisville hemp factory that employed sixteen slaves and ten whites, "there were six two-story dwellings in a row for the slaves, [and] a large frame building, two-stories put up as a boarding house for the white people." A Georgia railroad publicly assured owners of slave hirelings that they would be "worked separately and at a distance from any white laborers who will be employed in the same line of work." [19]

Such segregation was partly an expression of underlying racial hostility which sometimes dramatically surfaced. At the Tredegar Iron Works, in 1847, skilled white "puddlers" refused to train slave apprentices. Similarly, the hiring of a few Negroes by the New Castle and Frenchtown Turnpike-Railroad (virtually all of whose workmen were whites from Delaware, Maryland, and Pennsylvania), created such "apprehensions" of racial conflict that the blacks were discharged. During the depression of 1837-43, the apprenticing of slave Frederick Douglass to learn caulking at a Baltimore shipyard, where white and Negro craftsmen previously had worked together without any serious friction, precipitated a near-fatal attack on Douglass by four Irish artisans.[20] In the 1830's, the Gosport Navy Yard's integration of about one hundred slave common laborers with 130 white day laborers so incensed some white stonecutters that they petitioned the Navy Department, the President, and the Congress of the United States to exclude slave hirelings from federal projects. Despite such protests, however, the yard's chief engineer continued to employ an integrated work force, convinced that blacks worked as well as whites and were physically better suited to the tasks.[21]

Racial hostilities occurred, but they were much less significant than the striking extent of interracial harmony among workers at almost all integrated industries. Since whites were openly antagonistic to blacks only occasionally at integrated work places, the surprising fact is the depth of racial tolerance, considering the racist foundations upon which slavery rested.[22] For instance, hardly any violence was reported where Irish dockworkers, deckhands, and diggers worked side by side with slaves. Racial antagonisms subsided once such enterprises as the Tredegar Iron Works had been successfully integrated. Textile millers —black and white—labored together "without apparent repugnance or objection," reported Buckingham. A Georgia poet penned the following verse, suggesting the absence of racial conflict at integrated Southern gold mines:

> Wend you to the Cherokee? . . .
> Where . . . "chuck-luck" boxes loud are rattling;
> Where gin by the barrel full is drank,—
> And whites and blacks are all the same;
> Where no respect is paid to rank,
> But every one's of equal fame.[23]

Moreover, newspapers,[24] travelers,[25] and Southern businessmen[26] almost never reported racial hostilities.

A study of those racial antagonisms which did emerge suggests that they fall into several patterns. First, conflict between white workers and slaves was greatest when the Southern economy was most stagnant. Irish artisans attacked Frederick Douglass during the depression of the late 1830's, for example. Second, most racial friction seemed to occur in Maryland, Virginia, and Delaware, even though integrated work places were common in other Southern regions, including the Deep South. Third, most racial hostilities occurred when integration was first attempted—on the New Castle and Frenchtown line or at the Tredegar Iron Works, for instance. However, racial conflict failed to materialize at all when both races were working together under normal circumstances—as at Buckingham's textile mills and the Midlothian and Cherokee mines.

Racial antagonism at integrated work places was in part diminished because, during most of the ante-bellum period, Southern economic prosperity reduced competition for jobs between whites and slaves by creating work opportunities for both races. Racial tensions diminished further because slaves were after all a distinct caste, so firmly fixed in bondage that whites hardly felt threatened. Moreover, the proslavery argument convinced most nonslaveowners that economic advancement came through slaveownership, not through the abolition of slavery. So effective were the proslavery arguments that virulent racist ideologies, upon which those opposing integrated work forces could draw, were unneeded. Racism was, to be sure, common, but it hardened only after emancipation raised the specter of freedmen openly competing with whites. Neither legal proscription nor virulent racism was necessary, according to one authority,[27] so long as the status of Negroes was fixed by enslavement.

More important, since slaveowners so dominated the political economy of most Southern regions, they had the power to integrate work forces if they chose. Those opposing integration were powerless, and their objections went unheeded. In addition, since total segregation would have seriously obstructed the functioning of slavery, some physical association between whites and blacks was inevitable.[28]

Racial hostilities were more severe at integrated industrial establishments in the border slave states than in the Deep South, because slaveowners were often less powerful there. Moreover, the border states and New Orleans received large influxes of desperately poor European immigrants, who vigorously competed for jobs with Negroes and who sometimes precipitated racial violence. In any event, integration and racial harmony in ante-bellum Southern industries were more pronounced than might have been expected in a slave society.

It has long been understood that slavery was a means of "race adjustment" at the same time that it was always primarily a labor system. It is therefore not surprising that such post-bellum institutions as segregation partly originated in Old South industries and cities. However, the striking thing was the extent of racial harmony at integrated work places. Racial antagonisms certainly existed, but slave-employing industrialists and planters and sufficient economic and political power to use slave labor however they wished.

NOTES

1. See my manuscript, "Industrial Slavery in the Old South, 1790–1861," chap. 1. I would like to thank Professor Kenneth M. Stampp of the University of California, Berkeley, for his critical reading of this manuscript.

2. *Ibid.* chap. 1 and *passim*.

3. *Ibid.*; R. Wade, *Slavery in the Cities* (New York, 1964), chap. 1 and appendices.

4. C. V. Woodward, *The Strange Career of Jim Crow* (New York, 1955, 1967), 7, 11-13; J. Williamson, *After Slavery* (Chapel Hill, 1965), chap. 10; Wade, *Slavery in the Cities*, 266-78; L. Litwack, *North of Slavery* (Chicago, 1961); T. B. Wilson, *The Black Codes of the South* (University, Ala., 1965).

5. J. B. Smith Letterbooks and Papers (Duke Univ.); Silver Hill Mining Company Ledger, 1859–62 (Univ. of North Carolina, hereafter cited as UNC); F. Green, "Gold Mining in Ante-Bellum Virginia," *Virginia Magazine of History*, 45 (1937), 234, 363; Charleston *Courier*, July 18, 1845; *De Bow's Review*, 6 (1848), 295; Report of the Secretary of the Treasury, *House Exec. Doc.*, #6, 29 Cong., 1 sess., 1845, p. 660; M. Threlkel, "Mann's Lick," *Filson Club History Quarterly*, 1 (1927), 174; Letters and affidavits, 1815–22, Taliaferro Papers (Louisiana State Univ., hereafter cited as LSU); John Carter sawmill daybook, 1834–37 (Univ. of Georgia); D. Thomas and L. Beard sawmill book, 1838–39, vol. 7, Fisher Papers (UNC); Lumber Daybook of Plank Road Steam Mills, 1854–55, Jemison Papers (Univ. of Alabama); W. H. Fox to J. Fox, April 25, 1852, Fox Papers (Duke); sawmill account book, 1859–61, Affleck Papers (LSU).

6. P. Wager to A. Macomb, September 30, 1830, in J. W. Covington (ed.), "Letters from the Georgia Gold Regions," *Georgia Historical Quarterly*, 39 (1955), 407; *Harper's Monthly*, 15 (1857), 293; Gold Hill Mining Company Time Book, 1850–53 (UNC); Richmond *Whig*, January 2 and June 26, 1846; Richmond *Dispatch*, December 15 and 16, 1856.

7. Western North Carolina Railroad survey payroll, 1854, Treasurers Papers: Internal Improvements (North Carolina Archives); Raleigh and Gaston quarry time rolls, vols. 31 and 33, Hawkins Papers (UNC); reports of the Virginia Central, the Richmond and Petersburg, the Virginia and Tennessee, and the Richmond, Fredericksburg and Potomac railroads, Virginia *Board of Public Works Reports*, 1850–61.

8. Reports of the James River and Kanawha Canal, Virginia *Board of Public Works Reports*, 1820, 1854, and 1861; Report of Auditor of Public Accounts, pp. 20-43, Kentucky Legislature *Reports*, December 1849 session; Hardinsburg and Cloverport Turnpike Road Company Accounts, 1859-60 (Filson Club); B. L. C. Wailes Diary #16, Oct. 24, 1856 (Duke Univ.); New Orleans *Picayune*, November 27, 1845.

9. Statements and accounts, 1858 and July 13, 1860, and time and account books, vols. 42 and 43 (Hawkins Papers (UNC); statement, Aug. 11, 1855, Richardson Papers (Duke Univ.); Charleston *Mercury*, March 24, 1859; Jackson *Mississippian*, April 19, 1859.

10. F. L. Olmsted, *A Journey in the Seaboard Slave States* (New York, 1861), 607, 612; New Orleans *Picayune*, January 1, 1846; Report on Savannah River Improvement, *House Doc.*, #104, 21 Cong., 2 sess., 1831, p. 37; Report on Pilots' Association, Louisiana *Senate Journal*, 5 Legis., 1 sess., March, 1860, p. 91-2.

11. J. C. Robert, *Tobacco Kingdom* (Durham, 1938), tables; J. F. Hopkins, *A History of the Hemp Industry in Kentucky* (Lexington, 1951), *passim*.

12. H. A. Murray, *Lands of the Slave and the Free* (London, 1855), 168-9; Ford and Hawes Cash Book, 1844, Thruston Papers (Filson Club); H. T. Catterall (ed.), *Judicial Cases concerning American Slavery and the Negro*

(Washington, 1937), V, 290; Ebenezer Clark Ship Yard Account Books, 1838–41 and 1843–56 (Mississippi Archives); *De Bow's Review,* 14 (1853), 622-3.

13. J. Irwin to E. Irwin, May 20, 1839, Irwin Letters (Filson Club); G. M. Pennypacker to W. Weaver, November 4, 1831, W. W. Rex to D. Brady, September 6, 1860, and C. K. Gorgas to D. Brady, April 2, 1860, Weaver Papers (Duke Univ.); W. W. Rex to D. Brady, January 22, 1861, Weaver Papers (Univ. of Virginia).

14. C. Dew, Iron-Maker to the Confederacy, mss, chap. 2 and table 1; *Hunt's Magazine,* 28 (1853), 644-5, reported that 1045 whites and 1360 slaves worked the furnaces of Tennessee's Cumberland River iron region, while 260 whites and 410 slaves worked the forges, and 90 and 140 the rolling mills.

15. *Ibid.* 15 (1846), 598-9; R. W. Griffin and D. W. Standard, "The Textile Industry in Ante-Bellum North Carolina," *North Carolina Historical Review,* 34 (1957), 132-3; Jones, "Manufacturing in Richmond County, Georgia," *Georgia Historical Quarterly,* 78-9; D. Moore to T. Moore, November 5, 1817, Moore Papers (Duke Univ.).

16. Mill Ledger, 1856–70, pp. 86, 279, Wages Ledger, 1856–61, and letters dated June 2, 1861, March 13, 1862, and November 19, 1863, in Letterbook, 1859–64, Woolley Mill Papers (Univ. of Kentucky); *De Bow's Review,* 7 (1849), 372-3, 458; *Hunt's Magazine,* 22 (1850), 581-2; *Charleston Courier,* November 23, 1836; New Orleans *Picayune,* October 16, 1858; and *De Bow's Review,* 25 (1858), 717. Cf. Report of the Secretary of the Treasury, *House Exec. Doc.* #6, 29 Cong., 1 sess., 1845, p. 676; and B. Mitchell, *William Gregg* (Chapel Hill, 1928), 100.

17. J. S. Buckingham, *The Slave States of America* (London, 1842), II, 424, 411, and 112.

18. T. D. Jervey, *Robert Y. Hayne* (New York, 1909), 510-11, for example.

19. T. B. Searight, *The Old Pike* (Uuiontown, 1894), 109; Olmsted, *Seaboard Slave States,* 564; *Report of the Court of Claims,* #81, 34 Cong., 3 sess., 1857; R. B. Flanders, *Plantation Slavery in Georgia* (Chapel Hill, 1933), 198.

20. W. F. Holmes, "The New Castle and Frenchtown Turnpike and Railroad Company," *Delaware History,* 10 (1862–63), 172; Frederick Douglass, *Narrative* (Boston, 1845), 93-8. Douglass, a Negro slave hired to the shipyards by his owner to learn the caulker's trade, was apparently a victim of the competition for jobs between free Negro and white shipyard workers during the depression of 1837–43. When white workers struck to demand the discharge of the free Negroes, they did not object to Douglass's employment because he was a slave. According to Douglass, he was beaten up because he was a Negro. At the Tredegar Iron Works in Richmond, Virginia, in 1847, skilled white "puddlers" went out on strike when their employer, Joseph Reid Anderson, insisted that they train slaves as puddlers for a new rolling mill. Anderson dismissed the whites and employed slaves in their stead, insisting that he had the right to deploy his labor forces as he saw fit. This dramatic conversion from free labor to slave labor can be followed in the Richmond *Enquirer,* June 1, 11, and 15, 1847; Richmond *Whig,* May 28 and June 28, 1847. Cf. K. Bruce, *Virginia Iron Manufacture in the Slave Era* (New York, 1930), 224-37; C. Dew, "Iron-Maker to the Confederacy," mss, chap. 2.

21. "Memorandum of Work, February 1, 1831," and "Abstract from the Rolls of Labour on the Dry Dock in the Gosport Navy Yard," 1831–1832,

Baldwin Papers (Baker Library, Harvard Univ.); "Slaves on a Federal Project," Business Historical Society *Bulletin*, 8 (1934), 32-3.

22. For evidence of integration without antagonism at Old South ironworks, see: Cumberland Forge, Md., Daybook, 1802 (Library of Congress); Ridwell Furnace Book, and Shenandoah County, Va., Account Books vols. 3, 5, 6, 8 of "Pine Forge," 1804–1833 (UNC); payroll accounts with "Cesar a laborer," October 5, 1808, and March 25, 1809, Virginia Manufactory of Arms Papers, and letters of May 28, 1804, March 9, 1806, and January 29, 1808, and annual reports of December 25, 1804, and January 16, 1806, John Clarke Letterbook (Virginia State Library); Allatoona Iron Works Ledger, 1845 (Emory University); Report of the Secretary of the Treasury, *House Exec. Doc.*, #6, 29 Cong., 1 sess., (1845), 647-8; T. A. Moss account books, 1855–57, Fredericksburg, Va., Account Books (UNC); J. Bancroft, *Census of the City of Savannah* (Savannah, 1848), 36; Richmond *Dispatch*, January 14, 1858.

For mining: P. Ward to R. Leckie, October 25, 1818, Leckie Papers (Duke Univ.); J. G. Hamilton (ed.), *The Papers of William A. Graham* (Raleigh, 1957), I, 187; *Niles' Register*, 39 (1831), 334-5 and 40 (1831), 206; R. Smith Lead Mining Company Ledger, vol. 15, 1834–36 (Missouri Historical Society); *Mining Magazine*, 2 (1854), 304; F. Green, "Georgia's Forgotton Industry: Goldmining," *Georgia Historical Quarterly*, 19 (1935), 210-11.

For cotton mills: J. Stumpp and D. Ricketts Ledger, 1806–23 (New York Public Library); E. M. Coulter, "Scull Shoals," *Georgia Historical Quarterly*, 48 (1964), 41-3; Jones, "Manufacturing in Richmond County, Ga.," 81; I. Lippincott, *A History of Manufactures in the Ohio Valley* (New York, 1914), 169-70; W. Thomson, *A Tradesman's Travels* (Edinburgh, 1842), 112-15; Report of the Secretary of the Treasury, *House Exec. Doc.*, #6, 29 Cong., 1 sess., 1845, p. 649; Holt Diary, 1844–54 (UNC); *De Bow's Review*, 7 (1849), 458; R. S. Patterson to S. F. Patterson, January 7, 1855, Patterson Papers (Duke Univ.); vol. 38, Patterson Papers (UNC); Ivy Mills Ledger, 1858–63 (Georgia Archives); J. Webb Account Book, Vol. 8, 1852–63 (UNC).

For manufacturing and milling: Hopkins, *Hemp Industry*, 115; J. L. Mertens to W. W. Mertens, March 1, 1845, Mertens Papers (Duke Univ.); Olmsted, *Seaboard Slave States*, 346; Fogartie, Green & Co. Daybook, 1835 (Georgia Historical Society); J. H. Franklin, "Slaves Virtually Free in Ante-Bellum North Carolina," *Journal of Negro History*, 38 (1943), 299n.; account sheet, July 27, 1816, Kuntz Collection (Tulane Univ.); F. S. Klein, "Union Mills," *Maryland Historical Magazine*, 52 (1957), 293, 299; J. G. Taylor, *Negro Slavery in Louisiana* (Baton Rouge, 1963), 82.

For internal improvements projects: Expense Book of Saïd Plantation, November 12, 1806, McDonogh Papers (Tulane Univ.); G. R. Baldwin to J. F. Baldwin, February 5, 1837, vol. 25, Baldwin Papers (Baker Library, Harvard Univ.); *House Doc.* #201, 26 Cong., 1 sess., 1840, pp. 20ff; J. T. Hicks to S. S. Downey, March 25, 1838, Downey Papers (Duke Univ.); J. W. Livingood, "Chattanooga," *Tennessee Historical Quarterly*, 6 (1947), 245; W. H. Garland to wife, May 4, 1841, Garland Papers (UNC); reports of the Board of Internal Improvements, Kentucky *Legislative Reports*, 1841–42, pp. 265, 266; H. D. Dozier, *A History of the Atlantic Coast Line Railroad* (Boston, 1920), 45; *American Railroad Journal*, 21 (1848), 340-41, 361, and *American Railroad Journal*, 26 (1853), 622, 733; J. R. Kean, "The Development of the 'Valley Line' of the Baltimore and Ohio Railroad," *Virginia*

Magazine of History, 60 (1952), 541; V. McBee to V. A. McBee, November 9, 1851, McBee Papers (UNC); Charleston *Courier*, May 15, 1852; payrolls of surveys, October 29, 1853 and November 1, 1854, Treasurers Papers: Internal Improvements (North Carolina Archives); R. Bush to J. Buford, July 9, 1854, and T. W. Leftwich to J. Buford, December 4, 1854, Buford Papers (Duke Univ.); time rolls, vols. 31 and 38, Hawkins Papers (UNC); J. Stirling, *Letters from the Slave States* (London, 1857), 229; Report of the Little Rock and Napoleon Railroad, Arkansas *Journal of the Senate*, 11 sess., 1856–57, appendix, p. 129; Charleston *Mercury*, March 23, 1857; Treasurer's Report, table G, *Atlantic and North Carolina Railroad Report*, 1860; Western and Atlantic Railroad Payroll Books, 1852–64 (Georgia Archives); U. B. Phillips, *A History of Transportation in the Eastern Cotton Belt to 1860* (New York, 1908), 295; L. Armitage, "Louisa Railroad—1836–1850," Railroad and Locomotive Historical Society *Bulletin*, #65 (1944), 64; M. Chevalier, *Histoire et Description des Voies des Communications aux Etats-Unis* (Paris, 1841), II, 443; accounts, Cape Fear and Deep River Navigation Company Papers and London Papers (UNC and N.C. Archives).

23. Richmond *Whig*, June 26, 1846; Buckingham, *Slave States*, II, 112; a Milledgeville, Georgia, poet's verse in the Auraria, Ga., *Western Herald*, April 30, 1833, quoted in E. M. Coulter, *Auraria* (Athens, 1956), 58-9.

24. In 1858, the Petersburg *Express* reported that one tobacco manufacturer was employing forty white workers, whose department was kept very clean, "while all association with their 'odiferous' [black] co-laborers is entirely obviated."—quoted in E. A. Wyatt, "Rise of Industry in Ante-Bellum Petersburg," *William and Mary College Quarterly*, series 2, 17 (1937), 12-13. "A Southerner," writing to the Georgia *Citizen*, July 21, 1850, objected to the Atlanta *Intelligencer*'s advocacy of using slaves in cotton factories as follows: "*Negroes*, slaves, and White men, and *White Women*, cooperating in a cotton factory! What an association! Disgusting!"—quoted in Flanders, *Slavery in Georgia*, 205.

25. Olmsted, *Seaboard Slave States*, 48; F. L. Olmsted, *A Journey in the Back Country* (New York, 1907 edn.), II, 57; F. L. Olmsted, *A Journey Through Texas* (New York, 1857), 114-15; Taylor, *Slavery in Louisiana*, 83; R. B. Morris, "The Measure of Bondage in the Slave States," *Mississippi Valley Historical Review*, 41 (1954), 229; and F. Kemble, *Journal of a Residence* (New York, 1961 edn.), 104, 122-26, and 129, for protests by whites against slave competition or fear of racial hostility.

26. Negro Time Book, November 7 and 29, 1833, Graham Papers (Univ. of Virginia), for fight between "Capt. R." and "Bryce McC."; the objection by some Moravians to employing slaves, instead of whites, in textile mills, is recounted in A. L. Fries, "One Hundred Years of Textile in Salem," *North Carolina Historical Review*, 27 (1950), 13.

27. Woodward, *Strange Career of Jim Crow*, 13.

28. *Ibid.* 12.

• Arnold A. Sio's comparative analysis of the slave's legal status in Roman and American culture helps clarify the complex relationship existing between the bondsman's two definitions under law: as a person and as a chattel. Sio challenges the Tannenbaum-Elkins view that definitive differences existed between legal and social treatment of the slave in British America and Latin America. Compare this discussion with the support given to Tannenbaum and Elkins by Herbert Klein's examination of the economic status of the slave in Cuba and Virginia.

Interpretations of Slavery:
The Slave Status in the Americas

ARNOLD A. SIO

Recent interpretations of slavery in the United States suggest that we may be entering a new phase of scholarship on slavery as new approaches and categories are introduced by historians, and as anthropologists and sociologists again take up the study of an institution that was of such concern to their nineteenth century predecessors.

As an assessment of these interpretations, the concern of this essay is with those aspects of the legal status of the slave which appears as problematic or neglected. The purpose is to reformulate, refocus, and clarify rather than to introduce an alternative interpretation or to present new materials.[1]

Although the scholarship on slavery has tended to shift away from the strong moral bias as well as the categories of analysis carried over for so long from the pro-slavery and anti-slavery debates, those aspects of the slavery system traditionally at issue also constitute the problematic aspects in the more recent interpretations. These are the legal

From Arnold A. Sio, "Interpretations of Slavery," *Comparative Studies in Society and History*, VII (April 1965), 289-308. Reprinted by permission⌐. The Society for the Comparative Study of Society and History holds the copyright on this article.

status of the slave, the relations of masters and slaves, and the relation-ship between these two facets of the institution.[2]

I

The concept of slavery covers a considerable variety of social phenom-ena, but it is generally thought of as the practice of bringing strangers into a society for use in economic production and legally defining them in terms of the category of property. The complete subordination of the slave to the will of the master is regarded as a main defining feature of the institution.

> Subordination implies and is an aspect of authority. Authority is the socially recognized right to direct, control or manage some or all of the affairs of a person, or group, or thing. In this sense there is an overlap between property as a bundle of rights over things and the authority which is invested in some person over others as their slaves, with the result that such types of au-thority are treated as property at law.[3]

Slavery involves the "legal assimilation of interpersonal rights to the norm of property rights over things." [4]

This definition of the legal status of the slave has been taken in many studies as a basis for an interpretation solely in terms of the prop-erty component in the status.[5] Thus although the interpretations of slavery in the United States to be discussed in this essay involve both the historical and comparative methods and an emphasis on economic as well as ideological forces, they arrive at a similar conception of the legal status of the slave as property. This conception obscures signifi-cant differences between the property and racial components in the status, and circumvents critical evidence pertaining to the personal component in the status.[6]

In this essay an attempt is made to distinguish between the property and racial components in the status of the ante-bellum slave through a comparison with Roman slavery where the status involved a property but not a racial component. This is followed by a consideration of the evidence for a personal component in the definition of the slave status in the United States. The essay concludes with some re-examination of the status of the slave in Latin America in terms of the three components.

The interpretations of Frank Tannenbaum [7] and Stanley Elkins [8] exemplify the shift away from the moral approach to the institution of slavery and the introduction of new methods and categories. The treat-

ment in both is comparative. Why did slavery in the United States differ in form and consequences from the kind of servitude developed in
the Latin American colonies of Spain and Portugal? According to
Tannenbaum, there were at least three traditions or historical forces in
Latin America which prevented the definition of the slave there solely
as property; namely, the continuance of the Roman law of slavery as it
came down through the Justinian Code, the influence of the Catholic
Church, and the long familiarity of the Iberians with Moors and
Negroes.[9] Tannenbaum puts his emphasis on whether, "The law accepted the doctrine of the moral personality of the slave and made
possible the gradual achievement of freedom implicit in such a doctrine" and on a universalistic religion, i.e. Catholicism, in preventing
the definition of the slave solely as property.[10] In the United States
slavery developed in a legal and moral setting in which the doctrine
of the moral personality of the slave did not affect the definition of his
status in the society. "Legally he was a chattel under the law, and in
practice an animal to be bred for market." [11]

In comparing North American and Latin American slavery, Elkins
adds to Tannenbaum's earlier treatment. The legal status of the slave
in "the liberal, Protestant, secularized, capitalist culture of America"
is contrasted with that of the slave in "the conservative, paternalistic,
Catholic, quasi-medieval culture of Spain and Portugal and their New
World colonies." [12] Elkins concludes that in the absence of such restraining institutions in the United States the search for private gain
and profit was unlimited, and the law of slavery developed in such a
way as to eliminate the slightest hindrance to the authority of the
slaveholder over his slaves. The legal status of the slave developed exclusively in terms of property as the result of the demands of an
emerging capitalism. Slavery in the United States was "a system conceived and evolved exclusively on the grounds of property." [13]

For Elkins and Tannenbaum the definitive feature of the legal
status of the ante-bellum slave was the centrality of the property
component. The rights of personality were suppressed by the law, and
the legal subordination of the slave to the authority of the master in
the areas of parentage and kinship, property and other private rights,
and police and disciplinary power over the slave was developed to such
an extent as to make slavery in the United States a unique system.[14]
The entire institution became integrated around the definition of the
slave as property.

Kenneth Stampp's *The Peculiar Institution* [15] has been viewed as
one of the most important and provocative contributions since Ulrich

B. Phillips' *American Negro Slavery*.[16] Although it is organized essentially in terms of the categories used by Phillips and other earlier students of slavery, Stampp's study exceeds the earlier work in comprehensiveness, in presenting the response of the slave to the institution, and in its use of the available scientific evidence regarding race. In contrast to Elkins and Tannenbaum, Stampp takes up the social organization of slavery as well as its legal structure. His interpretation of the legal status of the slave is mainly in terms of economic values, and stresses the property component as do Elkins and Tannenbaum.[17] Unlike Elkins and Tannenbaum, however, he finds that the status also contained a personal element, which made for a certain degree of ambiguity in the status.[18]

In these interpretations, the initial status of the Negro is taken as having been neither that of a slave nor that of a member of a racial group against which discrimination was practised. The status of the Negro as a slave and his status as a member of a racial minority apparently developed concurrently, since there was no tradition of slavery or of racial discrimination in the colonies to inform the initial status of the Negro. The causal connection implied between slavery and racial discrimination is a widely held conception and needs to be reconsidered in the light of recent historical investigation and comparative evidence.

Much more difficult to grasp is the effect of racial discrimination on the definition of the slave status. Elkins refers to "the most implacable race-consciousness yet observed in virtually any society" as affecting the definition of the status, but the stress on economic values in his interpretation obscures any distinction that may have been intended between the property and racial components in the status.[19] Similarly, although Stampp refers to the fact "that chattel slavery, the caste system, and color prejudice" were a part of custom and law by the eighteenth century, no clear distinction is made between those features of the status which are to be attributed to the definition of the slave as property and those which are the consequence of racial discrimination.[20]

Tannenbaum is clearly concerned with the consequences of racial discrimination for the legal status of the Negro as slave and as freedman. He stresses the fact that slavery in the United States meant Negro slavery. In contrast to Latin America, slavery in the ante-bellum South involved "caste," "by law of nature," or "innate inferiority." [21] Slavery systems can be distinguished in terms of the ease and availability of manumission and the status of the freedman, as these indicate whether or not the law denied the moral personality of the slave.[22] In the United States the conception of the slave as a racial inferior led to severe restrictions on manumission and to a low status for free Negroes. At the same time, however, it is readily apparent from Tannenbaum's comparison with slavery in Latin America that in his view the conception of the ante-bellum Negro as innately inferior affected all the legal categories defining his status: the extent of the assimilation of his rights to property in law as well as manumission and the status of the freedman.[23] Racial discrimination accentuated the legal definition of the slave as property.

The slave as property is taken as the primary or exclusive component in these interpretations of the legal status of the slave in the United States. For Elkins and Stampp this is the consequence mainly of economic forces, while for Tannenbaum ideological forces are basic. The focus on the definition of the slave as property results in a tendency to fuse the property and racial components, and in a failure to consider the evidence bearing on the personal component in the legal status.

II

While the assimilation to property in law of the rights of slaves was common to slavery in classical antiquity and the United States, slavery in ancient society "was a type unfamiliar to Europeans and Americans of the last two centuries. It had no color line. (Therefore, *pace Aristotles*, it had no single and clearly defined race or slave caste.)" [24] Moreover, the law of slavery in ancient society did not deny the moral personality of the slave as, according to Roman law, the institution of slavery was of the *Ius Gentium* but at the same time contrary to the *Ius Naturale*, for all men were equal under natural law.[25] A comparison with slavery in Rome where slaves were defined as property in law but did not constitute a separate caste in the society, and where the legal suppression of the personality of the slave, as expressed in the attitude toward manumission and the status of the freedmen, did not occur, thus provides a method for distinguishing between the property and the racial components in the definition of the legal status. Since the categories of marriage and the family, property and other rights, and police and disciplinary powers over slaves are used by Elkins, Tannenbaum and Stampp in describing the status of the slave as property in the United States, these will guide the comparison with Rome.[26]

As to marriage and the family in the ante-bellum South, marriages between slaves had no legal standing. "The relation between slaves is

essentially different from that of man and wife, joined in lawful wed-
lock . . . with slaves it may be dissolved at the pleasure of either
party, or by the sale of one or both, depending on the caprice or necessity of the owners." [27] The denial of legal marriage meant, in conjunction with the rule that the child follow the condition of the mother,
that the offspring of slaves had no legal father, whether the father was
slave or free. The duration of the union between slaves depended on
the interests of the master or those of the slaves. The union was subject at any time to being dissolved by the sale of one or both of the
slaves. The children of these "contubernial relationships," as they were
termed, had no legal protection against separation from their parents.
In the law there was no such thing as fornication or adultery among
slaves. A slave could not be charged with adultery, and a male slave
had no legal recourse against another slave, free Negro, or white person for intercourse with his "wife." Nor could the slave present this
abuse as evidence in his defense in a criminal charge of assault and
battery, or murder.

Roman slaves were also legally incapable of marriage. Any union
between slaves or between slaves and free persons was differentiated as
contubernium as opposed to *conubium*. A marriage was terminated if
either party became enslaved. Infidelity between slaves could not be
adultery. Although a slave could be guilty of adultery with a married
free woman, it was not possible for an enslaved female to commit the
offense, or for it to be commited with her. The inheritance of slavery
followed the rule that the child follow the status of the mother, whatever the position of the father. A child born of a free father and a slave
mother was a slave and the property of the owner, while the child of a
slave father and a free mother inherited the free status of the mother.
The children of slaves were the property of the owner of the mother,
and, since the economic use of slaves during the Republic was at the
discretion of the master, slaves were bought and sold without regard
for their families. "There was nothing to prevent the legacy of a single
slave away from his connexions." [28]

According to the legal codes of the ante-bellum South, a slave "was
unable to acquire title to property by purchase, gift, or devise." [29] A
slave might not make a will, and he could not, by will, inherit anything. Slaves were not to hire themselves out, locate their own employment, establish their own residence, or make contracts for any
purpose including, of course, marriage. A slave "can do nothing,
possess nothing, nor acquire anything but what must belong to his
master." [30] He could engage in financial transactions, but only as his

master's agent. A slave could not be a party to a suit, except indirectly, when a free person represented him in a suit for freedom. Slaves might only be witnesses in court in cases involving slaves or free Negroes. When the testimony of a slave was allowed, he was not put under oath as a responsible person. Teaching slaves to read and write was prohibited, and instruction in religion was also subject to legal restrictions.

"Of the slave's position," in Rome, "it may be said that he had none." [31] A slave could not make a contract, he could be neither creditor nor debtor, he could not make a will, and if he became free, a will made in slavery was void. Slaves could in no way be concerned in civil proceedings which had to be made in the name of the master. A judgment against a slave was null and void and the pact of a slave was likewise void.

As to his participation in commerce, "his capacity here is almost purely derivative, and the texts speak of him as unqualified in nearly every branch of law." [32] Although the Roman slave could acquire possessions for the master, "the will of the slave and, in fact, his mental faculties in general, operate, in principle, where they operate at all, for the benefit of the master." [33] Legally the slave did not have possessory rights in the property acquired by him or granted to him. The *peculium* assigned to him by the master, to which the slave might add by investment, earnings, gift, interest, produce, or wages existed by the authority of the master and was subject to partial or total recall at the slaveowner's wish. The *peculium* was not alienable by the slave any more than other property. The *peculium* did not change the legal position of the slave. He was still a slave. No legal process which was closed to a slave without *peculium* was available to him if he had one. The *peculium* did not go with the slave upon manumission unless expressly given by the master.

Slaves were legally incapable of prosecution as accusers either on their own behalf or on behalf of others. As a general rule the evidence of slaves was not admissible in court, and when it was taken it was taken by torture, for it could not be received in any other form from slaves. Slaves were excluded from giving testimony on behalf of their masters.

The slave codes of the South supported the "full dominion" of the master in matters of policy and discipline. The slave's relationship with his master was expected to be one of complete subordination. Generally, homicide was the major crime that could be committed against an enslaved individual. The owner of a slave, however, could not be indicted for assault and battery on his own slave. "The power of the master must be absolute to render the submission of the slave perfect." [34] Furthermore, the master was not held responsible for the death of a slave as a consequence of "moderate correction," for "it cannot be presumed that prepensed malice (which alone makes murder felony)should induce any man to destroy his own estate." [35] The master was to recover damages caused by an assault or homicide against his slave.

During the Roman Republic there was no legal limitation on the power of the slaveowner: "his rights were unrestricted." [36] "Except in cases of revolt which endangered the government the Roman state left the problem of the discipline and punishment of slaves to their masters." [37] Sohm writes that as against his master, "a slave had no legal rights whatsoever." [38] In dealing with the offenses of slaves the owner's powers of punishment included corporal punishment, confinement in chains, confinement in the ergasulum, banishment from Rome and Italy, and the death penalty. Slaves, as possessions of value, were protected from mistreatment by persons other than their masters. In case of injury done to a slave "the master had cause of action for damages against the perpetrator." [39] If a slave was enticed into escaping or forcibly removed the owner might resort to both criminal and civil action.

These comparisons suggest that, on the legal evidence which defines the authority of the master in the areas of parentage and kinship, property and other rights, and police and disciplinary power over slaves, there is nothing sufficiently distinctive to distinguish the legal status of the slave as property in the United States from that in Rome.

Arnold Toynbee refers to the "Negro slave immigrant" as having been "subject to the twofold penalization of racial discrimination and legal servitude." [40] A society may extensively assimilate to property in law the rights of slaves, as indeed many have, but yet not restrict the status of slavery to members of a particular group for whom slavery is defined as natural, inevitable, and permanent as occurred in the United States. This was the introduction of caste into the status of the ante-bellum Negro, slave or free.[41] The Negro as slave occupied both a slave status and a caste status.[42] He was subject to disabilities in addition to those connected with the legal categorization of him as property, and these disabilities continued to define his status as a freedman. Caste law as well as slave law governed the status of the Negro.

The restriction of slavery to the Negro rested on the legal principle that it was a status properly belonging to the Negro as an innately (racially) inferior being. If slavery was a status attaching to a racial inferior, then it was inheritable even where one parent was white. Intermarriage between Negro slaves and whites was prohibited. Racial inferiority, legalized inheritance, and endogamy were related to another principle; namely, that slavery was the presumptive status of every Negro or person of color. The slave status was to follow naturally and inevitably from Negro ancestry.[43]

Although the slave and caste statuses were coextensive for the preponderant majority of ante-bellum Negroes, there were free Negroes in the North and South who, however, continued to be members of the lower caste. Caste was inclusive of the slave and free status. Thus the rule that the child follow the condition of the mother made slaves of the majority of Negroes and members of the lower caste of all Negroes. Negroes, slave or free, were legally prohibited from intermarrying with members of the dominant group. All members of the lower caste were presumed to be slaves unless they could establish that they should be legally free. There was a definite strain in the legal structure to establish slavery and caste as coextensive for all Negroes. The status of the free Negro is evidence of this strain. Although legally no longer an object of property rights, he was legally and socially a member of a lower caste and as such his life chances, whether he lived in the North or South, were held within narrow limits.[44]

Slavery in Republican Rome was not restricted to any particular group who ought properly to occupy the legal status of slaves. The legal restrictions on intermarriage of slave and free, on manumission, and on the status of freedmen, though at times severe, were not the consequence of a conception of the slave or former slave as innately inferior. Those who were enslaved in Rome did not constitute a caste in the society for whom the proper and permanent status was conceived to be slavery.[45]

It is not surprising that the highly perceptive Alexis de Tocqueville should have noticed this essential difference between slavery in antiquity and the United States. However, observing that discrimination against the Negro persisted in those parts of the United States where slavery had been abolished, he concluded that slavery must have given "birth" to "prejudice." [46] A causal relationship between slavery and racial discrimination is also implied in the interpretations under discussion.

Setting aside the conventional question as to "why slavery produced discrimination?" Carl Degler has separated the two elements, and, still treating the question historically, asks rather "which appeared first, slavery or discrimination?" His main argument is that from the beginning "the Negro was treated as an inferior to the white man, servant or free." [47] Caste or elements of caste antedated slavery, and as the legal status evolved "it reflected and included as a part of its essence, this same discrimination the white man had practiced against the Negro" from the outset in New England as well as the South.[48]

The colonists of the early seventeenth century not only were well aware of the distinction between indentured servitude and slavery, but they had ample opportunity to acquire the prejudical attitudes and discriminatory practices against Negroes through the slave trade and from Providence, Bermuda, Barbados, Jamaica, and the Spanish and Portuguese colonies.[49] Moreover, there was the inferior status ascribed to the non-Caucasian Indians and even their enslavement almost from the beginning of English settlement.

The evidence summarized by Degler indicates that Negroes were being set aside as a separate group because of their race before the legal status of slavery became fully crystallized in the late seventeenth century. There was legislation (1) preventing inter-racial marriages and sexual union; (2) declaring that the status of the offspring of a white man and a Negro would follow that of the mother and (3) establishing civil and legal disabilities applying to Negroes either free or in servitude.[50] As to the situation of the Negro in the North, "from the earliest years a lowly differentiated status, if not slavery itself, was reserved and recognized for the Negro—and the Indian, it might be added." [51] Degler concludes that "long before slavery or black labor became an important part of the Southern economy, a special and inferior status had been worked out for the Negroes. . . . it was a demand for labor which dragged the Negro to American shores, but the status he acquired cannot be explained by reference to that economic motive." [52]

Turning now to the personal component in the status of the ante-bellum slave, it is apparent that a conception of a legal relationship between persons or groups of persons is implied in the definition of slaves as a caste in the society. As we have seen, the ante-bellum slave was not uniformly regarded in the law as a person. There were certain situations and relationships, however, in which he was not regarded solely as property.

Kingsley Davis has observed that "slavery is extremely interesting precisely, because it does attempt to fit human beings into the category of objects of property rights. . . . Always the slave is given some rights, and these rights interfere with the attempt to deal with him solely as property." [53] Westermann found this to be a "constant paradox" in Greek and Roman antiquity, and "inherent in the very nature of the institution." "Theoretically," the slave was a chattel and subject only to the laws pertaining to private property, and in "actuality" he was "also a human being and subject to protective legislation affecting human individuals." [54] Isaac Mendelsohn refers to "the highly contradictory situation" in the slavery systems of the ancient Near East "in which on the one hand, the slave was considered as possessing qualities of a human being, while on the other hand, he was . . . regarded as a thing." [55] Under the law in Greek, Roman, and Near Eastern society the slave had an ambiguous status: he was both an object of property rights and a rudimentary legal person.

As to the personal component in the status of the slave in the United States, Elkins argues that as a consequence of the requirements of capitalistic agriculture "to operate efficiently and profitably," through the rational employment of slaves as economic instruments, any ambiguity in the legal status of the slave as property could not be tolerated.[56] Any rights of personality that remained to the Negro at the end of the seventeenth century had been suppressed by the middle of the eighteenth.[57] However they may differ as to causation, Elkins and Tannenbaum are in agreement that the status of the slave was determinate as property. For Tannenbaum the "element of human personality" had been lost in the definition of the slave in the United States.[58] Stampp, on the other hand, found a "dual character" in the legal codes. The legal authorities "were caught in a dilemma whenever they found that the slave's status as property was incompatible with this status as a person." [59] In a much earlier and very careful treatment of the personal component, Moore found that initially the question as to whether a slave was a person or a piece of property was involved in the difficult issue as to the status of the slave after conversion and baptism. Allowing the slave the privilege of salvation implied a recognition of him as a Christian person, and, by implication, as a legal personality. The idea that conversion and baptism altered the status of the slave as property was not easily changed, and the settling of the difficulty in favor of continued enslavement does not appear to have finally disposed of the matter.[60] "The persistence of this indeterminancy arising out of religious status," concludes Moore, "must be regarded as at least one source of the continued legislative and judicial declarations of the personality of the slave, despite other definitions and implications to the contrary." [61]

There are three aspects to be considered in taking up the matter of the doubtful status of the slave before the law. The most obvious, of course, is that the dual quality is inherent in the status itself. Slaves are conscious beings defined as economic property. On the one hand, the definition of the legal status conceives of them as objects of economic value. On the other hand, the slave as an item of economic value also remains a social object. The values he possesses as a conscious being can be utilized by the master, namely, his body, his skill, and his knowledge. The definition of the slave as a physical object overlaps that of the slave as a social object, since only social objects can perform and have intentions. The value of a slave as property resides in his being a person, but his value as a person rests in his status being defined as property.[62] The second aspect involves the recognition in the law not only of the humanity of the slave, but also that he may be the subject of rights of his own. In this connection, Stampp has noted a significant juxtaposition of two clauses in the legal code of Alabama in 1853. The first defines the status of the slave as property and establishes the owner's rights to the slave's "time, labor, and services," as well as the slave's obligation to comply with the lawful demands of the master. The second contains the personal element and states the master's obligation to be humane to his slaves and to provide them with adequate food, clothing, and with care during illness and old age.[63] Similarly a Kentucky court ruled in one case that "a slave by our code, is not a person, but (negotium) a thing," while in another case in the same state the court considered "slaves as property, yet recognizes their personal existence, and to a qualified extent, their natural rights." [64]

Cases clearly affirming that the slave was a person were also numerous during the ante-bellum period. One judgment in Tennessee held:

> A slave is not in the condition of a horse . . . he is made after the image of the Creator. He has mental capacities, and an immortal principle in his nature . . . the laws . . . cannot extenguish his high born nature, nor deprive him of many rights which are inherent in man.[65]

That the slave as an object of property rights was protected by law and by remedies the law provided whereby an owner could recover damages done to his property has already been discussed. A slave was also entitled in his own right to protection from malicious injury to his life and limb. The courts ruled that manslaughter against a slave "exists by common law: because it is the unlawful killing of a human being"; [66] that a slave is "a reasonable creature in being, in whose homicide either a white person or a slave may commit the crime of murder or manslaughter"; [67] and that "Negroes are under the protection of the laws, and have personal rights, and cannot be considered on a footing only with domestic animals." [68] The justification of the legal principle that a crime could be committed against an enslaved individual tended to shift, and in many cases revealed the ambivalence between the conception of the slave as property, and as a person. In a judgment acknowledging that an indictment for an assault upon a slave could be made, a Louisiana court ruled that "Slaves are treated in our law as property, and also, as persons. . . ." [69] As stated earlier, however, generally homicide was the major crime that could be committed against a slave, and the owner of a slave could not be indicted for assault and battery on his slaves.

Many of the laws also implied that a slave was a legal person in that he was capable of committing crimes and could be held to trial. Cases involving slave crimes were very numerous and frequently they turned on the conception of the slave as a person. In the judgment of a Georgia court in 1854:

> . . . it is not true that slaves are only chattels, . . . and therefore, it is not true that it is not possible for them to be prisoners . . . the Penal Code . . . has them in contemplation . . . in the first division . . . as persons capable of committing crimes; and as a . . . consequence . . . as capable of becoming prisoners.[70]

Another court held that a white man could be indicted and convicted as an accessory to a murder commited by a slave. The judgment stated that "Negroes are under the protection of the laws, and have personal rights. . . . They have wills of their own—capacities to commit crimes; and are responsible for offences against society." [71]

Again, however, there were limits on the extent to which the personality of the slave was recognized, and in defining these limits the courts frequently expressed the indeterminate character of the status:

> Because they are rational *human beings*, they are capable of committing crimes; and, in reference to acts which are crimes, are regarded as *persons*. Because they are *slaves*, they are . . . incapable of performing civil acts; and in reference to all such, they are *things*; not persons.[72]

That slaves were held to some of the responsibilities usually expected of persons in society and few of the privileges is further illustrated by the fact that slaves were persons who could abscond and commit capital crimes, but if killed or mained in capture or put to death by law, the slaveowner was reimbursed for the loss of his property.

The third aspect pertains to the cases of manumission by will, deed, and legislative action; the instances of successful suits for freedom; and the cases of self-purchase—all of which implied evaluation of the slave as a person with some legal capacity:

> They may be emancipated by their owners; and must, of course, have a right to seek and enjoy the protection of the law in the establishment of all deeds, or wills, or other legal documents of emancipation; and so far, they must be considered as natural persons, entitled to some legal rights, whenever their owners shall have declared . . . they . . . be free; and to this extent the general reason of policy which disables slaves as persons, and subjects them to the general reason of mere brute property, does not apply.[73]

Moreover, the presence of free Negroes in the population from the beginning; manumission; suits for freedom; and self-purchase indicated that slavery did not follow naturally and inevitably from Negro ancestry. The intrusion of the values of liberty and individual achievement into the legal structure meant that race and slavery were not coextensive for all Negroes. The law sanctioned the possibility of slaves legitimately aspiring to and attaining in attenuated form the culture goals of the enslaving group having to do with freedom and individual achievement. The status of the free Negro was real and symbolic evidence of the indeterminacy resulting from the attainment of goals that were presumably denied to Negroes and applicable only to whites.[74]

III

In the interpretations of Elkins, Tannenbaum, and Stampp much has been made of the legal status of the slave as property and the extent to which the rights of slaves were assimilated to property in law. As the preceding discussion has indicated, in the United States where slaves were conceived of as innately inferior they constituted a caste in the society and their rights were extensively assimilated to property in law. In Republican Rome where slaves were not conceived of as innately inferior to the enslaving group and did not form a separate caste an equally extensive assimilation of their rights to property occurred. In contrast to the United States, manumission was easily available to the Roman slave, and the freedman could look forward to assimilation into Roman society.

Although the slave status in Rome was not justified in terms of the innate inferiority of the slave, the assimilation of ownership in slaves to property was comparable to that in the United States. Roman law respected the moral personality of the slave, as reflected in the rules governing manumission and the status of the freed slave, but this did not prevent the assimilation of his rights to property in law.

In so far as the legal categorization of the slave as property is concerned we are dealing with a common social form in Rome and the United States. Caste produced the contrast between the legal structures of the two systems of slavery. The consequence of racial discrimination for the legal structure of ante-bellum slavery was the creation of a hereditary, endogamous and permanent group of individuals in the status of slaves who, moreover, continued as members of a lower caste in the society after freedom. Although the conception of the slave as innately (racially) inferior to the enslaving group had important consequences for manumission and for the status of freedmen, as Tannenbaum has indicated, the comparison with Rome suggests that it did not accentuate the assimilation of ownership in slaves to property. Racial discrimination does not appear to have affected the legal status of the slave as property.

Now slavery in Rome was not a single social phenomenon historically. Not until the first two centuries of the Empire did significant changes occur in the authority of the master over the rights of slaves. "In their ultimate legal formulation the changes found expression in the Codes of Theodosius and Justinian." [75] Up to that time, although Roman law respected the moral integrity of the slave, the subordination of the slave to the authority of the master was comparable to that in the United States. The slave law that came down through the Justinian Code to influence the Iberian law of slavery, later to be transferred to Latin America, contained not only the doctrine of the moral personality of the slave, but also embodied those changes in later Roman law which had "loosened the strict controls by which the slave element had formerly been bound to the will of the master group." [76]

According to the interpretations of slavery in Latin America by Tannenbaum and Elkins, it was this body of law in conjunction with certain traditions and institutional arrangements that functioned to protect the slaves both from an extensive assimilation to property in law and from a caste status. Some reference will be made in the concluding portion of this essay to the need for a revision of this interpretation on the basis of more recent research.

Considerable variation occurs among slavery systems in the extent to which the slave is assimilated to property in law. Variations in this component are generally taken to be related to "the level of technical development and the accompanying institutional apparatus, including the economic system." [77] Where slavery was a domestic system, as in China and the Near East, the assimilation of the slave to property in law was less extensive than in Rome and the United States where slavery was an industrial system.[78]

The property component in the status of the ante-bellum slave was undoubtedly related to economic values and the labor needs of an emerging capitalism, as Elkins and Stampp have emphasized, but the entire status cannot be derived from the operation of economic values. On the one hand, the extensive assimilation to property in law of the Roman slave did not generate a conception of him as innately inferior and create a caste of slaves and freedmen. On the other hand, the absence of certain institutions and traditions embodying values respecting the moral personality of the slave does not account for the conception of the Negro as inherently inferior and for caste. If these were absent, then the assimilation of ownership in slaves to property in law must have caused racial discrimination and caste. The historical evidence indicates rather that discrimination against the Negro occurred before the slave status was fully defined and before Negro labor became pivotal to the economic system.[79]

In the conception of the legal status of the slave as determinate in terms of property the slave has neither a juridical nor a moral personality. The values of the dominant group in the United States that had bearing on the law of slavery were, on the one hand, those which legitimatized slavery and the rigid system of stratification, and on the other hand, those values pertaining to freedom and individual dignity and worth. Although there was no complex of laws, traditions, and institutions pertaining to the institution of slavery as such that embodied these latter values, a significant element in the general value system of the South was an ethical valuation of the individual. The legal evidence indicates that these extra-legal values of the society were expressed in the legal definition and conception of slavery. The law of slavery shows the existence of an ethical norm, however vague and rudimentary, attaching value to the individual.[80]

The interpretation of the legal status of the slave primarily or wholly in terms of property has implications as well for the conception of the pattern of relations between masters and slaves. In discussing the connection between the legal structure and the master-slave relationship, David Potter has observed that "the human relationship within this legal context was complex and multiple." The relation between masters and slaves had "two faces—a paternalistic manorial one and an exploitative commercial one." [81]

In the interpretations of Tannenbaum, Elkins, and Stampp there is a close correspondence between the legal structure and the pattern of the master-slave relationship. Since, according to these writers, the slave status was governed by instrumental and economic values and not affected by the religious and ethical convictions of the dominant group attaching value to the individual, there was nothing to impede the rational use of slaves as economic instruments. The exploitative commercial pattern was expected to be followed in organizing the relations of masters and slaves. It was normatively and numerically the predominant pattern in the South.

Given this conception of the connection between the legal structure and the relations of masters and slaves, the paternalistic manorial pattern can only be interpreted as a deviation from the expected and approved pattern of the master-slave relationship. It is not interpreted as an equally recognized and approved mode of organizing and managing the relations of masters and slaves, but rather as the result of fortuitous circumstances. It is attributed to the smallness of the plantation or to the "personal factor." [82] According to this interpretation there was nothing in the law to sanction the paternalistic manorial pattern, while the commercial exploitative pattern was clearly compatible with the instrumental use of slaves as sanctioned in the definition of the slave as an object of property rights. Yet, the paternalistic manorial pattern was widespread in the South as an accepted and approved mode of organizing the master-slave relationship and represented, as did the personal component in the legal status, the intrusion of the valuation of the individual into a categorized relationship.[83]

IV

Since the contrast with slavery in Latin America is central to the interpretations of slavery in .the United States by Tannenbaum and Elkins, some reference may be made to the more recent studies of slavery and race relations in Latin America and the implications for a comparison with North America. The results of these studies appear to be consistent with those of this essay.

In connection with the interpretations of slavery in Latin America by Elkins and Tannenbaum, Mintz questions whether slavery in Latin America can be treated as a single phenomenon historically.[84] He points out that once slavery became a part of the industrial plantation system in Cuba and Puerto Rico, for example, an extensive assimilation to property in law of the rights of slaves occurred in spite of an institutional framework protecting the moral personality of the slave. Slavery in Cuba "dehumanized the slave as viciously as had Jamaican or North America slavery." [85] Much the same thing happened in Puerto Rico. Between 1803 and 1873 repressive laws were passed "more and more limiting the slaves' legal, social, economic status." [86] In connection with slavery on the sugar plantations and in the mines of Portuguese Brazil, E. R. Boxer writes that the widely accepted "belief that the Brazilian was an exceptionally kind master is applicable only to nineteenth-century slavery under the Empire" and not to the colonial period.[87] At the same time, however, "one of the few redeeming features in the life of slaves . . . was the possibility of their buying or being given their freedom at some time, a contingency which was much rarer in the French and English American colonies." [88]

As to the racial component in the slave status, investigations of race relations in Brazil, where most of the work has been done, indicate that during the colonial period slavery also involved a caste system between whites and Negro slaves, "based on white supremacy and the institutionalized inferiority of colored slaves." [89] Concubinage was widely practiced, but intermarriage was rare, "as the system demanded the separation of the two castes and the clearcut distinction of superiors and inferiors." [90] Colonial legislation discriminated against the free Negroes who "were often coupled with enslaved Negroes in the laws." [91] They were prevented from acquiring possessions or participating in activities in the society "which might tend to place them on a level with whites." [92] Mulattoes who attained positions of importance in Brazil "did so in spite of the official and social prejudices which existed against them throughout the whole of the colonial period." [93]

It is readily apparent from these studies that a much greater similarity existed between slavery in the United States and Latin America than heretofore suspected. The status of slaves in Latin America, as well as in Rome and the United States, indicates that whether or not the law respected the moral personality of the slave, an extensive assimilation of his rights to property in law occurred under slavery as an industrial system. Moreover, contrary to the widely held conception, racial discrimination was present in Latin America and had the consequence of creating a duality in the status of the slave as property and as a member of a racial caste.[94] These elements were apparently combined to some extent with a respect for the moral personality of the slave in the law.

Further comparative study of slavery in the United States and Latin America will enable us to delineate more precisely the differences and similarities in the property, racial, and personal components of the slave status in these societies. We may also expect such study to reveal, as this essay has attempted to do, that economic and ideological forces were not mutually exclusive in their consequences for the legal structure of slavery.

NOTES

1. The author wishes to acknowledge his obligations to M. I. Finley, John Hope Franklin, Robert Freedman, and Richard Robbins, among others, who have read and criticized this paper, and to the Research Council of Colgate University for a generous research grant.

2. See Stanley Elkins, *Slavery* (Chicago, 1959), Chap. I: Kenneth Stampp, "The Historian and Southern Negro Slavery," *American Historical Review*, LVII (April, 1952), pp. 613-24; Richard Hofstadter, "U. B. Phillips and the Plantation Legend," *Journal of Negro History*, XXIX (April, 1944), pp. 109-25.

3. M. G. Smith, "Slavery and Emancipation in Two Societies," *Social and Economic Studies*, III, Nos. 3 and 4 (1954), pp. 245-46.

4. *Ibid.*, p. 246.

5. The classic account is H. J. Nieboer, *Slavery as an Industrial System* (Rotterdam, 1910).

6. Wilbert Moore, "Slave Law and the Social Structure," *Journal of Negro History*, XXVI. (April, 1941), pp. 171-202.

7. *Slave and Citizen* (New York, 1947).

8. *Slavery*. Chap. 2. This discussion is limited to his treatment of the legal status of the slave. Elkins proposes an alternative to the established approach to slavery in the United States which, taking its stance from the debates over slavery, has been concerned mainly with the rightness or wrongness of the institution considered in terms of categories pertaining to the health and welfare of the slaves. The historical study of slavery has alternated over the years between a pro-slavery and an anti-slavery position, but the purpose and the categories of analysis have remained unchanged. The result has been a continuing confusion of the historical study of slavery with moral judgments about slavery. Elkins proposes discarding this approach and adopting instead the method of comparison as followed by Tannenbaum. Slavery as an evil is taken for granted. Elkins' treatment of slavery as analogous to the concentration camp in its effects on Negro personality is discussed in Earle E. Thorpe, "Chattel Slavery and Concentration Camps," *The Negro History Bulletin*, XXV (May, 1962), pp. 171-76.

9. Tannenbaum, pp. 43-65.

10. *Ibid.*, p. 8.

11. *Ibid.*, p. 82.

12. Elkins, p. 37.

13. *Ibid.*, p. 55.

14. *Ibid.*, p. 52. These categories are taken from Elkins, but they are also used by Stampp and Tannenbaum in describing the status of the slave.

15. (New York, 1957).

16. (New York, 1918).

17. Stampp, Chap. 5.

18. *Ibid.*, pp. 192-93.

19. Elkins, p. 61.

20. Stampp, p. 23.

21. Tannenbaum, pp. 55-56.

22. *Ibid.*, p. 69. See also William L. Westermann, *The Slave Systems of Greek and Roman Antiquity* (Philadelphia, 1955), p. 154.

23. Tannenbaum, p. 69.

24. William L. Westermann, "Slavery and Elements of Freedom in Ancient Greece," *Bulletin of the Polish Institute of Arts and Sciences in America*, I (Jan., 1943), p. 346. See also M. I. Finley, "Between Slavery and Freedom," *Comparative Studies in Society and History*, VI (Apr., 1964), p. 246.

25. Westermann, *The Slave Systems*, pp. 57, 80; W. W. Buckland, *The Roman Law of Slavery* (Cambridge, 1906), p. 1. The consequent ambiguity in the status of the slave as property and as a person in ancient society is discussed at a later point.

26. Materials for the description of the legal status of the ante-bellum slave are standard and taken from Elkins, Chap. 2; Stampp, Chap. 5; Tannenbaum, p. 69ff; and Helen T. Caterall, *Judicial Cases Concerning Slavery and the Negro* (Washington, 1926). Those for the Roman Republic are taken from the standard work by Buckland; R. H. Barrow, *Historical Introduction to the Study of Roman Law* (Cambridge, 1932); and Rudolph Sohm, *The Institutes* (Oxford, 1907).

27. *Howard v. Howard*, 6 Jones N.C. 235, December 1858. Caterall, II, p. 221.

28. Buckland, p. 77.

29. Stampp, p. 197.

30. The Civil Code of Louisiana quoted in John C. Hurd, *The Law of Freedom and Bondage in the United States* (Boston, 1858), II, p. 160.

31. Buckland, p. 82.

32. *Iibd.*, p. 82.

33. *Ibid.*, p. 82.

34. *State v. Mann*, 2 Deveroux 263, (N.C.), December 1829, Catterall, II, p. 57.

35. Virginia Act of 1669, Hurd, I, p. 232.

36. Buckland, p. 36.

37. Westermann, p. 75.

38. Sohm, p. 166.

39. Westermann. p. 83.

40. Arnold J. Toynbee, *A Study of History* (Oxford, 1934), II, p. 218.

41. There has been considerable disagreement as to whether the term "caste" is applicable to the American case. It has been insisted that it should be limited to India. The present writer agrees with Everett Hughes who writes: "If we grant this, we will simply have to find some other term for the kind of social

category into which one is assigned at birth and from which he cannot escape
by action of his own: and to distinguish such social categories from classes or
ranked groups, from which it is possible, though sometimes difficult, to rise."
Everett C. Hughes and H. MacGill Hughes, *Where Peoples Meet* (Glencoe,
1952), p. 111. Berreman has recently defined the term as to be useful cross-
culturally. He defines a caste system "as a *hierarchy of endogamous divisions in
which membership is hereditary and permanent.* Here hierarchy includes inequality both in status and in access to goods and services. Interdependence of
the subdivisions, restricted contracts among them, occupational specialization
and/or a degree of cultural distinctiveness might be added as criteria, although
they appear to be correlates rather than defining characteristics." Gerald D.
Berreman, "Caste in India and the United States," *American Journal of
Sociology*, LXVI (Sept., 1960), pp. 120-21, cf. Louis Dumont, "Caste, Racism,
and 'Stratification,' Reflections of a Social Anthropologist," *Contributions to
Indian Sociology*, V (Oct., 1961), pp. 20-43.

42. Moore, pp. 177-9.

43. *Ibid.*, 184-88. See also Winthrop D. Jordan, "American Chiaroscuro:
The Status and Definition of Mulattoes in the British Colonies," *William and
Mary Quarterly*, XIX, No. 2 (April, 1962), pp. 183-200.

44. John Hope Franklin, *The Free Negro in North Carolina* (Chapel Hill,
1943); Leon F. Litwack, *North of Slavery* (Chicago, 1961).

45. Westermann, p. 15, 23.

46. Alexis de Tocqueville, *Democracy in America* (New York, 1948), I,
pp. 358-60.

47. Carl N. Degler, "Slavery and the Genesis of American Race Prejudice,"
Comparative Studies in Society and History, II (Oct., 1959), p. 52. Cf. Oscar
and Mary F. Handlin, "Origins of the Southern Labor System," *William and
Mary Quarterly*, 3rd. Ser., VI (April, 1950), pp. 199-222; Winthrop D. Jordan,
"Modern Tensions and the Origins of American Slavery," *Journal of Southern
History*, XXVII (Feb., 1962), pp. 18-33.

48. Degler, p. 52.

49. *Ibid.*, pp. 53-56. See also Winthrop D. Jordan, "The Influence of the
West Indies on the Origin of New England Slavery," *William and Mary
Quarterly*, XVIII (April, 1961), pp. 243-250.

50. *Ibid.*, pp. 56-62. See also Moore, pp. 177-86.

51. Degler, p. 62.

52. *Ibid.*, p. 62. Jordan, *The Influence of the West Indies*, pp. 243-44, 250.

53. *Human Society* (New York, 1949), p. 456.

54. Westermann, p. 1.

55. *Slavery in the Near East* (New York, 1949), p. 64.

56. Elkins, p. 49, 53.

57. *Ibid.*, p. 42.

58. Tannenbaum, p. 97.

59. Stampp, pp. 192-93.

60. Moore, pp. 195-96.

61. *Ibid.*, p. 196. See also Charles Sellers, "The Travail of Slavery," in
Charles Sellers, ed., *The Southerner as American* (Chapel Hill, 1960), pp.
40-71.

62. Talcott Parsons and Neil J. Smelser, *Economy and Society* (Glencoe,
1956), p. 12.

63. Stampp, pp. 192-93. The following discussion is not intended to be

comprehensive. For a detailed treatment of the definition of the slave as a person see Moore, pp. 191-202.

64. *Jarman v. Patterson*, 7 T.B. Mon. 644, December 1828, (Ky.) Catterall, I, p. 311. See also *Catherine Bodine's Will*, 4 Dana 476, Oct. 1836, (Ky.) *Ibid.*, I, p. 334-35.

65. *Kennedy v. Williams*, 7 Humphreys, Sept., 1846 (Tenn.) *Ibid.*, II, p. 530.

66. *Fields v. State*, I Yerger 156, Jan., 1829 (Tenn.) *Ibid.*, II, p. 494.

67. *Hudson v. State*, 34 Ala. 253, June 1859, *Ibid.*, III, p. 233.

68. *State v. Cynthia Simmons and Laurence Kitchen*, I Brevard 6, Fall 1794 (So. Car.), *Ibid.*, II, p. 277.

69. *State v. Davis*, 14 La. An. 678, July 1859, *Ibid.*, III, p. 674.

70. *Baker v. State*, 15 Ga. 498, July 1854, *Ibid.*, III, p. 35.

71. *State v. Cynthia Simmons and Laurence Kitchen*, I Brevard 6, fall 1794 (So. Car.), *Ibid.*, II, p. 277.

72. *Creswell's Executor v. Walker*, 37 Ala. 229, January 1861, *Ibid.*, III, p. 247.

73. *Catherine Bodine's Will*, 4 Dana 476, October 1836, (Ken.), *Ibid.*, I, pp. 334-35.

74. Wilbert Moore and Robin Williams, "Stratification in the Ante-bellum South," *American Sociological Review*, VII (June, 1942), pp. 343-51. Cf. Douglas Hall, "Slaves and Slavery in the British West Indies," *Social and Economic Studies*, II, No. 4 (December, 1962), pp. 305-18.

75. Westermann, p. 140.

76. *Ibid.*, p. 140.

77. Sidney W. Mintz, Review of *Slavery* by Stanley Elkins, *American Anthropologist*, 63 (June, 1961), p. 580.

78. G. Martin Wilbur, *Slavery in China During the Former Han Dynasty* (Chicago, 1943), p. 243; Mendelsohn, pp. 121-22.

79. That the essential features of a caste status for the Negro may have preceded the full development of the slave status does not alter the widely accepted proposition that the initial status of the Negro was not that of a slave but rather that of an indentured servant or free man. Some aspects of caste appear to have developed later than others, but the main defining features were fixed early and before the complete development of the status of slavery. Racial segregation, although obviously foreshadowed in the status of the free Negro, did not appear as a part of the caste system until the late nineteenth and early twentieth centuries. The system of restricted contacts between Negroes and whites, clearly based on the long-standing assumption of the innate inferiority of the Negro, was simply the latest feature of caste to develop. See C. Vann Woodward, *The Strange Career of Jim Crow* (New York, 1957).

80. Moore, pp. 201-02. For another discussion of the alternative value systems and the resulting conflicts within Southern society and within individuals see Sellers, pp. 51-67. A similar ambiguity existed in connection with slavery in ancient society. In Roman law "slavery is the only case in which, in the extant sources . . . , a conflict is declared to exist between the *Ius Gentium* and the *Ius Naturale*." Buckland, p. 1. "No society," writes Finley, "can carry such a conflict within it, around so important a set of beliefs and institutions, without the stresses erupting in some fashion, no matter how remote and extended the lines and connections may be from the original stimulus." M. I. Finley, "Was

Greek Civilization Based on Slave Labour?," in M. I. Finley, ed. *Slavery in Classical Antiquity* (Cambridge, 1960), p. 162.

81. David M. Potter, Review of *The Peculiar Institution* by Kenneth Stampp, *Yale Review*, 46 (Winter, 1957), pp. 260-61.

82. Elkins, pp. 137-38.

83. The pattern of the master-slave relationships continues to be one of the most problematic and debated aspects of ante-bellum slavery. The exploitative commercial pattern tends to be taken as the predominant pattern and in accordance with the normative prescriptions of ante-bellum society, while the paternalistic manorial pattern is generally treated as the result of the intrusion of non-normative factors, and usually attributed to smallness of size. However, Franklin has pointed out that the bulk of the slaves were on small plantations. If so, then the paternalistic manorial pattern must have been exceedingly widespread. On the other hand, it has also been suggested that this pattern was to be found on the larger holdings. Phillips had this conception of the master-slave relationship on large plantations. It seems likely that both patterns were normative; that is, accepted and approved ways of organizing the master-slave relationship. If this was the case, then further investigation must be directed at ascertaining the determinants of these patterns on the concrete level. Size would be one among several determinants. See John Hope Franklin, *From Slavery to Freedom* (New York, 1952), pp. 185-86. Needless to say, the pattern of the master-slave relationship is significant for the impact of slavery upon the personality of the Negro. If the paternalistic manorial pattern was widely institutionalized in the ante-bellum South, then a very significant number of Negro slaves were able to escape the tendency for the system to absorb the personality. Cf. Elkins, pp. 137-138.

84. Useful summaries are to be found in Juan Comas, "Recent Research on Race Relations—Latin America," *International Social Science Journal*, XIII, No. 2 (1961), pp. 271-99; Oracy Nogueira, "Skin Color and Social Class," *Plantation Systems of the New World* (Washington, 1959), pp. 164-83; Roger Bastide, "Race Relations in Brazil," *International Social Science Bulletin*, IX, No. 4 (1957), pp. 495-512.

85. Mintz, p. 581.

86. *Ibid.*, p. 583, See also O. A. Sherrard, *Freedom from Fear* (London, 1959), p. 75.

87. *The Golden Age of Brazil* (Berkeley, 1961), p. 173. Gilberto Freyre's *The Masters and the Slaves* (New York, 1946), on which much of the existing conception of slavery in Brazil is based, wrote mainly about domestic slaves.

88. Boxer, p. 177.

89. Harley Ross Hammond, "Race, Social Mobility and Politics in Brazil," *Race*, IV, No. 2 (1962), p. 477. See Charles Wagley, "From Caste to Class in North Brazil," in Charles Wagley (ed.), *Race and Class in Rural Brazil* (New York, 1963), pp. 142-156.

90. *Ibid.*, p. 4.

91. Boxer, p. 17.

92. *Ibid.*, p. 17.

93. *Ibid.*, p. 17.

94. Nogueira, pp. 167-176, has attempted to distinguish race prejudice in Brazil from that in the United States. With reference to the origin of race prejudice in Brazil, James G. Leyburn, in his discussion of Nogueira's paper, questions whether it was slavery which produced prejudice. *Ibid.*, p. 181.

V. ASSESSMENTS

• The three reviews which follow present a small cross-section of the current dialogue among modern historians of slavery. The exchange between Genovese and Elkins may help the student to clarify some fundamental issues still being disputed by these and other American scholars. Finally, a leading historian of slavery in the ancient world, M. I. Finley, examines David Brion Davis's attempt at a new comparative treatment of the subject.

On Stanley M. Elkins's *Slavery, A Problem in American Institutional and Intellectual Life*

EUGENE D. GENOVESE

Elkins' *Slavery* is a well-written and absorbing examination of the social psychology of the Negro slave and of the institutional framework in which slavery developed. The principal idea is that the "Sambo" image of the antebellum Negro was essentially valid and must be accounted for by those who properly eschew racist mysticism. To demonstrate his point Elkins applies analytical methods borrowed from social psychology and refuses to genuflect before hallowed academic custom by making reference to plantation manuscripts and other primary sources, which, whatever their merits for other types of studies, are largely irrelevant here. This is a brave book, for it says a good deal of a man that he will defend an unpopular thesis, use an unfamiliar method certain to arouse the hostility of historians, and compound his crimes by refusing to disguise them with pseudo-scholarly paraphernalia.

Elkins is ideologically conservative and may win a hearing by his

From Eugene D. Genovese, review of Elkins, *Slavery* . . . , in *Science & Society*, XXV (Winter 1961), 41-7; Stanley Elkins, review of Genovese, *The Political Economy of Slavery* . . . , in *Commentary*, (July 1966), 73-5; Moses I. Finley, "The Idea of Slavery," a review of Davis, *The Problem of Slavery* . . . , in *New York Review of Books*, VIII (January 26, 1967), 6-9. All reprinted with permission.

defense of institutionalism and rejection of radical solutions to social problems. Conservative or no conservative, he has taken a new road and defied his profession to do so. He is surely sophisticated enough to know that his colleagues will be a long time in appreciating his achievement.

Elkins begins by denying that the Sambo image of a docile, child-like slave was simply a big lie repeated by persons of diverse temperaments, politics, and interests.[1] Why, he asks, was no Sambo image produced by Latin American slavery? He underscores his point by contrasting the few, scattered, weak slave rebellions in the United States with the heroic and massive rebellions in Brazil.[2] In Latin America, he notes, the feudal tradition expressed itself in a series of institutional arrangements mediating between master and slave. The Catholic church insisted on the Christianization of slaves, protected their right to marry and raise families, and used its influence to prevent arbitrary behavior by the masters. The Hispanic monarchies, with their administrative centralization, bureaucratization, and pretensions to the role of protector of the lowly, guaranteed the slaves certain minimum rights in court, to property ownership, and to a peculium.

In the United States slavery grew up under conditions of uncontrolled capitalism, in which economic motives were unchecked by adequate institutional arrangements. The master had supreme power over the slave. Elkins suggests that slavery in Virginia developed as an extension of British capitalism, that the mediating effects of church and patriarchal state were missing, and that the violent individualism and anti-institutionalism of Jacksonian America reinforced the dependence of the slave on his master. It is necessary for the next part of his thesis to show why abolition occurred in an orderly way in the British colonies and in a disorderly way in the United States. Here again he points to mediating institutions (the independence and prestige of the Anglican and dissenting churches, an intellectual and social elite with national influence, and so forth) to explain the difference. We shall examine the issue of abolition later; of immediate concern is Elkins' failure to explain adequately why British institutionalism established arrangements so much closer to Latin American models in the West Indies than in Virginia and South Carolina.

The trouble is that Elkins pays attention only to the capitalistic elements in Southern slavery, especially its commodity production, but neglects the noncapitalistic, aristocratic, patriarchal aspects to which he often alludes. The decisive feature of Southern development was not that a class of peculiar capitalists controlled the slave regime, but that an aristocracy roughly analogous to the Brazilian won political control over its territory and remade society in its own image. Just as Hispanic feudalism was local, individualistic, and despotic in its natural inclinations, despite the superimposition of a centralized state, so too was Southern slavery. That which made the Southern planters unusual and opened the way to absolute power over the slave was not the capitalist element but the political quasi-independence of the planters, who were fundamentally opposed to bourgeois values and society. Let us concede to Elkins that the general American phenomenon of institutional breakdown permitted the planters to go their own way without arousing much opposition for a long time. Let us concede, too, that his major point is sound: the Southern planter exercised far greater power over his slaves than did the Latin American.

Elkins is primarily interested in the effect of this total power on the Negro personality. The prime effect, he argues, was infantilization. First, the Negro underwent the shocks of capture, transportation to the sea, sale, the horrible Middle Passage, and resale to a plantation. These shocks annihilated much of his past, severed his personal ties, and deprived him of status. Then followed the subjection to an absolute authority: the slave in the United States depended on his master for his material existence; the master's rewards and approbations were the only ones he could receive; the master's values were the only ones he came to know.

Elkins overstates the contrast between American and Latin American slavery, for in practice the gap was far narrower. Much of Hispanic law was unenforced; not every Jesuit father consistently defended the faithful; [3] government officials could be and often were corrupt or indifferent. On the other hand, much of the arbitrariness of American slavery was mitigated by community pressure and the prevalent patriarchal ideology. Overstated or not, the contrast is sufficiently valid and needs to be qualified, not rejected.

Elkins opens himself to severe censure by drawing an extended analogy between American slaves and the inmates of Nazi concentration camps. He can deny saying that slavery was a concentration camp or even "like" a concentration camp. He can explain that he merely seeks to demonstrate that masses can be infantilized and that the vilest oppressor (*e.g.*, the S.S. officer) often emerges in the minds of the oppressed as a father image. I suspect that denials or no, he will be denounced for allegedly saying all the things he specifically repudiates. The analogy, in the careful, limited way in which he uses it, serves a good purpose. The vast literature on the concentration camps documents the possibility of mass infantilization and does show how a "childlike" devotion to an oppressor may result. Elkins' theory of infantilization, which can stand without reference to the concentration camps, provides a brilliant turning point in the discussion of antebellum slavery. Let us take Elkins at his word and use his controversial analogy in the restricted, suggestive way he asks.

Elkins uses Harry Stack Sullivan's theory of the "expectations of significant others" as well as role theory to explain the slave's personality development. Under the conditions of total power, previously described, the "significant others" became the master; hence, the American slave's personality rarely surpassed the level of childlike dependency.[4] Similarly, the American slave was deprived of roles other than that of child of the plantation-owner father. Unlike his Latin American counterpart, he could not function as a father, husband, or property owner.

Elkins realizes that the Negro may have acted the part of Sambo and hid his true personality. There is, he explains, "a broad belt of indeterminacy between 'mere acting' and the 'true self.' " To this layman, it seems probable that a lifetime of acting would transform the actor's "true personality" into that which he is acting out. Elkins realizes that urban slaves, artisans, and house slaves did not fit the stereotype but does not consider the undoubted exceptions among the field hands themselves.[5] Perhaps he would acknowledge such exceptions and insist that he is treating the main personality trait on the principle of one thing at a time, but we are concerned here with essentials, not shadings. If there were exceptions,[6] the social determinants of the Sambo personality must have been subject to counteracting forces. We have seen that Elkins underestimates the mitigating effects of community pressure; more surprisingly, he ignores the social life of the slaves—their leisure, holiday and Sunday activities, and the many less visible forms of interpersonal relations.

Is it realistic to assume that the slave's personality developed in response either to the social pressure for infantilization or to the counteracting pressures? Would it not be more realistic to assume that the personality of every slave responded to the tensions between the two but that the pressure emphasized by Elkins generally proved stronger? If we take this approach, we can examine the average plantation slave as a Sambo containing within himself an opposite tendency capable of realization under certain conditions. Elkins' assertion of "a broad belt of indeterminacy between 'mere acting' and the 'true self' " would then take on a newer, richer meaning.

The process by which the dependent laborer comes to self-consciousness through his labor has been the concern of social philosophers for centuries. If Elkins prefers not to begin with Marx or Engels, let him go to Hegel or Saint Simon. Hegel, after all, provided a useful starting point for an analysis of the psychological dependence of the slave on his master.[7] That very relationship of dependence turns into a sense of independence through the labor process, for the slave learns his strength and his power over the objects on which he labors. The master commands those objects and is independent of them; but simultaneously, he is dependent on the slave who produces them. The slave comes to self-consciousness by his participation in this two-fold process.

The last part of Elkins' book will win him praise from conservative writers who may recoil at the earlier chapters. He asserts that our intellectual reformers were largely declassed bourgeois without established institutional loyalties. To them, slavery was an absolute question of morality. Transcendentalists could not transcend their milieu and become abolitionists intent on saving their own souls and expurgating their own guilt. I cannot here do justice to Elkins' intelligent, well-argued, but unconvincing thesis. In general, he insists that Northern and Southern intellectuals should have fought to establish mediating institutions in the South to provide the slaves with religious training, marriages, a family, and a peculium. In this way, the Upper South might have been detached gradually from the Cotton Kingdom, and a transitional serfdom encroaching on slavery would have provided the slave with the time and conditions in which to emerge from his childlike dependency. The horrors of Civil War and Reconstruction could have been avoided as they were in the British colonies and in Brazil.

How sad that Elkins sees the moral issue of slavery purely as an expression of a guilt complex. Antislavery sentiment was the culmination of centuries of ideological conditioning—those values of Western, Christian civilization that we hear so much about—and cannot be so easily dismissed. Elkins seems to think that the guilt feelings were the important data and the moral revulsion merely an appearance or form of a deeper psychological phenomenon. That the sense of guilt was an important part of the abolitionists' psychological make-up we need not deny. Neither should we overlook the reality of the growing worldwide revulsion against slavery. It would seem more justifiable to assert that the revulsion was both genuine and proper and that the sense of guilt helped shape the particular form that it took in America.

This part of Elkins' book is weak for three other reasons. First, he is in danger of re-writing history to conform to his wishes when he tells us about might-have-beens, and worse, his speculations rest on a puz-

zling contradiction. On the one hand, man's freedom of action is ostensibly limited by his institutional arrangements, which in this case
were inadequate to the task. On the other hand, we are told that man
might have remade his institutions to deal with the problem confronting him. Elkins' appears to slide erratically between an institutional
determinism and a radical free-will doctrine; he cannot have it both
ways.

Secondly, he never analyzes the planters as a social class with a deep
ideological commitment to their way of life; he ignores their special
social psychology, which produced a fierce identification of slavery with
civilization itself. The reforms of which Elkins speaks would have been
a threat to the hegemony of the planters, who were neither so stupid
as to miss the implications nor so weak as to be unable to protect
themselves.

Thirdly, Elkins' tacit assumption that the abolitionists dominated
Northern politics and that the free soil movement was a transmission
belt developed by abolitionist tactics cannot be taken seriously. He
never analyzes the material interest of the Northern bourgeoise and the
farmers in the antislavery struggle. If he did, the entire abolitionist
ideology would emerge as only one part of a wider opposition not so
much to slavery as the power of the planters. The failure of Reconstruction resulted not from the failure of the antislavery forces to understand the special psychological needs of the freedmen but from the
interests of the social forces that emerged triumphant from the Civil
War. . . .

The peaceful solution in the British Caribbean—as Ragatz, whom
Elkins does not cite, has shown [8] —followed from the political weakness of the ruling planters. In Brazil, the slaveowners lacked a contigu-
ous territory and were isolated and subjected to a crushing defeatism by
the failure of the Confederate cause. Elkins' attempt to relate the
slave's personality development to wider questions of political history is
not, in my judgment, worthy of his considerable talent. That which
will survive in this generally remarkable book is the ingenious analysis
of the social psychology of the slave. Whatever the criticisms of that
analysis, it is a splendid beginning.

NOTES

1. He assumes that such a widely accepted stereotype must have some
validity, but this assumption is open to challenge. See John Harding, *et al.*,
"Prejudice and Ethnic Relations," *Handbook of Social Psychology*, ed. Gardner

Lindzey (2 Vols.; Cambridge, 1954), II, 1021-62, esp. p. 1024. Elkins does not bother to array evidence in support of his thesis that the slave did correspond to the Sambo stereotype. Yet, anyone familiar with the sources must concede that plenty of evidence exists and that the thesis is at least defensible.

2. Elkins draws heavily, with due acknowledgement on Frank Tannenbaum's important essay *Slave and Citizen* (New York, 1948), which admirably contrasts slavery in the United States with that in Latin America.

Elkins does not always make adequate use of the literature. He does not appear to read Portuguese; at least the only Brazilian works cited are those that have been translated. Such important studies as those of João Dornas Filho, Aderbal Jurema, and Bandeira de Mello are not cited. Note, for instance, that he mentions the participation of Moslem slaves in the Brazilian uprisings and the opposition of the Church to the importation of Moslems as slaves. Yet he attributes the ban on the importation of Moslems purely to religious pressure. There is reason to believe, as various studies point out, that the ban was largely due to the secular desire to shut out an ideology of rebellion.

Although Spanish works were consulted, there are important omissions. Of course, not every book read was cited, but Elkins often makes hasty generalizations that one suspects would not have been made if he had read as much as he might have.

3. Some of the Church plantations were noted for their cruelty toward the slaves. See, *e.g.*, Donald Pierson, *Negroes in Brazil, A Study of Race Contact at Bahia* (Chicago, 1932), pp. 54 f.

4. The word "childlike" is used by Elkins to mean docile, but even infants show ambivalence and hostility, as Elkins surely knows. Consideration of only one side of behavior patterns often leads him into trouble, as I shall try to show.

5. Similarly, he glosses over the tremendous number of exceptions to his generalizations about concentration camp inmates. Elkins does not do justice to the sections of Eugen Kogon's *The Theory and Practice of Hell* (New York, 1950) that discuss underground organization, resistance, and divergent personality patterns.

6. *Cf.*, Raymond A. Bauer and Alice H. Bauer, "Day to Day Resistance to Slavery," *Journal of Negro History* XXVII (Oct., 1942), 388-419; Bell Irvin Wiley, *Southern Negroes, 1861–1865* (New Haven, 1938).

7. G. W. F. Hegel, *The Phenomenology of Mind,* trans, J. B. Baillie (2nd ed. rev.; London, 1949), pp. 229-40. Hegel's chapter may prove even more fruitful as a starting point for an analysis of the social psychology of the master class.

8. Lowell Joseph Ragatz, *The Fall of the Planter Class in the British Caribbean, 1763–1833* (New York, 1928). Chapters I and II, for instance, give an excellent account of the political and economic dependence of the planters on the London interests.

On Eugene D. Genovese's *The Political Economy of Slavery: Studies in the Economy and Society of the Slave South*

STANLEY M. ELKINS

There was a time when Charles Beard's "Second American Revolution" chapter in *The Rise of American Civilization* passed for a "Marxist" interpretation of the Civil War, even with Marxists who ought to have known better. Beard argued that the "so-called Civil War" was no mere clash over constitutional principles or the morality of holding slaves. It was a revolutionary upheaval

> ending in the unquestioned establishment of a new power in the government, making vast changes in the arrangement of classes, in the accumulation and distribution of wealth, in the course of industrial development, and in the Constitution inherited from the Fathers. . . . Viewed under the light of universal history, the fighting was a fleeting incident; the social revolution was the essential portentous outcome.

But such language, which seemed to imply a line of interpretation suggested a half-century earlier by Marx and Engels themselves—that the American Civil War might best be understood as a struggle between an expanding, bourgeois North and a static, semi-feudal South—was misleading. For all his talk about underlying economic forces and social revolution, Beard found the classic Benthamite pleasure-pain calculus far more congenial to his own habits of mind than any Marxian dialectic. He could never grasp the subtle relationship between class interest, ideological conviction, and political action which Marx and Engels insisted upon. That a man living in a society wherein wealth, status, and self-esteem all rested on the possession of slaves might come to believe that slavery was a just and humane institution, and that such a man could be prepared on moral grounds to fight for its preservation, was a view of human psychology which Beard found incomprehensible. For Beard to see the connection between economic interest and political action, something more had to be at stake than "mere" ideological conviction, or even conviction rooted in the primary economic interests of a ruling class. He would finally conclude that the real key was not slavery at all (for all the bitter polemics, men never say what they really mean), but rather the tariffs, ship subsidies, bounties, and banking legislation (all "hard" things) that an industrializing North demanded and that an agrarian South, still in control of the federal government, could not afford to grant.

Eugene Genovese's *The Political Economy of Slavery* is an effort, by one far better versed in Marxist theory than Beard ever was, to put the argument back on the track and to reconsider the problem of meaningful connections between fundamental economic forces and the coming of the Civil War. Genovese is much too intelligent to pose the matter in terms of specific clashes of interest between North and South. Such clashes, in the light of the broader context, certainly created irritation but they were hardly central. What *was* central was the position of slave labor in the Southern economy. Bound up with this was, on the one hand, the slaveholder's power to impose himself and his values on Southern society, and, on the other, the inherent weakness of slavery as a labor system. "Slavery," according to Genovese, "gave the South a social system and a civilization with a distinct class structure, political community, economy, ideology, and set of psychological patterns [that set the South increasingly apart] from the rest of the nation and from the rapidly developing sections of the world." This happened because slavery was more than a system of labor. It was

> the foundation on which rose a powerful and remarkable social class: a class constituting only a tiny portion of the white population and yet so powerful and remarkable as to try, with more success than our neo-abolitionists care to see, to build a new, or rather to rebuild an old, civilization.

And yet that system upon which their economy, indeed their entire civilization, rested was woefully inefficient.

This fatal weakness, the full implication of which was the last thing the Southern elite was prepared to face, occupies most of the essays in Genovese's sharply and often brilliantly argued book. The slave was a careless and slovenly worker who needed constant supervision and could be trusted with only the most primitive of tools. He was especially hopeless at such work as animal husbandry, which required close attention and some sense of personal initiative. Southern agriculture had already completely adjusted to its labor force. It discouraged innovation, since the slave could barely cope with existing technology; it largely ignored crop rotation, which made economic sense only in conjunction with a thriving livestock industry; and it concentrated its energies on a few staples, mainly cotton, finding it cheaper to import food from the West. The result was a steady decline, which the planters were helpless to remedy, in the fertility of Southern soils.

Serious agricultural reform would have required skilled labor and commercial fertilizer, neither of which the South could afford; and a shift from cotton to truck would have required urban markets and proper transportation, neither of which the South had developed nor, with its existing economy, could hope to develop. The South's economic impasse, in short, was fundamental. It could only be remedied by measures which would have undermined the power and influence of the slaveholding elite. Such measures—emancipation, urban development, the systematic use of slaves in industry—would destroy the very thing the dominant class in the South had committed itself to building, an aristocratic, semi-feudal plantation society.

The one alternative that did not directly challenge the existing social arrangements was territorial expansion. If slave labor could be used on fresh lands in Cuba or Central America, or possibly in Western mines where it could be rigidly supervised and guarded, the South's most pressing problems might at least be postponed, if not solved. But when the Republican party moved to block even this distant hope, the stage was set for insurrection. The planters "could never agree to renounce the foundations of their power and moral sensibility and to undergo a metamorphosis into a class the nature and values of which were the inversion of their own." Given the choice of slipping into the bourgeoisie or fighting, they fought.

I am thoroughly persuaded by Genovese's analysis of the South's agricultural economy. He spells out the weakness of Southern farming in such specific terms as hogs that weighed from forty to fifty per cent less than those in the Midwest, a pitifully low production of butter and milk throughout the lower South, and a livestock industry so poorly managed that the South had to import substantial amounts of meat even though more than half of the country's cattle were located within its borders. He shows at every point the direct connection between such problems and slavery, and how the entire region was trapped by its commitment to a labor system both inefficient and economically stultifying—a dilemma doubly painful in view of the dynamic, expanding economies of the North and Midwest. Moreover, Genovese's discussion of the importance of territorial expansion in Southern thinking makes sense out of the South's seemingly irrational response to the free-soil movement and the Republican party.

Though his tone is frequently polemical, Genovese is always open-minded and flexible, and quite above squabbling with his many predecessors and contemporaries who have written on this same subject. His scholarship, indeed, is so thoroughly scrupulous that I believe it can be depended upon to reinforce conclusions quite different from his. He argues, in effect, that the plantation society of the ante-bellum South reflected a flawed form of latter-day feudalism, and that the flaw was slavery. A very slight change of definition would not in the least disturb the edifice of Genovese's scholarship, though I suppose it would threaten all his most basic theoretical convictions. Still, it seems to me just as plausible—indeed, more so—to say instead that the South reflected a flawed form of capitalism, and that the flaw was race.

Genovese's thesis that a dominant class can by an act of will "rebuild an old civilization" strikes me as gravely unhistorical. He argues that once a class becomes dominant in an economic order it is then in a position not only to impose its recently acquired values, standards, and beliefs on the entire society but also to shed its own past values with relatively little strain. The Southern planters had inherited a republican, bourgeois, contractual society many of whose intellectuals, such as Jefferson and Madison, continued to receive the deference of the ante-bellum South. To believe that these planters could in a single generation impose a set of quasi-feudal values and social arrangements on themselves and on the rest of society—that they could reverse the tide of history—is in itself almost an act of faith.

There were certainly Southerners who did think in such terms. George Fitzhugh was one, though I suspect Fitzhugh's relationship to the planter class was not unlike that between Barry Goldwater and today's business corporations—of a man who may be acceptable as a ceremonial spokesman but whose intellectual prescriptions are almost worthless as a basis for predicting actual behavior and polities. I am reluctant to take the Fitzhughs with a fully straight face, and in any case, I question the depth of the South's commitment to an organic, semi-feudal society in which both status and social responsibility would be fixed by law and custom.

Genovese is of the opinion that the South's basic values were "pre-capitalistic," and that even the aggressive "cotton snobs" of Alabama and Mississippi only needed a little time to wear down their rough edges before slipping naturally into the ranks of the aristocracy. But planting was a speculative business, and few planters were ever free from the shadow of crop failure and bankruptcy. What sort of aristocratic ethos is it possible to construct in a community where one or two bad crops can change a man from a rural magnate into just another farmer? How much mobility, in either direction or both, can a society absorb and still be described as semi-feudal?

Genovese explains the planters' desperate fear of emancipation by their determination to maintain the particular labor system on which depended their class position and their dreams of an organic feudal order. But the special quality of their desperation strikes me as very unfeudal. Their values were not those of a human organic community at all; they were far too bourgeois. Nobody could really see the Negro as an organic member, because every systematic effort had been made to define him as outside that community—as property. The underlying egalitarianism in Southern values was such, and the South's faith in barriers between classes was so limited, that once the Negro's bonds of chattel slavery were removed and once he was redefined as human, the first thing he was likely to do, for all anyone knew, was to marry somebody's daughter.

A true sense of stratified social hierarchy—as in Latin America, where the historical background was genuinely "feudal"—would have protected the Southerners from any such nightmare. They had no real faith in the justice of stability of their community, or any willingness to offer adequate human compensations for all of its members; no one could imagine the Negroes as a "loyal peasantry." An axiom of slave law was that if the master's power were relaxed in any way whatever, the whole system would collapse.

The Southern slaveholders, Genovese says, were a vital and dynamic class determined to create—or recreate—a society, and when it appeared that they were not to succeed, they fought rather than give up a cherished way of life. I should say they were a pathetic class, trapped by history, their minds frozen by the dilemma of race in a bourgeois culture. Their status, power, and pride, says Genovese, depended on their ownership of slaves, whose labor, as he shows so well, was under existing conditions very inefficient and less and less profitable. I should say that the irrational role of race in a contractual society, which defined the black slave as property, created such a narrow view of the Negro that the slaveholder could no longer be inventive. He could only develop a rigid and unimaginative system of labor and then try to justify it as a "way of life," even though it may be doubted whether in his heart he ever really believed it.

Otherwise, why the unwillingness to manipulate, to experiment? Why not some alternative arrangement short of full emancipation? A program of placing slaves and their families on individual plots of land? With some independence and adequate incentives, could they not have proven as efficient at growing cotton or caring for animals as they were in raising chickens or tending their gardens? Since this would in fact be done after emancipation, we know there was no inherent reason why it should not have worked. Indeed, all the precedents of feudalism pointed straight in that direction.

Instead, the South created for the slave the role of a helpless, pathetic dependent, insisted that he live up to it, and then justified the system to itself and to the world by claiming that the helpless Negro could survive under no other. But with slavery under attack from literally everywhere—destructive to retain, destructive to get rid of— it became an intolerable burden, and many a planter said so. This was the kind of tension that produced the Fitzhughs and the paranoia of the 1850's.

I agree with Genovese that the South's decision to fight represented the planters' final, superhuman effort in defense of slavery. I have followed his argument with admiration, and hold his skill and learning in the very highest respect. But I should think the test of the argument would be what happened after they lost their cherished institution. The reaction, if I read my postwar history right, was one of universal relief. For all the exasperating lost-cause sentimentalism of the New South, there was hardly a trace of an *ancien régime* mentality regarding slavery. "I am rejoiced," declared Robert E. Lee (along with many another aristocrat), "that slavery is abolished." George Fitzhugh was quickly forgotten. Slavery was gone; the South did not want to get it back; and no Southern leader, not the most passionate of the ante-bellum defenders, seriously proposed trying.

But they did set to work all over again, being just as implacably determined as they ever were, to avert what they had been convinced all along would be the real disaster, a mingling of two racial communities under a single set of standards. In this, as we know, they succeeded. Race was always the flaw in Southern capitalism, as it is still.

On David Brion Davis's *The Problem of Slavery in Western Culture*

M. I. FINLEY

In the year AD 61 the prefect of the city of Rome, Pedanius Secundus, was murdered by one of the slaves in his town house. Under the law, not only the culprit but all the other slaves in the household had to be executed, in this instance numbering four hundred. There was a popular outcry and the Senate debated the question. Some senators rose to plead clemency, but the day was carried by the distinguished jurist, Gaius Cassius Longinus, who argued that all change from ancestral law and customs is always for the worse. When a mob tried to prevent the sentence from being carried out, the emperor personally intervened on the side of the law, though he rejected another proposal that Pedanius ex-slaves should also be punished by banishment. That, he said, would be unnecessary cruelty.

The emperor was Nero and it has been suggested that one of the unsuccessful advocates of mercy may have been his closest adviser, the Stoic philosopher Seneca, in whose writings there are some powerful passages calling for the treatment of slaves as fellow-humans. Not once, however, did Seneca suggest that the institution itself was so immoral that it ought to be abolished. For that radical idea the western world still had to wait more than 1500 years, while philosophers, moralists, theologians, and jurists—save for an isolated voice here and there to whom no one listened—discovered and propagated a variety of formulas which satisfied them and society at large that a man could be both a thing and a man at the same time. This ambiguity or "dualism" is the "problem of slavery" to which Professor Davis has devoted a large, immensely learned, readable, exciting, disturbing, and sometimes frustrating volume, one of the most important to have been published on the subject of slavery in modern times.

The genesis of the book was a modest one. Professor Davis set out to make a comparative study of British and American antislavery movements. Gradually he began to appreciate that "the problem of slavery transcended national boundaries" in ways he "had not suspected." Slavery was brought to the New World at a time when it had disappeared from most of Europe; yet there were no hesitations, no gropings, because the heritage of the Bible, classical philosophy, and Roman law provided a ready-made set of regulations and a ready-made ideology. Differences within the New World, between the Anglo-Saxons in the north and the Latins in the south, between Protestant and Catholic colonies, appeared, on closer examination, to be tangential and far less significant than "their underlying patterns of unity." On this particular topic Professor Davis has now come forward with powerful support for a recent trend in scholarship running counter to the romantic idealized image of Latin American slavery, and in particular of race relationship in the southern hemisphere, which had long prevailed, a view perhaps best known from the works of the Brazilian Gilberto Freyre and from Frank Tannenbaum's seminal little book *Slave and Citizen*. In short, Professor Davis came to the conclusion that "there was more institutional continuity between ancient and modern slavery than has generally been supposed" and that "slavery has always raised certain fundamental problems that originated in the simple fact that the slave is a man."

From this conclusion a new and fundamental question followed. If the "legal and moral validity of slavery was a troublesome question in European thought from the time of Aristotle to the time of Locke," why was it that not until the 1770s were there "forces in motion that would lead to organized movement to abolish . . . the entire institutional framework which permitted human beings to be treated as things"? This development, he rightly says, "was something new to the world." Slavery had declined markedly in the later Roman Empire, not as a result of an abolitionist movement but in consequence of complex social and economic changes which replaced the chattel slave by a different kind of bondsman, the *colonus*, the *adscriptus glebi*, the serf. Modern slavery, in contrast, did not become slowly transformed. It was abolished by force and violence. Attempts to picture "anti-slavery and efforts to Christianize and ameliorate the condition of slaves as parts of a single swelling current of humanitarianism" falsify the historical record. "All such dreams and hopes ran aground on the simple and solid fact, which for centuries had been obscured by philosophy and law, that a slave was not a piece of property, nor a half-human instrument, but a man held down by force."

The book Professor Davis started to write was thus converted into a large project of which this is the first volume (though a self-contained one) carrying the story from antiquity to the early 1770s. The story, it must be stressed, is essentially one in the history of ideas. "A problem of moral perception" is how he himself phrases it.

> This book . . . makes no pretense of being a history of slavery as such, or even of opinion concerning slavery . . . I have been concerned with the different ways in which men have responded to slavery, on the assumption that this will help us to distinguish what was unique in the response of the abolitionist. I have also been concerned with traditions in thought and value from which both opponents and defenders of slavery could draw. I hope to demonstrate the slavery has always been a source of social and psychological tension, but that in Western culture it was associated with certain religious and philosophical doctrines that gave it the highest sanction.

As an essay in the history of ideas—more precisely, of ideology, a word which Professor Davis curiously shies away from—the book is brilliant, filled with detail yet never losing control of the main threads, subtle and sophisticated and penetrating. Even the relatively brief and derivative first part, on ancient and medieval thinking, has some fine insights. Then, with the discovery of America, Professor Davis comes into his own. No man, surely, has read so much or so deeply on the subject: the footnotes provide the most complete bibliography we have; too complete indeed, and one wishes he had been more discriminating in his selection of titles. It is impossible in a review to survey the ground covered or the multiplicity of fresh ideas and suggestions. But an example or two will indicate how complicated is the counterpoint that is woven throughout around the "dualism" concept. Early on the *leitmotif* emerges. The question is posed as to why in the later Roman Empire and the early Middle Ages, when "slavery all but disappeared from most parts of the Europe," we do not find "the Church turning away from its compromises with the Roman world and using its great moral power to hasten a seemingly beneficial change." Professor Davis answers:

> The most plausible explanation would seem to lie in the complex network of mental associations, derived from antiquity, which connnected slavery with ideas of sin, subordination, and the divine order of the world. To question the ethical basis of slavery, even when the institution was disappearing from view, would be to question fundamental conceptions of God's purpose and man's history and destiny. If slavery were an evil and performed no divinely appointed function, then why had God authorized

it in Scripture and permitted it to exist in nearly every nation? If slavery violated the natural law of equality and the divine law of human brotherhood, could not the same be said of the family, private property, social orders, and government?

The heretical sects were a threat all the time, for they seized on those ideas implicit in Christianity "that were potentially explosive when torn from their protective casings and ignited in the charged atmosphere of class rivalry and discontent." They had to be contained, and they were. Not until the middle of the eighteenth century did an English sect finally take a firm official stand against slavery (while the Church of England remained indifferent). The Quakers came to that after a long period of inner conflict on the subject, but by then society had been so transformed that the moral issues acquired new practical implications.

> In a period of intense soul-searching, of desire for self-purification and of concern over their image in the eyes of others, a decision to refrain from dealing in slaves was a means of reasserting the perfectionist content of their faith. It was a way of proscribing a form of selfish economic activity without repudiating the search for wealth; . . . a way of affirming the individual's moral will, and the historic mission of the church, without challenging the basic structure of the social order.

So bald a summary invites the charge of mere cynicism, but nothing would be more unjust. Behind the summaries lie meticulous accounts of the intense intellectual and moral struggles that went on in the search for a moral position. In all societies which are characterized by class or national conflicts and divergence of interests, ideology is necessarily ambivalent. No account is adequate which fails to reveal how ideology serves both to criticize and to preserve the social order at the same time, and the careless or blinkered observer automatically dismisses as cynicism any analysis which gives due weight to the second function. On the subject of slavery, the crowning paradox is that the rationalist attack on Christian theology in the eighteenth century brought the slave no nearer to freedom. Locke had already shown how a defense of slavery could be reconciled with natural rights. Now, "insofar as the Enlightenment divorced anthropology and comparative anatomy from theological assumptions, it opened the way for theories of racial inferiority."

And yet, at the point where this book ends, anti-slavery *had* become a program and eventually it was to become a successful major political issue. Slavery *was* finally abolished in the West. Why? It is on that decisive question that I find Professor Davis's account frustrating. "For some two thousand years men thought of sin as a kind of slavery. One day they would come to think of slavery as sin." Who are "they"? "By the early 1770s a large number of moralists, poets, intellectuals, and reformers had come to regard American slavery as an unmitigated evil." It is only a little unfair to remind Professor Davis of Jim Farley's remark, towards the close of Adlai Stevenson's first presidential campaign. Someone at a party was being jubilant over the fact that nearly all intellectuals were for Stevenson. "All sixty thousand of them," retorted Farley. Moralists, poets, intellectuals, and reformers did not destroy slavery. The Civil War did that, and Professor Davis himself has, as a by-product, delivered a crushing blow against the "unnecessary conflict" school of historians. I do not, of course, wish to deny the essential role of several generations of abolitionists. But nothing did or could happen until their moral fervor became translated into political and military action, and how that came about cannot be answered by the history of ideas. Nothing is more difficult perhaps than to explain how and why, or why not, a new moral perception becomes effective in action. Yet nothing is more urgent if an academic historical exercise is to become a significant investigation of human behavior with direct relevance to the world we now live in.

It would be gross injustice to call this book an academic historical exercise or to suggest that Professor Davis is unaware of the central question. Throughout the volume there are sharp comments very much to the point. In a brief note on the rather mechanical economic explanations in Eric Williams's *Capitalism and Slavery*, Davis joins the opposition but then adds that one cannot "get around the simple fact that no country thought of abolishing the slave trade until its economic value had considerably declined." He knows and uses the most recent discussions (down to Eugene Genovese's *Political Economy of Slavery*, published in 1965) of the profitability of slavery and its effects on economic growth. He agrees that it is "theoretically possible" that such divergences with respect to freed slaves as existed between North and South America "had less to do with the character of slavery in the two countries than with economic and social structures which defined the relations between colored freedmen and the dominant white society." He mentions the wars of the eighteenth century and the changes in the balance of power, which "brought a growing awareness of the instability and inefficiency of the old colonial system." And it may be that what I am looking for will find its proper place in the next volumes.

Yet the fact remains that the comments I have just quoted are really asides, often relegated to footnotes, and I do not think it is a sufficient defense that a man has a right to choose his own subject, in this case the history of ideas. Slavery is not an autonomous system; it is an institution embedded in a social structure. It is no longer the same institution when the structure is significantly altered, and ideas about slavery have to be examined structurally too. Only by remaining in the realm of abstractions can Professor Davis lay so much emphasis on the "institutional continuity" between ancient and modern slavery. He is in consequence led astray on several important aspects. His account of slavery among the Hebrews and other ancient Near Eastern societies suffers from precisely the weakness he has so effectively exposed in the case of Latin American slavery. He has allowed his authorities to mislead him into taking at face value pious hopes which he penetrates easily when they appear in Seneca or modern writers. And he has misjudged the social ambience by failing to appreciate sufficiently that for most of human history labor for others has been involuntary (quite apart from compulsions exercised by either family or wage-earning, which are of a different order from the kind of force that is the final sanction against slaves, serfs, peons, debt bondsmen, coolies, or untouchables). Slavery in that context must have different overtones from slavery in a context of free labor. The way slavery declined in the Roman Empire, to repeat an example I have already given, illustrates that. Neither moral values nor economic interests nor the social order were threatened by the transformation of slaves and free peasants together into tied serfs. They were—or at least many powerful elements in society thought they were —by proposals to convert slaves into free men.

What sets the slave apart from all other forms of involuntary labor is that, in the strictest sense, he is an outsider. He is brought into a new society violently and traumatically; he is cut off from all traditional human ties of kin and nation and even his own religion; he is prevented, insofar as that is possible, from creating new ties, except to his masters, and in consequence his descendants are as much outsiders, as unrooted, as he was. The final proof of non-status is the free sexual access to slaves which is a fundamental condition of all slavery (with complex exceptions in the rules regarding access of free females to slave males). When Professor Davis writes, "Bondwomen have always been the victims of sexual exploitation, which was perhaps the clearest recognition of their humanity," he has stood the situation on its head. Sexual *exploitation* is a denial, not a recognition, of a woman's humanity, whether she is slave or free.

I have stated the slave-outsider formula schematically and therefore too rigidly. Structural differences emerge clearly when one considers how much societies have differed with respect to the freed slave. At one extreme stood Rome, which not only allowed almost unlimited rights to individual masters to free their slaves but which also automatically enrolled the freedmen as citizens if their owners were citizens. At the other extreme was the American South. Professor Davis produces evidence that by 1860 there were more free Negroes, even in the South, than is often realized. Nevertheless, the emancipation process was hemmed in by very stringent regulations. And the fate of the freed slave in the United States hardly needs spelling out. What does need a careful look is the question of color, which is too central to be evaded out of sentimentality and on which Professor Davis has an important chapter (as usual, in the realm of ideas). Dr. Williams holds that "slavery was not born of racism, rather, racism was the consequence of slavery." One wishes profoundly that one could believe that. However, the slave-outsider formula argues the other way, as does the fact that as early as the 1660s southern colonies decreed that henceforth all Negroes who were imported should be slaves, but whites should be indentured servants and not slaves. The connection between slavery and racism has been a dialectical one, in which each element reinforced the other.

Racism has already outlived slavery by a century. Why, we are entitled to ask, did the "revolutionary shift in attitudes towards sin, human nature, and progress," which we may concede to have been a necessary condition of antislavery, not extend to racism? Is slavery any more a sin than the denial of civil rights, concentration camps, Hiroshima, napalm, torture in Algeria, or apartheid in South Africa or Rhodesia? Why did the new moral perception succeed in wiping out one sin and not the others? It is that question which makes this book a profoundly disturbing one. There is cold comfort here for anyone who trusts to the slow ameliorative process of a growing humanitarianism, of the "progressive development of man's moral sense" which Thomas Jefferson found in history. In Professor Davis's lapidary phrase, "faith in progress smothered [Jefferson's] sense of urgency" when it came to slavery.

A Selected Modern Bibliography

General Works

State and Local Studies of Slavery
    The North
    The South

The Antebellum Negro and the Problem of Race
    General studies
    Patterns of slave resistance
    Race relations
    Special studies

The Old South
    The slave trade
    General studies
    Special studies
    Collections and edited volumes

Guides to Further Reading
    Historiography
    Bibliographic aids

American Slavery in World Perspective
    Greece and Rome
    Latin America
    Other cultures

GENERAL WORKS

Alfred H. Conrad and J. R. Meyers, *The Economics of Slavery and Other Studies in Economic History* (Chicago, 1964).

David Brion Davis, *The Problem of Slavery in Western Culture* (Ithaca, 1966).

Thomas E. Drake, *Quakers and Slavery in America* (New Haven, 1950).

Stanley M. Elkins, *Slavery, A Problem in American Institutional and Intellectual Life* (Chicago, 1959).

Eugene D. Genovese, *The Political Economy of Slavery: Studies in the Economy and Society of the Slave South* (New York, 1965).

Barnett Hollander, *Slavery in America: Its Legal History* (New York, 1963).

Herbert S. Klein, *Slavery in the Americas: A Comparative Study of Cuba and Virginia* (Chicago, 1967).

Donald G. Mathews, *Slavery and Methodism: A Chapter in American Morality, 1780–1845* (Princeton, 1965).

Richard B. Morris, *Government and Labor in Early America* (New York, 1946).

Ulrich B. Phillips, *American Negro Slavery* (New York, 1918).

————, *Life and Labor in the Old South* (Boston, 1929).

Abbot Emerson Smith, *Colonists in Bondage: White Servitude and Convict Labor in America, 1607–1776* (Chapel Hill, 1947).

Kenneth M. Stampp, *The Peculiar Institution: Slavery in the Ante-bellum South* (New York, 1956).

Frank Tannenbaum, *Slave and Citizen: The Negro in the Americas* (New York, 1946).

Eric Williams, *Capitalism and Slavery* (Chapel Hill, 1944).

Arthur Zilversmit, *The First Emancipation: The Abolition of Negro Slavery in the North* (Chicago, 1967).

STATE AND LOCAL STUDIES OF SLAVERY

THE NORTH

Gwendolyn Evans Logan, "The Slave in Connecticut During the Revolution," *Connecticut Historical Society Bulletin*, XXX (July 1965).

Richard C. Twombly and Robert H. Moore, "Black Puritan: The Negro in Seventeenth-Century Massachusetts," *William and Mary Quarterly*, 3rd Series, XXIV (April 1967).

Lorenzo J. Greene, *The Negro in Colonial New England, 1620–1776* (New York, 1942).

Edgar J. McManus, *A History of Negro Slavery in New York* (Syracuse, N.Y., 1966).

THE SOUTH

Richard C. Wade, *Slavery in the Cities, The South, 1820–1860* (New York, 1964).

Charles S. Davis, *The Cotton Kingdom in Alabama* (Montgomery, Ala., 1939).

Weymouth T. Jordan, *Ante-Bellum Alabama, Town and Country* (Tallahassee, Fla., 1957).

James B. Sellers, *Slavery in Alabama* (Tuscaloosa, Ala., 1950).

Orville W. Taylor, *Negro Slavery in Arkansas* (Durham, N.C., 1958).

John A. Munroe, "The Negro in Delaware," *South Atlantic Quarterly*, LVI (1957).

William G. Proctor, Jr., "Slavery in Southwest Georgia," *Georgia Historical Quarterly*, XLIX (March 1965).

J. Winston Coleman, Jr., *Slavery Times in Kentucky* (Chapel Hill, 1940).

Joseph Karl Menn, *The Large Slaveholders of Louisiana, 1860* (New Orleans, 1964).

V. A. Moody, "Slavery on Louisiana Sugar Plantations," *Louisiana Historical Quarterly*, VII (1924).

John Milton Price, "Slavery in Winn Parish," *Louisiana History*, VIII (Spring 1967).

Robert C. Reinders, "Slavery in New Orleans in the Decade Before the Civil War," *Mid-America*, XLIV (October 1962).

Roger Shugg, *Origins of Class Struggle in Louisiana . . . 1840–1875* (Baton Rouge, La., 1939).

Charles S. Sydnor, *Slavery in Mississippi* (New York, 1933).

Lyle W. Dorsett, "Slaveholding in Jackson County, Missouri," *Bulletin of the Missouri Historical Society*, XX (October 1963).

Guion G. Johnson, *Ante-Bellum North Carolina: A Social History* (Chapel Hill, 1937).

Edward W. Phifer, "Slavery in Microcosm: Burke County, North Carolina," *Journal of Southern History* XXVIII (May 1962).

Rosser H. Taylor, *Slaveholding in North Carolina* (1926).

Robert E. Corlew, "Some Aspects of Slavery in Dickson County," *Tennessee Historical Quarterly*, X (September-December 1951).

Chase C. Mooney, *Slavery in Tennessee* (Bloomington, 1957).

Earl W. Fornell, "The Abduction of Free Negroes and Slaves in Texas," *Southwestern Historical Quarterly* (January 1957).

George R. Woolfolk, "Cotton Capitalism and Slave Labor in Texas," *Southern Social Science Quarterly* (June 1956).

————, "Sources of the History of the Negro in Texas, With Special Reference to Their Implications for Research in Slavery," *Journal of Negro History*, XLII (January 1957).

Susie M. Ames, *Studies of the Virginia Eastern Shore in the Seventeenth Century* (Richmond, Va., 1940).

Robert McColley, *Slavery and Jeffersonian Virginia* (Urbana, Ill., 1964).

Joseph Clarke Robert, *The Road from Monticello: A Study of the Virginia Slavery Debate of 1832* (Durham, N.C., 1941).

Constance McLaughlin Green, *Washington, Village and Capital, 1800–1878* (Princeton, 1962).

A number of older studies, many originally published as part of the Johns Hopkins University series of historical studies, are still useful to modern historians of the question. Among them are the following:

Bernard C. Steiner, *History of Slavery in Connecticut* (Baltimore, 1893).

Edward Ingle, *The Negro in the District of Columbia* (Baltimore, 1893).

N. Dwight Harris, *The History of Negro Servitude in Illinois, 1719–1864* (Chicago, 1904).

Ivan E. McDougle, *Slavery in Kentucky, 1792–1865* (Lancaster, Pa., 1918).

John H. T. McPherson, *History of Liberia* (Baltimore, 1891).

Jeffrey R. Brackett, *The Negro in Maryland* (Baltimore, 1904).
Eugene I. McCormac, *White Servitude in Maryland* (Baltimore, 1904).

Harrison A. Trexler, *Slavery in Missouri, 1804–1865* (Baltimore, 1914).

Henry S. Cooley, *Slavery in New Jersey* (Baltimore, 1896).
Edward Raymond Turner, *The Negro in Pennsylvania, 1639–1861* (American Historical Association, 1911).

John S. Bassett, *History of Slavery in North Carolina* (Baltimore, 1899).
R. H. Taylor, *Slaveholding in North Carolina: An Economic View* (Chapel Hill, 1926).

H. M. Henry, *Police Control of the Slave in South Carolina* (Emory, Va., 1914; Ph.D. Thesis, Vanderbilt University).
Edson L. Whitney, *Government in the Colony of South Carolina* (Baltimore, 1895).

Caleb P. Patterson, *The Negro in Tennessee, 1790–1865* (Austin, Texas, 1922).

THE ANTEBELLUM NEGRO AND THE PROBLEM OF RACE

GENERAL STUDIES

Herbert Aptheker, *A Documentary History of the Negro People in the United States*, 2 vols. (New York, 1951).
————, *Essays in the History of the American Negro* (New York, 1964).
Richard Bardolph, *The Negro Vanguard* (New York, 1959).
Benjamin F. Botkin (ed.), *Lay My Burden Down: A Folk History of Slavery* (Chicago, 1945).
Helen T. Catterall (ed.), *Judicial Cases Concerning American Slavery and the Negro*, 5 vols. (Washington, 1926–37).

Basil Davidson, *The Lost Cities of Africa* (Boston, 1959).

Dædalus, *The Negro in America*, 2 vols. (1966).

Leslie Fishel and Benjamin Quarles (eds.), *The Negro American: A Documentary History* (Chicago, 1967).

John Hope Franklin, *From Slavery to Freedom: A History of American Negroes*, 2nd ed., rev. (New York, 1963).

E. Franklin Frazier, *The Negro in the United States*, 2nd ed. (New York, 1957).

J. C. Furnas, *Goodbye to Uncle Tom* (New York, 1956).

Oscar Handlin, *Race and Nationality in American Life* (Boston, 1957).

Melville J. Herskovits, *The Myth of the Negro Past* (New York, London, 1941.)

Winthrop D. Jordan, *White Over Black: The Development of American Attiiuɹes ɹoward the Negro, 1550–1812* (Chapel Hill, 1968).

Abram Kardiner and Lionel Ovesey, *The Mark of Oppression; A Psycho-Social Study of the American Negro* (New York, 1951).

Leon Litwack, *North of Slavery: The Negro in the Free States, 1790–1860* (Chicago, 1961).

Gunnar Myrdal et al., *An American Dilemma; The Negro Problem and Modern Democracy*, 2 vols. (New York, London, 1944).

Charles H. Nichols, *Many Thousand Gone: The Ex-Slaves' Account of Their Bondage and Freedom* (Leiden, 1963).

Talcott Parsons and Kenneth B. Clark (eds.), *The Negro American* (New York, 1967).

Newton M. Puckett, *Folk Beliefs of the Southern Negro* (Chapel Hill, 1926).

"The Question of 'Sambo,'" A Report of the Ninth Newberry Library Conference on American Studies, *The Newberry Library Bulletin*, V (December 1958).

Carter Woodson, *The Mind of the Negro as Reflected in Letters Written during the Crisis, 1800–1860* (Washington, 1926).

Carter G. Woodson and Charles H. Wesley, *The Negro in Our History*, 10th ed. (Washington, 1962).

PATTERNS OF SLAVE RESISTANCE

Herbert Aptheker, *American Negro Slave Revolts* (New York, 1943).

———, *Nat Turner's Slave Rebellion . . .* (New York, 1966).

Raymond A. Bauer and Alice H. Bauer, "Day to Day Resistance to Slavery," *Journal of Negro History*, XXVII (October 1942).

Joseph C. Carroll, *Slave Insurrections in the United States, 1800–1865* (Boston, 1938).

Larry Gara, *The Liberty Line: The Legend of the Underground Railroad* (Lexington, Ky., 1961).

Nicholas Halasz, *The Rattling Chains: Slave Unrest and Revolt in the Antebellum South* (New York, 1966).

F. Roy Johnson, *The Nat Turner Slave Insurrection* (Murfreesboro, N.C., 1966).

Manon D. de B. Kilson, "Towards Freedom: An Analysis of Slave Revolts in the United States," *Phylon*, XXV, No. 2 (1964).

John Lofton, *Insurrection in South Carolina: The Turbulent World of Denmark Vesey* (Yellow Spring, Ohio, 1964).

Marion J. Russell, "American Slave Discontent in Records of the High Courts," *Journal of Negro History*, XXXI (October 1946).

Richard C. Wade, "The Vesey Plot: A Reconsideration," *Journal of Southern History*, XXX (May 1964).

Harvey Wish, "American Slave Insurrections before 1861," *The Journal of Negro History*, XXII (July 1937).

Civil War History (December 1967), Eugene Genovese, Aileen Kraditor, Christopher Lasch, and George Frederickson, articles on Elkins's *Slavery.* . . .

RACE RELATIONS

Dædalus, Color and Race (A Symposium), Spring 1967.

Carl N. Degler, "Slavery and the Genesis of American Race Prejudice," *Comparative Studies in Society and History*, II (October 1959).

Thomas F. Gossett, *Race, The History of an Idea in America* (Dallas, 1963).

Constance McLaughlin Green, *The Secret City; A History of Race Relations in the Nation's Capital* (Princeton, 1967).

Oscar and Mary Handlin, "Origins of the Southern Labor System," *William and Mary Quarterly*, 3rd Series, VII (April 1950).

Winthrop D. Jordan, "American Chiaroscuro: The Status and Definition of Mulattoes in the British Colonies," *William and Mary Quarterly*, 3rd Series, XIX (April 1962).

————, "Modern Tensions and the Origins of American Slavery," *Journal of Southern History*, XXVIII (February 1962).

Richard B. Morris, "The Measure of Bondage in the Slave States," *Mississippi Valley Historical Review*, XLI (September 1954).

Gilbert Osofsky (ed.), *The Burden of Race: A Documentary History of Negro-White Relations* (New York, 1967).

Rembert W. Patrick, *Race Relations in the South* (Tallahassee, Fla., 1958).

William R. Stanton, *The Leopard's Spots: Scientific Attitudes Toward Race in America, 1815–1859* (Chicago, 1960).

Mary W. Williams, "The Treatment of Negro Slaves in the Brazilian Empire: A Comparison with the United States," *Journal of Negro History*, XV (1930).

SPECIAL STUDIES

Dudley T. Cornish, *The Sable Arm: Negro Troops in the Union Army, 1861–1865* (New York, 1956).

Edwin A. Davis, "William Johnson: Free Negro Citizen of Ante-Bellum Mississippi," *Journal of Mississippi History*, XV (1953).

Edwin A. Davis and William R. Hogan, *The Barber of Natchez* (Baton Rouge, La., 1954).

Clement Eaton, "Slave-Hiring in the Upper South: A Step Toward Freedom," *Mississippi Valley Historical Review*, XLVI (March 1960).

Philip S. Foner, *Frederick Douglass* (New York, 1964).

John Hope Franklin, *The Free Negro in North Carolina, 1790–1860* (Chapel Hill, 1943).

Lorenzo J. Greene, *The Negro in Colonial New England, 1620–1776* (New York, 1942).

William R. Hogan and Edwin A. Davis (eds.), *William Johnson's Natchez* (Baton Rouge, La., 1951).

Luther Porter Jackson, . . . *Free Negro Labor and Property Holding in Virginia, 1830–1860* (New York, 1942).

G. B. Johnson, *Folk Culture on St. Helena Island, South Carolina* (Chapel Hill, 1930).

_____, *A Social History of the Sea Islands* (Chapel Hill, 1930).

James M. McPherson, *The Negro's Civil War; How American Negroes Felt and Acted During the War for the Union* (New York, 1965).

_____, *The Struggle for Equality; Abolitionists and the Negro in the Civil War and Reconstruction* (Princeton, 1964).

William Dostite Postell, *The Health of Slaves on Southern Plantations* (Baton Rouge, La., 1951).

Benjamin Quarles, *Frederick Douglass* (Washington, 1948).

_____, *Lincoln and the Negro* (New York, 1962).

_____, *The Negro in the American Revolution* (Williamsburg, Va., 1961).

_____, *The Negro in the Civil War* (Boston, 1953).

Willie Lee Rose, *Rehearsal for Reconstruction: The Port Royal Experiment* (Indianapolis, 1964).

M. Eugene Sirmans, "The Legal Status of the Slave in South Carolina, 1670–1740," *Journal of Southern History*, XXVIII (November 1962).

Emma L. Thornbrough, *The Negro in Indiana: A Study of a Minority* (Indianapolis, 1957).

Bell I. Wiley, *Southern Negroes, 1861–1865* (New Haven, 1938).

THE OLD SOUTH

THE SLAVE TRADE

Frederic Bancroft, *Slave-Trading in the Old South* (Baltimore, 1931).

Reginald Coupland, *The British Anti-Slavery Movement* (London, 1933).

_____, *East Africa and its Invaders* . . . (Oxford, England, 1956).

Basil Davidson, *Black Mother: The Years of the African Slave Trade* (Boston, 1961).

Kenneth G. Davies, *The Royal African Company* (London, 1957).

Elizabeth Donnan (ed.), *Documents Illustrative of the History of the Slave Trade to America*, 4 vols. (Washington, 1930–35)

W. E. B. Du Bois, *The Supression of the African Slave Trade to the United States of America, 1638–1870* (New York, 1896).

Peter Duignan and C. Clendenen, *The United States and the African Slave Trade, 1619–1862* (Stanford, Calif., 1963).

Daniel Mannix, *Black Cargoes: A History of the Atlantic Slave Trade, 1518–1865* (New York, 1962).

Wendell H. Stephenson, *Isaac Franklin, Slave Trader and Planter of the Old South* (Baton Rouge, La., 1938).

Howard S. Warren, *American Slavers and the Federal Law, 1837–1862* (Berkeley, Calif., 1963).

H. A. Wyndham, *The Atlantic and Slavery* (London, 1935).

GENERAL STUDIES

Carl Bridenbaugh, *Myths and Realities: Societies of the Colonial South* (Baton Rouge, La., 1952).
Wilbur J. Cash, *The Mind of the South* (New York, 1941).
William E. Dodd, *The Cotton Kingdom* (New Haven, 1919).
Clement Eaton, *The Growth of Southern Civilization, 1790–1860* (New York, 1961).
————, *A History of the Old South*, 2nd ed., rev. (New York, 1966).
John Hope Franklin, *The Militant South, 1800–1861* (Cambridge, Mass., 1956).
Lewis C. Gray, *History of Agriculture in the Southern United States in 1860*, 2 vols. (Washington, 1933).
Frank L. Owsley, *Plain Folk of the Old South* (Baton Rouge, La., 1949).
Fabian Linden, "Economic Democracy in the Slave South: An Appraisal of Some Recent Views," *The Journal of Negro History*, XXXI (April 1946).
Francis B. Simkins, *A History of the South*, 2nd ed., rev. (New York, 1953).
Wendell H. Stephenson, *A Basic History of the Old South* (Princeton, 1959).
————, *The South Lives in History* (Baton Rouge, La., 1955).
C. Vann Woodward, *The Burden of Southern History* (Baton Rouge, La., 1960).

SPECIAL STUDIES

Chronological

Wesley Frank Craven, *The Southern Colonies in the Seventeenth Century, 1607–1689* (Baton Rouge, La., 1949).
John R. Alden, *The South in the Revolution, 1763–1789* (Baton Rouge, La., 1957).
Thomas P. Abernethy, *The South in the New Nation, 1789–1819* (Baton Rouge, La., 1961).
William W. Freehling, *Prelude to Civil War: The Nullification Crisis in South Carolina, 1816–1836* (New York, 1966).
Charles S. Sydnor, *The Development of Southern Sectionalism, 1819–1848* (Baton Rouge, La., 1948).
Avery O. Craven, *The Growth of Southern Nationalism, 1848–1861* (Baton Rouge, La., 1953).

Topical

Aubrey C. Land, *The Dulanys of Maryland* (Baltimore, 1955).
Arthur Pierce Middleton, *Tobacco Coast: A Maritime History of Chesapeake Bay in the Colonial Era* (Newport News, Va., 1953).
Louis Morton, *Robert Carter of Nomini Hall: A Virginia Planter of the Eighteenth Century* (Williamsburg, Va., 1941).
John H. Moore, *Agriculture in Ante-Bellum Mississippi* (New York, 1958).
Joseph C. Robert, *The Tobacco Kingdom: Plantation, Market, and Factory in Virginia and North Carolina, 1800–1860* (Durham, N.C., 1938).

William K. Scarborough, *The Overseer: Plantation Management in the Old South* (Baton Rouge, La., 1966).

Joseph C. Sitterson, *Sugar Country: The Cane Sugar Industry in the South, 1753–1950* (Lexington, Ky., 1953).

Articles

Douglas F. Dowd, "A Comparative Analysis of Economic Development in the American South and West," *Journal of Economic History*, XVI (December 1956).

Stanley L. Engerman, "The Effects of Slavery Upon the Southern Economy: A Review of the Recent Debate," *Explorations in Entrepreneurial History*, 2nd Series, Vol. 4 (Winter 1967).

Ulrich B. Phillips, "The Central Theme of Southern History," *American Historical Review*, XXXIV (October 1928).

Charles Grier Sellers, Jr., "The Travail of Slavery," in Sellers (ed.), *The Southerner as American* (Chapel Hill, 1960).

Richard Stutch, "The Profitability of Ante-Bellum Slavery—Revisited," *Southern Economic Journal* (April 1965).

Edgar T. Thompson, "The Natural History of Agricultural Labor in the South," in David K. Jackson (ed.), *American Studies in Honor of William Kenneth Boyd* (Durham, N.C., 1940).

Robert W. Vogel and Stanley L. Engerman (eds.), *The Reinterpretation of American Economic History* (New York, 1968). Part VII, "The Economics of Slavery."

Harold D. Woodman, "The Profitability of Slavery: A Historical Perennial," *Journal of Southern History*, XXIX (August 1963).

COLLECTIONS AND EDITED VOLUMES

Thomas D. Clark, *Travels in the Old South: A Bibliography*, 3 vols. (Norman, Okla., 1956–59).

Katherine M. Jones (ed.), *The Plantation South* (Indianapolis, 1957).

Eric McKitrick (ed.), *Slavery Defended: The Views of the Old South* (Englewood Cliffs, N.J., 1963).

Willard Thorp (ed.), *A Southern Reader* (New York, 1955).

Ina W. Van Noppen, *The South, A Documentary History* (Princeton, 1958).

Harvey Wish (ed.), *Slavery in the South: A Collection of Contemporary Accounts . . .* (New York, 1964).

Harold D. Woodman (ed.), *Slavery and the Southern Economy* (New York, 1966).

C. Vann Woodward (ed.), George Fitzhugh, *Cannibals All! or Slaves Without Masters* (Cambridge, Mass., 1960).

GUIDES TO FURTHER READING

HISTORIOGRAPHY

James C. Bonner, "Plantation and Farm: The Agricultural South," in Arthur S. Link and Rembert W. Patrick (eds.), *Writing Southern History:*

Essays in Historiography in Honor of Fletcher M. Green (Baton Rouge, La., 1965).

Louis R. Harlan, "The Negro in American History," Service Center for Teachers of History, Publication Number 61 (Washington, 1965).

Richard Hofstadter, "U. B. Phillips and the Plantation Legend," *Journal of Negro History*, XXIX (April 1944).

Ruben F. Kugler, "U. B. Phillips' Use of Sources," *Journal of Negro History*, XLVII (July 1962).

Staughton Lynd, "On Turner, Beard and Slavery," *Journal of Negro History*, XLVIII (October 1963).

Chase C. Mooney, "The Literature of Slavery: A Re-evaluation," *Indiana Magazine of History*, XLVII (September 1951).

Arnold A. Sio, "Interpretations of Slavery," *Comparative Studies in Society and History*, VII (April 1965).

Kenneth M. Stampp, "The Historian and Southern Negro Slavery," *American Historical Review*, LVII (April 1952).

Bennett H. Wall, "African Slavery," in Link and Patrick (eds.), *Writing Southern History: Essays in Historiography in Honor of Fletcher M. Green* (Baton Rouge, La., 1965).

Harold D. Woodman, "The Profitability of Slavery: A Historical Perennial," *Journal of Southern History*, XXIX (August 1963).

Stanley M. Elkins, *Slavery, A Problem in American Institutional and Intellectual Life*, David Brion Davis, *The Problem of Slavery in Western Culture*, and Eugene D. Genovese, *The Political Economy of Slavery* also contain valuable historiographic commentaries.

BIBLIOGRAPHIC AIDS

W. E. B. Du Bois *et al.*, *Encyclopedia of the Negro: Preparatory Volume with Reference Lists and Reports* (New York, 1946).

The Journal of Negro History (1916–present).

Elizabeth W. Miller (compiler), *The Negro in America: A Bibliography* (Cambridge, Mass., 1966).

Monroe N. Work, *A Bibliography of the Negro in Africa and America* (New York, 1928).

Excellent bibliographies of American slavery can be found in the footnotes of two previously cited works: Stanley M. Elkins, *Slavery* . . . , and David Brion Davis, *The Problem of Slavery in Western Culture*. All of the historiographic articles listed also contain good bibliographies.

AMERICAN SLAVERY IN WORLD PERSPECTIVE

GREECE AND ROME

Moses I. Finley (ed.), *Slavery in Classical Antiquity: Views and Controversies* (Cambridge, England, 1960).

————, *The World of Odysseus* (Meridian Paperback Ed., New York, 1959).

William Linn Westerman, *The Slave Systems of Greek and Roman Antiquity* (Philadelphia, 1955).

LATIN AMERICA

C. R. Boxer, *The Golden Age of Brazil, 1690–1750: Growing Pains of a Colonial Society* (Berkeley, Calif., 1962).

————, *Race Relations in the Portugese Empire, 1415–1825* (Oxford, England, 1963).

Gilberto Freyre, *The Masters and the Slaves: A Study in the Development of Brazilian Civilization* (New York, 1946).

Marvin Harris, *Patterns of Race in the Americas* (New York, 1964).

James F. King, "The Negro in Continental Spanish America: A Select Bibliography," *Hispanic American Historical Review,* XXIV (August 1944).

Herbert S. Klein, *Slavery in the Americas: A Comparative Study of Cuba and Virginia* (Chicago, 1967).

Alexander Marchant, *From Barter to Slavery: The Economic Relations of Portugese and Indians in the Settlement of Brazil, 1500–1580* (Baltimore, 1942).

Vienna Moog, *Bandeirantes and Pioneers* (New York, 1964).

Magnus Morner, "The History of Race Relations in Latin America," *Latin American Research Review,* I (1966).

Oriol Pi-Sunyer, "Historical Background to the Negro in Mexico," *Journal of Negro History,* XLII (October 1957).

Stanley J. Stein, *Vassouras: A Brazilian Coffee County, 1850–1900* (Cambridge, Mass., 1957).

Frank Tannenbaum, *Slave and Citizen: The Negro in the Americas* (New York, 1946).

OTHER CULTURES

Abd el-Moshen Bakir, *Slavery in Pharaonic Egypt* (Cairo, 1952).

Dev Raj Chanana, *Slavery in Ancient India, As Depicted in Pali and Sanskrit Texts* (New Delhi, 1960).

Hannah S. Goldman, "American Slavery and Russian Serfdom: A Study in Fictional Parallels" (Unpublished Ph.D. Thesis, Columbia University, 1955, University Microfilms No. 11, 453).

Melville J. Herskovits, *Dahomey: An Ancient West African Kingdom* (New York, 1938).

Isaac Mendelsohn, *Slavery in the Ancient Near East: A Comparative Study of Slavery in Babylonia, Assyria, Syria, and Palestine, from the Middle of the Third Millennium to the End of the First Millennium* (New York, 1949).

E. G. Pulleyblank, "The Origins and Nature of Chattel Slavery in China," *Journal of the Economic and Social History of the Orient,* I, pt. 2 (1958).

Lowell J. Ragatz, *The Fall of the Planter Class in the British Caribbean, 1763–1833* (New York, 1928).

C. Martin Wilbur, *Slavery in China During the Former Han Dynasty, 206 B.C.–A.D. 25* (Chicago, 1945).

The excellent bibliographic footnotes in David Brion Davis, *The Problem of Slavery in Western Culture*, contain a much more complete listing of books and articles on slavery in other cultures.